Accounting and Corporate Finance for Lawyers

ASPEN COURSEBOOK SERIES

Accounting and Corporate Finance for Lawyers

Stacey L. Bowers

Associate Professor of the Practice
University of Denver Sturm College of Law

 Wolters Kluwer

Published by Wolters Kluwer in New York.

Wolters Kluwer Legal & Regulatory U.S. serves customers worldwide with CCH, Aspen Publishers, and Kluwer Law International products. (www.WKLegaledu.com)

To contact Customer Service, e-mail customer.service@wolterskluwer.com, call 1-800-234-1660, fax 1-800-901-9075, or mail correspondence to:

Wolters Kluwer
Attn: Order Department
PO Box 990
Frederick, MD 21705

Printed in the United States of America.

1 2 3 4 5 6 7 8 9 0

ISBN 978-1-4548-7897-1

Library of Congress Cataloging-in-Publication Data
Names: Bowers, Stacey L., author.
Title: Accounting and corporate finance for lawyers / Stacey L. Bowers.
Description: New York. : Wolters Kluwer, [2019] | Series: Aspen coursebook
  series | Includes bibliographical references.
Identifiers: LCCN 2018023675 | ISBN 9781454878971
Subjects: LCSH: Lawyers—Accounting. | Corporations—Finance.
Classification: LCC HF5686.L35 B69 2019 | DDC 657.024/34—dc23
LC record available at https://lccn.loc.gov/2018023675

About Wolters Kluwer Legal & Regulatory U.S.

Wolters Kluwer Legal & Regulatory U.S. delivers expert content and solutions in the areas of law, corporate compliance, health compliance, reimbursement, and legal education. Its practical solutions help customers successfully navigate the demands of a changing environment to drive their daily activities, enhance decision quality, and inspire confident outcomes.

Serving customers worldwide, its legal and regulatory portfolio includes products under the Aspen Publishers, CCH Incorporated, Kluwer Law International, ftwilliam.com, and MediRegs names. They are regarded as exceptional and trusted resources for general legal and practice-specific knowledge, compliance and risk management, dynamic workflow solutions, and expert commentary.

For Jeff McClelland, my significant other.
I couldn't have done this project without his unending support,
encouragement, and good humor.

Summary of Contents

Contents

3 OVERVIEW OF ACCOUNTING AND AUDITING PRINCIPLES   41

5 DIVIDEND DISTRIBUTIONS   163

6 ANALYSIS OF FINANCIAL STATEMENTS   189

9 FINANCIAL TERMS AND COVENANTS IN CONTRACTS   263

Preface

Accounting and corporate finance concepts are knowledge bases that law students should master on their path to becoming well-rounded lawyers, no matter their chosen practice area. These practical skills form the basis for understanding business concepts and businesses — skills that clients have grown to expect of their lawyers and skills that allow lawyers to bring added value to the lawyer-client relationship.

The basic idea behind this text was to create a book that law students, who often have little to no background in the areas of accounting or finance, could easily read and understand on their journey to mastering concepts that are not the norm in the law school setting and skills that are often viewed as foreign and scary by law students because they involve math. The impetus for this book rests with a number of law students in my early Accounting for Lawyers classes who encouraged me to write a book that approached the topic from my teaching style, which according to the students was easy to follow and understand.

While my law students were the original impetus, it was David Herzig at Wolters Kluwer and his encouragement to submit a proposal that helped to bring this book to fruition. This book would also not have happened without the help, input, and problem-solving skills of my dedicated research assistants over the past two years, Joe Bone and Ryan Cordsen. Additionally, two of my professional colleagues and friends who are corporate paralegals, Nanci Lilja and Cathy Hulsey, read every chapter and offered great suggestions and much needed support. Also, many of my Accounting for Lawyers students took time out of their busy schedules to give me feedback, offer ideas, and provide edits to drafts of various chapters. Lastly, the support of my colleagues who teach as a part of the corporate and commercial law certificate program helped to guide and motivate me over the course of this project.

This book is meant to provide an overview of what I view as some of the most important accounting and finance skills that soon-to-be lawyers should know. While it is not possible in a semester-long course to cover every concept that a practicing lawyer may face, this text attempts to introduce students to many accounting and corporate finance situations they may encounter in their representation of future clients and, in particular, businesses. My goal is by no means to turn law students into accountants or corporate finance experts. However, I do hope that after reading this text, law students, who are our future practicing lawyers, will be conversant and able to hold a well-informed conversation with their clients, other lawyers, or accountants regarding the concepts covered.

It was hard to know the best order in which to cover the topics contained within this text, and I reordered the chapters and shifted content between chapters too many times to count before I ultimately settled on the current structure. I attempted to write this text in a way that would allow users to selectively choose which chapters or concepts to cover and to be able to do so in the order written or in their own sequencing. Chapter 1 provides a brief history of accounting, touches on some of the more recent accounting scandals, and emphasizes why law students should learn and hone these skill sets. Chapter 2 provides an overview of the four primary financial statements in order to establish a fundamental knowledge base for Chapter 3, which introduces students to accounting and auditing principles, and Chapter 4, where students learn how to record financial transactions and prepare balance sheets and income statements. Chapter 5 covers dividend distributions, and Chapter 6 looks at financial statement analysis through the use of various trend and ratio assessments. Chapter 7 introduces students to the concepts of commitments and contingencies and the role that attorneys play in regard to the assessment and disclosure of contingent obligations in an entity's financial statements and footnote disclosures. Chapter 8 discusses the concepts of interest, time value of money principles, and bond valuation. Chapter 9 attempts to familiarize students with some of the main contracts where they may encounter and work with financial terms and covenants. Chapter 10 addresses basic business valuation methodologies, and Chapter 11 touches on those concepts that did not fit elsewhere, such as capital versus operating leases, the financial markets, methods of raising capital through debt and equity, and derivative instruments. Throughout the text there are multiple examples to demonstrate concepts, as well as problems so that students can practice and reinforce what they have learned. I have also included exhibits as supplements to concepts covered in various chapters and a glossary. My experience in teaching Accounting for Lawyers over the past four years played a significant role in how I structured this text, including its style and voice. My goal was to create a student-friendly book and one where law students did not feel overwhelmed by the concepts.

Stacey Bowers
June 2018

Accounting and Corporate Finance for Lawyers

Overview of Accounting

A. INTRODUCTION

Accounting is often referred to as "the language of business," meaning that business people communicate information about the operations and financial status of the business through the use of accounting concepts and practices to produce financial reports. According to one business dictionary, accounting is the "systematic process of identifying, recording, measuring, classifying, verifying, summarizing, interpreting, and communicating financial information" about an entity's condition.[1] Entities present this information to users in the form of financial statements and reports. In order to understand financial reports, lawyers must have a basic understanding of accounting and finance concepts, meaning they must speak "the language of business."

B. BRIEF HISTORY OF ACCOUNTING

The advent of accounting can be traced back over 6,000 years ago to the ancient civilizations of Mesopotamia and Egypt, where records indicate it was used to track expenditures, as to well as track goods received and traded in commerce.[2] During those early years, young boys were selected to become "scribes" and trained in the arts of reading, writing, and calculating.[3] Upon completion of their training, scribes often worked for the local governments, as well as served roles in public administration and commerce, by keeping accurate business records

---

[1] *Accounting,* BusinessDictionary.com, *available at* http://www.businessdictionary.com/definition/accounting.html (last visited Aug. 24, 2017).
[2] The History of Accounting: An International Encyclopedia (Michael Chatfield & Richard Vangermeersch eds., 2015).
[3] *Id.*

and accounts of transactions.[4] This role of single-entry bookkeeping, or simply maintaining a transaction ledger, continued into the twelfth century.[5] However, in the early 1200s, things began to change as trade and the flow of currency increased, which resulted in the keeping of better accounts and records ranging from financial accounts, to rental contracts, to legal records.[6] In conjunction with private merchants maintaining better records, governments started to do the same and also utilized the concept of audits, whereby tax collectors and treasurers would check the accounts of government officials for accuracy.[7] Yet, the concepts of accounting were still difficult to employ as most societies relied on Roman numerals, which made it quite difficult to track monetary transactions due to the numeric symbols and lack of fractions or decimals.[8] Imagine trying to add the Roman numbers MCCLXXVI (1,276) and CMXXXVIII (938), which equals MMCCXIV (2,214).

Yet, this all changed in the late twelfth and thirteenth centuries as Italy began to emerge as one of the wealthiest countries and epicenters in Europe, mainly due to its shipping and banking industries.[9] As these industries grew, new accounting techniques were needed to manage and track the large amounts of money that changed hands in the shipping industry and to allocate the profits and losses to the partners of the banks.[10] In 1202, Leonardo Fibonacci, an Italian merchant, wrote his formative work on calculation with Arabic numbers and the use of the abacus, which greatly enhanced the practice and ease of mathematics.[11] By the end of the 1200s, schools teaching mathematics through the use of the abacus were widespread, and many merchants trained there.[12] All of these factors ultimately led to the development of double-entry bookkeeping, which allowed for great advancement in the world of accounting and record keeping, and for the first time, an accounting system existed that established a method for the calculation and determination of profits and losses for businesses.[13] The earliest records of double-entry bookkeeping date back to the start of the 1300s, employed by Italian merchants and city stewards.[14] While the precise date of the first use of double-entry bookkeeping cannot be pinpointed, in 1494 Luca Pacioli published the first accounting textbook that described double-entry bookkeeping and the technique of recording a balancing entry with both debits and credits.[15] The earliest double-entry bookkeeping entries were written in paragraph form with corresponding debit and credit paragraphs, which later became written as descriptions of transactions in side-by-side columns and ultimately written solely in Arabic numbers in side-by-side columns.[16] Although

---

[4]*Id.*
[5]Jacob Soll, The Reckoning: Financial Accountability and the Rise and Fall of Nations 7-8 (2014).
[6]*Id.* at 8.
[7]*Id.*
[8]*Id.* at 9.
[9]Doug Bennett, *A History of Accounting*, 60 Armed Forces Comptroller 6, 7 (Winter 2015).
[10]*Id.* at 7.
[11]Soll, *supra* note 5, at 10.
[12]*Id.* at 10-11.
[13]*Id.* at 11.
[14]*Id.*
[15]Bennett, *supra* note 9, at 7.
[16]Soll, *supra* note 5, at 12.

double-entry bookkeeping had been born, it would take time for the practice to spread and be widely used throughout the world. However, it still remains as the underlying framework for recording most financial transactions today.

Through the next centuries, the concepts of accounting and tracking finances grew in importance, particularly in governments where accountants were often appointed to oversee receipts and expenditures of funds, and in large enterprises, such as the Dutch East India Company.[17] Keeping track of government finances was of such importance that one of the first acts of the United States Congress in 1776 was to create the U.S. Treasury and the position of Auditor General to oversee the treasury.[18] The Industrial Revolution created more demand for accounting and auditing, and accounting became more readily recognized and regarded as a profession in the early 1900s.[19]

The crash of the U.S. stock markets in the late 1920s and the Great Depression, which followed, led to the passage of the Securities Act of 1933, the Exchange Act of 1934, and the creation of the U.S. Securities and Exchange Commission on June 6, 1934.[20] One of the underlying goals of the securities legislation and establishment of the SEC was to begin the process of restoring a level of confidence in the U.S. financial markets and to create a standardized system of accounting and reporting requirements for entities that were publicly traded. The original drafters of the legislation believed that an effective market mandated competent and honest experts, such as lawyers, bankers, accountants, and others, and that the laws should protect investors from false and misleading information by requiring these experts to meet new standards.[21] While the SEC was granted the power to create the professional standards that accountants must adhere to in regard to their roles with publicly traded entities, since the 1940s the SEC has opted to defer most of that power to the relevant accounting professional organizations.

The accounting profession and its reputation grew from the 1940s through the 1960s, and accountants were once again viewed as trusted experts.[22] The profession continued to boom but became increasingly more competitive, and as a result the "Big Eight" auditing firms took on more consulting work for the same clients for which they acted as auditors, thus blurring the role of outside accountant independence.[23] As a result, the 1970s saw some of the first big accounting scandals as auditors failed to catch the use of "creative accounting" methods by entities that they audited.[24] Due to these early scandals and a government report criticizing auditing firms for their lack of independence and conflicts due to making significantly more fees from the consulting services than the auditing services they provided, the reputations of the "Big Eight" and

---

[17]Bennett, *supra* note 9, at 8.
[18]*Id.*
[19]Chatfield and Vangermeersch (eds.), *supra* note 2.
[20]*Id.*
[21]*Id.*
[22]Soll, *supra* note 5, at 194.
[23]*Id.* at 196.
[24]*Id.*

accountants again took a downward turn.[25] The "Big Eight" soon became the "Big Six" in the late 1980s and continued to earn most of their revenues as consultants versus auditors, yet firm profits continued to drop as competition kept increasing and the auditing market held little room for growth.[26] This inherent conflict of acting as an "independent auditor" and consultant for their clients continued into the early 2000s but was quickly dismantled in 2002 with the passage of the Sarbanes-Oxley Act in the wake of the Enron and WorldCom accounting scandals and subsequent bankruptcy filings, as well as Arthur Andersen LLP's demise as an auditing firm.

C. ACCOUNTING SCANDALS

Accounting scandals are nothing new and long pre-date the modern era. Whether as misrepresenting income and expenditures to the local tax collectors during the Roman Empire rule, preparing false books and reports by publicly reporting entities in the early 1920s, or failing to disclose certain transactions to investors in the 2000s, accounting fraud was, and is likely to remain, an ongoing issue in the global world of business and government.

Scandals often emanate from what is generically referred to as "creative accounting," referring to methods that are frequently used by businesses to bolster their actual financial results and are often easily or well hidden from the entity's auditors. A few of the methods that entities employ to "creatively account" for their financial results include (i) inflating revenues; (ii) overvaluing assets; (iii) underreporting expenses; and (iv) understating liabilities.[27] An entity can increase its worth, or stockholders' equity, as reported on its balance sheet, by overvaluing its assets or understating its liabilities. Additionally, an entity can increase its bottom-line net income, or profit, as reflected on its income statement, by inflating its revenues or decreasing its expenses for the period. In any case, by engaging in creative accounting, the entity's reported results are not accurate or indicative of its true financial condition. While creative accounting is often within the bounds of the pertinent accounting rules or relevant regulations and does not rise to the level of fraud, in some circumstances it is one and the same, and in others it is the precursor to an entity's stepping over the line and engaging in actual financial fraud.[28]

While a business may engage in creative accounting or even fraud for a plethora of reasons, there are a few common rationales that seem to motivate these practices. These rationales often include the entity's need to (i) meet financial analysts' expectations to protect the entity's stock price; (ii) ensure that bonus plan incentives are met; (iii) prevent a default under a commercial loan agreement; or (iv) engage in an actual cover-up.[29] In today's world, there

---

[25]*Id.* at 197-198.
[26]*Id.* at 199-200.
[27]Michael Jones, Creative Accounting, Fraud and International Accounting Scandals 12-13 (2011).
[28]*Id.* at 43-44.
[29]*Id.* at 32-33.

have been and continue to be far too many accounting scandals to even scratch the surface in this introductory chapter, but some of the bigger scandals in the United States since the late 1990s and into the 2000s will be presented to provide a modicum of insight into how such events can occur in entities utilizing a wealth of experts from accountants, to lawyers, to consultants, and that are governed by financial information reporting rules and regulations as well as governmental agencies.

1. Waste Management, Inc.

Waste Management, Inc. is a Texas-based publicly traded company that provides both residential and business waste management services. During the 1990s, Waste Management, Inc.'s high-ranking executives, while Arthur Andersen LLP was the company's auditor, manipulated the company's financial results and statements through the use of improper accounting. As a result, the SEC instituted a number of actions. The first occurred in early June 2001 when the SEC filed an administrative proceeding against Arthur Andersen LLP and a number of current and former partners of the firm alleging that they "knowingly and recklessly issued false and misleading unqualified audit reports" that indicated that Waste Management's financial statements were presented fairly.[30] The SEC quickly reached a settlement with the firm and some of the partners in mid-June 2001, with the firm paying a civil penalty in the amount of $7.0 million and being enjoined from engaging in further improper professional conduct.[31]

The following year, in March of 2002, the SEC filed a lawsuit against Waste Management's founder and five former top executive officers claiming that the former executives "engaged in a systematic scheme to falsify and misrepresent Waste Management's financial results between 1992 and 1997."[32] In its complaint, the SEC stated that "[f]or years, these defendants cooked the books, enriched themselves, preserved their jobs, and duped unsuspecting shareholders."[33] These five executives manipulated Waste Management's financial statements to meet analysts' expectations and did so through a number of improper accounting methods, which included among others (i) manipulating depreciation expense on garbage trucks by inflating salvage values and extending useful life; (ii) failing to record expenses associated with landfills; (iii) capitalizing expenses that should have been recognized immediately; and (iv) failing to establish sufficient reserves for taxes and other expenses.[34] These fraudulent accounting practices resulted in a $1.7 billion pretax earnings restatement in 1998 upon discovery by an accounting review ordered by the company's new

---

[30]SEC Litigation Release, Arthur Andersen LLP, Litig. Rel. No. 17039 (June 19, 2001), *available at* https://www.sec.gov/litigation/litreleases/lr17039.htm (last visited Aug. 24, 2017).
[31]*Id.*
[32]SEC Press Release, Waste Management Founder, Five Others Sued for Massive Fraud, *available at* https://www.sec.gov/news/headlines/wastemgmt6.htm (last visited Aug. 24, 2017).
[33]*Id.*
[34]*Id.*

chief executive officer.[35] The SEC ultimately settled with four of the five former executives for $30.8 million and barred each from acting as an officer or director of a public company.[36] Additionally, the corresponding shareholder class action suit cost Waste Management more than $450 million, a small portion of which was recouped from Arthur Andersen.[37]

2. Enron Corp.

Enron Corp. was a Texas-based publicly traded company that, at the time of its demise, was primarily engaged in energy trading. During the late 1990s and into the early 2000s, Enron and its management, while Arthur Andersen LLP was the company's auditor, engaged in a variety of fraudulent accounting practices, including creating fictitious income, incorrectly reporting cash flow, and moving liabilities off its balance sheet.[38] Management created a number of "special purpose entities" that were used to hide the company's significant debt load and generate fictitious income, and were structured in such a way that Enron did not have to consolidate the special-purpose entities and report those entities' financial results with its own in a consolidated manner.[39] In conjunction with the special purpose entities, Enron undertook such actions as guaranteeing commercial bank loans, which accounted for 97 percent of one entity's total financing, or selling Enron's assets to these special purpose entities at a gain, even though there should have been no gain recognized.[40] The guaranteed loans were a major reason for Enron's bankruptcy filing in late 2001, which cost its investors and employees more than $70 billion, including the loss of many employees' entire retirement savings.

The SEC ultimately filed a noteworthy number of lawsuits against various parties associated with Enron, including a number of its former executive officers, in-house accountants, in-house lawyers, and other high-level employees; Arthur Andersen LLP and various current and former partners of the firm; Merrill Lynch and various executives of the firm; J.P. Morgan Chase; as well as others. Some of the larger monetary settlements attained by the SEC included (i) Andrew Fastow, Enron's former chief financial officer, who disgorged more than $23 million and agreed to a ten-year prison term; (ii) J.P. Morgan Chase, which disgorged $135 million; and (iii) Citigroup, which disgorged $120 million.[41] Many more Enron executives and affiliated parties agreed to other types of penalties, such as consenting (i) to not violate Section 10(b) of the

---

[35]*Id.*
[36]SEC Litigation Release, Waste Management, Inc. Founder and Three Other Former Top Officers Settle SEC Fraud Action for $30.8 Million, Litig. Rel. No. 19351 (Aug. 29, 2005), *available at* https://www.sec.gov/litigation/litreleases/lr19351.htm (last visited Aug. 24, 2017).
[37]Calmetta Coleman, *Waste Management to Pay $457 Million to Settle Shareholder Class-Action Suit*, WALL ST. J. (Nov. 8, 2001), *available at* http://www.wsj.com/articles/SB1005139585747973440 (last visited Aug. 24, 2017).
[38]Jones, *supra* note 27, at 420.
[39]*Id.*
[40]*Id.*
[41]SEC Litigation Release, Andrew S. Fastow, Litig. Rel. No. 18543 (Jan. 14, 2004), *available at* https://www.sec.gov/litigation/litreleases/lr18543.htm (last visited Aug. 24, 2017); SEC Press Release, SEC

Securities Exchange Act of 1934; (ii) to never serve in the capacity of an officer or director of a publicly traded company; (iii) to not violate the antifraud provisions of the federal securities laws; and (iv) to being barred from appearing or practicing before the SEC. Additionally, Jeffrey Skilling, Enron's former president, chief executive, and chief operating officer, and Kenneth Lay, Enron's former chairman and chief executive officer, were sentenced to significant jail terms for fraud and insider trading, though Lay died before serving his sentence.

In the midst of Enron's downward spiral toward bankruptcy, Arthur Andersen LLP, the entity's auditor, destroyed a significant amount of documentation related to Enron and its financial information, which destruction continued well after Enron knew it was being investigated by the SEC and, quite probably, after Arthur Andersen was served with a subpoena by the SEC for Enron's records. Arthur Andersen was ultimately convicted of obstruction of justice in 2002 and, effective August 31, 2002, surrendered its license to practice before the SEC and to audit publicly traded companies.[42]

Today, Enron is synonymous with accounting fraud, but sadly was just a tip of the iceberg. Accounting scandals and fraud continued to follow in its wake in the United States and throughout the world.

3. WorldCom, Lehman Brothers, and More

In 2002, WorldCom's internal auditors uncovered a fraud of more than $3.5 billion as a result of the entity inflating the values of its assets through improper capitalization of costs, inflating revenues, and manipulating reserves, during a time period that Arthur Andersen LLP was the outside auditor.[43] WorldCom settled with the SEC in July 2003 and agreed to a civil penalty of $2.25 billion, but would only be obligated to pay $500 million under the terms of its bankruptcy settlement.[44] It was shortly after the Enron and WorldCom accounting scandals that the SEC passed the Sarbanes-Oxley Act of 2002, which introduced sweeping reforms in an attempt to deal with fraudulent financial statements and general accounting fraud.

In 2008, both the Lehman Brothers and Madoff Securities International Ltd. accounting scandals occurred. Lehman Brothers sold "toxic assets," meaning assets whose value had significantly declined, to Cayman Island banks, with the banks believing that such assets would be repurchased, which allowed Lehman Brothers to appear to have $50 billion more in cash than it actually held.[45] Lehman Brothers ultimately filed for bankruptcy but was not prosecuted by the SEC. Madoff Securities, through its founder Bernard Madoff, ran a

---

Settles Enforcement Proceedings Against J.P. Morgan Chase and Citigroup, Rel. No. 2003-87 (July 28, 2003), *available at* https://www.sec.gov/news/press/2003-87.htm (last visited Aug. 24, 2017).

[42]ABC News, Arthur Andersen Goes Out of Business, ABC NEWS (2009), *available at* http://abcnews.go.com/Business/Decade/arthur-andersen-business/story?id=9279255 (last visited Aug. 24, 2017).

[43]The 10 Worst Corporate Accounting Scandals of All Time, *available at* https://visual.ly/community/infographic/business/10-worst-corporate-accounting-scandals-all-time (last visited Aug. 24, 2017).

[44]SEC Litigation Release, WorldCom Inc., Litig. Rel. No. 18219, AAER-1811 (July 7, 2003), *available at* https://www.sec.gov/litigation/litreleases/lr18219.htm (last visited Aug. 24, 2017).

[45]The 10 Worst Corporate Accounting Scandals of All Time, *supra* note 43.

ponzi scheme, where early investors were compensated with newer investors' funds, which ultimately cost investors more than $50 billion.[46] Bernard Madoff, whose sons turned him into the SEC after he confided in them regarding his scheme, was sentenced to life in prison. As a result of the Madoff Securities ponzi scheme, the SEC found itself under investigation and tarnished in the public's eye for failing to uncover the ongoing fraud even after having received a significant number of allegations and complaints from investors regarding Madoff Securities over the course of 16 years.[47]

More recently, between 2011 and 2015, Wells Fargo, through its employees, created an estimated 2 million fake checking and credit card accounts. The employees created the fake accounts in order to meet unrealistic sales quotas instituted by executives, which resulted in greatly inflated revenues for the bank.[48] Many of the customers, who were victims of the fake accounts, were charged fees or had their credit rating impacted as a result of the fraud. Wells Fargo returned $5 million in illegal fees to the wronged customers and paid over $186 million in fines.[49] In addition, the chief executive officer lost his job, and the bank is in the midst of settling a class action suit, which is likely to cost it more than $140 million.[50]

The above are simply a few examples of accounting scandals that have occurred in the United States in the past two decades. Many more have occurred both domestically and internationally and continue to occur as this book is being written. Ongoing accounting fraud includes schemes that involve falsifying accounts, documents, and financial statements; overstating the value of assets; overstating revenues; overstating profits; making illegal payments; and more. While it seems logical that the notoriety of the scandals and the various pieces of legislation that have been put in place to curtail them might have reduced the number of or dollar amounts associated with accounting fraud, that has not been the case. It seems that business entities' use of creative accounting methods, whether rising to a level of fraud or not, is here to stay and that the auditors (and lawyers) will continue to face the challenges of spotting and addressing these issues in an attempt to prevent even more scandals in the future.

---

[46]SEC Press Release, SEC Charges Bernard L. Madoff for Multi-Billion Dollar Ponzi Scheme, Rel. No. 2008-293 (Dec. 11, 2008), *available at* https://www.sec.gov/news/press/2008/2008-293.htm (last visited Aug. 24, 2017).

[47]Zachary A. Goldfarb, *The Madoff Files: A Chronicle of SEC Failure*, Wash. Post (Sept. 3, 2009), *available at* http://www.washingtonpost.com/wp-dyn/content/article/2009/09/02/AR2009090203851.html (last visited Aug. 24, 2017).

[48]Matt Eagan, *Wells Fargo Victims Get Closer to Paycheck in $142 Million Settlement*, CNN Money (July 10, 2017), *available at* http://money.cnn.com/2017/07/10/investing/wells-fargo-fake-account-settlement/index.html (last visited Aug. 18, 2017).

[49]*Id.*

[50]*Id.*

D. IMPORTANCE OF ACCOUNTING AND FINANCE LITERACY FOR LAWYERS

In early 2014, three professors from Harvard Law School published the results of an online survey conducted during 2013 in which over 120 attorneys at major law firms were asked to provide information regarding the most valuable business-oriented courses that law students should take in preparation for practice.[51] The survey asked the practicing attorneys to rate how useful seven specific business-oriented courses[52] would be for law students on a scale of "1-to-5."[53] The courses that were rated of most importance were "Accounting and Financial Reporting" and "Corporate Finance," with overall ratings of 4.38 and 4.21, respectively.[54] The results were further subdivided between responses from lawyers practicing in areas of corporate and transactional law or in litigation. Transactional lawyers ranked "Accounting and Financial Reporting" at a 4.62, and litigation lawyers ranked it at 4.15.[55] In a follow-up question regarding which three of the seven listed classes were most important, an average of 83 percent of the lawyers surveyed indicated that students should take "Accounting and Financial Reporting" (86 percent of transactional lawyers and 85 percent of litigation lawyers).[56] In this same survey, attorneys ranked the importance of certain business-oriented skills and knowledge bases[57] and once again Accounting and Financial Statement Analysis skills were at the top of the list with an overall ranking of 4.3 out of 5.0.[58] What is overwhelmingly clear from the results of this survey is that practicing attorneys deem accounting and corporate finance classes a critical component of a student's law school education and the related knowledge bases and critical skills that law students should learn before entering the practice of law.

In 2013, the American Bar Association (ABA) created a task force to assess the key competencies for business lawyers across a variety of practice areas and settings.[59] The task force elucidated what it viewed as essential components of problem solving for business lawyers. Those components include (i) possessing basic business knowledge; (ii) understanding the client's business and industry; (iii) understanding the parties' relationships in a transaction; (iv) understanding the parties' motivations in a transaction; (v) understanding

---

[51]John Coates, Jesse Fried, & Kathryn Spier, *What Courses Should Law Students Take? Lessons from Harvard's BigLaw Survey*, 64 J. LEGAL EDUC. 443, 443-445 (2015).

[52]The seven specific courses were "Accounting and Financial Reporting," "Corporate Finance," "Negotiation Workshop," "Business Strategy for Lawyers," "Analytical Methods for Lawyers," "Leadership in Law Firms," and "Statistical Analysis/Quantitative Analysis."

[53]Coates, Fried, & Spier, *supra* note 51, at 445.

[54]*Id.* at 445-446.

[55]*Id.* at 446.

[56]*Id.*

[57]The skills and knowledge bases were "Accounting/Financial Statement Analysis," "Teamwork," "Financial Markets/Products," "Negotiations," "Business Strategy/Industry Analysis," "Statistical/Quantitative Analysis," and "Legal Services Industry."

[58]Coates, Fried, & Spier, *supra* note 51, at 449.

[59]Business Law Educ. Comm., American Bar Assn., Report of the Task Force on Defining Key Competencies for Business Lawyers, *Defining Key Competencies for Business Lawyers*, 72 BUS. LAW. 101, 102-103 (2016).

transactions generally; and (vi) understanding the client's specific transaction.[60] The task force further elaborated that business lawyers should, at a minimum, have an understanding of accounting concepts, including reading and understanding financial statements and the related footnotes, as well as having a basic knowledge regarding Generally Accepted Accounting Principles.[61] Further, depending on the lawyers' areas of practice, they should also understand various corporate finance concepts, business structures, business valuation techniques, time value of money concepts, and economics.[62]

If law students want to understand businesses and effectively counsel their clients who are business entities or are involved with business entities, they must understand the language of business. Armed with business knowledge, whether in the form of industry, accounting, finance, or other related concepts, a lawyer is in a better position to meet the client's needs. One of these critical business knowledge bases for lawyers is financial acumen and literacy.[63] According to an educator and former practicing lawyer, every lawyer should have a basic understanding of accounting concepts and know how to read and interpret financial statements.[64] In other words, today's lawyers practicing in an increasingly interdisciplinary world need to develop financial literacy.[65]

---

[60]*Id.* at 115-117.
[61]*Id.* at 116.
[62]*Id.*
[63]Praveen Kosuri, *Beyond Gilson: The Art of Business Lawyers*, 19 Lewis & Clark 463, 485 (2015).
[64]*Id.* at 476.
[65]*Id.* at 485.

Understanding the Basics of Financial Statements

A. INTRODUCTION

Financial statements are one way in which an entity presents its financial position and results of operations. These statements provide users, whether the executive officers of the entity, an investor, or a lender, with insight into the entity's current financial condition and performance. Financial statements can also be used to make predictions regarding an entity's future performance. As discussed in Chapter 3, many entities prepare their financial statements in accordance with Generally Accepted Accounting Principles in order to provide consistency in the presentation of results.

B. PRIMARY FINANCIAL STATEMENTS

There are four primary financial statements that a business entity might prepare in order to represent and evaluate the financial condition of its business — the balance sheet, income statement, statement of cash flows, and statement of changes in stockholders' equity. Each financial statement represents a specific set of information regarding the financial condition of the entity and can be used to understand various aspects of the entity and its business operations. Different financial statements are prepared based on the needs or requirements of the business. Many businesses, no matter their size or structure, prepare the balance sheet and income statement. However, not all businesses prepare the statement of cash flows or statement of changes in stockholders' equity. In many cases only large companies or publicly traded companies prepare the statement of changes in stockholders' equity.

EXAMPLE 2.1   **FINANCIAL STATEMENTS PREPARED**

The following table sets forth the type of business entity and the financial state-ments that the entity might prepare to reflect its financial condition.

Type of Business	Balance Sheet	Income Statement	Statement of Cash Flows	Statement of Changes in Stockholders' Equity
Small Private Company	S	S	N	N
Medium Private Company	S	S	M	N
Large Private Company	S	S	S	M
Publicly Traded Company	R	R	R	R

M = Might prepare this financial statement; N = Not likely to prepare this financial statement; R = Required to prepare this financial statement; S = Should prepare this financial statement

Practicing lawyers often encounter and work with financial statements. A transactional lawyer may need to review a client's financial statements to assist in the capital-raising process. A family lawyer with a divorce client who has a number of small business entities must review the financial statements of each of those entities to establish their value as a part of a divorce proceeding. A litigator with a client who wishes to sue an entity for intellectual property infringement may examine the defendant's financial statements as part of the trial preparation process. These are but a few situations in which practicing lawyers may interact with financial statements.

For the remainder of this chapter, the financial statements of Retailers, Inc., found in **Exhibit A** and the excerpts included throughout the chapter, will be utilized to illustrate specific aspects of each financial statement. All of the financial information is reflected in thousands except share or stock data. Retailers, Inc. is a fictitious entity that sells retail products, both directly and indirectly through third-party resellers, to the consumer. Retailers, Inc. sells athletic apparel, footwear, and other related products. Retailers, Inc. owns intel-lectual property associated with its apparel, including patents and trademarks. Retailers, Inc. periodically purchases other small companies in the same or related industry to add to its holdings and available product offerings.

1. Balance Sheet

The balance sheet is a reflection of the financial condition of an entity at a sin-gle point in time. It represents the underlying structure of the business entity and reflects the monetary value of each of its components. It also indicates the size of each part in relation to its categorization and in relation to the over-all balance sheet. In essence, the balance sheet reflects what the entity owns (assets), what it owes (liabilities), and the difference between what it owns and owes (equity). The balance sheet provides information regarding an entity's financial position and reflects the entity's book value, indicating what the entity is worth on paper.

This financial statement speaks as of a specific point or date in time and represents a snapshot of the entity at that date, whether month-end, quarter-end, or year-end. As a result, by the time the balance sheet is prepared, it is generally out of date as the entity may be days, weeks, or months past the pre-pared balance sheet's date.

The balance sheet contains disclosure regarding three main categories: assets, liabilities, and equity. Each of these is further broken down into subparts. Just as its name implies, the balance sheet always balances, meaning that assets must equal the sum of liabilities plus equity. This is known as the fundamental accounting equation:

$$\text{Assets = Liabilities + Equity}$$

or put another way

$$\text{Assets - Liabilities = Equity}$$

This fundamental accounting equation is represented in the same format in which most balance sheets are prepared, with assets listed on the left-hand side and liabilities and equity listed on the right-hand side. Alternatively, assets may be listed in the top half and liabilities and equity listed in the bottom half of the balance sheet.

EXAMPLE 2.2   **BALANCE SHEET DEPICTIONS**

The following two examples illustrate the two ways in which a balance sheet can be presented, as well as represent the fundamental accounting equation.

SIDE-BY-SIDE BALANCE SHEET DEPICTION

Assets	$5,000	Liabilities	$3,500
		Equity	$1,500
Total Assets	**$5,000**	**Total Liabilities & Equity**	**$5,000**

TOP AND BOTTOM BALANCE SHEET DEPICTION

Assets	$5,000
Total Assets	**$5,000**
Liabilities	$3,500
Equity	$1,500
Total Liabilities & Equity	**$5,000**

a. Components of the Balance Sheet

The three main categories reflected on an entity's balance sheet are assets, liabilities, and equity. Most entities will further divide these main categories into subcategories. An entity will subcategorize in a way that makes sense for its business and operations.

i. Assets

Assets at their most basic represent those things that the entity owns. They may be tangible, meaning you can see or touch them (e.g., inventory or equipment) or intangible, meaning you cannot see or touch them (e.g., a patent or goodwill). Some of the most common types of assets are cash and cash equivalents (cash and short-term liquid investments held by the entity); accounts receivable (money owed to the entity by customers); inventory (raw materials and goods held by the entity for sale); prepaid expenses (expenses paid in advance by the entity, such as its business insurance premium); property, plant, and equipment (land, buildings, machinery, furniture, and fixtures owned by the entity); long-term investments (investments in stocks and bonds held by the entity for the long-term); and intangibles (intellectual property owned by the entity and goodwill, or the premium paid for the purchase of another entity).

In order for an entity to classify an item as an asset of its business and report it on the balance sheet, that entity must (i) control the asset; (ii) believe the asset will provide a future economic value to the business; and (iii) be able to measure the value of the asset and reflect that value in dollars as a result of a past transaction.[1] Once it has been determined that an asset meets these criteria, the entity reflects the asset on its balance sheet. Most assets are recorded at historical cost (the amount of money the entity paid for that asset when it was purchased) and not current market value.

If an asset does not meet the three criteria stated above, it cannot be reflected on the entity's balance sheet. This means the entity does not benefit from being able to recognize that item as an asset of the business or something the business owns that adds economic value. Some items that fall into the category of non-recordable assets include the benefits an entity derives from its brand name recognition, the positive morale of its workforce, or the overall satisfaction of its customer base with the products or services it provides. All of these items have the potential to benefit the entity's reputation, business, and financial results; however, none of them can be reflected as an asset of the business because the entity does not directly control the assets, the assets do not provide future value, and the assets did not involve a past transaction that permits the entity to measure and value them.

---

[1] Robert Libby, Patricia A. Libby, & Daniel G. Short, Financial Accounting 46 (7th ed. 2011).

Assets are typically broken into two categories on an entity's balance sheet: current assets and long-term assets.

(a) Current Assets

Current assets are those items that the entity can readily access or convert to cash in 12 months or less. Current assets are listed first in the asset category of the entity's balance sheet and are generally listed in order of their liquidity, meaning those assets that are most easily converted to cash are listed first. The most common current assets are cash and cash equivalents, accounts receivable, inventory, and prepaid expenses.

EXAMPLE 2.3 **RETAILERS, INC. CURRENT ASSETS EXCERPT**

The following excerpted section of Retailers, Inc.'s balance sheet reflects the current assets for the current and prior fiscal years ending December 31. Retailers, Inc. has increased all of its current assets from last year to this year, meaning that each asset has grown or increased over the course of the year. For example, Retailers, Inc. grew its cash and cash equivalents $3,376 during the period, meaning it has a greater amount of cash and cash equivalents on hand that it can utilize in its business and operations. In addition, Retailers, Inc.'s accounts receivable increased by $699 during the period, indicating that it is owed more money from its customers at the end of the current year than it was owed at the end of the prior year. Retailers, Inc. also increased the amount of inventory it has on hand by $677, indicating it has an increased amount of inventory that it can sell to its customers. Lastly, Retailers, Inc.'s prepaid expenses and other current assets increased by $2,319, indicating that it prepaid additional expenses during the period and acquired other short-term assets.

	December 31 Current Year	December 31 Prior Year
Current Assets		
Cash and cash equivalents	$6,850	$3,474
Accounts receivable	2,798	2,099
Inventory	5,367	4,690
Prepaid expenses and other current assets	8,717	6,398
Total current assets	$23,732	$16,661

(b) Long-Term Assets

Long-term assets include those items that cannot be easily converted to cash in 12 months. These assets are generally meant to have a useful life of more than one year and are often utilized by the entity for the business's ongoing operations. Long-term assets are generally categorized as long-term investments; property, plant, and equipment; and intangibles.

EXAMPLE 2.4   **RETAILERS, INC. LONG-TERM ASSETS EXCERPT**

The following excerpted section of Retailers, Inc.'s balance sheet reflects the long-term assets for the current and prior fiscal years ending December 31. Retailers, Inc. increased all of its long-term assets from last year to this year. For instance, the balance sheet reflects that Retailers, Inc. acquired additional property in the amount of $75 and additional equipment in the amount of $72 during the current fiscal year that it now has on hand to utilize in its business operations. Retailers, Inc.'s intangible assets remained the same. Lastly, Retailers, Inc. acquired $952 of other long-term assets during the period, such as the purchase of additional long-term investments.

	December 31 Current Year	December 31 Prior Year
Property	$1,050	$975
Equipment	2,605	2,533
Less: Depreciation	(550)	(520)
Net equipment	2,055	2,013
Goodwill	1,232	1,222
Intangible assets	1,809	1,809
Less: Amortization	(653)	(600)
Net intangible assets	1,156	1,209
Other long-term assets	$5,706	$4,754

ii. Liabilities

Liabilities reflect what the entity owes to another party. Some of the most common types of liabilities are accounts payable (money owed by the entity to its creditors); other payables (money owed by the entity to pay such items as employee salaries or income taxes); unearned income (money received by the entity for goods or services not yet delivered or provided); and long-term debt (money owed by the entity to its commercial lenders).

In order for an entity to classify an item as a liability of the business and report it on the balance sheet, the entity (i) cannot avoid the duty to meet the liability or obligation; (ii) must pay or meet the obligation and provide an economic benefit to another party in the future; and (iii) must be able to measure the value of the liability or obligation as a result of a past transaction.[2] Once it has been determined that a liability meets these criteria, the entity records the transaction and reflects the liability on its balance sheet. Like assets, liabilities are recorded at cost or the amount of obligation the entity incurred in relation to that liability.

If a liability does not meet the three criteria stated above, it cannot be reflected on the entity's balance sheet, which means the entity does not

---

[2]*Id.* at 47.

recognize the future detriment to the business of owing and paying that liability. One liability that is non-recordable is the right to future borrowings under a commercial loan or line of credit facility. Even though the entity is entitled to borrow the funds in the future, the liability is not recordable until the money is actually borrowed. Another example of a non-recordable liability may be a contingent liability. A contingent liability is one of which the entity is aware (e.g., litigation) but for which it might not yet be able to estimate or measure the value. While these types of liabilities have the ability to detrimentally impact the entity, its reputation, business, and financial results, they cannot be reflected on the balance sheet because the entity does not yet owe the obligation or it cannot be valued.

As with assets, liabilities are typically broken into two categories: current liabilities and long-term liabilities.

(a) Current Liabilities

Current liabilities are those obligations that the entity must pay in the next 12 months or less. Current liabilities are listed first in the liability category of the entity's balance sheet and are often listed in order of greatest to least amount owed. The most common current liabilities are accounts payable, accrued liabilities or other payables, and the current portion of long-term debt (meaning that amount which matures and is due in the next 12 months).

EXAMPLE 2.5 **RETAILERS, INC. CURRENT LIABILITIES EXCERPT**

The following excerpted section of Retailers, Inc.'s balance sheet reflects current liabilities for the current and prior fiscal years ending December 31. Most of Retailers, Inc.'s current liabilities increased from last year to this year, indicating that it owes a greater amount in short-term obligations at the end of the current year. The exception is the revolving credit facility (Retailers, Inc.'s line of credit), where the liability is now zero, indicating that Retailers, Inc. paid the credit facility in full during the current fiscal year. Retailers, Inc.'s accounts payable increased $450, reflecting that it owes more money to its creditors and suppliers at the end of the current fiscal year as compared to the prior year. This may be the result of the purchase of additional inventory or property and equipment, which asset accounts both increased during the current fiscal year. Retailers, Inc.'s accrued expenses and other payables increased $139 during the period, indicating that it owes more at the end of the current fiscal year for those items, which may be the result of additional salary expenses or tax liabilities. Lastly, Retailers, Inc.'s current portion of long-term debt and other current liabilities also increased $1,454 and $1,209, respectively, which means that it owes more to its lenders and incurred additional obligations owed to other short-term creditors during the next 12 months than it did at the end of the prior year.

	December 31 Current Year	December 31 Prior Year
Current Liabilities		
Revolving credit facility	--	$750
Accounts payable	2,104	1,654
Accrued expenses and other payables	1,476	1,337
Current portion of long-term debt	1,951	497
Other current liabilities	3,456	2,247
Total current liabilities	$8,987	$6,485

(b) Long-Term Liabilities

Long-term liabilities are those obligations that are not due in the next 12 months. The most common long-term liabilities are long-term debt (money owed by the entity to its commercial lenders); bonds (money owed by the entity to the bond holders); deferred bonuses (money owed by the entity to employees for bonus obligations); or pension obligations (money owed by the entity to employees in the future under the entity's pension plan). Other long-term liabilities include the entity's commitments and contingencies (the entity's future obligations or possible future losses), when those obligations are probable and can be reasonably estimated.

EXAMPLE 2.6   **RETAILERS, INC. LONG-TERM LIABILITIES EXCERPT**

The following excerpted section of Retailers, Inc.'s balance sheet reflects the long-term liabilities for the current and prior fiscal years ending December 31. Retailers, Inc.'s long-term liabilities have grown from last year to this year, indicating it owes more money to its creditors in the long term. In particular, the amount of long-term debt has grown $1,500 from the prior fiscal year to the current fiscal year, which reflects an increase in Retailers, Inc.'s borrowings from its commercial lender. In addition, Retailers, Inc.'s other long-term liabilities increased by $181 during the period, indicating it may owe additional money as deferred bonus payments or to its employee pension fund.

	December 31 Current Year	December 31 Prior Year
Long-term debt, net of current maturities	$6,295	$4,795
Other long-term liabilities	679	498

iii. Equity

Equity is what remains after the total of all liabilities are deducted from the total of all assets of the entity. This amount reflects the residual interest of the owners of the entity, meaning that if the entity were to liquidate, receive full value for the assets, and pay off all of its liabilities, the remainder would represent the amount that would be distributed to the owners of the entity on a pro rata basis—thus equity. This residual interest is often referred to as the book value of the entity and reflects what the entity is worth on paper. Unlike assets and liabilities, the specific terminology used in the equity section on the balance sheet differs depending on the specific type of entity structure. To explain the different terminology, the next sections outline the components of the equity section of a balance sheet of four frequently encountered business types.

(a) Sole Proprietorship

A sole proprietorship is formed and owned by one individual. Generally that individual is responsible for the day-to-day management and operation of the business, though the individual may hire employees to assist with the operations. The residual interest in a sole proprietorship is called **proprietorship** and represents the money or property contributed by the owner to the business, the profits or losses incurred by the business over time, and the money or property withdrawn from the business by the owner. The equity section of the balance sheet of a sole proprietorship would have one line titled **proprietorship** that reflects all those amounts combined.

(b) Partnership

A partnership is an entity formed and owned by two or more persons with the intent to jointly operate a business for profit. Generally the partners are responsible for the day-to-day management and operation of the business, though the partners may hire employees to assist with the operations. The residual interest in a partnership is called **partners' equity** and represents the money or property contributed by all of the partners to the business, the profits or losses incurred by the business over time, and the money or property withdrawn from the business by all of the partners. The equity section of the balance sheet for a partnership often has one line titled **partners' equity** or **partners' capital** that reflects all of those amounts combined. However, the entity would maintain a separate account for each partner of the partnership as a part of its internal books and records. Those internal accounts, titled **partner's capital – [last name of partner]**, reflect each individual partner's contributions, withdrawals, and portion of the profits or losses of the entity. The portion of profits or losses allocated to an individual partner is based upon that partner's percentage of ownership interest.

(c) Limited Liability Company

A limited liability company is an entity formed pursuant to state law and owned by at least one or more persons or entities. The residual interest in a limited liability company is called **members' equity** and represents the money or property contributed by all of the members to the entity, the profits or losses incurred by the entity over time, and the money or property distributed or withdrawn from the entity by all of the members. The equity section of the balance sheet for a limited liability company generally has one line titled **members' equity** or **members' capital** that reflects all of those amounts combined. However, the entity maintains a separate account for each member of the limited liability company as a part of its internal books and records. Those internal accounts, titled **member's capital – [last name of member]** or **membership interest – [last name of member]**, reflect each individual member's contributions, distributions or withdrawals, and portion of the profits or losses of the entity. The portion of profits or losses allocated to an individual member is generally, though not always, based upon that member's percentage ownership interest.

(d) Corporation

A corporation is an entity formed pursuant to state law and owned by at least one or more persons or entities. The residual interest in a corporation is called **shareholders' equity** or **stockholders' equity** and represents the money or property contributed by all of the shareholders of the entity, the net income or loss incurred by the entity over time, and the money or property distributed by the entity to the shareholders (e.g., a dividend distribution). The equity section of the balance sheet for a corporation generally includes multiple accounts, and the amounts in all of the accounts combined represent the overall stockholders' equity. A corporation does not maintain a separate internal account for each stockholder as a partnership or limited liability company does for its partners or members. However, a corporation does track the ownership of its stock, either internally or through a third party called a transfer agent. The equity section of a corporation generally includes a combination of the following accounts:

(i)   Common Stock — The amount in this account reflects the number of shares of common stock that the corporation has sold (or issued) multiplied by the par value of the stock.

(ii) Preferred Stock — The amount in this account reflects the number of shares of preferred stock that the corporation has sold (or issued) multiplied by the par value of the stock.

(iii) Additional Paid-In-Capital — The amount in this account reflects the amount of money that the corporation received upon the sale of its common stock or preferred stock in excess of that stock's par value.

(iv) Treasury Stock — The amount in this account reflects the amount of money the corporation has spent to repurchase shares of its stock from its shareholders.

(v)   Retained Earnings or Accumulated Loss — The amount in this account reflects the amount of net income or net loss that the corporation has accrued since its inception. If the amount is positive, the account is called retained earnings, and if the amount is negative, the account is called accumulated loss.

(vi) Accumulated Other Comprehensive Income or Loss — The amount in this account reflects the amount of other income or loss that the corporation has accrued since its inception that does not directly relate to the entity's business operations. Amounts reflected in other comprehensive income or loss include such items as foreign currency adjustments, gains or losses on foreign currency transactions, and gains or losses on derivative instruments. If the amount is positive, the account is called accumulated comprehensive income, and if the amount is negative, the account is called accumulated comprehensive loss.

EXAMPLE 2.7 **RETAILERS, INC. EQUITY EXCERPT**

The following excerpted section of Retailers, Inc.'s balance sheet reflects the stockholders' equity for the current and prior fiscal years ending December 31. Retailers, Inc. has one class of stock — common stock. The amount indicated in common stock reflects the number of shares issued and outstanding (7,295,988 and 6,628,708, respectively) multiplied by the par value per share ($0.01), with the remainder of money earned from the sale of stock reflected in the additional paid-in-capital account. As evidenced in the balance sheet, Retailers, Inc. issued additional shares of common stock during the current fiscal year as the number of shares issued and outstanding (as reflected in the description of the stock) increased by a total of 667,280 shares. As a result, the common stock value and additional paid-in-capital value grew from the end of the prior fiscal year to the end of the current fiscal year to reflect the money received as a result of the sale of additional shares of common stock, $7 and $1,845, respectively.

Additionally, Retailers, Inc. increased retained earnings by $2,062 during the fiscal year, indicating that it had net income during the current fiscal year and thus increased its total retained earnings.

	December 31 Current Year	December 31 Prior Year
Stockholders' Equity		
Common stock, $0.01, par value, 40,000,000 shares authorized; 7,295,988 issued and outstanding as of December 31 Current Year and 6,628,708 issued and outstanding as of December 31 Prior Year	$73	$66
Additional paid-in-capital	6,687	4,842
Retained earnings	12,210	10,148
Total stockholders' equity	$18,970	$15,056

b. Application to Practice

While the balance sheet may not be the primary financial statement that an investor is interested in, it is often the financial statement with the most importance to lawyers. The balance sheet provides insight into the entity's overall financial health. It indicates the amount of cash and cash equivalents that the entity currently has on hand, as well as the value of all of the assets that it holds. These details often provide the financial background that helps a litigator determine whether it is economically viable to file a lawsuit against an entity or whether an award is collectible. For example, if the entity has a minimal amount of cash on hand or holds few assets with significant value, it may not be cost effective to bring a suit against that entity, as there is little of value to attach against in the event of a damages award.

A transactional lawyer may utilize the information contained on the balance sheet to assist a client that is interested in acquiring another entity. The lawyer may be able to point out potential financial concerns to the client based on a review of the target entity's balance sheet. For example, the target may have liabilities that are greater than its assets, indicating that the target owes more money than what it owns and so may not be able to meet its obligations. A review of the balance sheet can reveal the amount of long-term debt the target is carrying and whether it appears to have sufficient assets or resources to cover that future debt obligation. Ultimately, this glimpse at the financial health and condition of a business entity is important in many aspects of a lawyer's practice.

Balance Sheet Problems

Problem 2.1

Classify the following balance sheet accounts as assets, liabilities, or equity.

Accounts Payable	Inventory
Accumulated Loss	Long-Term Debt
Additional Paid-In-Capital	Marketable Securities *A*
Building	Prepaid Insurance *A*
Cash	Salaries Payable *L*
Common Stock	Unearned Income *L*
Contingency — *footnote disclosure*	

Problem 2.2

Indicate whether the following assets and liabilities are short-term or long-term and explain your reasoning.

Accounts Receivable	Prepaid Expense
Current Portion of Long-Term Debt	Property, Plant, & Equipment
Deferred Bonuses	Short-Term Investment
Intellectual Property	Taxes Payable
Pension Liability	Note Receivable

Problem 2.3

Indicate the amount that should be reflected in each partners' capital account at the end of the calendar year based upon the following information:

John Smith and Jane Williams started a partnership on January 1 of this year. John contributed $60,000 cash (60 percent ownership) and Jane contributed $40,000 cash (40 percent ownership) to fund the partnership's business and operations. During the course of the year, John took two withdrawals from the partnership of $2,500 and $5,000 and Jane took one withdrawal from the partnership of $7,500. The partnership made $30,000 in net profits as of the end of the calendar year.

What is the balance in John Smith's capital account as of December 31?

What is the balance in Jane Williams' capital account as of December 31?

2. Income Statement

The income statement (also referred to as the "profit and loss statement," "statement of operations," "statement of income," or "statement of earnings") reflects the net income or net loss of the entity for a period of time. The income statement reflects the revenue and gains that the entity made during the period and the expenses and losses the entity incurred during the period. The difference between the total of all revenues and gains and the total of all expenses and losses is the net income or net loss for the period or, in other words, the bottom line.

Unlike the balance sheet, which speaks as of a particular date, the income statement covers a period of time and reflects those events that occurred during the entire period, whether a month, quarter, or year. There are three main categories of items reflected on an entity's income statement: revenues, expenses, and other gains and losses.

a. Revenues

Revenues are always the first amount reported on an entity's income statement and reflect the dollar value of all of the products or services the entity sold during that particular period of time. Revenues are sometimes referred to as "sales," or in the case of a business that only provides services (e.g., law firm or accounting firm) the entity may call revenues "professional income." All of these terms are interchangeable and represent the same thing — the total amount of income for that period that resulted from the entity's sales of its primary products or services. In some cases, there may be a deduction from revenues called "returns and allowances" that reflects the dollar value of those products that were returned or the value of discounts or allowances the entity provided to its customers as part of the sales process. The difference between revenues and returns and allowances reflects the "net revenues" of the entity. Some entities may only record net revenues on their income statement.

EXAMPLE 2.8 **RETAILERS, INC. REVENUES EXCERPT**

The following excerpted section of Retailers, Inc.'s income statement reflects the revenues for the current and prior fiscal years ending December 31. Retailers, Inc.'s overall revenues and net revenues increased by $7,598 and $7,523, respectively, during the course of the year, indicating that it increased sales of its retail products during the period. Returns and allowances also increased by $75 as a result of additional product returns by customers or greater allowances provided by Retailers Inc., possibly to third-party resellers who bought in bulk quantities.

	December 31 Current Year	December 31 Prior Year
Revenues	$31,151	$23,553
Less: returns and allowances	(308)	(233)
Net revenues	$30,843	$23,320

b. Expenses

An entity reports a variety of costs and expenses on its income statement for those items that result in an actual or anticipated cash expenditure during that particular period. Expenses result from the entity's principal business operations and are reflected in two main categories on the income statement: cost of goods sold and operating expenses.

i. Cost of Goods Sold

Cost of goods sold (COGS) or cost of sales (COS) reflects the costs directly associated with producing the product or service that the entity sells. Examples of various costs that are included in COGS or COS are the cost to purchase the raw materials to manufacture the product, the cost of the direct labor to produce the product, the cost to purchase the product that is resold, or the cost to purchase inventory for use or sale. Only those COGS or COS associated with the revenues for that particular period are reflected as expenses on the income statement. The difference between revenues or net revenues and COGS or COS is the entity's "gross profit" for that period, which is a reflection of the profit the entity earned based on the sales and expenses directly associated with its products or services. Generally a manufacturer will use the term COGS, whereas a retailer may use the term COS. Some entities, such as professional organizations, may not have or reflect COGS or COS on their income statements.

EXAMPLE 2.9 RETAILERS, INC. COST OF GOODS SOLD EXCERPT

The following excerpted section of Retailers, Inc.'s income statement reflects the net revenues, COGS, and gross profit for the current and prior fiscal years ending December 31. Retailers, Inc.'s COGS grew by $3,768 during the period. As evidenced by Retailers, Inc.'s results, when an entity has increased sales of its products (increase in revenues) it will generally also have an increase in COGS because it requires additional raw materials and direct labor to produce the product that is sold, or the entity incurs additional costs to purchase the product that is resold to meet the increased sales demand.

	December 31 Current Year	December 31 Prior Year
Net revenues	$30,843	$23,320
Cost of goods sold	15,721	11,953
Gross profit	$15,122	$11,367

ii. Operating Expenses

Operating expenses reflect the costs the entity incurs as a result of running its business on a day-to-day basis that are not included in COGS or COS. Operating expenses are often combined and listed as selling, general, and administrative expenses (SG&A) on the income statement and include those costs related to the entity's efforts to sell its products or services and the costs related to the general operation of the entity. Examples of costs included in SG&A are sales commissions, marketing and advertising, research and development, depreciation and amortization, salaries, rent, utilities, office supplies, accounting and legal services, and licenses and fees. The difference between gross profit and operating expenses is "operating income" for that period, which is a reflection of the entity's profit from running its business on a day-to-day basis before taking into account other gains and losses, interest expense, and income tax expense.

EXAMPLE 2.10 RETAILERS, INC. OPERATING EXPENSES EXCERPT

The following excerpted section of Retailers, Inc.'s income statement reflects the gross profit, SG&A expenses, and operating income for the current and prior fiscal years ending December 31. Retailers, Inc.'s SG&A increased by $2,867 during the period, indicating an increase in those expenses associated with running the business on a day-to-day basis, such as an increase in marketing costs, research and development costs, or executive salaries.

	December 31 Current Year	December 31 Prior Year
Gross profit	$15,122	$11,367
Selling, general, and administrative expenses	11,582	8,715
Operating income	$3,540	$2,652

c. Other Income or Gains and Other Expenses or Losses

An entity must also report on its income statement other income or gains it recognizes, as well as other expenses or losses it incurs during that period of time. These items are tangential to the entity's business and do not result from its principal business operations. As a result, the items cannot be reflected in any of the previously discussed categories (revenues, COGS or COS, or SG&A). Items that may be reflected as other income or gains include dividend income (a cash dividend received by the entity); interest income (interest paid by a third party to the entity); gain on the sale of an asset (money received by the entity due to the sale of property or equipment); or other gains (gains resulting from derivative instruments or foreign currency fluctuations). Items that may be reflected as other expenses or losses include interest expense (money paid by the entity to its lenders); loss on the sale of an asset (loss recorded by the entity due to the sale of property or equipment); or other losses (losses resulting from derivative instruments or foreign currency fluctuations). The difference between operating income and other gains and losses is "income before income taxes" for that period.

EXAMPLE 2.11   **RETAILERS, INC. OTHER INCOME AND EXPENSE EXCERPT**

The following excerpted section of Retailers, Inc.'s income statement reflects the operating income, interest expense, other expenses, and income before income taxes for the current and prior fiscal years ending December 31. Retailers, Inc.'s interest expense increased by $24 during the period, indicating that it owed additional interest on its long-term borrowings during the current fiscal year. In addition, Retailers, Inc. had an increase of $53 in other expenses for the period, indicating that it incurred more additional expenses during the current fiscal year as compared to the prior year, such as a loss on a derivative instrument held for investment purposes.

	December 31 Current Year	December 31 Prior Year
Operating income	$3,540	$2,652
Interest expense	53	29
Other expenses	64	11
Income before income taxes	$3,423	$2,612

d. Income Tax Expense

Income tax expense reflects an estimate of the entity's income taxes for that particular period of time. The difference between income before income taxes and income tax expense is the "net income" or "net loss" for that particular period. If the difference is a positive amount, the entity made a profit, and if the difference is a negative amount, the entity suffered a loss.

EXAMPLE 2.12 **RETAILERS, INC. INCOME TAX EXPENSE EXCERPT**

The following excerpted section of Retailers, Inc.'s income statement reflects the income before income taxes, estimated income tax expense, and net income for the current and prior fiscal years ending December 31. Retailers, Inc.'s income tax expense increased during the current year by $375, indicating that it owed a greater amount of income taxes during the current fiscal year. In addition, Retailers, Inc. recognized a net income for the period, indicating that it made a bottom-line profit as a result of its overall business operations.

	December 31 Current Year	December 31 Prior Year
Income before income taxes	$3,423	$2,612
Provision for income taxes	1,361	986
Net Income	$2,062	$1,626

EXAMPLE 2.13 **INCOME STATEMENT PROFIT LEVELS AND TERMINOLOGY**

The following table sets forth a snapshot of the various profit, or income, levels on the income statement of an entity.

Net Revenues	$1,000,000
Less: Cost of Good Sold	($600,000)
Gross Profit	$400,000
Less: Selling, General, & Administrative	($250,000)
Operating Income	$150,000
Less: Other Gains (and Losses)	($10,000)
Earnings Before Interest and Taxes	$140,000
Less: Interest Expense	($15,000)
Less: Income Tax Expense	($33,000)
Net Income (Net Loss)	**$92,000**

e. Application to Practice

The income statement is most often sought out and examined to determine how much revenue the entity generated by selling its products or services, how much it spent to cover the expenses of running the business, and the amount of profit (or loss) the entity incurred for the given period. Ultimately, the income statement indicates whether or not the entity is making a profit, which is valuable information in many contexts.

A transactional lawyer assisting a client with obtaining a long-term loan or line of credit will need to examine and understand the income statement (as well as other financial statements) in conjunction with the various financial covenants and restrictions contained in the loan agreement, because many of these covenants and restrictions will mandate that certain financial thresholds and benchmarks be maintained by the client. A litigator representing an employee who claims he should have received a bonus because the entity he works for met the required financial benchmarks (e.g., a certain level of net revenues, gross profit, operating income, or net income) will need to examine the income statement and assess whether the required benchmarks were met.

Income Statement Problems

Problem 2.4

Classify the following income statement accounts as revenues, cost of goods sold, cost of sales, operating expenses, other income or gains, or other expenses or losses:

Advertising
Cost of Raw Materials
Depreciation
Dividend Income
Gain on the Sale of a Short-Term
  Investment
Interest Expense

Officers' Salaries
Production Workers' Wages
Professional Income
Cost of Inventory
Rent Expense
Utilities Expense

Problem 2.5

Fill in the blanks with the corresponding terms to track the flow of income through the income statement:

Revenues

Less ~~returns & allowances~~

= ~~Net Rev~~

Less ~~COGS~~

= ~~Gross Prof.~~

Less ~~SG&A~~

= ~~Op Income~~

Less ~~Other gains & losses~~

= ~~IBIT~~

Less ~~Int. Exp.~~

= ~~IBT~~

~~Less Taxes~~

~~= N.I~~

Net Income (Net Loss)
Gross Profit
Income Tax Expense
Net Revenues
Other Gains and Losses
Operating Income
Income Before Interest and Taxes
Revenue Returns and Allowances
Cost of Goods Sold
Interest Expense
Selling, General, and Administrative

Problem 2.6

Assume that Zero Corporation incurred the costs or expenses set forth below for the accounting period. Indicate its total Cost of Goods Sold (COGS) and Operating Expenses (SG&A) for the period.

Costs or Expenses	Amount
Costs of Raw Materials	$545,000
Rent Expense	$37,000
Salary Expense	$43,000
Direct Labor	$160,000
Interest Expense	$6,800
Tax Expense	$64,905
Marketing Expense	$18,000
Loss on Sale of Equipment	$27,000
Revenue Returns & Allowances	$5,500

Handwritten annotations: COGS, SG&A, ", COGS, Neither, SG&A, Extraordinary, Neither

Problem 2.7

Assume Zero Corporation had revenues of $1,275,000 for the accounting period. Using this information and the information from Problem 2.6, prepare an income statement and determine if Zero Corporation had a net income or net loss for the period.

3. Statement of Cash Flows

The statement of cash flows reflects the movement of cash within the entity as it shows the amount of cash inflows or cash receipts and the amount of cash outflows or cash payments for a period of time. In essence, the statement of cash flows reflects the changes that took place in the entity's cash balance from the beginning of the period to reach the entity's cash balance at the end of the period through a reconciliation process. The statement of cash flows reflects three main categories of information: (i) cash from or used in operating activities; (ii) cash from or used in investing activities; and (iii) cash from or used in financing activities.

a. Operating Activities

Operating activities reflect those transactions that are generally related to the principal business operations of the entity (producing the product or providing the services offered) or those events that allowed the entity to realize net income for the period.[3] This section of the statement of cash flows can be prepared in two different ways, utilizing the direct method or the indirect method.

i. Direct Method

The direct method reflects those items that directly impact cash flow from transactions that involve cash receipts by the entity and transactions that involve cash expenditures by the entity.[4] An entity that utilizes the direct method for operating activities would reflect the following transactions: (i) cash received from customers; (ii) cash received from the payment of interest or dividends to the entity; (iii) cash received from other operating activities; (iv) cash paid by the entity to its employees or short-term creditors; (v) cash expended for interest payments due; (vi) cash expended for income taxes due; and (vii) cash expended for other operating activities.[5]

EXAMPLE 2.14 **DIRECT METHOD EXAMPLE**

An example of the operating activities section of the statement of cash flows of an entity prepared using the direct method is set forth below:[6]

---

[3]ACCOUNTING STANDARDS CODIFICATION, Statement of Cash Flows, ASC §230-10-20 (Fin. Accounting Found. 2017).
[4]*Id.* §230-10-45.
[5]*Id.*
[6]This example does not utilize the financial statements and information provided in Exhibit A.

	December 31 Current Year	
Cash Flows from Operating Activities		
Cash received from sales of goods	$385,000	
Cash received from interest income	12,500	
Cash received from dividend income	18,000	
Cash provided by operating activities		$415,500
Cash paid to short-term creditors	$115,000	
Cash paid for operating expenses	89,500	
Cash paid for interest expense	14,750	
Cash paid for income tax expense	22,500	
Cash disbursed for operating activities		($241,75)
Net cash provided by operating activities		$173,750

ii. Indirect Method — starting from net income

The indirect method reflects the difference between net income as reported on the income statement and net cash flows determined from the entity's accounting information versus actual cash receipts and expenditures.[7]

In order to determine net cash flows from operating activities under the indirect method, the entity must adjust net income at the end of the period for (i) those items that did not affect cash or are noncash transactions, such as depreciation or amortization expense; (ii) gains or losses on the sale of equipment, as those transactions do not relate to the entity's principal business operations; and (iii) changes in its current asset and liability accounts, such as changes in accounts receivable, inventory, prepaid expenses, accounts payable, and other short-term payables.[8] Cash flows from operating activities ultimately reflects the amount of cash that is generated from the entity's principal business operations, which hopefully is an ongoing source of cash.

Preparing the operating activities section of the statement of cash flows using the indirect method is a bit tricky. The first concept to keep in mind is that while net income is a product of the income statement, the changes in an entity's operating asset and liability accounts only impact the balance sheet and not the income statement. As a result, net income must be adjusted to reflect the changes in the balances of those accounts from the beginning of the period to the end of the period in order to determine net cash flows from operating activities.

Except for cash and cash equivalent accounts, if an asset account (e.g., accounts receivable) increases from the beginning to the end of the period, that indicates that the entity spent cash to increase the asset (e.g., increased the amount of accounts receivable due from customers). That expenditure of cash, which is not reflected in the entity's net income, must be subtracted from

---

[7]Accounting Standards Codification, *supra* note 3, §230-10-45.
[8]*Id.*

net income as part of the reconciliation process. In the alternative, if an asset account (e.g., inventory) decreases from the beginning to the end of the period, that indicates that the entity spent less cash on that asset (e.g., decreased the amount of inventory on hand). In that case, the entity did not spend cash, and the difference must be added to net income to reflect the fact that the entity did not use, or freed up, cash which was not reflected in net income.

If a liability account (e.g., accounts payable) decreases from the beginning to the end of the period, that indicates that the entity expended cash to reduce that particular liability (e.g., paid an obligation due a supplier), which cash reduction was not reflected in net income. As a result, that decrease must be subtracted from net income as part of the reconciliation process. In the alternative, if a liability account (e.g., income taxes payable) increases from the beginning to the end of the period, that indicates that the entity did not pay that liability or expend cash (e.g., deferred paying income taxes). As a result, the entity must add back that difference to net income to reflect the fact that it did not use up that cash during the period.

EXAMPLE 2.15   **OPERATING ACTIVITIES ADJUSTMENTS**

The following table summarizes the adjustments an entity makes to its net income (or loss) in the operating activities section of the statement of cash flows.

Balance Sheet Account	Change in Account's Balance	Adjustment to Net Income
Asset	Increase in Balance	Subtract from Net Income
Asset	Decrease in Balance	Add to Net Income
Liability	Increase in Balance	Add to Net Income
Liability	Decrease in Balance	Subtract from Net Income

The entity would follow this process for each of its asset and liability accounts on the balance sheet that pertain to the entity's principal business operations. Those adjustments, in conjunction with the adjustments for noncash transactions and the sale of long-term assets, ultimately result in the amount of net cash flows from operating activities for the period.

EXAMPLE 2.16   **RETAILERS, INC. CASH FLOWS FROM OPERATING ACTIVITIES EXCERPT**

The following excerpted section of Retailers, Inc.'s statement of cash flows reflects cash flows from operating activities for the current fiscal year ending December 31. This section leads off with net income for the period, which is reflected on Retailers, Inc.'s income statement. Next, adjustments are made for those items reflected on the income statement that did not impact Retailers, Inc.'s cash balance or are not attributable to its primary business operations.

Using Retailers, Inc.'s cash flows from the operating activities excerpt below, depreciation and amortization are added back to net income, as each of these items was reflected as an expense on its income statement and each is a non-cash transaction. Next, Retailers, Inc. adjusts for changes in its operating asset and liability accounts. Retailers, Inc.'s asset accounts of accounts receivable, inventories, and prepaid expenses and other assets increased from the prior fiscal year to the current fiscal year end, which indicates that it spent cash, so those increases are deducted from net income. Additionally, Retailers, Inc.'s current liability accounts, which include accounts payable and accrued expenses and other liabilities, increased from the prior fiscal year to the current fiscal year end, which indicates that it spent less cash, so these increases are added back to net income. After taking into account all of the adjustments, Retailers, Inc. can determine that it had net cash used in operating activities of $523, meaning its primary operations did not generate cash for the period.

	December 31 Current Year
Cash Flows from Operating Activities	
Net income	$2,062
Adjustments to reconcile net income to net cash used in operating activities:	
Depreciation and amortization	83
Changes in operating assets and liabilities, net of effects of acquisitions:	
Accounts receivable	(699)
Inventories	(677)
Prepaid expenses and other current assets	(3,271)
Accounts payable	450
Accrued expenses and other current liabilities	1,529
Net cash used in operating activities	($523)

b. Investing Activities

Investing activities reflect those activities that arise in connection with the purchase or sale of items for the purpose of generating returns that are not directly related to the entity's principal business operations. Examples of cash inflows from investing activities include collection of loans made to other entities; sales of short-term investments or bonds; sales of property, plant, and equipment; or the sale of a business unit.[9] Examples of cash outflows from investing activities include loans to other entities; purchases of short-term investments or

---

[9]ACCOUNTING STANDARDS CODIFICATION, Statement of Cash Flows, ASC §230-10-45 (Fin. Accounting Found. 2017).

bonds; purchases of property, plant, and equipment; or the purchase of another business.[10]

EXAMPLE 2.17 **RETAILERS, INC. CASH FLOWS FROM INVESTING ACTIVITIES EXCERPT**

The following excerpted section of Retailers, Inc.'s statement of cash flows reflects cash flows from investing activities for the current fiscal year ending December 31. During the current fiscal year, Retailers, Inc. made a number of cash expenditures. It purchased $147 worth of new property and equipment and acquired a business for $10. Since Retailers, Inc. engaged in these purchases, it expended cash and reflects a deduction, and as a result the net cash used in investing activities is $157.

	December 31 Current Year
Cash Flows from Investing Activities	
Purchases of property and equipment	($147)
Purchase of business	(10)
Net cash used in investing activities	($157)

c. Financing Activities

Financing activities reflect those activities that directly affect the entity's owners or creditors as a result of the entity's need for financing. Examples of cash inflows from financing activities include the receipt of proceeds from the sales of stock or other equity, proceeds from the issuance of debt, and proceeds from long-term borrowings.[11] Examples of cash outflows from financing activities include the repurchase of the entity's stock, redemption of the entity's debt instruments, repayment of long-term borrowings, and payment of cash dividends.[12]

EXAMPLE 2.18 **RETAILERS, INC. CASH FLOWS FROM FINANCING ACTIVITIES EXCERPT**

The following excerpted section of Retailers, Inc.'s statement of cash flows reflects cash flows from financing activities for the current fiscal year ending December 31. During the current fiscal year, Retailers, Inc. paid off its revolving credit facility, made payments on its long-term debt obligation, and paid debt financing costs. As these are all cash expenditures, each is represented as a

[10]*Id.*
[11]*Id.*
[12]*Id.*

deduction. On the other hand, Retailers, Inc. borrowed additional money and received proceeds from the exercise of stock options and stock issuances. As these are all cash receipts, each is represented as an increase. After taking into account all cash receipts and expenditures, Retailers, Inc. recognized $4,056 in net cash provided by financing activities.

	December 31 Current Year
Cash Flows from Financing Activities	
Payments on revolving credit facility	($750)
Proceeds from long-term debt	3,931
Payments on long-term debt	(870)
Proceeds from exercise of stock options and other stock issuances	1,852
Payments of debt financing costs	(107)
Net cash provided by financing activities	$4,056

d. Net Increase or Decrease in Cash

The final step in the statement of cash flows is to determine the amount by which the entity's cash increased or decreased for that period of time in order to reconcile the change in the entity's cash balance. In order to determine net cash flow, the entity must add together net cash from operating activities, investing activities, and financing activities, which is then added to or subtracted from the cash balance at the beginning of the period to reconcile to the cash balance at the end of the period.

EXAMPLE 2.19 **RETAILERS, INC. NET CASH INCREASE OR DECREASE EXCERPT**

The following excerpted section of Retailers, Inc.'s statement of cash flows reflects the final adjustments and reconciliation of cash at the beginning of the period to cash at the end of the period. For clarity, the net cash used or provided from operating, investing, and financing activities is included in this excerpt. After totaling net cash from operating activities, investing activities, and financing activities, Retailers, Inc. had a net increase in cash and cash equivalents of $3,376 during the current fiscal year. By adding the net cash increase to the cash and cash equivalents balance of $3,474 at the beginning of the fiscal year, it reconciles to the cash and cash equivalents balance of $6,850 at the end of the fiscal year.

	December 31 Current Year
Net cash used in operating activities	($523)
Net cash used in investing activities	(157)
Net cash provided by financing activities	4,056
Net increase in cash and cash equivalents	3,376
Cash and Cash Equivalents	
Beginning of period	$3,474
End of period	$6,850

e. Application to Practice

The statement of cash flows is the financial statement that lawyers may utilize the least as compared to the balance sheet and income statement. While the statement of cash flows is critical in that it sets out how the entity is generating cash and where that cash comes from, as well as how and where the entity is spending cash, it likely has less relevance for lawyers. However, it does provide a picture of whether or not the entity is generating cash and how it is generating or using cash, and can indicate if the entity is positioned to meet its debt obligations, purchase new PP&E, pay a cash dividend, or continue operations without relying on additional financing.

    The statement of cash flows can be important to a transactional lawyer engaged in a merger and acquisition context, as it can be critical to understand how the target entity is generating cash — from its operations (or primary business) or from borrowings and sales of additional stock (outside financing). An entity generating cash from its operations as opposed to one that is overdependent on borrowings may indicate a financially healthier target. As a result, the statement of cash flows is relevant to a lawyer's practice, but just not utilized as frequently as the balance sheet and income statement.

Cash Flow Problems

Problem 2.8

Classify the following items into the appropriate section of the statement of cash flows: operating activities, investing activities, or financing activities:

Proceeds from Stock Option
  Exercises F
Accounts Receivable Change O
Purchase of New Property Inv
Paying Down a Line of Credit F
Prepaid Expenses Change O

Sale of a Business Unit Inv.
Inventory Change O
Sale of a Piece of Equipment Inv.
Sale of Corporate Bonds Inv.
Accounts Payable Change O
Repurchase of Common Stock F.

Problem 2.9

Zero Corporation has provided the information below. Use that information to reconcile cash and cash equivalents at the beginning of the period to the end of the period through the creation of a simple statement of cash flows.

Beginning Cash & Cash Equivalents Balance	$935,000
Ending Cash & Cash Equivalents Balance	$903,000
Net Income	$43,000
Depreciation Expense	$31,000
Changes in Operating Assets & Liabilities, net	($90,000)
Net Cash Used/Provided by Investing Activities	($24,000)
Net Cash Used/Provided by Financing Activities	$8,000

4. Statement of Changes in Stockholders' Equity

The statement of changes in stockholders' equity reflects a detailed summary of the changes that occurred in the stockholders' equity accounts for a period of time. It presents the balances in various equity accounts at the beginning of the period and sets out the changes that occurred during the period to arrive at the ending balances for the period. There are two main types of changes that occur to stockholders' equity: changes that occur as a result of transactions with the entity's shareholders during the period, and changes that occur as a result of changes in the entity's comprehensive income for the period.

The statement of changes in stockholders' equity will reflect how those components in the equity section of the entity's balance sheet changed from the beginning to the end of the current fiscal year. That means this particular financial statement may reflect changes to the following accounts: common stock, preferred stock, additional paid-in-capital, treasury stock, and retained earnings. Changes that result from transactions with the entity's shareholders include the sale of capital stock (whether common or preferred), the issuance and exercise of shares pursuant to stock option plans, the payment of other share-based compensation, and the purchase or sale of treasury stock. Changes that result from transactions affecting the entity's comprehensive income include such items as the entity's recognizing net income or net loss for the period, revaluing a fixed asset, incurring other gains or losses, and restating financial statements.

EXAMPLE 2.20   **RETAILERS, INC. STATEMENT OF CHANGES IN STOCKHOLDERS' EQUITY EXCERPT**

The following excerpted section of Retailers, Inc.'s statement of changes in stockholders' equity reflects changes in stockholders' equity from the end of the prior fiscal year to the end of the current fiscal year. The following transactions, which occurred during the current fiscal year, impacted Retailers, Inc.'s equity account balances.

Employees of Retailers, Inc. exercised 600,000 common stock options during the period for an increase in value of common stock of $6 and additional paid-in-capital of $1,550. Retailers, Inc. issued 67,280 shares of common stock, which resulted in an increase of $1 and $295 in the value of common stock and additional paid-in-capital, respectively. Lastly, Retailers, Inc. recognized an increase in retained earnings of $2,062, its net income for the period. As a result of these changes in stockholders' equity during the period, overall equity increased $3,914 from $15,056 at the end of the prior fiscal year to $18,970 at the end of the current fiscal year.

	Common Stock		Additional Paid-In Capital	Retained Earnings	Total Stockholders' Equity
	Shares	Amount			
Balance as of End of Prior Fiscal Year	$6,628	$66	$4,842	$10,148	$15,056
Exercise of stock options	600	6	1,550	-	1,556
Issuance of common stock	67	1	295	-	296
Net income (loss)				2,062	2,062
Balance as of End of Current Fiscal Year	$7,295	$73	$6,687	$12,210	$18,970

5. Interconnections Between the Financial Statements

While it may not be obvious when examining each financial statement individually, there are connections between the four financial statements. This section discusses some of those interconnections utilizing Retailers, Inc.'s financial statements.

a. Balance Sheet and Income Statement

The main connection between the balance sheet and income statement pertains to the equity section of the balance sheet and the net income or net loss reflected on the income statement. At the end of each accounting period, the net income or net loss is added to or subtracted from the retained earnings or accumulated loss account in the equity section of the balance sheet.

retained earnings

EXAMPLE 2.21 **RETAILERS, INC.'S BALANCE SHEET AND INCOME STATEMENT INTERCONNECTION**

Utilizing Retailers, Inc.'s financial statements, the $2,062 in net income for the current fiscal year end will be added to the retained earnings account on

Retailers, Inc.'s balance sheet. This tracks with the increase in retained earnings of $2,062 from the end of the prior fiscal year to the end of the current fiscal year.

b. Balance Sheet and Statement of Changes in Stockholders' Equity

There is a direct connection between the balance sheet and the statement of changes in stockholders' equity, as the latter statement sets out all of the changes that occurred in the entity's equity accounts (or the equity section of the balance sheet) during the period.

EXAMPLE 2.22 **RETAILERS, INC.'S BALANCE SHEET AND STATEMENT OF CHANGES IN STOCKHOLDERS' EQUITY INTERCONNECTION**

For instance, Retailers, Inc.'s common stock account on its balance sheet increased by $7 from $66 at the end of the prior fiscal year to $73 at the end of the current fiscal year, which is detailed on the statement of changes in stockholders' equity as stock option exercises of $6 and issuance of common stock of $1. Retailers, Inc.'s additional paid-in-capital account increased $1,845 as a result of the stock option exercises and sales of additional shares of common stock of $1,550 and $295, respectively.

Also, Retailers, Inc.'s retained earnings balance increased $2,062 during the fiscal year from $10,148 at the end of the prior year to $12,210 at the end of the current year. This change was a result of the net income for the period of $2,062 as reflected on its income statement.

When all of the above transactions are accounted for, the results track with Retailers, Inc.'s overall change in equity from $15,056 at the end of the prior year to $18,970 at the end of the current year, or a $3,914 increase.

c. Balance Sheet and Statement of Cash Flows

There are a number of connections between an entity's balance sheet and the operating activities section of the statement of cash flows. In particular, the changes in the operating asset and liability accounts from the end of the prior period to the end of the current period are reflected in the operating activities section of the statement of cash flows, if the indirect method is used.

EXAMPLE 2.23 **RETAILERS, INC.'S BALANCE SHEET AND STATEMENT OF CASH FLOWS INTERCONNECTION**

The following excerpted portion of Retailers, Inc.'s statement of cash flows indicates that accounts receivable, inventories, and prepaid expenses and other current assets increased during the period in the amounts of $699, $677, and

$3,271, respectively. Accounts payable and accrued expenses and other current liabilities also increased during the period in the amounts of $450 and $1,529, respectively. In examining the excerpted current assets and current liabilities sections of the balance sheet, those changes can be calculated by subtracting the balance in the prior fiscal year from the current fiscal year.

EXCERPT FROM THE OPERATING ACTIVITIES SECTION OF A STATEMENT OF CASH FLOWS

Operating Activities	
Changes in operating assets and liabilities:	
Accounts receivable	($699)
Inventory	(677)
Prepaid expenses and other current assets	(3,271)
Accounts payable	450
Accrued expenses and other current liabilities	1,529

EXCERPT FROM CURRENT ASSETS SECTION OF A BALANCE SHEET

	December 31 Current Year	December 31 Prior Year	Difference Between Current and Prior Year
Current Assets			
Accounts receivable	$2,798	$2,099	$699
Inventories	$5,367	$4,690	$677
Prepaid expenses and other current assets	$14,423	$611,152	$3,271

EXCERPT FROM CURRENT LIABILITIES SECTION OF A BALANCE SHEET

	December 31 Current Year	December 31 Prior Year	Difference Between Current and Prior Year
Current Liabilities			
Accounts payable	$2,104	$1,654	$450
Accrued expenses and other current liabilities	$5,611	$4,082	$1,529

Overview of Accounting and Auditing Principles

A. INTRODUCTION

Accounting and auditing principles and standards are important components of the accounting profession. Accounting principles were developed to assist entities in the preparation of their financial statements and reports and to provide accountants with standards to utilize. Accounting principles, generally, are the standards that an entity follows in the preparation of its financial statements, whether that entity uses Generally Accepted Accounting Principles or some other type of accounting standards. By utilizing these standards, and doing so in a consistent manner from period to period, the entity can create financial statements that are more easily readable and understood by the users of those financial statements. Additionally, when prepared consistently, financial statements can be used as a tool to compare and contrast an entity's results across time.

Auditing principles were developed to provide guidance to independent accountants in the performance and conduct of an audit. Generally Accepted Auditing Standards and Public Company Accounting Oversight Board Auditing Standards are the guidelines that auditors follow to ensure that an entity's financial statements have been prepared accurately and consistently. These guidelines cover the process of an audit from start to finish.

B. ACCOUNTING BODIES

The primary entity that establishes Generally Accepted Accounting Principles (GAAP), the standards for businesses and nonprofit organizations, is the

Financial Accounting Standards Board (FASB). FASB is an independent, not-for-profit organization that was established in 1973.[1] While the U.S. Securities and Exchange Commission (SEC) has the authority to establish accounting standards for publicly traded or SEC reporting companies, the SEC recognizes the GAAP standards established by FASB as authoritative and supplements those GAAP standards through SEC-promulgated regulations. The Governmental Accounting Standards Board (GASB), also an independent, nonprofit organization, establishes GAAP standards for state and local governments.

The Financial Accounting Foundation (FAF), which was established in 1972, is the independent, not-for-profit body that oversees both FASB and GASB.[2] The FAF is in charge of the oversight and administration of both FASB and GASB, and appoints the members who serve on the boards of both bodies.[3] FASB is made up of seven board members, each of whom must sever all ties with firms or institutions with which they previously worked and commit to serving in a full-time capacity.[4] The diverse board, as a whole, must have a collective knowledge of "accounting, finance, business, accounting education, and research" and serve the public's interest in matters relating to financial information reporting.[5] FASB board members serve for terms of five years and may serve for up to ten years.[6] The overarching mission of FASB and GASB, with the oversight of the FAF, "is to establish and improve financial accounting and reporting standards to provide useful information to investors and other users of financial reports and educate stakeholders on how to most effectively understand and implement those standards."[7]

In addition to the FAF and the FASB board members, FASB Advisory Groups serve as a FASB resource.[8] These advisory groups provide advice on many issues, including technical matters; project priorities; investor, not-for-profit, and small business perspectives; private company matters; and emerging issues.[9]

1. Generally Accepted Accounting Principles

An entity prepares financial statements and reports in order to provide information about its financial condition and results of operations, whether a public or private entity. This information provides a reader with knowledge of the entity's financial position through its balance sheet, its results of operations through its income statement, its generation and use of cash through its statement of cash flows, and its changes in equity through its statement of changes in stockholders' equity. In order to assist entities in preparing these financial

---

[1] FASB, About the FASB, *available at* http://www.fasb.org/jsp/FASB/Page/LandingPage&cid=1175805317407.
[2] *Id.*
[3] *Id.*
[4] *Id.*
[5] *Id.*
[6] *Id.*
[7] *Id.*
[8] *Id.*
[9] *Id.*

statements and the accompanying footnote disclosure, accounting standards were developed and established. These accounting standards are known as GAAP. GAAP is the product of standards and conventions developed over time to provide entities with guidance in how to prepare and present information in their financial statements. GAAP establishes a consistent way for entities to measure and disclose their financial results.

a. FASB Accounting Standards Codification

The sole source for GAAP standards is the FASB Accounting Standards Codification (Codification). The Codification, which became effective on September 15, 2009, sets out all authoritative GAAP standards with the exception of the rules issued by the SEC, which only apply to SEC reporting companies. The Codification is organized by topics, which significantly differs from the prior organization of GAAP by individual standards.

FASB also issues Concepts Statements, which are intended to set forth objectives and concepts that FASB will use in its determination and development of future GAAP accounting standards.[10] These Concepts Statements inform the public about current matters that FASB believes warrant recognition or measurement for financial reporting purposes.[11] Concepts Statements, in and of themselves, do not create authoritative GAAP standards. To date, FASB has issued eight Concepts Statements, some of which supersede or replace prior statements.

When a change is made to the Codification, FASB issues an Accounting Standards Update (ASU) that sets forth the change, the rationale for the change, and the date the change becomes effective.[12] An ASU is not an authoritative standard — it is not until the change becomes effective and part of the Codification that it is an authoritative GAAP standard.[13]

C. ACCOUNTING ASSUMPTIONS, PRINCIPLES, AND CONSTRAINTS

In addition to the basic objectives regarding an entity's financial reporting, there are also a number of accounting assumptions, principles, and constraints that must be taken into consideration. Any entity preparing its financial statements in accordance with GAAP should take these principles and guidelines into account as a part of that financial statement preparation and reporting

---

[10]FASB Concepts Statements, *available at* http://www.fasb.org/jsp/FASB/Page/PreCodSectionPage&cid=1176156317989.
[11]*Id.*
[12]FASB Accounting Standards Updates Issued, *available at* http://www.fasb.org/jsp/FASB/Page/SectionPage&cid=1176156316498.
[13]*Id.*

process. These principles and guidelines represent the "conceptual framework" of financial reporting for business entities.[14]

1. General Assumptions

There are four general accounting assumptions that address how an entity operates and how financial transactions are recorded. In essence, these assumptions are rules of conduct for the business more so than actual accounting principles. In the event that one of these assumptions is violated, an entity's financial statements may be inaccurate or misleading.

a. Business Entity Assumption

The business entity assumption sets forth the concept that the business entity is distinct and separate from the owners of the entity, whether shareholders, partners, or members, as well as separate from any other businesses.[15] The idea is that the business entity must track its financial transactions and accounts separately from the owners and related businesses, meaning that the entity operates as a stand-alone "person."[16] The business entity and the owners' financial transactions and accounts should not be intermingled because, if intermingled, the business entity cannot accurately reflect its financial condition and operations. This underlying assumption holds true for corporations, partnerships, limited liability companies, and sole proprietorships. With that said, generally a parent entity will prepare consolidated financial statements for the parent and its subsidiaries, and this consolidated reporting does not violate the business entity assumption. The business entity assumption allows users of the entity's financial statements to understand how the entity itself, as a stand-alone business, is operating and performing.

b. Going Concern Assumption

The going concern assumption sets forth the concept that it is presumed that a business entity will operate indefinitely with no predetermined end date.[17] In other words, the entity will continue as a going concern into the foreseeable future with no intention of ceasing business operations in the near term. This assumption allows an entity to engage in the prepayment of or accrual for certain expenses, as well as to recognize depreciation and amortization of its assets. If an entity did not intend to continue operations, there would be no valid rationale to engage in those types of accounting practices.

---

[14]ROBERT LIBBY, PATRICIA A. LIBBY, & DANIEL G. SHORT, FINANCIAL ACCOUNTING 45 (7th ed. 2011).
[15]*Id.* at 45-46.
[16]*Id.*
[17]*Id.* at 46.

c. Monetary Unit Assumption

The monetary unit assumption sets forth the concept that a business entity will record its financial transactions using one stable monetary unit or currency.[18] The presumption is that the chosen monetary unit (e.g., U.S. dollars) is a stable currency and that all financial transactions can be reported in that currency notwithstanding the effects of inflation. If a financial transaction cannot be expressed in terms of the chosen currency, it cannot be recorded. As a result of this assumption, assets purchased years apart are recorded at their historical costs and not periodically adjusted for inflation, meaning a piece of equipment bought in 1990 for $30,000 is reflected the same as a piece of equipment bought in 2015 for $30,000.

d. Time Period Assumption

The time period assumption, also known as the periodicity assumption, sets forth the concept that the activities of a business entity can be parsed into artificial periods of time, or accounting periods (month, quarter, or year).[19] As a result, the entity's financial results are measured and reported for each of those accounting periods even though the entity continues to operate indefinitely into the future. This assumption allows users of an entity's financial statements to review its performance for those periods of time and to compare the entity's performance from one period to the next.

2. General Principles

There are four general accounting principles that address how an entity must record and report its financial transactions. These principles are rules that an entity must follow and provide a basis for consistent and accurate reporting of financial transactions.

a. Historical Cost Principle

The historical cost principle requires a business entity to record assets at their historical costs or original purchase prices.[20] The entity continues to reflect its assets on its balance sheet at those historical costs rather than reporting their current fair market values. While not generally an accurate reflection of the value of the assets, it does provide a reliable and consistent presentation of financial information. It also prevents an entity from having to constantly undertake an assessment and valuation of its assets each accounting period so those items can be reflected at fair value. Additionally, using historical costs

---

[18]*Id.*
[19]*Id.* at 104.
[20]*Id.* at 46-47.

limits the entity's discretion in reporting fair market value and curtails the subjectivity in the value of those items reported on its balance sheet.

b. Revenue Recognition Principle

The revenue recognition principle requires a business entity to record and recognize revenue only if it has been earned and can be measured.[21] Revenue is generally earned when the product has been sold or the service has been performed (meaning it is realizable and realized). As a result, an entity records earned revenue even if it has not received payment from the customer. The revenue recognition principle is a key concept of accrual-based accounting and allows an entity to record and recognize revenue before payment is actually received.

c. Matching Principle

The matching principle requires a business entity to match expenses with the revenues that those expenses helped to generate.[22] As a result, expenses are recorded with their corresponding revenues and not necessarily when the entity incurs or pays for the expense. If an expense cannot be tied to revenues (e.g., administrative personnel salaries), it should be recorded and recognized in the current period. The matching principle is also a key concept of accrual-based accounting and allows an entity to tie direct expenses to revenues no matter when those expenses were actually incurred or paid.

d. Full Disclosure Principle

The full disclosure principle requires a business entity to disclose important and relevant information in its financial statements or related footnotes if the entity believes such information would matter to a user of its financial statements.[23] As a result, users of an entity's financial statements have a full picture of the entity and its operations. Information may be disclosed on the face of the financial statements, may be included in the related footnotes, or may be provided as supplemental information.

3. General Constraints

There are six general accounting constraints that address principles an entity should adhere to in recording and reporting financial transactions. These

---

[21] *Id.* at 108-109.
[22] *Id.* at 111-112.
[23] *Id.* at 236.

constraints permit an entity to provide useful financial information to users by modifying and limiting the general accounting assumptions and principles.

a. Materiality Constraint

The materiality constraint requires an entity to disclose all material information in its financial statements if such information would impact the opinion of a user.[24] Or on the flip side, it allows an entity to not disclose information that is immaterial in its financial statements or immaterial to a user of its financial statements. Materiality is a relative concept, and what is material to one entity may be immaterial to another entity. As a result, an entity has to make a case-by-case assessment of whether the information is material or immaterial in light of its financial position and context to determine if it should be included and disclosed.

b. Conservatism Constraint

The conservatism constraint requires an entity to err on the side of conservatism and to choose the accounting methodology that is least likely to result in an overstatement of assets and gains or an understatement of liabilities and losses.[25] In addition, an entity should employ this constraint when reflecting estimates in its financial statements, such as allowances for doubtful accounts or contingencies. The idea is that it is better to be conservative than aggressive in reporting financial results.

c. Industry Practices Constraint

The industry practices constraint requires an entity to take into consideration industry practices even if such practice deviates from GAAP.[26] The concept is that an entity should report its financial information in a manner that is consistent with how the industry as a whole reports the financial information. This adherence to industry practices provides for a more accurate presentation of industrywide financial information and results for users.

d. Consistency Constraint

The consistency constraint requires an entity to follow the same accounting practices from period to period so that accounting principles are consistently applied to the entity's financial transactions, and thus financial statements are more readily comparable across time.[27] Notwithstanding this constraint, if a

---

[24]*Id.* at 237.
[25]*Id.*
[26]*Id.* at 236.
[27]*Id.*

more relevant accounting principle exists, an entity should not refrain from implementing the new principle due to consistency constraints.

e. Cost Constraint

The cost constraint requires an entity to weigh the costs and benefits of providing information in its financial statements to assess whether the costs outweigh the benefits.[28] The idea is that it would be cost prohibitive if an entity had to report every single piece of information, and so the entity has the freedom to assess whether the information is of the type that requires a greater cost to gather and report than the value derived by the users of the financial statements if that piece of information was included.

f. Objectivity Constraint

The objectivity constraint requires an entity to record its financial transactions and present its financial statements based on reliable, objective, and unbiased evidence.[29] Financial statements should be prepared with researched and fact-based evidence and not based upon an unsubstantiated opinion. This constraint ultimately results in financial statements with greater accuracy and reliability.

D. AMERICAN INSTITUTE OF CERTIFIED PUBLIC ACCOUNTANTS

The American Institute of Certified Public Accountants (AICPA) was founded in 1887 and is the entity that establishes rules and standards regarding services provided by certified public accountants (CPAs) to their clients, including audits of private companies.[30] In particular, the AICPA establishes Generally Accepted Auditing Standards (GAAS). Additionally, the AICPA engages in advocacy, provides educational publications, develops and scores the CPA exam, and oversees CPA compliance with the profession's technical as well as ethical standards.[31] The organization is made up of staff and volunteers who oversee and carry out its mission and objectives. The AICPA Governing Council sets the organization's programs and policies in compliance with the AICPA bylaws and is composed of 265 members who serve terms of varying lengths.[32] The AICPA Board of Directors acts as the primary executive committee for the Governing

---

[28]*Id.*
[29]*Id.*
[30]AICPA Mission and History, *available at* http://www.aicpa.org/About/MissionandHistory/Pages/default.aspx.
[31]*Id.*
[32]AICPA Governing Council, *available at* http://www.aicpa.org/ABOUT/GOVERNANCE/AICPACOUNCIL/Pages/default.aspx.

Council and is made up of elected and appointed members from across the United States and its territories.[33]

1. Generally Accepted Auditing Standards

GAAS are standards utilized by auditors in the undertaking and performance of an audit of a private (non-publicly traded or reporting) entity. GAAS, developed by the AICPA, establish the objectives for independent auditors and explain how an audit should be designed in order for the auditor to meet those objectives.[34] In addition to setting standards for how an audit should be conducted, GAAS contain requirements regarding an independent auditor's general responsibilities.[35] While GAAS are initially issued as Statements on Auditing Standards, these statements are later codified in a topical manner as sections that are delineated by the moniker, "AU-C Section #."

E. PUBLIC COMPANY ACCOUNTING OVERSIGHT BOARD

The primary entity that establishes Auditing Standards (AS) for registered public accounting firms is the Public Company Accounting Oversight Board (PCAOB). The PCAOB is a nonprofit entity established under the Sarbanes-Oxley Act of 2002 to oversee audits of public companies.[36] The Dodd-Frank Wall Street Reform and Consumer Protection Act amended the Sarbanes-Oxley Act, giving the PCAOB authority to also oversee audits of brokers and dealers.[37] The SEC is the body responsible for overseeing the PCAOB and for appointing the members of the PCAOB Board, as well as approving the organization's rules, standards, and budget.[38] The PCAOB Board is made up of five members appointed by the SEC for staggered five-year terms.[39] There are also two advisory groups that provide advice to the PCAOB Board. The Investor Advisory Group provides advice regarding broad policy issues, and the Standing Advisory Group provides advice regarding auditing and professional standards.[40]

The PCAOB is tasked with the following four main functions: (i) registration of accounting firms auditing public companies and brokers and dealers; (ii) inspections of registered accounting firms; (iii) establishment of auditing, quality controls, ethics, and other independence standards; and (iv) investigation

---

[33]*Id.*

[34]Codification of Statements on Auditing Standards, Overall Objectives of the Independent Auditor and the Conduct of an Audit in Accordance with Generally Accepted Auditing Standards, AU-C §200 (Am. Inst. of Certified Pub. Accountants 2016).

[35]*Id.*

[36]About the PCAOB, *available at* https://pcaobus.org:443/About.

[37]Public Company Accounting Oversight Board, Public Company Accounting Oversight Board Strategic Plan: Improving the Quality of the Audit for the Protection and Benefit of Investors 2016-2020 (Nov. 18, 2016).

[38]About the PCAOB, *supra* note 36.

[39]PCAOB: The Board, *available at* https://pcaobus.org:443/About/Board/Pages/default.aspx.

[40]About the PCAOB, *supra* note 36.

and discipline of registered accounting firms in regard to law, rule, or professional standard violations by the registered firm or individuals who work for the registered firm.[41]

1. PCAOB Auditing Standards

AS are standards developed by the PCAOB and utilized by registered public accounting firms in the undertaking and performance of an audit of a public company. The AS consist of two types, GAAS as developed by the AICPA and adopted by the PCAOB and standards that are specifically developed and issued by the PCAOB.[42] Similar to the reorganization of GAAP into the Codification, the PCAOB reorganized the AS into a topical format, with those changes effective December 31, 2016. In addition to setting standards for how an audit should be conducted, the AS contain requirements regarding an independent auditor's general responsibilities in the conduct of audits of public companies or brokers and dealers.

F. AUDITING PROCESS

An audit is an examination of an entity's financial reports to ensure that those reports fairly present the financial results of the entity. The audit is undertaken in order to provide those persons who use the financial statements with an opinion from the auditor as to whether the financial statements, in all material respects, fairly present the results of operations and the financial condition of the entity being audited. When the auditor performs the audit in compliance with GAAS (for a private entity) or with the AS (for a public entity), the auditor is in a position to form and issue an opinion regarding the fair presentation of the financial statements of the audited entity.[43] While GAAS and AS establish standards for the performance of an audit, they do not establish the standards that management of the entity must utilize in the preparation of the entity's financial statements.

The overarching objectives of the audit, whether of a private or public entity, are: (i) to enable the auditor to "obtain reasonable assurance about whether the financial statements as a whole are free from material misstatement, . . . thereby enabling the auditor to express an opinion on whether the financial statements are presented fairly . . . ," and (ii) to permit the auditor to communicate and report the audit findings.[44] The auditor reports the findings through

---

[41]Public Company Accounting Oversight Board, *supra* note 37.
[42]Public Company Accounting Oversight Board, Reorganization of PCAOB Auditing Standards and Related Amendments to PCAOB Standards and Rules, PCAOB Rel. No. 2015-002 (Mar. 31, 2015).
[43]Codification of Statements on Auditing Standards, Overall Objectives of the Independent Auditor and the Conduct of an Audit in Accordance with Generally Accepted Auditing Standards, AU-C §200 (Am. Inst. of Certified Pub. Accountants 2016); Auditing Standards, Responsibilities and Functions of the Independent Auditor, AS §1001 (Am. Inst. of Certified Pub. Accountants 2002).
[44]Codification of Statements on Auditing Standards, *supra* note 43; Auditing Standards, *supra* note 43.

the issuance of an "audit report" to the entity once the audit is completed. This report sets forth the auditor's opinion regarding whether the financial statements fairly present the results of operations in all material respects based upon the findings and results of the audit.

1. Planning the Audit

In order to undertake an audit, the auditor must first establish an audit strategy for that particular entity (or client) and develop an audit plan. The strategy should set forth the "scope, timing, and direction of the audit" in order for the auditor to develop the actual audit plan so that the audit is performed in an effective manner.[45] The audit plan should address details regarding the overall audit structure, design, risk identification procedures, timing, and extent of planned audit procedures, but at the same time allow for flexibility so that the plan can be updated and adapted as necessary as the audit progresses.[46] A critical component of the audit plan is the procedures the auditor will utilize to assess the risks of a material misstatement in the entity's financial statements.[47] Once the preliminary audit plan is in place, the audit can commence with the understanding that the audit plan may evolve and change as the audit progresses based on information discovered or learned by the audit team.

2. Audit Risk

A crucial consideration for every audit is the determination of the audit risk for that particular engagement. Audit risk is the risk that the auditor renders an inaccurate audit opinion as a result of financial statements that are materially misstated.[48] Overall audit risk has two separate components — risk of a material misstatement and detection risk.[49]

a. Risk of a Material Misstatement

The risk of a material misstatement arises as a result of an entity's financial statements containing a material misstatement prior to the start of the audit. The auditor should assess the potential risk at two distinct levels — the financial statement level and the assertion level, meaning management's direct or indirect assertions regarding the entity's financial statements and related

---

[45]CODIFICATION OF STATEMENTS ON AUDITING STANDARDS, Planning an Audit, AU-C §300 (Am. Inst. of Certified Pub. Accountants 2016); AUDITING STANDARDS, Audit Planning, AS §2101 (Am. Inst. of Certified Pub. Accountants 2010).
[46]Codification of Statements on Auditing Standards, *supra* note 45; Auditing Standards, *supra* note 45.
[47]Codification of Statements on Auditing Standards, *supra* note 45; Auditing Standards, *supra* note 45.
[48]Codification of Statements on Auditing Standards, *supra* note 43; AUDITING STANDARDS, Audit Risk, AS §1101 (Am. Inst. of Certified Pub. Accountants 2010).
[49]Codification of Statements on Auditing Standards, *supra* note 43; Auditing Standards, *supra* note 45.

disclosures. The risk of a material misstatement at the assertion level includes both inherent risk and control risk, which are risks of the entity itself.[50]

Inherent risk is the "susceptibility of an assertion . . . to a misstatement that could be material, either individually or when aggregated with other misstatements, before consideration of any related controls."[51] Inherent risk is assessed based on evidence gathered as a part of the auditor's risk assessment procedures.[52]

Control risk is "the risk that a misstatement that could occur in an assertion . . . that could be material, either individually or when aggregated with other misstatements, will not be prevented or detected and corrected, on a timely basis by the entity's internal controls."[53] The auditor assesses control risk by utilizing the evidence garnered from testing the entity's internal controls.[54]

b. Detection Risk

Detection risk is the risk that the procedures put in place by the auditor to reduce the audit risk to an acceptable low level will not actually detect a material misstatement, either individually or when aggregated with other misstatements.[55] Detection risk is directly related to the effectiveness of the audit plan and established procedures, and can be mitigated through sufficient audit planning, engaging the proper audit team, applying professional judgment and skepticism to the audit process, and adequate supervision of team members' work.[56] Detection risk and risk of a material misstatement have an inverse relationship: the greater the risk of a material misstatement, the lower the level of acceptable detection risk and vice versa.[57]

Once the auditor has determined the overall level of audit risk, the auditor will take that assessment into consideration in the design of the audit plan, and that risk assessment will play a role in the type and extent of audit procedures undertaken as a part of that specific engagement.

G. AUDIT PROCEDURES

Audit procedures are the methods the auditor utilizes to gather the necessary audit evidence in order to have a basis upon which to render its opinion and report. There are two main categories of audit procedures — risk assessment procedures (discussed above) and other audit procedures.[58] Other audit

---

[50]Codification of Statements on Auditing Standards, *supra* note 43; Auditing Standards, *supra* note 45.
[51]Codification of Statements on Auditing Standards, *supra* note 43.
[52]Auditing Standards, *supra* note 45.
[53]Codification of Statements on Auditing Standards, *supra* note 43.
[54]Auditing Standards, *supra* note 45.
[55]Codification of Statements on Auditing Standards, *supra* note 43.
[56]*Id.*
[57]*Id.*
[58]CODIFICATION OF STATEMENTS ON AUDITING STANDARDS, Performing Audit Procedures in Response to Assessed Risks and Evaluating the Audit Evidence Obtained, AU-C §330 (Am. Inst. of Certified Pub. Accountants 2016); AUDITING STANDARDS, Audit Evidence, AS §1105 (Am. Inst. of Certified Pub. Accountants 2010).

procedures include test of control procedures, or procedures that are meant to evaluate the effectiveness of the internal controls that prevent or detect and correct material misstatements, and substantive procedures, or procedures that are meant to discover material misstatements.[59] The other audit procedures should be planned and undertaken based upon the assessed audit risk. Types of specific audit procedures that might be employed to gather audit evidence during the course of an audit include: (i) inspection; (ii) observation; (iii) inquiry; (iv) confirmation; (v) recalculation; and (vi) analytical procedures.[60]

1. Test of Controls

A test of controls audit procedure is one that is meant to evaluate how successful the entity's internal controls are at preventing a material misstatement or identifying and correcting of a material misstatement.[61] In essence, the auditor is attempting to determine the amount of reliance that can be placed on the entity's internal controls to prevent material misstatements in order to assess the extent of substantive testing procedures required as a part of the audit. The auditor can use a variety of techniques to determine the effectiveness of the entity's internal controls, including interviewing the entity's employees, examining pertinent documents, and observing the internal control processes.[62] As a part of the internal controls testing, the auditor should assess the manner in which and consistency with which the entity's internal controls were applied during the period being audited, as well as assess the individuals applying the controls in conjunction with their authority level and aptitude in regard to the internal controls and the manner in which such individuals applied the necessary internal controls.[63] If the entity's internal controls are deemed inadequate or unreliable, the auditor may have to expand the scope of the audit and substantive procedures and test not only material classes of transactions but also each line item reported on the entity's balance sheet.[64]

2. Substantive Procedures

A substantive audit procedure is one that is meant to identify material misstatements and includes testing of material groups of financial transactions, reported account balances, and other financial disclosures.[65] Examples of substantive testing procedures include, without limitation: (i) the confirmation of accounts receivable balances, accounts payable balances, bank balances, and loan balances by contacting the relevant third party; (ii) observing the entity's inventory

[59] Codification of Statements on Auditing Standards, *supra* note 58; Auditing Standards, *supra* note 58.
[60] Auditing Standards, *supra* note 58.
[61] Codification of Statements on Auditing Standards, *supra* note 58.
[62] D. Edward Martin, Attorney's Handbook of Accounting, Auditing, and Financial Reporting §12.02 (Rel. No. 19, Dec. 2011).
[63] Codification of Statements on Auditing Standards, *supra* note 58.
[64] Martin, *supra* note 62, §12.02.
[65] Codification of Statements on Auditing Standards, *supra* note 58.

counting and tracking procedures; (iii) reconciling the disclosures in the financial statements with the entity's accounting books and records; (iv) assessing reported estimates by examining management's methodologies in determining estimates, verifying management's calculations, and independently developing an estimate based on industry and historical knowledge; and (v) examining and verifying that the entity's various journal and adjusting entries are accurately reflected in and support the preparation of its financial statements.[66]

a. Audit Evidence

Audit evidence is the information that an auditor obtains as a part of the audit process, whether it is obtained from the audit procedures or other sources such as previous audits, a specialist, or the entity's accounting books and records.[67] Audit evidence includes evidence that supports and validates the financial statements prepared by management, including the underlying assertions and the entity's internal control processes and procedures, as well as evidence that does not support or disputes those financial statement assertions or internal controls.[68] The auditor relies on this audit evidence to support the auditor's opinion and audit report.

As a result, the auditor must establish and undertake audit procedures that gather the necessary audit evidence to enable the auditor to establish a basis for its opinion.[69]

Audit evidence must be both sufficient and appropriate. The concept of sufficiency assesses the quantity of the audit evidence.[70] The quantity of audit evidence required is correlated to the audit risk assessment and to the quality of the evidence obtained.[71] In the case of an audit that is determined to contain a high risk of a material misstatement or an increased risk regarding the entity's internal control processes, the auditor will require a greater quantity of audit evidence to support the auditor's opinion versus an audit with a lower risk determination in regard to both of those items.[72] The quality of the audit evidence also has a direct impact on the quantity required. The higher the quality of evidence obtained by the auditor, the less audit evidence needed to support the auditor's opinion and vice versa.[73]

The concept of appropriateness assesses the quality of the audit evidence.[74] In order for audit evidence to be deemed appropriate, it must be both relevant

---

[66]Martin, *supra* note 62, §12.02.
[67]CODIFICATION OF STATEMENTS ON AUDITING STANDARDS, Overall Objectives of the Independent Auditor and the Conduct of an Audit in Accordance with Generally Accepted Auditing Standards, AU-C §200 (Am. Inst. of Certified Pub. Accountants 2016); AUDITING STANDARDS, Audit Evidence, AS §1105 (Am. Inst. of Certified Pub. Accountants 2010).
[68]Codification of Statements on Auditing Standards, *supra* note 67; Auditing Standards, *supra* note 67.
[69]Auditing Standards, *supra* note 67.
[70]Codification of Statements on Auditing Standards, *supra* note 67; Auditing Standards, *supra* note 67.
[71]Codification of Statements on Auditing Standards, *supra* note 67; Auditing Standards, *supra* note 67.
[72]Codification of Statements on Auditing Standards, *supra* note 67; Auditing Standards, *supra* note 67.
[73]Codification of Statements on Auditing Standards, *supra* note 67; Auditing Standards, *supra* note 67.
[74]Codification of Statements on Auditing Standards, *supra* note 67; Auditing Standards, *supra* note 67.

and reliable in offering support for the auditor's opinion.[75] Relevance assesses whether the audit evidence is related to the assertion or internal control being tested by the auditor.[76] Reliability assesses whether the evidence was derived from an adequate source, as well as takes into consideration the circumstances surrounding the source and the evidence to determine whether the source is knowledgeable and independent, or whether the evidence is obtained directly or indirectly.[77]

The auditor must utilize professional judgment and skepticism in assessing the sufficiency and appropriateness of the audit evidence obtained through the audit and the established audit procedures. This is critical as all of the audit evidence obtained acts as an underlying basis and support for the auditor to issue its opinion regarding the entity's fair presentation of its financial statements and results of operations.

3. Management's Representations

One of the final pieces of the audit is the requirement that the auditor obtain written representations from the entity's management that set forth management's responses to both the auditor's written and oral questions that occurred over the course of the audit.[78] This letter, setting forth management's representations, does not take the place of auditing procedures but is instead a supplement to those procedures and acts as audit evidence.[79] Management's representation letter, which cannot be dated earlier than the auditor's report, is addressed directly to the auditor and is generally executed by the chief executive officer and chief financial officer of the entity.

While the written representations vary depending on the specific entity and audit engagement and are limited to an established level of materiality, some items typically covered in management's representation letter include: (i) management's acknowledgment that it is responsible for the fair presentation of the entity's financial information in accordance with GAAP (or other appropriate financial reporting framework); (ii) management's belief that the financial statements fairly present the entity's results in accordance with GAAP (or other appropriate financial reporting framework); (iii) representations regarding the availability and completeness of the information provided to the auditors as a part of the audit process; (iv) representations regarding management's obligations to implement and maintain internal controls; (v) representations regarding any potential fraud or suspected fraud; (vi) representations concerning related-party transactions and guarantees; (vii) representations regarding estimates; (viii) representations regarding potential legal violations, unasserted

---

[75]Codification of Statements on Auditing Standards, *supra* note 67; Auditing Standards, *supra* note 67.
[76]Codification of Statements on Auditing Standards, *supra* note 67; Auditing Standards, *supra* note 67.
[77]Codification of Statements on Auditing Standards, *supra* note 67; Auditing Standards, *supra* note 67.
[78]AUDITING STANDARDS, Management Representations, AS §2805 (Am. Inst. of Certified Pub. Accountants 2001, 2004).
[79]*Id.*

claims, and other accrued liabilities; (ix) representations about subsequent events; and (x) any other relevant or requested representations.[80]

In the event that management refuses to provide written representations or is not willing to provide all written representations deemed necessary by the auditor, this results in a limitation on the audit scope and generally prevents the auditor from issuing an unqualified opinion.[81] In the case where management refuses to provide any written representations (not just limited written representations), the auditor may find it necessary to disclaim an opinion or even withdraw and terminate the audit engagement.[82]

4. Audit Inquiry Letters

The audit inquiry letter is the primary method that auditors use to obtain information about litigation, claims, and assessments that their client, the entity, may be facing. In particular, the auditor must obtain information regarding the existence of matters that may result in a possible loss by the entity, the time frame in which such matter occurred, the probability assessment of a negative outcome, and the potential amount of the loss.[83] This information serves as a means for the auditor to confirm the information that management of the entity provided and is necessary for the auditor to complete its audit and issue an opinion regarding the entity's financial statements and results of operations.[84]

This inquiry letter (an example of which is found in **Exhibit B**), which is prepared by the entity's management on behalf of its auditors, is sent to all of the entity's lawyers that were consulted during the audit period concerning litigation, claims, and assessments, including both in-house and outside counsel. Management of the entity should include the following information in each inquiry letter: (i) name of the entity, any subsidiaries, and the audit date; (ii) a list describing and evaluating pending and threatened litigation, claims, and assessments for which that particular lawyer has been consulted or engaged or a request that the lawyer prepare and provide this list; (iii) a list describing and evaluating unasserted claims and assessments that rise to the level of a probable assertion for which that particular lawyer has been consulted or engaged; and (iv) a statement that the entity understands that the lawyer will advise the entity if it believes the entity should include disclosure in its financial statements regarding unasserted claims or assessments.[85]

The inquiry letter should request that the lawyer comment on those pending and threatened matters listed in the letter and include the following details, when applicable, regarding each pending or threatened matter: (i) a description; (ii) the progress of the case; (iii) the entity's intended course of action in

---

[80]*Id.*
[81]*Id.*
[82]*Id.*
[83]Auditing Standards, Inquiry of Client's Lawyer Concerning Litigation, Claims, and Assessments, AS §2505 (Am. Inst. of Certified Pub. Accountants 1996).
[84]*Id.*
[85]*Id.*

regard to the case; (iv) the likelihood that the outcome will be unfavorable; (v) an estimate of the amount or range of the loss, if feasible; and (vi) a statement that the list provided by management is complete or, in the alternative, a list of those pending or threatened matters that were omitted.[86] The inquiry letter should also request that the lawyer provide an opinion regarding unasserted claims and assessments if such opinion differs from what management stated in the letter, that the lawyer confirm the client's understanding regarding disclosure recommendations concerning unasserted claims or assessments by the lawyer, and that the lawyer identify any inquiry letter response limitations.[87]

What should be evident is that the request of the entity's lawyers, through the audit inquiry letter, to provide information to the entity's auditors results in the potential waiver of the right to the confidence of attorney-client communications and right to attorney-client privilege. Pursuant to the Code of Professional Responsibility, only the client can voluntarily waive privilege with its lawyer, and the request of its lawyers to make these disclosures to a third party, the auditor, may destroy that privilege as well as the privilege for other communications regarding the same subject matter.[88]

The audit inquiry letter process is thus viewed as potentially impacting open communications between a client and its lawyers and as a process that may result in management not feeling free to discuss potential litigation matters with counsel for fear of such future disclosure to its auditors.[89] However, the American Bar Association (ABA) also recognizes that the public must be able to rely on and have confidence in an entity's financial statements, and one of the ways that happens is through the audit process.[90] And so a dichotomy clearly exists between these two purposes — open communication between a client and its lawyers and the public's trust that an entity's financial statements fairly present its results.

a. Attorney Responses to Audit Inquiry Letters

As a result of this dichotomy between the auditors and the lawyers for the entity, the ABA attempted to differentiate between pending litigation, including matters where the entity is aware of a party's present intention to commence litigation, and other possible legal contingencies.[91] While the ABA agrees that an entity's lawyers are in the best position to address pending litigation, it disagrees with that assessment in regard to other legal contingencies.[92] Based on these assessments, the ABA adopted a Statement of Policy (Policy) regarding

---

[86]*Id.*
[87]*Id.*
[88]AMERICAN BAR ASS'N, ABA STATEMENT OF POLICY REGARDING LAWYERS' RESPONSES TO AUDITORS' REQUESTS FOR INFORMATION (1976, 1998, 2003).
[89]*Id.*
[90]*Id.*
[91]*Id.*
[92]*Id.*

the audit inquiry letter that advises the entity's lawyer on how best to respond to such letters. Specifically the Policy stipulates the following:

(i)   the lawyer must first obtain the client's consent to respond to the audit inquiry letter, which consent can be included in the inquiry letter itself or can be obtained directly and outside the inquiry letter;

(ii)   the lawyer should remember that its evaluation of the matters might be used by the adverse party against the entity in the proceeding as a potential admission of liability or responsibility by the entity;

(iii) the lawyer should consider requesting that the entity review its response to the audit inquiry letter before such response is submitted to the auditors;

(iv)   the lawyer should include any appropriate limitations on the scope of its response, as well as indicate that it is undertaking no obligation to update the auditor after the date of the response letter;

(v)   the lawyer should indicate if its response is limited to only those matters that it deems material;

(vi)   the lawyer should address only those loss contingencies for which the lawyer has been engaged;

(vii) the lawyer should include a limitation on the use of its response and, in particular, that it is for the auditor's information only in connection with the audit and that it cannot be quoted from or referred to without the lawyer's prior written consent; and

(viii) the lawyer should include any other information it deems relevant to its response.[93]

In responding to loss contingencies, the Policy states that lawyers should address the following matters as a part of the response to the audit inquiry letter: (i) overtly threatened or pending litigation (whether specified or omitted by the client in the inquiry letter); (ii) contractually assumed obligations specifically identified by the client in the inquiry letter; and (iii) unasserted claims or assessments specifically identified by the client in the inquiry letter, but only if the claim or assessment is judged probable, the outcome is determined to be one that will be unfavorable, and the potential loss will be material.[94] An example of a lawyer's audit response letter is found in **Exhibit C**.

While the ABA's guidance through its Policy is crucial in assisting lawyers with how best to respond to audit inquiry letters, it is not necessarily definitive. In some instances the lawyer may have to provide more information, per the auditor's request and with the entity's consent, in order for the entity to receive an unqualified opinion from its auditors. As a result, at the end of the day it is a delicate balancing act between providing only the information that is necessary while protecting the entity's confidences with its lawyers and responding adequately so that it does not result in the entity receiving a qualified opinion from its auditors.

---

[93]*Id.*
[94]*Id.*

5. Audit Documentation

During all stages of the audit, the auditor should keep detailed written records of its processes. These written records should include, but are not limited to, the audit plan, the risk assessment analysis, the audit procedures performed and evidence obtained, the record of communications between the auditor and management, and the auditor's conclusions regarding the audit.[95] These records, often referred to as audit documentation or working papers, form the basis for the auditor's ultimate conclusions regarding the audit and whether the entity's financial statements are fairly presented in all material respects.[96] In addition to establishing evidence and supporting the auditor's conclusions, the audit documentation should establish that the auditor followed GAAS or AS in conducting the audit and that the entity's accounting books and records agreed with or were reconciled to the entity's financial statement disclosures.[97] The audit documentation, which may comprise both hard copy and electronic records, should be timely organized upon completion of the audit and maintained in the auditor's archives for the proper retention period, but for no less than five years from completion of the audit.[98]

6. Audit Report and Opinion

In conjunction with an audit, one of the auditor's responsibilities is to form an opinion regarding whether the entity's financial statements fairly present its financial position and results of operations in compliance with GAAP. The auditor utilizes all of the evidence collected during the audit to form that opinion. Once the audit is complete and the auditor has reached an opinion regarding the entity's financial statements' presentation, the auditor will issue a written report that sets forth the auditor's opinion, as well as the basis for the opinion.

a. Audit Report

The audit report is a fairly standard written report and follows a similar format whether it is a report for an audit of a publicly traded entity, a privately owned entity, or some other type of organization. The written audit report should contain the following items:

(i)   a title that incorporates the word "independent" to indicate that the auditor is acting independently of the audited entity;

---

[95]CODIFICATION OF STATEMENTS ON AUDITING STANDARDS, Audit Documentation, AU-C §230 (Am. Inst. of Certified Pub. Accountants 2016); AUDITING STANDARDS, Audit Documentation, AS §1215 (Am. Inst. of Certified Pub. Accountants 2004).
[96]Codification of Statements on Auditing Standards, *supra* note 95; Auditing Standards, *supra* note 95.
[97]Codification of Statements on Auditing Standards, *supra* note 95; Auditing Standards, *supra* note 95.
[98]Codification of Statements on Auditing Standards, *supra* note 95; Auditing Standards, *supra* note 95.

(ii)   an opening paragraph that identifies both the audited entity and that the financial statements identified in the written report were audited;

(iii)   a statement that management of the entity is responsible for the preparation of the financial statements as well as maintaining internal controls and that the auditors are simply expressing an opinion on the management-prepared financial statements based upon the audit;

(iv)   a statement that the audit was conducted in accordance with GAAS or AS and that those standards require the auditor to follow the requisite procedures in planning and performing the audit to obtain reasonable assurance that the entity's financial statements do not contain a material misstatement;

(v)   a statement that sets forth a description of the audit procedures;

(vi)   a statement that the auditor believes that the completed audit places the auditor in a position to render an opinion;

(vii)   a paragraph that sets forth the auditor's opinion as to whether the financial statements "fairly present" the entity's financial position and results of operations, whether an unqualified, unqualified with explanatory language, qualified, or adverse opinion; and

(viii)   the date of the report, the location of the auditor (city and state), and the auditor's signature.[99]

i. Unqualified Opinion

When the auditor determines that the entity's "financial statements present fairly, in all material respects, an entity's financial position, results of operations, and cash flows in conformity with Generally Accepted Accounting Principles," the auditor will issue a standard report containing an unqualified or clean opinion.[100] This type of opinion can only be issued if the audit was undertaken and performed in compliance with GAAS or AS.[101] An unqualified opinion, which is the best opinion for an entity, also indicates that the entity's financial records and statements have been prepared in accordance with GAAP. An example of an unqualified audit opinion is found in **Exhibit D**.

ii. Unqualified Opinion with Explanatory Language

In certain circumstances, the auditor may issue an unqualified opinion that contains explanatory language. The explanatory language does not change or negate the unqualified opinion, it simply provides additional relevant information that a reader of the financial statements should be aware of and take into consideration. Circumstances that may give rise to explanatory language include, but are not limited to, the current auditor's use of another auditor's

---

[99]CODIFICATION OF STATEMENTS ON AUDITING STANDARDS, Forming an Opinion and Reporting on Financial Statements, AU-C §700 (Am. Inst. of Certified Pub. Accountants 2016); AUDITING STANDARDS, Reports on Audited Financial Statements, AS §3101 (Am. Inst. of Certified Pub. Accountants 2001, 2002, 2003, 2004).

[100]Auditing Standards, *supra* note 99.

[101]Codification of Statements on Auditing Standards, *supra* note 99; Auditing Standards, *supra* note 99.

report, the auditor's concern as to whether the entity will continue as a "going concern," a material change in accounting methods or principles from one period to the next, a correction of a material misstatement in the entity's prior financial statements, or other information the auditor wishes to further explain and emphasize.[102] While the auditor's opinion is still an unqualified one, it is critical to closely examine any explanatory language to further understand the entity's financial condition and results of operations. An example of an unqualified audit opinion with explanatory language is found in **Exhibit E**.

iii. Qualified Opinion

In some situations, the auditor may issue a qualified opinion. A qualified opinion must indicate the specific matters that gave rise to the qualification and that other than those matters, the entity's financial statements "fairly present" its financial position and results of operations.[103] The auditor will include a separate paragraph in the audit report that discloses the rationale for the qualified opinion, and such paragraph should precede the auditor's opinion and make it clear that this particular information represents an exception to the auditor's overall opinion.[104] An auditor typically issues a qualified opinion when there are limitations on the scope of the audit or when the financial statements are not prepared in accordance with GAAP.[105] Limitations on the scope of the audit may result from actions of or restrictions imposed by the client or particular circumstances related to the audit, and include such matters as the auditor's inability to observe physical inventory or to confirm various accounts receivable balances.[106] In essence, the auditor is unable to obtain sufficient audit evidence to complete the audit in a manner that allows it to reach an unqualified opinion. An example of a qualified audit opinion is found in **Exhibit F**.

iv. Adverse Opinion

In the case where the entity's financial statements, assessed as a whole, do not present fairly its financial position and results of operations in accordance with GAAP, the auditor must issue an adverse opinion.[107] The adverse opinion specifically indicates that the entity's financial statements "do not present fairly the financial position or the results of operations or cash flows in conformity with Generally Accepted Accounting Principles."[108] An adverse opinion is the worst type of opinion that an entity can receive and prevents a public company from filing its annual report on Form 10-K with the SEC, and may also result in delisting from an exchange. Similar to a qualified opinion, the auditor must include a paragraph that specifically sets forth the reasons for the adverse opinion and how those matters affect the entity's financial position, if

---

[102] Auditing Standards, *supra* note 99.
[103] *Id.*
[104] *Id.*
[105] *Id.*
[106] *Id.*
[107] *Id.*
[108] *Id.*

possible.[109] This paragraph must precede the auditor's opinion paragraph, and, in addition, the opinion paragraph should cross-reference the paragraph that sets forth the reasons for the adverse opinion.[110] An adverse opinion is a rare occurrence, as generally the entity's management will correct the problems or conditions in the financial statements in order to avoid the issuance of such opinion. An example of an adverse audit opinion is found in **Exhibit G**.

v. Disclaimer of Opinion

In limited situations, the auditor may not be in a position to express an opinion and so disclaims an opinion as to whether the entity's financial statements fairly present the entity's financial condition and results of operations.[111] In this circumstance, the audit report should set forth the specific reasons as to why the auditor is disclaiming an opinion. A disclaimer of an opinion occurs if the auditor is unable to perform the audit in such a manner as to obtain sufficient evidence to issue an opinion, which is typically the result of a client's limitation on the scope of the audit.[112] An example of a disclaimer of audit opinion is found in **Exhibit H**.

H. AUDITOR'S LIABILITY

Like many professions, an auditing firm faces as one of its major concerns the potential for a liability claim as a result of an audit engagement. These claims may arise directly from the client's dissatisfaction or indirectly from a third party's dissatisfaction with the auditor's rendered opinion. There are many costs involved in these potential liability claims, including actual costs and inherent costs. Actual costs include attorneys' fees and expenses, as well as judgments, penalties, or settlements. The inherent costs are more than monetary in nature and include lost time and productivity of audit firm partners and staff, as well as the impact to the auditing firm's reputation. According to claim data, as of October 2016, 23 percent of the open claims against certified public accounting firms were related to audit and attestation services (16 percent) or accounting services (5 percent).[113] As a result, audit services present an area of potential liability and require audit firms to be vigilant, as they are often viewed as the party that has "deep pockets" in lawsuits brought by clients, investors, regulators, lenders, and other third parties. Auditor liability arises in two distinct ways — through a lawsuit by the client or through a lawsuit by a third party.

---

[109]*Id.*
[110]*Id.*
[111]*Id.*
[112]*Id.*
[113]Sarah Beckett Ference, CPA Professional Liability Risk Resolutions for 2017, J. Accт. (2017), *available at* https://www.journalofaccountancy.com/issues/2017/jan/liability-risk-resolutions-for-2017.html.

1. Liability to Clients

An independent accountant may be liable to the client if the accountant fails to perform the professional services for which it was engaged in an adequate or proper manner, with one such service being the audit engagement. The contract (or engagement letter) between the client and the independent accountant creates a relationship of privity and thus allows the client to bring a claim under a breach of contract theory. In order for the client to bring a cause of action against the independent accountant for negligent performance of professional services, the client must establish the following: (i) a contract existed between the client and accountant; (ii) the accountant breached the contract; (iii) the accountant's breach was the proximate cause of the client's injuries; and (iv) the client suffered injuries or damages as a result of the breach.[114] The contract between the client and independent accountant establishes the express duties that the accountant owes to the client, which are supplemented by the accountant's duty to perform the services in a skilled manner and to exercise the same skill and care as other like accountants.[115] If the client is successful in a breach of contract case, the available remedies include damages, restitution, and specific performance, with damages and restitution being the most typical.[116]

A client may also bring actions against the independent accountant under the theories of negligent misrepresentation or fraudulent misrepresentation. In order to establish a cause of action for negligent misrepresentation, the client must prove: (i) that the accountant misrepresented a material fact; (ii) the accountant knew or should have known of the misrepresentation; (iii) the accountant intended the misrepresentation to induce the client to act or rely on it; and (iv) the client justifiably relied on the misrepresentation and was injured.[117] The remedy for negligent misrepresentation is damages for the actual (or economic) losses suffered by the client as a result of the misrepresentation.[118] In order to establish a cause of action for fraudulent misrepresentation, the client must prove: (i) the accountant made a misrepresentation of a material fact, either knowingly or recklessly, and (ii) the client justifiably relied on the intentional misrepresentation and was injured.[119] The remedies for fraudulent misrepresentation include both actual and punitive damages, thus opening the door for a larger award for the client and greater penalty for the independent accountant.

---

[114] 15 CAUSES OF ACTION 2D *Cause of Action Against Accountant for Negligent Performance of Professional Services* §3 (2000).
[115] *Id.* §5.
[116] D. EDWARD MARTIN, ATTORNEY'S HANDBOOK OF ACCOUNTING, AUDITING, AND FINANCIAL REPORTING §15.02 (Rel. No. 19, Dec. 2011).
[117] Causes of Action 2d, *supra* note 114, §4.
[118] Martin, *supra* note 116, §15.02.
[119] *Id.*

2. Liability to Third Parties

An independent accountant may also be liable to third parties who do not have a contractual relationship (or direct privity) with the accountant. Since direct privity does not exist, as there is no contract between the third party and the accountant, two primary theories are used to hold the accountant liable to third parties. The first theory, known as the restatement standard, stems from §522 of the Restatement (Second) of Torts.[120] The second theory, known as the reasonably foreseeable standard, stems from the relationship between the third party and accountant.[121]

Under the restatement standard, a professional (i.e., an independent accountant) who provides false information for the use of others regarding business transactions and does so without exercising reasonable care or professional competence may be liable for the economic losses of the third parties who justifiably relied on the information.[122] Under this theory, which a number of jurisdictions have adopted, those third parties whom the accountant is aware of and who intend to rely on the accountant's opinion, or those third parties whom the client intends to rely on the accountant's opinion, can bring a cause of action.[123] In other words, it is irrelevant whether the accountant knows the identity of the third party; it is simply enough that the third party relied on the information — no direct privity is required.

Under the reasonably foreseeable standard, the independent accountant may be liable to a third party if it was foreseeable that the third party would request, be provided with, and rely on the client's financial statements and auditor's opinion, or if the accountant fails to limit the client's dissemination of the financial statements and auditor's opinion.[124] This standard, which has been adopted in a limited number of jurisdictions, does not require privity but does require the third party to be of a class of reasonably foreseeable persons.[125] In other words, it is not enough for a third party to simply access the client's financial statements and auditor's opinion once released; the third party must be one that the independent accountant would expect the client to provide the financial statements and audit opinion to directly, such as the client's commercial lender or a majority shareholder.

In addition to these two theories, a number of states have enacted statutes that specifically govern the liability of independent accountants to third parties. In some states, the accountant must specifically know the identity of the third party receiving and relying on the client's financial statements. In other states, it may be adequate that the accountant knew the client's intent was to provide a benefit for or influence the third party bringing the cause of action.[126]

---

[120] RESTATEMENT (SECOND) OF TORTS: INFORMATION NEGLIGENTLY SUPPLIED FOR THE GUIDANCE OF OTHERS §522 (1977).
[121] 15 CAUSES OF ACTION 2D, *supra* note 114, §6.
[122] *Id.* §7.
[123] Martin, *supra* note 116, at §15.02.
[124] CAUSES OF ACTION 2D, *supra* note 114, §6.
[125] *Id.*
[126] *Id.* §9.

Lastly, an independent accountant may be liable to a third party based upon a claim of fraudulent misrepresentation. In those instances, the third party must establish the same requirements as the accountant's client discussed above.

3. **Statutory Liability**

Independent accountants may also be liable to third parties pursuant to the Securities Act of 1933 and the Securities Exchange Act of 1934. In particular, accountants may find themselves liable to those third parties who purchased securities pursuant to a registration statement or those third parties who purchased or sold securities in reliance on Forms 10-K or 10-Q.

Pursuant to §11(a) of the Securities Act of 1933, a purchaser of securities may bring a cause of action if the registration statement, upon its effective date, contained an untrue statement of a material fact or omitted to state a material fact.[127] Since an entity is required to provide audited financial statements in its registration statement, the independent accountant who performs the audit may be liable for misrepresentations or omissions in those financial statements. The third party must prove the following: (i) that the third party purchased a security in connection with a false registration statement; (ii) that the auditor's opinion was incorrect as a result of the fact that the financial statements were materially misstated or contained a material omission; (iii) that the falsity can be linked to the accountant; and (iv) that the third party was injured or suffered damages as a result.[128] The auditor can avoid liability by establishing that the third party knew the information was false or omitted, that the third party's damages resulted from relying on information other than the financial statements, or that the auditor acted in good faith and exercised due diligence in auditing the financial statements.[129]

Pursuant to §10(b) of the Securities Exchange Act of 1934 and Rule 10b-5, a purchaser or seller of securities may bring a cause of action if a filing or communication contained an untrue statement of a material fact or omitted to state a material fact that would prevent the statement from being misleading or if there was an act of fraud or deceit.[130] The third party must prove the following: (i) the filing contained a material misrepresentation or omission or other fraudulent device; (ii) the securities were bought or sold in connection with the fraudulent scheme; (iii) the accountant intended to make the material misrepresentation or omission (i.e., there was scienter); (iv) the transaction involved the use of interstate commerce; (v) the third party justifiably relied on the fraudulent device; and (vi) the third party was injured or suffered damages as a result.[131] Liability under Rule 10b-5 extends to any false statement and not just those contained in a filing with the SEC.

---

[127]Securities Act of 1933 §11(a), 15 U.S.C. §§77a et seq.
[128]Martin, *supra* note 116, at §15.03.
[129]*Id.*
[130]17 C.F.R. §240.10b-5 (2017).
[131]Martin, *supra* note 116, §15.03.

Pursuant to §18 of the Securities Exchange Act of 1934, a purchaser or seller of securities may bring a cause of action for a false or misleading statement of material fact contained in a filing with the SEC. The third party must prove the following: (i) the financial statements were misrepresented or the auditor provided false advice; (ii) the third party justifiably relied on the false statements or advice; and (iii) the third party was injured or suffered damages as a result.[132] The independent accountant can avoid liability if the accountant can prove that the third party knew the statement was false or misleading or that the accountant acted in good faith without knowledge that the statement was false or misleading.[133]

4. Criminal Liability

In the circumstance where an independent accountant is found statutorily liable, the accountant may also be held criminally liable. Under §24 of the Securities Act of 1933, an accountant can be criminally liable for willfully making a false statement or omitting a material fact in connection with a registration statement, and under §32(a) of the Securities Exchange Act of 1934 an auditor can be criminally liable for willfully making a false or misleading statement in reports filed under the Exchange Act.[134] If found criminally liable under either of these sections, an accountant can face a fine of up to $10,000, five years in prison, or both.[135]

What should be apparent is that independent accountants may face liability from a variety of parties and circumstances. As such, independent accountants should pay particular attention to their roles and responsibilities so as to mitigate that potential liability.

I. AUDIT ALTERNATIVES

An audit is just one type of service that accounting firms offer, which is known as an assurance engagement, meaning the auditor issues a report regarding the state of the financial statements. While many entities are required to prepare audited financial statements — such as those entities that are publicly traded or are under a contractual obligation to do so (e.g., as required by a commercial loan agreement covenant) — there are many entities that prepare unaudited financial statements. Accounting firms also provide services to entities that do not require an audit, which accounting services result in a lesser level of review and assessment of an entity's financial statements and a lower risk for

---

[132]Jay Alix, Robert J. Rock, & Ted Stenger, Financial Handbook for Bankruptcy Professionals: A Financial and Accounting Guide for Bankruptcy Judges, Attorneys, and Accountants §12.26 (2d ed. 1996).
[133]Martin, *supra* note 116, §15.03.
[134]Securities Act of 1933, *supra* note 127, §24; Securities Exchange Act of 1934 §32(a), 15 U.S.C. §78a et seq.
[135]Alix, Rock, & Stenger, *supra* note 132, §12.27.

the accounting firm. In particular, these audit alternatives include a compilation or review of an entity's financial statements.

1. Compilation Engagement

A compilation is a service provided by an independent accountant with the objective of assisting "management in presenting financial information in the form of financial statements without undertaking to obtain or provide any assurance that there are no material modifications that should be made to the financial statements in order for the statements to be in conformity with the applicable financial reporting framework."[136] During the course of a compilation, the accountant does not assess the entity's internal controls or risk of fraud, nor does the accountant undertake testing or other audit procedures in regard to the information underlying the financial statements.[137] Instead, the accountant simply assists management in compiling and presenting the entity's financial statements. As a result, a compilation is not an assurance engagement, but rather is an attestation engagement.[138] The accountant will issue a compilation report that indicates that: (i) the financial statements are prepared and presented by management of the entity, and (ii) the accountant offers no assurances or opinion regarding the financial statements.[139]

2. Review Engagement

A review is a service provided by an independent accountant with the objective of providing "limited assurance that there are no material modifications that should be made to the financial statements in order for the statements to be in conformity with the applicable financial reporting framework."[140] During the course of a review, the accountant collects sufficient evidence in order to provide this limited assurance. However, the accountant does not engage in assessing the entity's internal controls or risk of fraud, nor does it engage in testing procedures or other methods utilized in the course of audit.[141] As a result, the accountant can only provide limited assurance and not attest to the financial statements being free of material misstatements. The accountant will issue a review report that indicates that: (i) the financial statements are prepared and presented by management of the entity; (ii) the accountant's review primarily included the application of analytical procedures to the financial information provided by management; (iii) the accountant's review is significantly less than in an audit engagement; and (iv) the accountant provides limited assurance that it is not aware of any material modifications that should be made to the

---

[136]STANDARDS FOR ACCOUNTING AND REVIEW SERVICES, Framework for Performing and Reporting on Compilation and Review Engagements, AR §60 (Am. Inst. of Certified Pub. Accountants 2016).
[137]*Id.*
[138]*Id.*
[139]*Id.*
[140]*Id.*
[141]*Id.*

financial statements in order for the statements to be in compliance with the entity's chosen financial reporting scheme.[142]

J. COST OF AN AUDIT

Any entity that undertakes an audit, whether due to the fact that it is a publicly reporting company, as a result of a contractual obligation, or voluntarily, is likely to face significant fees. Fees charged by auditing firms vary depending on whether such fees are specifically tied to the audit (e.g., audit services, comfort letters, or attestation services), are related to an audit (e.g., due diligence review, internal control review, or employee benefit plan services), or are non-audit related. Audit and audit-related fees for publicly reporting companies initially increased after the passage of the Sarbanes-Oxley Act in 2002, but then began to decrease starting in 2009 for a number of years.[143] This trend ended in 2013 when audit fees began a steady increase, which continued through 2017, though the rate of increase slowed from 2016 to 2017.[144]

The audit fees for publicly reporting companies vary depending on the entity's filing status as a large accelerated (greater than $700 million in public float), accelerated ($75 million to $700 million in public float), or non-accelerated (less than $75 million in public float) filer. The average audit fees in 2016 for all publicly reporting companies were $7,446,739, with an average fee of $10,021,524 for large accelerated filers, $1,594,728 for accelerated filers, and $365,717 for non-accelerated filers.[145] The average audit fees in 2016 for all private companies were $163,993, which represented a decrease from 2015, when the average audit fees were $258,935.[146] Audit fees are also directly tied to the entity's revenues. For instance, a public company with more than $50 billion in revenues paid an average audit fee of $23,217,750, and a private company with revenues in the $5 million to $15 million range paid an average audit fee of $1,160,000.[147]

What is evident from the results of this recent survey is that auditing fees generate a significant expense for any company, whether public or private. While fees may be increasing at a slower rate or decreasing for some entities, particularly private companies, the cost to undertake an audit is often quite burdensome.

---

[142]STANDARDS FOR ACCOUNTING AND REVIEW SERVICES, Review of Financial Statements, AR-C §90 (Am. Inst. of Certified Pub. Accountants 2016).
[143]Terry Sheridan, *Audit Fees Continue Their Increase* (Jan. 18, 2018), *available at* https://www.accountingweb.com/aa/auditing/audit-fees-continue-their-increase.
[144]Dave Pelland, Financial Execs. Research Found., *2017 Audit Fee Survey Report* 2, *available at* https://www.workiva.com/sites/workiva/files/pdfs/thought-leadership/fei-audit-fee-2017-report-final.pdf.
[145]*Id.* at 3.
[146]*Id.* at 6.
[147]*Id.* at 33.

K. INTERNATIONAL ACCOUNTING STANDARDS BOARD

The entity that establishes International Financial Reporting Standards (IFRS) for the global community for use in the preparation of public company financial statements is the International Accounting Standards Board (IASB). IASB is an independent body, which was formed in 2001 to replace the International Accounting Standards Committee, and operates under the oversight of the IFRS Foundation, a nonprofit organization also founded in 2001.[148] IASB is responsible for developing and issuing IFRS in accordance with established processes, as well as developing its agenda and approving interpretations prepared by the IFRS Interpretations Committee.[149] IASB is composed of up to a maximum of 16 experts in the accounting field with a commitment to engaging board members from diverse geographic locales.[150] The IFRS Foundation consists of 22 trustees, with the foundation appointing and overseeing IASB and its members, as well as raising funds to support the organizations.

IASB works closely with its global stakeholders, including investors, regulators, businesspersons, and the accounting profession to develop and set IFRS.[151] A variety of advisory committees, many of which were established by IASB, assist the board in its work on a regular basis and do so in a public forum context.[152] One of the primary responsibilities of IASB is to develop IFRS utilizing its "due process" procedure, which comprises six steps: (i) setting an agenda; (ii) planning; (iii) preparing and disseminating the discussion paper; (iv) preparing and disseminating the exposure draft; (v) preparing and disseminating the new standard; and (vi) undertaking the post-standard-setting procedures.[153]

1. International Financial Reporting Standards

IFRS are a set of accounting standards and requirements that entities must utilize in the preparation of their financial statements. IFRS are applicable to entities that are publicly traded, as well as entities that fall in the financial institutions category.[154] Unlike GAAP, IFRS are global standards, and more than 149 jurisdictions use these standards, with 125 of those jurisdictions requiring the use of IFRS.[155] IFRS are developed with the goals of transparency and public input, and one of the ways that is achieved is through the use of IASB due process procedures.[156] These standards result in financial statements that are prepared in a comparable manner across entities and thus allow users of the financial statements to more readily understand an entity's financial disclosures.

---

[148]IFRS, IASB, *available at* http://www.ifrs.org/groups/international-accounting-standards-board/.
[149]*Id.*
[150]*Id.*
[151]IFRS, Consultative Bodies, *available at* http://www.ifrs.org/about-us/consultative-bodies.
[152]*Id.*
[153]IFRS, How We Set IFRS Standards, *available at* http://www.ifrs.org/about-us/how-we-set-standards.
[154]IFRS, Who We Are, *available at* http://www.ifrs.org/about-us/who-we-are.
[155]*Id.*
[156]*Id.*

IFRS are supplemented by authoritative interpretations of the standards, which are prepared by the IFRS Interpretations Committee and approved by IASB.[157] IFRS are replacing many countries' local accounting standards and are rapidly becoming the mainstream accounting standards used by entities around the world.

Audit Opinion and Response Problems

These problems address audit opinion issues and audit response letters.

Problem 3.1

You work for Big Law Firm, PC, and your firm represents Beta Company in regard to much of its day-to-day litigation, including employment-related matters and claims. Beta Company is currently undergoing its year-end audit for the year ended December 31, 20X1. Big Law Firm received the audit inquiry letter from Beta Company on behalf of Small Audit Firm, LLC, Beta Company's auditors, regarding contingencies. The audit inquiry letter was dated January 5, 20X2, and was from Jamie Jones, Beta Company's President and Chief Executive Officer. Beta Company did not complete the "pending and threatened litigation" section, but instead requested that Big Law Firm, LLC provide that information to the auditors on its behalf, as Beta Company does not have an in-house counsel to rely on in that regard. The response letter is due to Small Audit Firm no later than February 12, 20X2. The partner has asked you to prepare Big Law Firm's initial draft of the audit response letter to Small Audit Firm, LLC and provided you with the following information in regard to litigation matters under Big Law Firm's purview:

Pending Litigation Matters
Smith v. Beta Company — Smith is suing Beta Company over a product defect, the trial date is set, management intends to proceed to trial, and the partner at Big Law Firm believes it is likely that there will be an unfavorable outcome in this matter, somewhere in the range of $350,000 to $625,000, which the partner believes is material to Beta Company.

McClelland v. Beta Company — McClelland, a customer of Beta Company, is suing Beta Company for contract breach. The lawsuit was filed last week, so the case has just begun and management has not yet determined how it will respond. The partner at Big Law Firm is not yet able to determine the likelihood of an unfavorable outcome or what the potential loss may be, but does believe this lawsuit could be material to Beta Company.

---

[157]*Id.*

Threatened Litigation Matters

Beta Company's landlord, Real Estate Corp., for its main facility has written a demand letter to Beta Company indicating that Beta owes it $23,000 for repairs that were made by Real Estate Corp. but were Beta Company's responsibility. The demand letter indicated that if Beta Company does not pay within ten days of the letter's date, Real Estate Corp. will file a lawsuit. Beta Company does not believe it owes the landlord any money and is not willing to pay Real Estate Corp. Big Law Firm does not believe the demand claim or threatened litigation will be material to Beta Company.

Unasserted Claims and Assessments

Big Law Firm is not aware of any unasserted claims or assessments in regard to Beta Company.

Using the above information, prepare a draft of Big Law Firm, PC's audit response letter to Small Audit Firm, LLC.

Problem 3.2

For each of the scenarios below, indicate the type of audit opinion the auditor would issue and explain your rationale.

Part A: Beta Company and its management prepare the financial statements in accordance with GAAP and have been doing so for the past five years. Beta Company's management selects those GAAP standards that it believes make the most sense for Beta Company's business model. In the current year, Beta Company opted to make some changes and adopted three new GAAP standards in conjunction with its financial statement preparation. One of the GAAP changes was as a result of a new accounting pronouncement, and the other two changes were elected by management because management thought the changes would result in more accurate financial statement disclosures.

Part B: Omega Company and its management prepare the financial statements in accordance with GAAP and have been doing so for the past three years. Omega Company's management carefully selects those GAAP standards that it believes best reflect industrywide usage and rarely deviates from the accounting methods other companies in the industry are using.

Part C: Sigma, Inc. and its management prepare the financial statements in accordance with GAAP, but for the current year decided to deviate from a GAAP standard as all the other companies in the industry were doing the same thing, since it seemed to better reflect the financial results of companies in this industry. Sigma, Inc.'s management thinks that a new GAAP standard will be put in place next year allowing for this type of reporting; however, management is not certain that will happen.

Part D: Epsilon Corp. and its management prepare the financial statements in accordance with GAAP and have been doing so since the entity was incorporated. During the current fiscal year, Epsilon realized it had made a material mistake in the prior year's financial statements and so elected to restate those financial statements to correct the material misstatement.

Financial Statement Preparation

A. INTRODUCTION

Chapter 2 introduced the primary financial statements — the balance sheet, income statement, statement of cash flows, and statement of changes in stockholders' equity. This chapter introduces the various transactions that affect a business entity's accounting books and records, as well as the process of recording those day-to-day transactions so that an entity can prepare financial statements at the end of the accounting period.

In order to prepare financial statements and reports, an entity must first maintain its books and records on a continuous basis. This includes recording its financial transactions through double-entry bookkeeping, preparing and recording adjusting entries, closing the accounts for the period, and preparing its financial statements. As a part of those processes, the entity must track and value its inventory, compute and record depreciation and amortization expenses, recognize revenues and expenses, and more. The beginning step to financial statement preparation is the entity's internal bookkeeping.

B. BOOKKEEPING

Bookkeeping is not synonymous with accounting. Bookkeeping is a part of the accounting process in which an entity records financial transactions of the business in order to keep the entity's internal books and records up to date and accurate. Accounting, on the other hand, is the preparation of an entity's financial statements and reports, as well as analysis of financial data. While technically two different processes, bookkeeping and accounting are intertwined. Before an entity can prepare financial statements and undertake analyses, it must first perform proper bookkeeping to keep its books and records current and accurate.

Today, most bookkeeping happens electronically through some type of accounting-based software. Many of the most common software tools blur the line between bookkeeping and accounting processes. For example, in traditional bookkeeping, recording a transaction requires you to update all of the entity's related accounts one at a time. This process ultimately allows for the preparation of the financial statements once the accounting period has ended and all relevant transactions have been entered and posted. By contrast, accounting software streamlines the process whereby recording the transaction automatically updates all the related accounts. While this makes entering and recording financial transactions easier, the user must understand how to properly prepare those transactions and enter them into the system correctly so that the entity's financial statements are an accurate reflection of its business and operations. Additionally, most bookkeeping and accounting software does not have the ability to indicate whether a transaction has been entered accurately (e.g., correct accounts or correct dollar amounts), whether a transaction that should have been entered was missed, whether a transaction was mistakenly entered more than once, or whether an invalid transaction was entered. As a result, the bookkeeping entries as well as the financial statements are only as accurate as the information and transactions that are entered into the system. Thus, in order to utilize any accounting software correctly and accurately, and to rely on the financial statements produced by the software, one must understand how to prepare the financial transactions that are the underlying basis for that information.

1. Double-Entry Bookkeeping

Double-entry bookkeeping is the standard manner in which an entity's financial transactions are recorded. At its most basic, it simply means that a transaction must impact at least two separate accounts and that the dollar value of the debit entries must equal the dollar value of the credit entries.

EXAMPLE 4.1   **DOUBLE-ENTRY BOOKKEEPING**

The below table illustrates examples of financial transactions and the two accounts that are impacted by each transaction—in other words, double-entry bookkeeping.

Financial Transaction Details	Account Impacted (Debit)	Account Impacted (Credit)
Business purchases $10,000 worth of inventory for cash	Inventory account increase of $10,000 (debit entry)	Cash account decrease of $10,000 (credit entry)
Business pays its outstanding utilities bill in the amount of $4,500	Utilities payable account decrease of $4,500 (debit entry)	Cash account decrease of $4,500 (credit entry)
Business borrows money from its commercial lender in the amount of $125,000	Cash account increase of $125,000 (debit entry)	Long-term debt account increase of $125,000 (credit entry)

In order to properly prepare the financial transactions, one must engage in double-entry bookkeeping, but must also understand the concept of debits and credits so that the transactions can be entered accurately and balance, meaning they have equal debits and credits.

---

2. Debits and Credits

While many people have preconceived notions regarding debits and credits as a result of their use of a debit card or credit card, when these terms are used in regard to double-entry bookkeeping and accounting the concept is much simpler and always the same. A debit is an entry to the left-hand side of an account and a credit is an entry to the right-hand side of an account.

In the world of double-entry bookkeeping, every financial transaction must have an equal value or amount of debits and credits; in other words, debits must equal credits for every transaction recorded. In order to accurately record the debit and credit entries for an entity's financial transactions, accountants utilize what are referred to as "T-accounts," which are symbolized by a capital letter "T." Every financial transaction will result in a debit to at least one account and a credit to at least one account. In each instance, and no matter the account impacted, the debit entry will be registered on the left side of the T-account and the credit entry will be registered on the right side of the T-account.

T-Account

Debits	Credits

3. Accounts

Every entity that maintains books and records creates a list of all accounts that are used to enter the various financial transactions of the business. These accounts are listed in what is called a "chart of accounts" and are classified into the following main categories: assets, liabilities, equity, revenues, expenses, gains, and losses.

The chart of accounts contains a list of all the potential accounts an entity uses in the preparation of its bookkeeping entries. As a result, the chart of accounts will contain many more accounts than what are actually reflected on that entity's balance sheet or income statement at any given time because not every account is utilized each accounting period. In addition to listing the names of all the accounts, each account will also have a number that is associated with that specific account and, in some instances, a brief description of the account. The chart of accounts is not a static list but rather can be changed or expanded as needed by the entity.

The general ledger is a list of all the accounts that are currently in use by the entity (which would be fewer than the full number listed in the chart of accounts) and the summary of all the financial transactions that have occurred. Each financial transaction is first entered as a journal entry in a general journal. The general journal records all the transactions of the entity in date order. The journal entries are then posted to their respective accounts in the general ledger, and at the end of the accounting period, the total of all the debit entries in the general ledger must equal the total of all the credit entries. If debits do not equal credits, then the general ledger does not balance. In that case, the mistake or mistakes must be located and corrected before the entity is in a position to close its books for the accounting period and prepare its financial statements. The balances in the general ledger accounts are ultimately utilized to prepare the balance sheet and income statement of the entity at the end of the accounting period.

The balance sheet accounts (assets, liabilities, and equity) are often referred to as permanent accounts, because the balances in these accounts carry forward from period to period, as well as from year to year, and the accounts are never closed as a part of the closing process at the end of each accounting period. While the balance in a balance sheet account may become zero due to the fact that it has no balance — for instance, the entity may not currently have any office supplies and so the balance for that asset account is zero — the account is still not closed and its zero balance carries forward for the account's use in future periods just like balance sheet accounts that retain a balance.

On the other hand, the income statement accounts (revenues, expenses, other gains, and other losses) are often referred to as temporary accounts, because the balances in these accounts do not carry forward from period to period or year to year. Instead, these accounts are closed as a part of the closing process at the end of each accounting period. At the end of the accounting period, each income statement account is ultimately closed into the entity's equity account (retained earnings if a corporation, proprietorship or owner's equity if a sole proprietorship, or members' or partners' equity if a limited liability company or partnership) so that each income statement account balance becomes zero and is closed for that particular accounting period. As a result, the income statement accounts are opened as new accounts with no balances at the start of each new accounting period.

C. BALANCE SHEET ENTRIES AND PREPARATION

As a refresher: the balance sheet speaks as of a specific date in time and reflects what the entity owns (assets), what it owes (liabilities), and the difference between what it owns and owes (equity). This concept is represented by the fundamental accounting equation: Assets – Liabilities = Equity. As discussed in

Chapter 2, these three main balance sheet categories are further divided into subparts.

In order to better understand how to record debit and credit entries, it is helpful to examine the setup of the T-account for each of three main balance sheet components. T-accounts can be used in conjunction with the general ledger (as a checks and balances system) or in lieu of the general ledger. For purposes of this text, T-accounts will be used in lieu of the general ledger.

Assets reflect those items that an entity owns. The opening balance in every asset account is reflected on the left or debit side of the T-account. If the entity increases an asset, meaning it receives cash or purchases inventory or equipment, that entry is logged as a debit or increase to the asset account. On the other hand, if the entity decreases an asset, meaning it spends cash or sells inventory or equipment, that entry is logged as a credit or decrease to the asset account.

Asset Accounts

Debit	Credit
Opening Balance	
Increase/+	Decrease/-

Liabilities are those items that an entity owes, and equity is the difference between total assets and total liabilities, or the residual interest of the owners. The opening balance in every liability and equity account is reflected on the right or credit side of the T-account. One primary exception to that rule results from an entity that has an accumulated loss versus retained earnings. In that case, the equity account of accumulated loss reflects a debit, or negative balance.

If the entity increases a liability, meaning it incurs an additional obligation to a creditor or increases its long-term debt, that entry is logged as a credit or increase to the liability account. On the other hand, if the entity decreases a liability, meaning it pays a creditor or pays down the principal on its long-term debt, that entry is logged as a debit or decrease to the liability account.

If the entity increases an equity account, meaning it sells additional shares of stock or has net income for the period (increase to retained earnings), that entry is logged as a credit or increase to the equity account. On the other hand, if the entity repurchases shares of its stock or has a net loss for the period (decrease to retained earnings), that entry is logged as a debit or decrease to an equity account.

Liability & Equity Accounts

Debit	Credit
	Opening Balance
Decrease/-	Increase/+

1. Preparing Journal Entries

Journal entries are records of financial transactions recorded in the general journal in chronological order for the accounting period. Journal entries typically include the following information: (i) date of the transaction; (ii) the amount and accounts debited; (iii) the amount and the accounts credited; and (iv) a short description of the transaction. At the end of the accounting period, the journal entries are posted to their respective accounts in the general ledger, and in some cases, to T-accounts.

EXAMPLE 4.2   **SMITH & SONS, INC. JOURNAL ENTRIES**

To demonstrate the concept of journal entries, the table below presents how the following transactions would be logged in a general journal utilizing double-entry bookkeeping for Smith & Sons, Inc. for the month of January:

- Smith & Sons, Inc. purchases a new machine that costs $79,000 from Thrift Corporation on account on January 5
- Smith & Sons, Inc. receives a $67,000 payment on January 13 from Big Machinery Company to pay off a portion of its outstanding accounts receivable
- Smith & Sons, Inc. sells an additional 100,000 shares of its common stock (par value $0.01) for a cash payment of $300,000 on January 28

SMITH & SONS, INC.—GENERAL JOURNAL

Date	Account	Debit	Credit
1/5	Equipment	$79,000	
	Accounts Payable—Thrift Corp (purchase of equipment on account from Thrift Corp)		$79,000
1/13	Cash	$67,000	
	Accounts Receivable—Big Machinery Company (receipt of cash from Big Machinery Company as payment on its receivable)		$67,000
1/28	Cash	$300,000	
	Common Stock		$1,000
	Additional Paid-In-Capital (sale of common stock for cash)		$299,000
Total		$446,000	$446,000

On January 5, Smith & Sons, Inc. records a debit (increase) to its equipment asset account to reflect that it bought and now owns a new piece of equipment and records a credit (increase) to its accounts payable account to reflect that it owes money to Thrift Corporation for the purchase.

- Impacts one asset and one liability account

On January 13, Smith & Sons, Inc. records a debit (increase) to its cash account to reflect that Big Machinery Company paid off a portion of its accounts receivable due Smith & Sons, Inc. and records a credit (decrease) to its accounts receivable account to reflect that it is no longer owed that amount.

• Impacts two asset accounts

On January 28, Smith & Sons, Inc. records a debit (increase) to its cash account to reflect the receipt of cash from the sale of its common stock and reflects a credit (increase) to common stock (amount received based on par value) and a credit to additional paid-in-capital (amount received in excess of par value) to reflect that it sold additional shares of common stock.

• Impacts one asset and two equity accounts

While each of the examples above impacts a different set of balance sheet accounts, one thing remains true — the total debit entries equal the total credit entries for each and every transaction. While all the journal entries for the accounting period would be posted into the general ledger, where the overall debits and credits would equal each other or balance for the period, this text does not include the general ledger but instead relies on posting the journal entries to T-accounts.

2. Posting Journal Entries to T-Accounts

Once all the journal entries for the accounting period have been logged in the general journal, those entries must be posted to either the general ledger accounts or T-accounts. The posting of the entries to their respective accounts ultimately allows the entity to know the balance in each account and prepare the balance sheet for the period.

EXAMPLE 4.3 **SMITH & SONS, INC. POSTED JOURNAL ENTRIES**

The following T-accounts, which include each account's opening balance, reflect how the three transactions in Example 4.2 would be posted to Smith & Sons, Inc.'s T-accounts for the month of the January:

Cash		Accounts Payable	
Op. Bal. $5,533,000			$2,026,000 Op. Bal.
1/13 67,000			79,000 1/5
1/28 300,000			

Accounts Receivable		Common Stock	
			$12,000 Op. Bal.
Op. Bal. $2,817,000	67,000 1/13		1,000 1/28

Equipment		Additional Paid-in-Capital	
Op. Bal. $1,681,000			$4,224,000 Op. Bal.
1/5 79,000			299,000 1/28

EXAMPLE 4.4 **BALANCE SHEET ACCOUNT TRANSACTION IMPACTS**

When preparing transactions that impact only balance sheet accounts, the table below sets forth the predominant ways in which entries may impact the asset, liability, and equity accounts.

Asset Accounts		Liability Accounts		Equity Accounts	
Debit (increase/+)	Credit (decrease/–)	Debit (decrease/-)	Credit (increase/+)	Debit (decrease/–)	Credit (increase/+)
A	A				
B			B		
C					C
	D	D			
	E			E	
			F	F	

The following sets forth an example representing each potential entry listed in the above table:

A: Company purchases inventory for cash thus converting one asset into another: debit to inventory/credit to cash

B: Company purchases inventory on account thus increasing an asset, but also increasing a liability for the purchase of the inventory: debit to inventory/ credit to accounts payable

C: Company receives cash for sale of stock thus increasing an asset for selling an ownership stake and increasing equity: debit to cash/credit to common stock and additional paid-in-capital

D: Company pays off an accounts payable balance thus decreasing a liability, but also decreasing an asset to pay the liability: credit to cash/debit to accounts payable

E: Company pays cash for the repurchase of shares of its common stock thus decreasing an asset for the repurchase of shares and decreasing equity: credit to cash/debit to treasury stock

F: Company issues a promissory note for the repurchase of shares of its common stock thus increasing a liability for the repurchase of the shares and decreasing equity: credit to note payable/debit to treasury stock

Now that you have been introduced to the concept of double-entry bookkeeping, debits and credits, general journal entries, and T-accounts, the next step is to put all that information together in the form of a simple example utilizing only balance sheet accounts.

| ILLUSTRATION 1 | **BALANCE SHEET ONLY TRANSACTIONS** |

The following illustration walks through the process of creating balance sheet T-accounts, preparing and logging journal entries for the month of February, posting journal entries to the respective T-accounts, and preparing the simple balance sheet for the month of February.

ILLUSTRATION EXAMPLE 1.1

SMITH & SONS, INC.—OPENING BALANCE SHEET

The balance sheet for Smith & Sons, Inc. as of January 31 is set forth below. The balance of each asset, liability, and equity account as of January 31 is set forth and these balances reflect the cumulative balance for each account since the inception of Smith & Sons, Inc.

SMITH & SONS, INC. BALANCE SHEET AS OF JANUARY 31

	January 31
Assets	
Cash and cash equivalents	$5,900,000
Accounts receivable	2,750,000
Property	1,050,000
Equipment	1,760,000
Furniture	325,000
Total assets	**$11,785,000**
Liabilities and Stockholders' Equity	
Liabilities	
Accounts payable	$2,105,000
Note payable	480,000
Long-term debt	1,135,000
Total liabilities	**$3,720,000**
Stockholders' equity	
Common stock, $0.01 par value; 4,000,000 shares authorized; 1,300,000 issued and outstanding as of January 31	$13,000
Additional paid-in-capital	4,523,000
Retained earnings	3,529,000
Total stockholders' equity	**$8,065,000**
Total liabilities and stockholders' equity	**$11,785,000**

ILLUSTRATION EXAMPLE 1.2

SMITH & SONS, INC.—FEBRUARY TRANSACTION LIST

The following Smith & Sons, Inc. financial transactions occurred during the month of February:

February 3	Smith & Sons, Inc. sent a payment to Thrift Corporation for $79,000 to pay the portion of its outstanding accounts payable that was due on or before February 5.
February 8	Big Machinery sent a payment of $83,000 to Smith & Sons, Inc. to pay the portion of its outstanding accounts receivable that was due on or before February 10.
February 11	Smith & Sons, Inc. purchased new furniture for its corporate offices, for which it paid $17,450 in cash.
February 16	Smith & Sons, Inc. sold an additional 15,000 shares of common stock, $0.01 par value, to a venture capitalist for $3.75 per share, which was paid for in cash.
February 18	Smith & Sons, Inc. paid its lender $45,000 as a payment on its note payable.
February 22	Smith & Sons, Inc. purchased $39,450 worth of equipment on account from Office Suppliers, Inc.
February 25	Smith & Sons, Inc. borrowed an additional $105,000 in long-term debt from its commercial lender.
February 27	Smith & Sons, Inc. utilized $103,000 of the additional long-term debt borrowing on February 25 to purchase an adjacent piece of property to expand its corporate offices, for which it paid cash.

ILLUSTRATION EXAMPLE 1.3

SMITH & SONS, INC.—FEBRUARY GENERAL JOURNAL

The following general journal sets forth the recorded financial transactions for the month of February based on the information provided in Illustration Example 1.2.

SMITH & SONS, INC. GENERAL JOURNAL—FEBRUARY

Date	Account	Debit	Credit
2/3	Accounts Payable	$79,000	
	Cash		$79,000
2/8	Cash	$83,000	
	Accounts Receivable		$83,000
2/11	Furniture	$17,450	
	Cash		$17,450
2/16	Cash	$56,250	
	Common Stock Additional-Paid-In-Capital		$150 $56,100
2/18	Note Payable	$45,000	
	Cash		$45,000
2/22	Equipment	$39,450	
	Accounts Payable		$39,450
2/25	Cash	$105,000	
	Long-Term Debt		$105,000
2/27	Property	$103,000	
	Cash		$103,000

ILLUSTRATION EXAMPLE 1.4

SMITH & SONS, INC.—FEBRUARY T-ACCOUNTS

The following T-accounts set forth the opening balance for each Smith & Sons, Inc. balance sheet account as set forth on the January 31 balance sheet and reflect the transactions posted to each T-account for the month of February based on the general journal entries set forth in Illustration Example 1.3.

Cash and Cash Equivalents					Accounts Payable		
Op. Bal.	$5,900,000	79,000	2/3	2/3	79,000	$2,105,000	Op. Bal.
2/8	83,000	17,450	2/11			39,450	2/22
2/16	56,250	45,000	2/18			$2,065,450	Balance
2/25	105,000	103,000	2/27				
Balance	$5,899,800						

Note Payable			
2/18	45,000	$480,000	Op. Bal.
		$435,000	Balance

Accounts Receivable			
Op. Bal.	$2,750,000	83,000	2/8
Balance	$2,667,000		

Long-Term Debt		
	$1,135,000	Op. Bal.
	105,000	2/25
	$1,240,000	Balance

Property		
Op. Bal.	$1,050,000	
2/27	103,000	
Balance	$1,153,000	

Common Stock		
	$13,000	Op. Bal.
	150	2/16
	$13,150	Balance

Equipment		
Op. Bal.	$1,760,000	
2/22	39,450	
Balance	$1,799,450	

Additional Paid-In-Capital		
	$4,523,000	Op. Bal.
	56,100	2/16
	$4,579,100	Balance

Furniture		
Op. Bal.	$325,000	
2/11	17,450	
Balance	$342,450	

Retained Earnings		
	$3,529,000	Op. Bal.
	$3,529,000	Balance

ILLUSTRATION EXAMPLE 1.5

SMITH & SONS, INC.—CLOSING BALANCE SHEET

The balance sheet for Smith & Sons, Inc. as of February 28 is set forth below and reflects all the changes that took place during the month of February to each balance sheet account.

SMITH & SONS, INC. BALANCE SHEET AS OF FEBRUARY 28

	February 28
Assets	
Cash and cash equivalents	$5,899,800
Accounts receivable	2,667,000

continued

Property	1,153,000
Equipment	1,799,450
Furniture	342,450
Total assets	**$11,861,700**
Liabilities and Stockholders' Equity	
Liabilities	
Accounts payable	$2,065,450
Note payable	435,000
Long-term debt	1,240,000
Total liabilities	**$3,740,450**
Stockholders' equity	
Common stock, $0.01 par value; 4,000,000 shares authorized; 1,315,000 issued and outstanding as of February 28	$13,150
Additional paid-in-capital	4,579,100
Retained earnings	3,529,000
Total stockholders' equity	**$8,121,250**
Total liabilities and stockholders' equity	**$11,861,700**

EXPLANATION OF ILLUSTRATION 1

The following discusses and explains in detail the process for preparing the books and records for Smith & Sons, Inc. for the month of February:

Step 1: Record opening balances. The first step in the process of managing the transactions for the month of February is to create a T-account for each asset, liability, and equity account listed on the January 31 balance sheet for Smith & Sons, Inc. After creating the T-accounts, the opening balances (ending balance from the January 31 balance sheet) should be recorded in the respective T-accounts and are labeled as "Op. Bal." (see Illustration Example 1.4 above). All asset accounts' opening balances are reflected as debits (entries on the left-hand side of the respective T-account). All liability and equity accounts' opening balances are reflected as credits (entries on the right-hand side of the respective T-account).

Step 2: Record February transactions in the general journal and post transactions to the proper T-accounts. The next step is to record the February financial transactions based on the information provided. Each transaction is recorded in the general journal and then subsequently posted to the appropriate T-account reflecting the date on which the transaction occurred (see Illustration Example 1.3 and Illustration Example 1.4 above, respectively). An explanation of each journal entry follows:

February 3: Smith & Sons, Inc. made a payment to one of its creditors and as a result it records a $79,000 debit to accounts payable to reflect that it reduced the amount it owes to its creditors and records a $79,000 credit to cash to reflect that it expended cash to make the payment to the creditor, Thrift Corporation.

It reflects a debit (left side entry) to the accounts payable T-account and reflects a credit (right side entry) to the cash T-account.

February 8: Smith & Sons, Inc. received a payment from one of its customers and as a result it records an $83,000 debit to cash to reflect that it received a cash payment and records an $83,000 credit to accounts receivable to reflect that it is now owed less from its customers.

It posts a debit (left side entry) to the cash T-account and posts a credit (right side entry) to the accounts receivable T-account.

February 11: Smith & Sons, Inc. purchased new furniture and paid in cash and as a result it records a $17,450 debit to furniture to reflect that it now owns more furniture and records a $17,450 credit to cash to reflect that it expended cash to purchase the furniture.

It posts a debit (left side entry) to the furniture T-account and posts a credit (right side entry) to the cash T-account.

February 16: Smith & Sons, Inc. sold additional shares of its common stock for a cash investment and as a result it records a $56,250 debit to cash to reflect that it received cash for the stock and records a $150 credit to common stock (15,000 shares × $0.01 par value) and a $56,100 credit to additional paid-in-capital (15,000 shares × $3.74 (sales price of $3.75 less $0.01 par value)) to reflect the sale of additional shares of common stock.

It posts a debit (left side entry) to the cash T-account and posts a credit (right side entry) to both the common stock and additional paid-in-capital T-accounts.

February 18: Smith & Sons, Inc. made a payment to the lender on the outstanding balance owed on its note and as a result it records a $45,000 debit to note payable to reflect that it reduced the amount it owes and records a $45,000 credit to cash to reflect the payment on the note.

It posts a debit (left side entry) to the note payable T-account and posts a credit (right side entry) to the cash T-account.

February 22: Smith & Sons, Inc. purchased new equipment on account from Office Suppliers, Inc. and as a result it records a debit to equipment to reflect that it now owns additional equipment and records a credit to accounts payable to reflect that it now owes an additional amount to its creditors.

It posts a debit (left side entry) to the equipment T-account and posts a credit (right side entry) to the accounts payable T-account.

February 25: Smith & Sons, Inc. borrowed additional money under its long-term credit facility and so it records a $105,000 debit to cash to reflect that it received those funds from its lender and records a $105,000 credit to long-term debt to reflect that it now owes more to its commercial lender.

It posts a debit (left side entry) to the cash T-account and posts a credit (right side entry) to the long-term debt T-account.

February 27: Smith & Sons, Inc. utilized its recent cash borrowings to purchase a new piece of property and so it records a $103,000 debit to property to reflect that it now owns additional property and records a $103,000 credit to cash to reflect that it expended cash to purchase the property.

It posts a debit (left side entry) to the property T-account and posts a credit (right side entry) to the cash T-account.

Step 3: Total each balance sheet T-account. The next step is to total the balance of each T-account in order to have the information needed to prepare the February month-end balance sheet. Asset accounts should reflect a debit balance (left side balance) and so all the debit entries should be added together and all the credit entries should then be subtracted to determine the overall debit balance for the T-account. Liability and equity accounts should reflect a credit balance (right side balance) and so all credit entries should be added together and all the debit entries should then be subtracted to determine the overall credit balance for the T-account (see Illustration Example 1.4 above).

Step 4: Prepare the balance sheet for Smith & Sons, Inc. as of February 28. The final step is to utilize the balances from the asset, liability, and equity T-accounts to prepare the balance sheet for the month ended February 28 (see Illustration Example 1.5 above).

Balance Sheet Problems 4.1 to 4.3

Problems 4.1 to 4.3: Background Information

Alan, Barry, and Charles Williams, three brothers, are forming ABC, Inc. to manufacture custom furniture that the three brothers design. ABC, Inc. is a traditional C Corporation with two classes of stock authorized, common stock (par value $0.10, 4,000,000 shares authorized) and preferred stock (par value $2.50, 500,000 shares authorized). ABC, Inc. is formed in early January and January is the first month of its corporate existence and operations.

The following three problems, 4.1, 4.2, and 4.3, all focus on ABC, Inc. and build on each other, so must be completed in sequence.

Problem 4.1

For the January transactions set forth below, prepare the journal entries for the month of January in a general journal, post the journal entries to the respective

T-accounts, total the T-accounts as of the end of January, and prepare a balance sheet as of January 31.

January Transactions

January 2: The three brothers, Alan, Barry, and Charles, incorporate ABC, Inc., and upon incorporation, ABC, Inc. issued 10,000 shares of common stock to each brother (for a total issuance of 30,000 shares of common stock) in exchange for $30,000 from each brother (for a total of $90,000).

January 4: ABC, Inc. borrowed $110,000 from Western Bank to fund the first phase of growth for the new business.

January 7: ABC, Inc. purchased $96,000 worth of machinery on account from Big Machinery Company.

January 13: Sally Jones bought 3,000 shares of preferred stock from ABC, Inc. for $40,500. Sally paid half in cash and owes $11,000 on January 25 with the remainder due on February 2.

January 16: ABC, Inc. spent $3,670 in cash to purchase new furniture for its corporate offices from the OF Warehouse.

January 18: ABC, Inc. sent a payment to Big Machinery Company for $22,000 in payment of the portion of its outstanding accounts payable that was due on or before January 20.

January 25: Sally Jones sent a payment of $11,000 to ABC, Inc. to pay her second payment due on the purchase of the preferred stock on January 13.

Problem 4.2

For the February transactions set forth below, prepare the journal entries for the month of February in a general journal, post the journal entries to the respective T-accounts (you should utilize your T-accounts from the month of January and add new T-accounts as needed), total the T-accounts as of the end of February, and prepare a balance sheet as of February 28.

February Transactions

February 2: Sally Jones paid ABC, Inc. $9,250, the remainder of her outstanding balance due for the purchase of the preferred stock on January 13.

February 6: Worried about its financial condition and cash position, ABC, Inc. sold 50,000 shares of common stock to Fran Financer for $78,000, for which Fran paid cash.

February 8: ABC, Inc. made a payment of $39,000 to Big Machinery Company on the portion of its outstanding accounts payable that was due.

February 11: ABC, Inc. purchased $36,780 worth of materials (or inventory) from Fine Wood Warehouse to build furniture that it will sell. ABC, Inc. paid cash for the materials.

February 12: Randy Reese, a good friend of the brothers, bought 180,000 shares of ABC, Inc. common stock for $27,000 pursuant to an interest-free promissory note. He agreed to pay the promissory note in two equal installments with one payment due in March and one due in April.

February 17: ABC, Inc. sold 5,000 shares of its preferred stock to Susie Williams, who is the sister of Alan, Barry, and Charles, for $20,000 cash.

February 19: ABC, Inc. bought $104,300 worth of equipment for the business from Equipment Sales, Inc. and paid cash for it.

February 23: ABC, Inc. purchased three office chairs on account from Chairs-R-Us, one for each brother, for a cost of $1,300 per chair.

February 26: ABC, Inc. made a payment of $35,000 to Big Machinery Company to pay the remaining outstanding amount of its accounts payable due.

Problem 4.3

For the March transactions set forth below, prepare the journal entries for the month of March in a general journal, post the journal entries to the respective T-accounts (you should utilize your T-accounts from the month of February and add new T-accounts as needed), total the T-accounts as of the end of March, and prepare a balance sheet as of March 31.

March Transactions

March 3: Maxine Merger, who is a friend of the Williams brothers, wants to help out their business and buys 50,000 shares of common stock for $100,000 and 65,000 shares of preferred stock for $227,500, paying cash for both purchases.

March 7: ABC, Inc. paid $2,000 toward its outstanding accounts payable balance due Chairs-R-Us.

March 12: Randy Reese made a promissory note payment of $13,500 to ABC, Inc. for the stock he purchased on February 12.

March 18: ABC, Inc. made a large equipment purchase of $183,700 from Big Machinery Company. Big Machinery Company required ABC, Inc. to make a 15 percent down payment. The remainder was put on account.

March 24: ABC, Inc. paid $5,000 to Western Bank on its principal balance for its loan.

March 29: ABC, Inc. purchased $78,000 worth of materials (or inventory) from The Lumber Supplier to begin building an order of custom furniture. ABC, Inc. bought the materials on account.

March 30: ABC, Inc. received an early promissory note payment from Randy Reese for $13,500 for the stock he purchased on February 12.

D. INCOME STATEMENT ENTRIES AND PREPARATION

As a refresher: the income statement reflects the net income or net loss of an entity for a specific period of time. It reflects the revenues and gains as well as the expenses and losses of the entity for the period. The difference between all the revenues and gains and all the expenses and losses is the net income (if a positive amount) or net loss (if a negative amount) for the period.

In order to expand on how to record debit and credit entries as a part of logging a transaction when the income statement is impacted, it is helpful to examine the setup of the T-account for the main income statement components. The structure of the T-account does not change just because it reflects income statement accounts — the left side is still a debit and the right side is still a credit. However, income statement accounts are different from balance sheet accounts in that an income statement account never has an opening balance as each of these accounts is closed at the end of the accounting period, meaning it is zeroed out and closed for the period. As a result, an opening balance is never reflected in an income statement T-account.

Revenues reflect the value of all of the business's primary products or services that the entity sold. On the other hand, gains represent the value of those items that created earnings for the business but are tangential, meaning they are not revenues. Gains include such items as dividend income, interest income, or gain on a sale of an asset. If an entity increases revenues or recognizes a gain, that entry is logged as a credit to the revenue or gain account.

Revenue and Gain Accounts	
Debit	Credit
Decrease/–	Increase/+

Expenses are costs of the business resulting from the entity's principal business operations, whether directly related to revenue (cost of goods sold or COGS) or not directly related to revenue (operating expenses). Losses and other expenses are those costs of the entity's business that do not fall into the category of COGS or operating expenses. Losses and other expenses include such items as dividend expense, interest expense, or loss on the sale of an asset. If an entity incurs an expense or loss, that entry is logged as a debit to the expense or loss account.

Screwed up graphic

Expense and Loss Accounts	
Debit	Credit
Decrease/–	Increase/+

1. Cash Versus Accrual Accounting Methodology

There are two distinct accounting methodologies that entities can utilize in tracking the revenues and expenses of the business: cash basis accounting or accrual basis accounting.

a. Cash Basis Accounting

Cash basis accounting is the simpler of the two methods and focuses on when the entity receives or expends cash, or in other words, when cash changes hands. Under this type of system, an entity recognizes revenues when it receives the cash payment and expenses when it makes the cash payment. In other words, revenues are recognized in the accounting period when the cash is actually received and deposited in the entity's bank account and expenses are allocated to the accounting period when the entity expends the cash from its bank account to make the payment. As a result, the entity's cash account on the balance sheet and its bank account balance match, so its cash account reflects the actual amount of cash it has on hand in the bank to meet the business's ongoing needs. Small businesses may elect to utilize cash basis accounting due to its simplicity in maintaining the entity's books and records. However, due to its limitations, an entity rarely uses cash basis accounting.

EXAMPLE 4.5 **CASH BASIS ACCOUNTING**

Cash basis accounting for revenues. Assume an entity sells $25,000 worth of products to a customer on January 15 and includes an invoice with the delivery of the products. Even though the entity has sold its products on January 15, it does not recognize the $25,000 of revenues as the customer has not yet paid. Assume further that the customer pays the entity in full via wire transfer on February 5. It is on that date that the entity will recognize the $25,000 of revenues even though the sale happened in the prior month. In other words, the entity recognizes the revenues in a different accounting period (February) than the accounting period when the actual sale took place (January).

Cash basis accounting for expenses. Assume an entity receives its utility bill on March 30 in the amount of $3,250 for utilities it consumed during the month of March. Even though the entity consumed the utilities in March and received the bill, it does not recognize the expense of $3,250 as the entity has not yet paid the bill. Assume further that the entity pays the utility bill in full on April 24. It is on that date that the entity will recognize the $3,250 utilities expense even though it consumed the utilities in the prior month. In other words, the entity allocated the expense in a different accounting period (April) than the accounting period when it actually benefited from the utilities (March).

b. Accrual Basis Accounting

Accrual basis accounting is the more complicated of the two methods and focuses on when the revenues are earned and the expenses are incurred versus when cash changed hands. Under this type of system, an entity recognizes revenues when it has earned those revenues and allocates expenses when incurred or when the expense provides a benefit to the entity even if no cash has been exchanged in the transaction. In other words, revenues are recognized in the accounting period when the entity earns the revenues and expenses are allocated to the accounting period when the entity incurs or benefits from the expenses.

An entity that utilizes this accounting methodology engages in what is known as accruing and deferring revenues and expenses. Unlike cash basis accounting, it is irrelevant whether the customer has paid for a product or service or the entity has paid a bill—it only matters whether the revenue is earned or the expense is incurred. Most businesses utilize accrual basis accounting. While complicated, accrual basis accounting provides a more realistic perspective of an entity's financial position.

EXAMPLE 4.6   **ACCRUAL BASIS ACCOUNTING**

Accrual basis accounting for revenues. Assume an entity sells $25,000 worth of products to a customer on January 15 and includes an invoice with the delivery of the products. Even though the entity has not received a cash payment from the customer for the products sold on January 15, the entity still recognizes $25,000 of revenue and creates an accounts receivable due from the customer on that date. Assume further that the customer pays the entity in full via wire transfer on February 5. On that date, the entity will recognize the receipt of the cash payment and eliminate the customer's accounts receivable balance, but will not recognize revenue as the entity already did so in January. In other words, the entity recognizes revenue in the accounting period it was earned (January) rather than the accounting period when it was actually paid for the products (February).

Accrual basis accounting for expenses. Assume an entity receives its utility bill on March 30 in the amount of $3,250 for utilities it consumed during the month of March. Even though the entity has not paid the utility bill in March, the entity still recognizes $3,250 of expenses for the month as it incurred or received the benefit of those expenses and creates an accounts payable due the utility company. Assume further that the entity pays the utility bill in full on April 24. On that date, the entity will recognize the payment of cash and eliminate the accounts payable due the utility company, but will not recognize an expense as the entity already did so in March. In other words, the entity recognizes the expense in the accounting period it was used (March) rather than the accounting period in which the entity actually paid for the expense (April).

i. Revenue and Gain Recognition

Pursuant to Generally Accepted Accounting Principles (GAAP), an entity can only recognize revenue, whether that revenue is from selling a product or a service, when two conditions are met.[1] Those conditions are that the revenue (i) must be realizable or realized, and (ii) has been earned.[2] Revenue is realizable or realized when the product, merchandise, or service is exchanged for cash or claims to cash (a right to receive cash).[3] Revenue is earned when the entity has substantially completed the requirements of the sale such as producing and delivering the product or providing the service.[4] Accordingly, these two conditions are typically met "by the time product or merchandise is delivered or services are rendered to customers."[5]

The U.S. Securities and Exchange Commission (SEC) has also provided guidance regarding revenue recognition and the two conditions. The SEC believes

[1] ACCOUNTING STANDARDS CODIFICATION, Revenue Recognition, ASC §605-10-45 (Fin. Accounting Found. 2017).
[2] Id.
[3] RECOGNITION AND MEASUREMENT IN FINANCIAL STATEMENTS OF BUSINESS ENTERPRISES, Statement of Financial Accounting Concepts No. 5, §83(a) (Fin. Accounting Standards Bd. 2008).
[4] Id. §83(b).
[5] Id. §84(a).

that revenue can be recognized when four criteria have been met: (i) there is persuasive evidence that an arrangement exists, meaning that a final understanding between the parties regarding the nature and terms of the transaction has been agreed upon; (ii) delivery has occurred or the services have been rendered, meaning the seller has substantially completed its obligations; (iii) the seller's price to the buyer is fixed or determinable, meaning that the price is a set amount and is not subject to a refund or adjustment; and (iv) collectibility is reasonably assured, meaning the seller is reasonably confident it can collect the payment.[6]

Gains are treated similarly for GAAP purposes. In order to recognize a gain, it must also be realizable or realized, and earned. A gain is realizable or realized when an asset is exchanged for cash or a claim to cash.[7] As gains generally do not result in earnings, the condition of being earned is less important than the condition of being realizable or realized.[8] Traditionally, gains are recognized at the time of the actual sale or transaction.[9]

The concept of revenue and gain recognition is important, as an entity is not entitled to recognize revenues or gains during the accounting period unless it has met the recognition conditions. In the case where the entity has not met the two conditions, it will have to defer recognition of the revenue or gain to a future accounting period when the conditions have been satisfied.

Revenue recognition is an area that is ripe with potential fraud, as it is easy for an entity to recognize revenue in an incorrect accounting period, whether intentionally or unintentionally. For example, in order to meet earning expectations, an entity may choose to recognize revenue in the current accounting period to increase its net income even though the entity has not substantially completed the work and thus the revenue has not been earned. On the other hand, an entity may defer revenue that has been earned to a future accounting period in order to miss certain financial target levels that would require the entity to pay bonuses to its employees. In either circumstance, an entity can often establish a justification as to why revenue should or should not be reported in a particular accounting period.

ii. *Expense and Loss Allocation*

Pursuant to GAAP, an entity should recognize expenses and losses when the entity's economic benefits are used up in delivering or producing the product, in rendering the services, or when an asset is expected to provide reduced or no further benefits.[10]

According to the matching principle, an entity should recognize expenses of the business in the same accounting period, as it recognizes the revenues that are related to those expenses. For instance, cost of goods sold (i.e., inventory, direct labor, etc.) should be matched to the revenues that directly result from those expenses. If an expense cannot be matched to specific revenues,

---

[6]SEC Staff Accounting Bull. No. 104, S.E.C. Rel. No. SAB-104 (Dec. 17, 2003).
[7]Recognition and Measurement in Financial Statements of Business Enterprises, *supra* note 3, §83(a).
[8]*Id.* §83(b).
[9]*Id.* §84(a).
[10]*Id.* §85.

the entity should recognize the expense in the accounting period in which the expense is incurred, whether cash is expended or a liability is created.[11] Other costs and expenses that are not directly related to revenue, such as depreciation, are allocated in a systematic and rational manner over a set period of time, meaning the time that such asset is expected to provide a benefit to the entity.[12]

Expense recognition is also an area where misreporting by the entity can occur. For example, in order to meet earning expectations an entity may choose to defer an expense of the current accounting period to a future accounting period to prevent such expense from impacting its net income for the period. On the other hand, an entity may recognize an expense in the current accounting period, which is not associated with revenues or actually incurred, in order to miss certain financial target levels that would require the entity to pay bonuses to its employees.

c. Basic Accrual Concepts at Work

Accrual is the process through which an event is recognized in the current accounting period even though the cash related to that event will not be received or paid until some future accounting period. It is the process through which an entity recognizes revenues as earned in the current accounting period even though the entity has not received payment for the sale of that product or service. It is also the process through which incurred expenses of the entity are recognized in the current accounting period even though the entity has not yet rendered a payment for those expenses.

EXAMPLE 4.7   **BASIC ACCRUAL CONCEPT OF WORK BEFORE PAYMENT**

In this scenario, the entity produces and delivers the good or performs the service on June 20 and invoices the customer in the amount of $75,000 on that same date. The customer pays the entity $75,000 on July 15. Because the entity earned the revenue in June, it recognizes that revenue and creates an accounts receivable due from that customer in the month of June even though it does not receive payment until July. When the customer pays the entity on July 15, the entity will recognize the cash payment and the elimination of the receivable, but not recognize the revenue, as it already did so in June. The following journal entries represent these financial transactions:

Date	Account	Debit	Credit
6/20	Accounts Receivable	$75,000	
	Revenue		$75,000
7/15	Cash	$75,000	
	Accounts Receivable		$75,000

---

[11] *Id.* §86(b).
[12] *Id.* §86(c).

EXAMPLE 4.8   **BASIC ACCRUAL CONCEPT OF USE BEFORE PAYMENT**

In this scenario, the entity has been fortunate to enter into a lease arrangement where it pays rent of $4,000 per month on or before the fifth day of the following calendar month (in other words, one month in arrears). The entity pays the lessor the July rent payment of $4,000 on August 5. Even though the entity did not pay for the July rent expense until August, it must still recognize that rent expense and create a rent payable in the month of July, as it has incurred the expense or benefited from the use of the space in July. When the entity pays the lessor on August 5, the entity will recognize the cash payment and the elimination of the payable, but not recognize the expense, as it already did so in July. The following journal entries represent these financial transactions:

Date	Account	Debit	Credit
7/31	Rent Expense	$4,000	
	Rent Payable		$4,000
8/5	Rent Payable	$4,000	
	Cash		$4,000

d. Basic Deferral Concepts at Work

Deferral is the process through which an event is not recognized until a future accounting period even though the cash related to that event is received or paid in the current accounting period. It occurs when an entity receives cash in the current accounting period for products that will not be delivered or services that will not be provided until a future accounting period. It also occurs when the entity prepays for expenses in the current accounting period that will not be incurred or benefited from until a future accounting period.

EXAMPLE 4.9   **BASIC DEFERRAL CONCEPT OF PAYMENT BEFORE WORK**

In this scenario, the entity receives a prepayment of $63,000 from a customer on September 10 for products or services the entity will deliver in the future. On October 15, the entity delivers $63,000 worth of products or services to the customer. Even though the entity was paid in September, it cannot recognize that cash payment as revenue, as it has not yet earned that revenue. Instead, the entity will recognize unearned revenue or unearned income during the September accounting period. When the entity delivers the products or performs the services in October, it will recognize the revenue at that point in time as it has been earned and eliminate the unearned revenue liability. The following journal entries represent these financial transactions:

Date	Account	Debit	Credit
9/10	Cash	$63,000	
	Unearned Revenue		$63,000
10/15	Unearned Revenue	$63,000	
	Revenue		$63,000

EXAMPLE 4.10   **BASIC DEFERRAL CONCEPT OF PAYMENT BEFORE USE**

In this scenario, on April 23 the entity prepays its business insurance monthly premium of $2,600 for the month of May. The monthly premium is not due until the third day of each month to cover the insurance expense for that given month. Even though the entity has paid its insurance provider in April, it cannot recognize the expense, as the entity has not yet incurred or received the benefit of that expense. Instead, the entity will recognize prepaid insurance during the April accounting period. In the month of May, when the insurance premium is due, the entity will recognize the insurance expense and eliminate the prepaid insurance asset. The following journal entries represent these financial transactions:

Date	Account	Debit	Credit
4/23	Prepaid Insurance	$2,600	
	Cash		$2,600
5/3	Insurance Expense	$2,600	
	Prepaid Insurance		$2,600

e. Accrual and Deferral in More Detail

The examples above illustrate basic accrual and deferral concepts where an entity accrues a single amount for a set period or defers a single amount for a set period. However, the business world is not generally so simple and oftentimes an entity receives a prepayment that it uses up over multiple periods or prepays an expense for an entire year. In those cases, the concept of accrual and deferral becomes slightly more complicated and impacts more than one or two accounting periods. In some of those instances, the entity will have to make an adjusting entry at the end of the month to recognize an expense.

i. Prepaid Expenses

The concept of a prepaid expense as an asset of the business is one that is often difficult to grasp, as it is not intuitive. A prepaid expense, which is an asset of the business, arises when an entity prepays for a future expense of the business.

Those future expenses could be rent obligations, insurance premiums, professional dues, or something else.

When an entity prepays for an expense, it records that prepayment as an asset of the business (debit entry) and recognizes the cash payment (credit entry). The rationale for this is that the entity is not yet in a position to recognize an expense, as it has not incurred or received the benefit of the expense, yet it has already paid and so must reflect that prepayment in its accounting books and records. As a result, the entity creates an asset account for the prepaid expense due to the fact that if the entity never incurs the expense or uses the benefit of the prepaid expense, the entity is entitled to a refund of all or that portion of the prepayment that it has not used up. Because the entity could be entitled to a refund, the prepaid expense is reflected as an asset of the business until used. As the entity uses up the prepaid expense, the entity reduces the prepaid expense asset account and recognizes and records the appropriate portion of the recognized expense. The reason the prepaid expense asset account is reduced is that the entity has used up part of that asset (because it incurred or benefited from a portion of the expense) and thus no longer has that asset and is no longer entitled to a refund for that portion.

Prepaid expenses bring another accounting process into the mix—adjusting entries. Because the entity has recorded a prepaid expense that it will use up over the course of time, the entity must recognize that usage and record the necessary expense. The entity undertakes that process through an adjusting entry that it makes at the end of the accounting period in which a portion of the prepaid expense was used. Adjusting entries for prepaid expenses require the entity to record an expense for the period as a debit entry and to record the use of the prepaid expense as a credit entry. The cash account is not impacted as a part of the adjusting entry, as the entity already recognized the cash expenditure when it initially prepaid the expense.

ii. Deferred or Unearned Revenue

The concept of deferred or unearned revenue as a liability of the business is another idea that is not always easy to understand. Unearned revenue arises when an entity receives a prepayment for future goods or services it must provide to a customer.

When an entity receives a prepayment for future goods or services, it recognizes the cash receipt immediately (debit entry) and records that prepayment as a liability of the business (credit entry). The rationale for this is that the entity is not yet in a position to recognize the revenue, as it has not delivered the goods or provided the services and so has not earned the revenue, yet the entity has already received payment and must reflect that prepayment in its accounting books and records. As a result, the entity creates a liability account for the unearned revenue due to the fact that if the entity never delivers the goods or provides the services, the entity must refund all or the portion of the prepayment that it has not earned. Because the entity may have to make a refund, that unearned revenue is a liability of the business until it is earned. As the entity delivers the goods or provides the services, the entity has earned the revenue and reduces the unearned revenue liability account and recognizes and records the appropriate amount of earned revenue. The reason the unearned revenue account is reduced is that the entity has earned that revenue (because it delivered the good or provided the service) and thus no longer has that liability and would not be required to refund that portion.

Deferred or unearned revenue also requires an adjusting entry, which is generally made at that point in the accounting period when the entity has earned the revenue. Because the entity has recorded unearned revenue that it will earn over the course of time, the entity must recognize and record that portion of the revenue as it is earned. This type of adjusting entry requires the entity to record a reduction of unearned revenue for the period as a debit entry and to record the amount of revenue earned as a credit entry. The cash account is not impacted as a part of the adjusting entry, as the entity already recognized the cash payment when it initially received the prepayment.

iii. Advanced Accrual and Deferral Concepts at Work

The following examples address those facets of the accrual and deferral process that are more prototypical of the way in which transactions occur in the business world. In particular, they examine the concepts of accrual and deferral over multiple accounting periods.

EXAMPLE 4.11 **ADVANCED ACCRUAL CONCEPT OF WORK BEFORE PAYMENT**

In this scenario, the entity produces and delivers goods on October 10 and invoices the customer in the amount of $98,000. The customer pays the entity $49,000 on November 11 and $49,000 on December 14. Because the entity has earned the revenue, it recognizes that revenue in the month of October even though it does not receive payment until November and December. The following journal entries represent these financial transactions:

Date	Account	Debit	Credit
10/10	Accounts Receivable	$98,000	
	Revenue		$98,000
11/11	Cash	$49,000	
	Accounts Receivable		$49,000
12/14	Cash	$49,000	
	Accounts Receivable		$49,000

On October 10 the entity recognizes the full amount of $98,000 as revenue, as it has produced and delivered the goods to the customer. That revenue was earned in the month of October and must be recognized. It is irrelevant that the customer does not pay the entity until November and December for the goods.

In November and December when the customer pays the entity, the entity will recognize receipt of the cash payment and reduce the accounts receivable account to reflect the fact that it is now owed less from the customer.

EXAMPLE 4.12 ADVANCED ACCRUAL CONCEPT OF USE BEFORE PAYMENT

In this scenario, the entity has been fortunate to enter into a lease arrangement where it pays its rent in arrears at the end of each calendar quarter, meaning it pays for January, February, and March rent on March 31. The total rent for the quarter is $22,500, or $7,500 per month. Even though the entity is not paying for its rent until the end of the quarter, it must still recognize an expense as a result of the fact that it is utilizing a benefit each month (the space it leases) and record a liability to reflect the fact that it will owe a payment to the lessor at the end of the quarter.

The following journal entries represent the recognition of the expense even though the entity has not yet paid its rent:

Date	Account	Debit	Credit
1/1	Rent Expense	$7,500	
	Rent Payable		$7,500
2/1	Rent Expense	$7,500	
	Rent Payable		$7,500
3/1	Rent Expense	$7,500	
	Rent Payable		$7,500

The following journal entry represents the entity's cash payment to the lessor for the rent for January, February, and March:

Date	Account	Debit	Credit
3/31	Rent Payable	$22,500	
	Cash		$22,500

EXAMPLE 4.13 ADVANCED DEFERRAL CONCEPT OF PAYMENT BEFORE WORK

In this scenario, the entity receives a prepayment of $105,000 from a client on March 1 for services the entity will provide over the next three months. At the end of March, April, and May, the entity has performed $33,000, $48,000, and $34,000 worth of services, respectively. In each instance, the entity sends an invoice to the client indicating the amount of services performed and the client's remaining prepayment balance or the amount due. On June 10, the client remits payment for the full amount due as noted on the May invoice, as at that point the client had utilized the services of the entity in excess of its initial prepayment amount. The entity cannot recognize revenue until March 31, April 30, and May 31 when it submits an invoice to the client for services performed during the month. The following journal entries represent all of the above financial transactions:

Date	Account	Debit	Credit
3/1	Cash	$105,000	
	Unearned Revenue		$105,000
3/31	Unearned Revenue	$33,000	
	Revenue		$33,000
4/30	Unearned Revenue	$48,000	
	Revenue		$48,000
5/31	Unearned Revenue Accounts Receivable	$24,000 $10,000	
	Revenue		$34,000
6/10	Cash	$10,000	
	Accounts Receivable		$10,000

On March 1 the entity recognizes the cash payment of $105,000 from the client and creates a liability—unearned revenue—due to the fact that if the entity does not perform any services or performs services less than the value of the prepayment, the entity would be required to refund that unearned revenue to the client.

On March 31 and April 30 the entity recognizes revenue for the services performed during the month and utilizes the prepayment amount held in the unearned revenue account. On May 31, the entity recognizes revenue for the services performed during the month, utilizes the remaining prepayment amount of $24,000 in the unearned revenue account, and records an accounts receivable in the amount of $10,000 for the services provided that exceed the remaining prepayment amount reflected in unearned revenue. At that point, because the client has utilized services in excess of the prepayment balance, the client now owes the entity $10,000. On June 10 the client pays its receivable and the entity recognizes the receipt of cash and payment of the accounts receivable. In each case, the entity recognizes the revenue only after it has been earned.

EXAMPLE 4.14   **ADVANCED DEFERRAL CONCEPT OF PAYMENT BEFORE USE**

In this scenario, on June 1 the entity prepays its business insurance premium for three months in the amount of $18,000 ($6,000 per month) for the months of June, July, and August. Even though the entity has paid its insurance provider on June 1, it cannot recognize the expense, as the entity has not yet incurred or received the benefit of that expense. Instead, the entity will recognize prepaid insurance for the full payment on June 1. At the end of each of the three months, the entity will record an adjusting entry to recognize the fact that it used up one-third of the benefit of that insurance for the accounting period (or incurred an expense of $6,000 for that period). The following journal entry represents the original financial transaction where the entity prepaid its insurance provider:

Date	Account	Debit	Credit
6/1	Prepaid Insurance	$18,000	
	Cash		$18,000

The following journal entries represent the adjusting entries the entity would record at the end of June, July, and August in order to recognize its use of one-third of the insurance for each of the accounting periods:

Date	Account	Debit	Credit
6/30 (adjusting entry)	Insurance Expense	$6,000	
	Prepaid Insurance		$6,000
7/31 (adjusting entry)	Insurance Expense	$6,000	
	Prepaid Insurance		$6,000
8/31 (adjusting entry)	Insurance Expense	$6,000	
	Prepaid Insurance		$6,000

In the original journal entry on June 1, the entity reflects the cash payment to its insurance provider for three full months of premium at the cost of $6,000 per month or $18,000 in total. The entity creates an asset account—prepaid insurance—to reflect the fact that it has paid for its insurance in advance. If the entity were to cancel that insurance policy, it would be entitled to a refund for that portion of the premiums that it did not utilize (thus this prepayment becomes an asset of the business until it is used up).

In each adjusting entry on June 30, July 31, and August 31, the entity reflects the fact that it used up or received the benefit of one-third of its insurance premium by reducing prepaid insurance and recording insurance expense, as that expense was incurred during the month. At the end of August, the entity's prepaid insurance account would have a zero balance, as the entity has used up the benefit in full.

Whenever an entity creates a prepaid asset account, whether through the prepayment of rent, insurance premiums, professional dues, or a subscription, the entity will have to make an adjusting entry at the end of the month recognizing an expense for the portion of the prepaid expense that was utilized or benefited from during the month. The entity will make this adjusting entry until the entire prepayment has been used up and reflected as an expense of the business.

f. Bad Debt Expense

Bad debt expense is the expense an entity incurs when certain of its accounts receivable, meaning sales made on account, are not collected. In a perfect world, an entity would collect all of its outstanding accounts receivable; however, that is an unlikely scenario, as customers go out of business, have insufficient funds to pay, or simply choose not to pay. As a result, an entity, if it can make an estimate, must reflect an expense to the business for its potential uncollectible receivables.

While it is impossible to know which specific receivables or the dollar value of the receivables that the entity will fail to collect at the time of the sales, the entity should be in a position to make an estimate based on its past experience or experiences of similar companies in the same industry. And pursuant to the matching principle, expenses should be matched with their corresponding revenues whenever possible. As a result, at the end of the accounting period the entity estimates its bad debt expense and records an adjusting entry.

Since the specific uncollectible accounts receivable cannot be identified at the time of the sale, the entity creates a contra account to accounts receivable called "allowance for doubtful accounts" to reflect the amount it anticipates will not be collected and immediately recognizes an expense to the business. Generally, an entity's accounts receivable account is reflected on the balance sheet as net of allowance for doubtful accounts, with the amount estimated as uncollectible described in its footnotes.

When the entity determines the specific customer that will not pay its accounts receivable, then that customer's accounts receivable is written off (credit to accounts receivable) and the allowance for doubtful accounts amount is eliminated (debit to allowance for doubtful accounts). Since the bad debt expense associated with this uncollected accounts receivable was already recognized at the time of the sale, there is no additional impact to the income statement.

i. Estimating Bad Debt Expense

An entity can estimate its bad debt expense in two primary ways: the percentage of credit sales or aging of accounts receivable methods.

(a) Percentage of Credit Sales Method

If an entity utilizes the percentage of credit sales method, it establishes an estimate by using the average percentage of accounts receivable it has failed to collect in the past, which is determined by dividing its sales on credit by the actual amount uncollected. Once it has established that estimate, it multiplies its current sales on credit by the established percentage to determine its bad debt expense for the period. This method is more easily determined, but generally results in a less accurate estimate of bad debt expense, as it is a broad-based estimate.

EXAMPLE 4.15 **PERCENTAGE OF CREDIT SALES**

Assume that Smith & Sons, Inc. failed to collect an average of 2 percent of its sales on credit in the prior fiscal year and uses that percentage to estimate its bad debt expense for the current year. Smith & Sons, Inc. had $135,000 worth of credit sales for the month of October. Smith & Sons, Inc. would calculate October bad debt expense as follows:

$$\text{October Bad Debt Expense} = \$135,000 \times .02$$
$$= \$2,700$$

The following month-end adjusting entry reflects the recognition of the bad debt expense estimate for the month of October.

Date	Account	Debit	Credit
10/31	Bad Debt Expense	$2,700	
	Allowance for Doubtful Accounts		$2,700

(b) Aging of Accounts Receivable Method

If the entity utilizes an aging of accounts receivable method, it establishes an estimate by breaking its outstanding accounts receivable into periods of time based on days outstanding. One typical breakdown is accounts receivable (i) due in 30 days or less (meaning not yet overdue), (ii) overdue for 31 to 90 days, and (iii) overdue more than 90 days. The entity then estimates the amount of receivables from each period of time that it deems uncollectible based on its past experiences. It establishes an estimate by using the average percentage of accounts receivable it has failed to collect in the past for each period of days outstanding. Once it has established the estimates, it multiplies accounts receivable for each time period by the requisite percentage to determine its bad debt expense for the period. This method is more difficult to determine but generally results in a more accurate estimate of bad debt expense and becomes even more accurate when the entity uses a greater number of time periods to reflect days accounts receivable are outstanding.

EXAMPLE 4.16 **AGING OF ACCOUNTS RECEIVABLE**

Assume that Smith & Sons, Inc. has an accounts receivable balance of $1,220,000 for the period January 1 to October 31 broken down as follows: $732,000 not yet due, $366,000 in the 31- to 90-day overdue range, and $122,000 more than 90 days overdue. Assume that it estimates that 1 percent of the not yet due, 6 percent of the 31- to 90-day overdue, and 9 percent of the more than 90 days overdue will be uncollectible. Smith & Sons, Inc. would calculate bad debt expense for the period January 1 to October 31 as follows:

$$\text{Bad Debt Expense} = (\$732,000 \times .01) + (\$366,000 \times .06) + (\$122,000 \times .09)$$
$$\text{(January − October)} = \$7,320 + \$21,960 + \$10,980$$
$$= \$40,260$$

This amount, $40,260, represents Smith & Sons, Inc.'s bad debt expense for the period of January through October as it takes into account all outstanding accounts receivable from the start of the current fiscal year.

Now assume that Smith & Sons, Inc. has a net balance in its allowance for doubtful accounts for the year to date of $36,400, meaning it has previously recognized that amount of bad debt expense for the fiscal year. In order to determine the amount of bad debt expense it must recognize for the month of October, Smith & Sons, Inc. would make the following calculation:

$$\text{Bad Debt Expense for October} = \text{Total Bad Debt Expense to Date −}$$
$$\text{Allowance for Doubtful Accounts Balance}$$
$$= \$40,260 − \$36,400$$
$$= \$3,860$$

The following month-end adjusting entry reflects the recognition of the bad debt expense estimate for the month of October.

Date	Account	Debit	Credit
10/31	Bad Debt Expense	$3,860	
	Allowance for Doubtful Accounts		$3,860

ii. Accounts Receivable Write-Offs

While the methods described above are used to estimate the entity's bad debt expense, the entity must still recognize an accounts receivable write-off when it has determined that a customer will not pay a portion or all of its outstanding receivable. At that point in time where it becomes clear that a customer is not going to pay its accounts receivable, the entity must write off that receivable on its books. Keep in mind that the entity has already recognized the bad debt expense, so this entry does not impact the income statement.

EXAMPLE 4.17 **ACCOUNTS RECEIVABLE WRITE-OFF**

Assume that Smith & Sons, Inc. learns on November 22 that one of its customers, Sigma Company, finalized its bankruptcy petition and that as a result Smith & Sons, Inc. received a payment of $525 on Sigma Company's $2,600 outstanding accounts receivable. In order to recognize the partial payment and write-off of Sigma Company's accounts receivable, Smith & Sons, Inc. would make the following journal entry:

Date	Account	Debit	Credit
11/22	Cash	$525	
	Allowance for Doubtful Accounts	$2,075	
	Accounts Receivable		$2,600

The above entry reflects the fact that Smith & Sons, Inc. received $525 in the bankruptcy settlement and eliminated Sigma Company's outstanding accounts receivable of $2,600. The difference between the total outstanding accounts receivable and the amount received ($2,600 - $525 = $2,075) reduces the allowance for doubtful accounts contra account. Smith & Sons, Inc. recognized an expense for this bad (or uncollected) debt in a prior period.

g. Posting Adjusting Entries

As noted above, when an entity prepays an expense and creates a prepaid asset account on its books, it must record an adjusting entry at the end of the month to recognize the expense that represents that portion of the prepaid asset that was used up during the month. Adjusting entries for prepaid expenses are recorded in the general journal after all the financial transactions for the month have been recorded and are generally posted on the last day of the month. The adjusting entries must be calculated and posted before the entity can commence the process of closing its books for the month.

Also, as noted above, when an entity receives a prepayment for goods or services and creates an unearned revenue liability account on its books and records, it must record an adjusting entry at that point in time when the entity earns a portion of the revenue, whether that occurs in the middle or at the end of the accounting period. Adjusting entries for unearned revenue are generally recorded in the general journal, as they occur during the accounting period as opposed to on the last day of the month.

h. Closing the Income Statement Accounts

As noted earlier in the chapter, income statement accounts do not maintain an ongoing balance like balance sheet accounts, which are permanent. Instead, income statement accounts are temporary accounts that are closed at the end of each accounting period, meaning each account is zeroed out. The income statement accounts are then reopened at the start of the next accounting period with no preexisting balance. The income statement ultimately reflects the total net income or net loss that an entity had during the accounting period. Once the entity has determined the amount of its net income or net loss, that amount is transferred (or closed) to the entity's equity account, or the retained earnings account (or accumulated loss account) in the case of a corporation. It is through the closing process of the income statement accounts that the entity's net income or net loss is ultimately transferred, or closed, into the equity section of the balance sheet. This closing process is completed at the end of each accounting period.

While the income statement accounts could be closed directly to the entity's retained earnings account (or accumulated loss account) on the balance sheet, most entities choose to close the income statement accounts to a temporary account called "income summary" or "profit and loss" in order to effect the closing process. This allows the entity to create a trail of all its revenues and gains, as well as its expenses and losses for the accounting period. In addition, it results in a single entry to the retained earnings (or accumulated loss) account, thus eliminating the need to clutter the retained earnings (or accumulated loss) account with multiple entries at the end of each accounting period.

The following T-account depicts the fact that expenses and losses reduce an entity's retained earnings, whereas revenues and gains increase an entity's retained earnings. The difference between revenues and gains and expenses and losses is the net income or net loss for the period, which is ultimately closed into the retained earnings (accumulated loss) account. This account reflects the total of the entity's profits and losses since commencement of its business operations.

In essence, the entity is closing all expense and loss income statement accounts to the debit side of its retained earnings (accumulated loss) account and all revenue and gain income statement accounts to the credit side of its retained earnings (accumulated loss) account.

Retained Earnings/Accumulated Loss

Debit	Credit
Decrease/–	Increase/+
Expenses/Losses	Revenues/Gains

Debit	Credit	Debit	Credit
Decrease/–	Increase/+	Decrease/–	Increase/+

i. Income Tax Calculations and Entries

Income taxes are an expense of the business and require the entity to recognize an expense each accounting period and accrue a liability on its balance sheet for the taxes that it will owe in the future as a result of its profits. After an entity has recorded all its financial transactions for the accounting period, including recording any necessary adjusting entries, and closed its income statement accounts to the profit and loss holding account, it is in a position to calculate its income tax expense for the period as the entity now knows its net income or net loss before taxes for the period. An entity only calculates income tax expense when it has net income before taxes for the period.

In order to calculate the income tax expense for the accounting period, two pieces of information are required: (i) the net income before taxes for the period and (ii) the entity's effective tax rate. With that information the entity can determine the tax expense for the accounting period using the following formula:

Income Tax Expense = Net Income Before Taxes × Effective Income Tax Rate

Once the entity has determined its income tax expense for the period, it must record an additional adjusting and closing entry to reflect the tax expense for the period and close the additional income statement account (income taxes expense) to the profit and loss holding account. The reason the entity must prepare and record an adjusting entry is that most entities only pay income tax annually, yet it is an expense of the business that must be recognized each accounting period. As a result, the entity must record that expense during the accounting period it is incurred and accrue an income tax liability on its balance sheet to reflect that it owes that amount in taxes and will make the payment in the future.

EXAMPLE 4.18   **INCOME TAX EXPENSE**

Assume an entity had net income of $1,225,000 for the accounting period ended March 30 and has an effective income tax rate of 25 percent. It would calculate its income tax expense as follows:

$$\text{Income Tax Expense} = \$1,225,000 \times .25$$
$$= \$306,250$$

The following journal entries reflect the adjusting and closing entries for the entity based on the above information:

Date	Account	Debit	Credit
3/30 (adjusting entry)	Income Tax Expense	$306,250	
	Income Tax Payable		$306,250
3/30 (closing entry)	Profit and Loss	$306,250	
	Income Tax Expense		$306,250

The first entry on March 30 reflects the adjusting entry to record the income tax expense for the period and create an income tax liability to reflect that the entity will have to pay income taxes in the future.

The second entry on March 30 reflects the closing entry to close the income tax expense account to the profit and loss holding account. As income tax is an expense account (or temporary account), it must be closed at the end of the accounting period to the profit and loss account so that the entity can determine its net income or net loss after taxes for the period.

ii. Closing Profit and Loss Account

Once the entity has closed all the income statement accounts, including income tax expense, to the profit and loss account, it is in a position to complete the closing process. In order to close the books and zero out all the income statement accounts, the entity must close the profit and loss balance to the equity section of the balance sheet, meaning to the retained earnings or accumulated loss account. If the profit and loss account has a credit balance, the entity had net income for the period, and if the profit and loss account has a debit balance, the entity had a net loss for the period.

ILLUSTRATION 2 | **BALANCE SHEET AND INCOME STATEMENT TRANSACTIONS**

The following example will build on Illustration 1, utilizing Smith & Sons, Inc.'s balance sheet for February 28 (see Illustration Example 1.5). This example will reiterate the steps introduced in Illustration 1, but will incorporate financial transactions for the month of March that impact both balance sheet and income statement accounts, as well as the concepts of prepaid expenses and unearned revenue. It will also demonstrate the process of opening and posting current balance sheet account balances to T-accounts, preparing and logging general journal entries for the month of March, preparing and logging adjusting entries for the month of March, preparing closing entries for the income statement accounts for the month of March, calculating and recording the tax expense for the month of March, closing the books for the month of March, and preparing a simple balance sheet and income statement for the month of March.

ILLUSTRATION EXAMPLE 2.1

SMITH & SONS, INC.—MARCH TRANSACTION LIST

The following Smith & Sons, Inc. financial transactions occurred during the month of March:

March 1	Smith & Sons, Inc. paid its insurance premium of $7,500 for the months of March and April ($3,750 per month).
March 8	Big Machinery purchased $45,000 worth of products on account from Smith & Sons, Inc., which were immediately delivered.

continued

March 19	Smith & Sons, Inc. received a prepayment of $57,000 from Thrift Corporation for products that Smith & Sons, Inc. will deliver to Thrift in late March and early April.
March 25	Smith & Sons, Inc. sold $13,250 worth of its products to Newco, Inc. for cash.
March 28	Smith & Sons, Inc. received its utility bill in the amount of $2,670 for the month of March, which is not due until April 15, at which time Smith & Sons, Inc. will pay it.
March 29	Smith & Sons, Inc. delivered $30,000 worth of products to Thrift Corporation that Thrift prepaid for on March 19.

ILLUSTRATION EXAMPLE 2.2

SMITH & SONS, INC.—MARCH GENERAL JOURNAL

The following general journal sets forth the recorded financial transactions for the month of March based on the information provided in Illustration Example 2.1:

SMITH & SONS, INC.—GENERAL JOURNAL

Date	Account	Debit	Credit
3/1	Prepaid Insurance	$7,500	
	Cash		$7,500
3/8	Accounts Receivable	$45,000	
	Revenue		$45,000
3/19	Cash	$57,000	
	Unearned Revenue		$57,000
3/25	Cash	$13,250	
	Revenue		$13,250
3/28	Utility Expense	$2,670	
	Utility Payable		$2,670
3/29	Unearned Revenue	$30,000	
	Revenue		$30,000

ILLUSTRATION EXAMPLE 2.3

SMITH & SONS, INC.—ADJUSTING JOURNAL ENTRIES

The following general journal sets forth the adjusting entries for the month of March.

SMITH & SONS, INC.—ADJUSTING ENTRIES—MARCH

Date	Account	Debit	Credit
3/31	Insurance Expense	$3,750	
	Prepaid Insurance		$3,750

ILLUSTRATION EXAMPLE 2.4

SMITH & SONS, INC. —MARCH T-ACCOUNTS

The following T-accounts set forth the opening balance for each Smith & Sons, Inc. balance sheet account as set forth on the February 28 balance sheet (see Illustration Example 1.5) and reflect the transactions posted to each balance sheet and income statement T-account for the month of March based on the journal entries set forth in Illustration Example 2.2, adjusting entries set forth in Illustration Example 2.3, and the closing entries set forth in Illustration Examples 2.5, 2.6, and 2.7.

Balance Sheet Accounts

Cash and Cash Equivalents			
Op. Bal.	$5,899,800	$7,500	3/1
3/19	$57,000		
3/25	$13,250		
Balance	$5,962,550		

Accounts Receivable			
Op. Bal.	$2,667,000		
3/8	45,000		
Balance	$2,712,000		

Property		
Op. Bal.	$1,153,000	
Balance	$1,153,000	

Equipment		
Op. Bal.	$1,799,450	
Balance	$1,799,450	

Furniture		
Op. Bal.	$342,450	
Balance	$342,450	

Prepaid Insurance			
Op. Bal.	$0.00	$3,750	3/31
3/1	7,500		
Balance	$3,750		

Accounts Payable		
	$2,065,450	Op. Bal.
	$2,065,450	Balance

Note Payable		
	$435,000	Op. Bal.
	$435,000	Balance

Long-Term Debt		
	$1,240,000	Op. Bal.
	$1,240,000	Balance

Unearned Revenue			
3/29	$30,000	$0.00	Op. Bal.
		$57,000	3/19
		$27,000	Balance

Utility Payable		
	$0.00	Op. Bal.
	$2,670	3/28
	$2,670	Balance

Income Tax Payable		
	$0.00	Op. Bal.
	$16,366	(c)
	$16,366	Balance

Common Stock		
	$13,150	Op. Bal.
	$13,150	Balance

Additional Paid-In-Capital		
	$4,579,100	Op. Bal.
	$4,579,100	Balance

Income Statement Accounts

Insurance Expense			
3/31	$3,750		
Balance	$3,750	$3,750	(a)
	-0.00-		

Retained Earnings		
	$3,529,000	Op. Bal.
	$ 65,464	(e)
	$3,594,464	Balance

Utility Expense			
3/28	$2,670		
Balance	$2,670	$2,670	(a)
	-0.00-		

Revenue			
		$45,000	3/8
		$13,250	3/25
		$30,000	3/29
(b)	$88,250	$88,250	Balance
		-0.00-	

Income Tax Expense			
(c)	$16,366		
Balance	$16,366	$16,366	(d)
	-0.00-		

Profit and Loss			
(a)	$6,420	$88,250	(b)
(d)	$16,366		
(e)	$65,464	$65,464	Balance
		-0.00-	

ILLUSTRATION EXAMPLE 2.5

SMITH & SONS, INC.—CLOSING JOURNAL ENTRIES

The following general journal sets forth the closing entries for the month of March:

SMITH & SONS, INC.—GENERAL JOURNAL—CLOSING ENTRIES

Date	Account	Debit	Credit
(a)	Profit and Loss	$6,420	
	Insurance Expense		$3,750
	Utility Expense		$2,670
(b)	Revenue	$88,250	
	Profit and Loss		$88,250

ILLUSTRATION EXAMPLE 2.6

SMITH & SONS, INC.—GENERAL JOURNAL—TAX ENTRIES

The following general journal sets forth the tax entries for the month of March, assuming that Smith & Sons, Inc. has an effective income tax rate of 20 percent. Net income before taxes was $81,830 ($88,250 – $6,420) and $81,830 × .20 = $16,366.

SMITH & SONS, INC.—GENERAL JOURNAL—TAX ENTRIES

Date	Account	Debit	Credit
(c)	Income Tax Expense	$16,366	
	Income Tax Payable		$16,366
(d)	Profit and Loss	$16,366	
	Income Tax Expense		$16,366

ILLUSTRATION EXAMPLE 2.7

SMITH & SONS, INC.—GENERAL JOURNAL—FINAL CLOSING ENTRY

The following general journal sets forth the final closing entry for the month of March to close the profit and loss account, which has a credit balance, so reflects net income for the month, to retained earnings:

SMITH & SONS, INC. — GENERAL JOURNAL — FINAL CLOSING ENTRY

(e)	Profit and Loss	$65,464	
	Retained Earnings		$65,464

ILLUSTRATION EXAMPLE 2.8

SMITH & SONS, INC.—CLOSING BALANCE SHEET

The balance sheet for Smith & Sons, Inc. as of March 31 is set forth below and reflects all the changes that took place during the month of March to each balance sheet account.

SMITH & SONS, INC. BALANCE SHEET AS OF MARCH 31

	March 31
Assets	
Cash and cash equivalents	$5,962,550
Accounts receivable	2,712,000
Property	1,153,000
Equipment	1,799,450
Furniture	342,450
Prepaid insurance	3,750
Total assets	**$11,973,200**
Liabilities and Stockholders' Equity	
Liabilities	
Accounts payable	$2,065,450
Note payable	435,000
Unearned revenue	27,000
Income tax payable	16,366
Utility payable	2,670
Long-term debt	1,240,000
Total liabilities	**$3,786,486**
Stockholders' equity	
Common stock, $0.01 par value; 4,000,000 shares authorized; 1,315,000 issued and outstanding as of March 31	$13,150
Additional paid-in-capital	4,579,100
Retained earnings	3,594,464
Total stockholders' equity	**$8,186,714**
Total liabilities and stockholders' equity	**$11,973,200**

ILLUSTRATION EXAMPLE 2.9

SMITH & SONS, INC.—INCOME STATEMENT

The following income statement for Smith & Sons, Inc. for the period ended March 31 reflects the net income for the period:

SMITH & SONS, INC. INCOME STATEMENT FOR THE PERIOD ENDED MARCH 31

	March 31
Revenues	$88,250
Less operating expenses:	
Insurance expense	3,750
Utility expense	2,670
Net income before taxes	$81,830
Less income tax expense	16,366
Net income	**$65,464**

EXPLANATION OF ILLUSTRATION 2

The following discusses and explains in detail the process for preparing and closing the books and records of Smith & Sons, Inc. for the month of March:

Step 1: Record opening balances. Utilizing the balance sheet for February 28 set forth in Illustration Example 1.5, a T-account is created for each asset, liability, and equity account reflecting the opening balance (closing balances from February 28) for each account.

Step 2: Record March transactions in the general journal and post transactions to the proper T-accounts. The next step is to record the financial transactions based on the information provided. Each transaction is recorded in the general journal and subsequently posted to the appropriate T-account, reflecting the date on which the transaction occurred (see Illustration Examples 2.2 and 2.4, respectively). In some instances, a new T-account had to be created to reflect the transaction. An explanation of each journal entry follows:

March 1: Smith & Sons, Inc. made a payment of $7,500 to its insurance company to prepay its premium for the months of March and April. As this premium is an expense that is being prepaid for two months, it is an asset of the business. It records a debit of $7,500 to prepaid insurance to reflect the fact that it has prepaid its insurance premium for two months and records a credit of $7,500 to cash to reflect the fact that it expended cash to make the prepayment to its insurance company.

It posts a debit (left side entry) to the prepaid insurance T-account (a balance sheet account) and posts a credit (right side entry) to the cash T-account (a balance sheet account).

March 8: Smith & Sons, Inc. sold $45,000 worth of its products to Big Machinery on account and so it records a debit of $45,000 to accounts receivable to reflect the fact that it is owed that amount from the customer and records a credit of $45,000 to revenue to reflect the fact that it made a sale of its products.

It posts a debit (left side entry) to the accounts receivable T-account (a balance sheet account) and posts a credit (right side entry) to the revenue T-account (an income statement account).

March 19: Smith & Sons, Inc. receives a prepayment of $57,000 from one of its customers for products it will deliver later this month and the following month. As this revenue has not yet been earned, it must defer recognizing the revenue until it delivers the products. It records a debit of $57,000 to cash to reflect the fact that it received the cash payment from the customer, and records a credit of $57,000 to unearned revenue to reflect the fact that it now has a liability (or obligation) to fulfill the order and deliver the products, but if it does not do so, it is obligated to refund the payment.

It posts a debit (left side entry) to the cash T-account (a balance sheet account) and posts a credit (right side entry) to the unearned revenue T-account (a balance sheet account).

March 25: Smith & Sons, Inc. sold $13,250 worth of its products to Newco for cash, so it records a debit of $13,250 to cash to reflect the fact that it received a cash payment for the sale and records a credit of $13,250 to revenue to reflect the fact that it made a sale of its products.

It posts a debit (left side entry) to the cash T-account (a balance sheet account) and posts a credit (right side entry) to the revenue T-account (an income statement account).

March 28: Smith & Sons, Inc. received its utility bill of $2,670 for the month of March. As this bill is for an expense incurred in the month of March, it must be recognized in that month. It records a debit of $2,670 to utility expense to reflect the fact that it incurred that expense during the month, and records a credit of $2,670 to utility payable to reflect that it owes this bill and will pay it in the future.

It posts a debit (left side entry) to the utility expense T-account (an income statement account) and posts a credit (right side entry) to the utility payable T-account (a balance sheet account).

March 29: Smith & Sons, Inc. delivers $30,000 worth of the products that Thrift Corporation prepaid for on March 19. As Smith & Sons, Inc. has now earned this revenue, it must be recognized. It records a debit of $30,000 to unearned revenue to reflect that it has earned that portion and would no longer be required to refund it, and records a credit of $30,000 to revenue to reflect that it has been earned.

It posts a debit (left side entry) to the unearned revenue T-account (a balance sheet account) and posts a credit (right side entry) to the revenue T-account (an income statement account).

Step 3: Prepare and post the adjusting entries. The next step is to prepare the adjusting entries for the month. As Smith & Sons, Inc. prepaid an expense and has now used up one month's worth of that prepayment, it must prepare an adjusting entry and post it to the appropriate T-accounts (see Illustration Examples 2.3 and 2.4).

March 31: Smith & Sons, Inc. has used up or benefited from one month, or $3,750 worth, of its prepaid insurance and must reflect that in an adjusting entry. It records a debit of $3,750 to insurance expense to reflect the fact that the expense was incurred (or benefited from during March) and records a credit of $3,750 to prepaid insurance to reflect the fact that it used up one month's worth of its insurance and would no longer be entitled to a refund for that amount.

It posts a debit (left side entry) to the insurance expense T-account (an income statement account) and posts a credit (right side entry) to the prepaid insurance T-account (a balance sheet account).

Step 4: Total each balance sheet and income statement T-account. The next step is to total the balance sheet and income statement T-accounts in order to have the information needed to prepare the March closing entries as well as prepare the March balance sheet and income statement.

Asset and expense accounts should reflect a debit balance (left side balance). All the debit entries should be added together and all the credit entries should then be subtracted to determine the overall debit balance for the account. Liabilities, equity, and revenue accounts should reflect a credit balance (right side balance), except in the case of an accumulated loss, which has a debit balance (left side balance). All credit entries should be added together and all the debit entries should then be subtracted to determine the overall credit balance for the account (see Illustration Example 2.4).

Step 5: Prepare and post the closing entries. The next step is to prepare the initial closing entries to close each of the income statement accounts into the holding account called profit and loss, which will allow Smith & Sons, Inc. to calculate its income tax expense for the period (see Illustration Examples 2.4 and 2.5).

Closing Entries: Smith & Sons, Inc. closes the expense accounts — insurance expense of $3,750 and utility expense of $2,670 — to the profit and loss account for a total of $6,420 and closes the revenue account to the profit and loss account for a total of $88,250.

It posts a debit (left side entry) to the profit and loss T-account and posts a credit (right side entry) to the insurance expense and utility expense T-accounts. As the expense accounts maintain a debit balance, each account must be credited to cause the account balance to be zero and offset with a debit to profit and loss to close the accounts for the period.

It posts a debit (left side entry) to the revenue T-account and posts a credit (right side entry) to the profit and loss T-account. As the revenue account maintains a credit balance, it must be debited to cause the account balance to be zero and offset with a credit to profit and loss to close the account for the period.

Step 6: Prepare and post income tax entries. The next step is to calculate the income taxes for the period, prepare the tax entries, and post the entries to the appropriate T-accounts (see Illustration Examples 2.4 and 2.6).

After preparing and posting the initial closing entries (see Illustration Examples 2.4 and 2.5), the balance in the profit and loss account reflects Smith & Sons, Inc.'s net income before taxes for the period (credit balance). Since the profit and loss account had a credit balance of $81,830, Smith & Sons, Inc. had income before taxes for the accounting period and must calculate its estimated tax expense by multiplying income before taxes by its effective tax rate ($81,830 × .20 = $16,366).

Smith & Sons, Inc. must prepare an entry to recognize its tax expense of $16,366 for the period and then close the additional expense account to profit and loss to complete the closing process for the period. It records a debit of $16,366 to income tax expense to reflect the fact that the expense was incurred and records a credit of $16,366 to income tax payable to reflect the fact that it will owe that income tax in the future.

It posts a debit (left side entry) to the income tax expense T-account (an income statement account) and posts a credit (right side entry) to the income tax payable T-account (a balance sheet account).

Smith & Sons, Inc. now closes the tax expense of $16,366 to the profit and loss account. It records a credit of $16,366 to income tax expense and records a debit of $16,366 to profit and loss.

It posts a debit (left side entry) to the profit and loss T-account and posts a credit (right side entry) to the income tax expense T-account. As the income tax expense account maintains a debit balance, it must be credited to cause the account balance to be zero and offset with a debit to profit and loss to close the account for the period.

Step 7: Prepare and post final closing entry. The last step is to prepare the final closing entry closing the profit and loss balance to retained earnings, now that the tax entries have been posted to the appropriate T-accounts (see Illustration Examples 2.4 and 2.7). As the profit and loss T-account for Smith & Sons, Inc. reflected a credit balance after all closing entries were posted, that indicates that Smith & Sons, Inc. had net income for the period.

Since Smith & Sons, Inc. had net income after taxes for the accounting period of $65,464 ($81,830 – $16,366), which results in a credit balance, it must debit profit and loss to cause the holding account balance to be zero and offset with a credit to the retained earnings account for the period as it moves the net income for the period to the retained earnings account on the balance sheet, which results in the income statement bottom line being closed to the balance sheet equity section for the accounting period.

It posts a debit (left side entry) to the profit and loss T-account and posts a credit (right side entry) to the retained earnings T-account.

Step 8: Prepare the balance sheet and income statement for Smith & Sons, Inc. for the month of March. The final step is to utilize the balances from the asset, liability, and equity T-accounts to prepare the balance sheet as of March 31 (see Illustration Example 2.8) and to utilize the balances from the revenue and expense accounts (prior to the closing entries) to prepare the income statement for the period ended March 31 (see Illustration Example 2.9).

Balance Sheet and Income Statement Combined Problems 4.4 and 4.5

Problems 4.4 and 4.5 both focus on CPAs for Lawyers, Inc. and build on each other, so must be completed in sequence.

Problems 4.4 and 4.5: Background Information

CPAs for Lawyers, Inc. (CFL) is a traditional C Corporation with one class of stock — common stock (par value $0.01, 500,000 shares authorized). CFL has three common stock shareholders who each own 50,000 shares for a total of 150,000 shares issued and outstanding. CFL was formed more than three years ago and has been in business since that time. CFL specializes in providing accounting services for lawyers and law firms.

CFL secured a loan for $60,000 from Southern Bank, which loan is a term loan that bears simple interest at the rate of 3 percent per annum and requires CFL to make a monthly interest payment on the last day of each month or the immediately preceding business day if the last day is a Saturday, Sunday, or legal holiday.

For purposes of these two problems, CFL does not depreciate its office equipment or furniture.

CFL accrues monthly for its income taxes at an effective tax rate of 20 percent and rounds the result to an even number (no cents) based on traditional rounding conventions.

Problem 4.4

CFL provided its balance sheet as of May 31. For the month of June, open T-accounts based upon the May 31 balance sheet, prepare the journal entries for the transactions set forth below for the month of June in a general journal, post the journal entries to the respective T-accounts, prepare any necessary adjusting entries for the month of June and post the adjusting entries to the respective T-accounts, total the T-accounts as of the end of June, close the books for the month of June (i.e., prepare the closing entry transactions, including the tax entries, and post the entries to the respective T-accounts), prepare a balance sheet as of June 30, and prepare an income statement for the period ended June 30.

CPAS FOR LAWYERS, INC. BALANCE SHEET AS OF MAY 31

	May 31
Assets	
Current Assets	
Cash and cash equivalents	$236,230
Accounts receivable	91,880
Total current assets	$328,110

Fixed Assets	
Office equipment	47,520
Furniture	66,000
Total fixed assets	$113,520
Total assets	**$441,630**
Liabilities and Stockholders' Equity	
Liabilities	
Current Liabilities	
Accounts payable	$74,400
Taxes payable	4,125
Total current liabilities	$78,525
Long-Term Liabilities	
Long-term debt	$60,000
Total liabilities	**$138,525**
Stockholders' Equity	
Common stock, $0.01 par value; 500,000 shares authorized; 150,000 issued and outstanding as of May 31	$1,500
Additional paid-in-capital	148,500
Retained earnings	153,105
Total stockholders' equity	**$303,105**
Total liabilities and stockholders' equity	**$441,630**

June Transactions

June 1: CFL purchased $6,000 of office equipment from the Equipment Warehouse on account.

June 3: CFL provided services to Big Law Firm in the amount of $11,300, which the law firm paid for immediately.

June 8: CFL returned a defective piece of the office equipment it purchased on June 1 from Equipment Warehouse, which cost $1,500, and Equipment Warehouse issued CFL a credit on its account.

June 16: CFL paid salaries to its employees in the amount of $3,850 for the first half of the month.

June 22: CFL renewed its business liability insurance policy, which runs from July 1 to June 30, and sent a check to its insurance provider in the amount of $11,640. This is the first time CFL prepaid its insurance.

June 25: CFL provided services to Small Law, LLC in the amount of $6,800, half of which Small Law paid for immediately and half of which was put on its account.

June 26: CFL received a partial payment for an outstanding accounts receivable from the Springer Law Firm in the amount of $23,000.

June 28: CFL received and immediately paid its June telephone and Internet bill in the amount of $386.

June 29: CFL received its June utility bill in the amount of $440 (due on or before July 15), which it will pay in July.

June 30: Because the last day of the month fell on a Sunday, CFL did not pay its employees the $3,800 in salaries due for the second half of the month of June. It will pay those salaries on July 1.

June 30: CFL made its monthly interest payment to Southern Bank.

Problem 4.5

For the month of July, prepare the journal entries for the transactions set forth below in a general journal, post the journal entries to the respective T-accounts (you should utilize your T-accounts from the month of June and add new T-accounts as needed), prepare any necessary adjusting entries for the month of July and post the adjusting entries to the respective T-accounts, total the T-accounts as of the end of July, close the books for the month of July (i.e., prepare the closing entry transactions, including the tax entries, and post the entries to the respective T-accounts), prepare a balance sheet as of July 31, and prepare an income statement for the period ended July 31.

July Transactions

July 1: CFL paid the salaries it owed its employees for the second half of June in the amount of $3,800.

July 3: CFL made a payment of $33,000 to the Equipment Warehouse on its outstanding account balance.

July 7: CFL provided services to Lawyers & Daughters, PC in the amount of $74,320, which the client paid for immediately.

July 12: CFL received a payment of $43,400 from Small Law, LLC to cover its total outstanding receivable of $3,400 and to prepay for future accounting services.

July 13: CFL paid the salaries to its employees for the first half of July in the amount of $3,800.

July 14: CFL paid its June utility bill in the amount of $440.

July 18: CFL made a payment of $27,500 to High Quality Furniture on its outstanding accounts payable balance.

July 20: CFL provided services in the amount of $24,800 to Specialty Law Shop, which was given 30 days to pay for those services.

July 23: CFL provided a cash refund of $3,320 to one of its clients as a result of a mistake in its quarterly financial statements caused by a CFL accountant.

July 26: CFL received its phone and Internet bill for $198 and its utilities bill for $420, both of which it will pay in August.

July 29: CFL made its monthly interest payment to Southern Bank.

July 30: CFL paid the salaries to its employees for the second half of July in the amount of $3,850.

July 30: CFL provided services in the amount of $13,860 to Small Law, LLC and utilized Small Law, LLC's prepayment funds received on July 12.

E. ACCOUNTING FOR INVENTORY

Inventory is often one of the largest current assets that many entities carry on their balance sheet, particularly for those entities that engage in a retail (or merchandise business) or a manufacturing business. Inventory consists of tangible personal property that has any one of the following three traits: (i) it is held for sale in the ordinary course of business; (ii) it is in the process of being produced for sale in the ordinary course of business; or (iii) it is currently utilized in the production of goods or services that will be offered for sale in the ordinary course of business.[13] Thus, inventory includes (i) goods that are currently available for sale, whether produced by the entity or purchased by the entity for resale (finished goods); (ii) goods that are in the process of being produced for sale (work in progress); and (iii) materials that are utilized in the production process (raw materials).[14]

1. A Merchandise Business

A merchandise business is one where the entity sells merchandise or products as its primary business. It may be a retail entity that sells the merchandise directly to the customer or it may be a wholesale entity that sells the merchandise to other retailers or wholesalers that then sell it downstream. The

---

[13]Accounting Standards Codification, Inventory, ASC §330-10-20 (Fin. Accounting Found. 2017).
[14]*Id.*

merchandise can be of almost any nature, such as clothing, shoes, sports equipment, books, office supplies, or nuts and bolts. In addition, the merchandise may be sold through a traditional brick-and-mortar store or it may be sold online. In any case, a merchandise business generally maintains a significant amount of inventory on hand in order to fulfill the demands of its business and customers.

As is true of any business, the entity must accurately reflect the amount of inventory it holds on its balance sheet for the period, as well as reflect the amount of the cost of goods sold (COGS) for the period (discussed below). The entity accounts for COGS as an expense that is reported on its income statement. In a merchandise business, COGS generally consists of the costs to purchase the goods that are being sold directly or indirectly to the customer, the costs to ready the goods for sale (if any), the costs of freight to bring the goods to the retail location for sale, and the costs of freight to ship the merchandise to the customer or reseller.

2. A Manufacturing Business

A manufacturing business is one where the entity utilizes raw materials and other supplies to manufacture a finished product as its primary business. It may sell those finished products directly to the customer or to other businesses that use the product or then sell it downstream. Similar to a merchandise business, a manufacturing business may produce many different types of finished products, such as cars, mountain bikes, heavy machinery, or golf clubs. A manufacturing business also maintains a significant amount of inventory, in the form of raw materials, goods in progress, and finished goods, in order to produce the product and ultimately fulfill the demands of its business and customers.

Just as a merchandise business does, a manufacturing business must account for its inventory on hand on its balance sheet and for the cost of the inventory, or its finished goods, that it sells, and report that COGS expense on its income statement. In a manufacturing business, COGS generally consists of all the materials and direct costs associated with manufacturing the finished good. This includes the cost of the supplies, materials, and components to produce the good, as well as direct labor costs and manufacturing overhead.

3. Ownership of Inventory

When an entity has inventory, it must assess what it should and should not include in its inventory account. In order for an item to be included in an entity's physical inventory and reflected on the balance sheet, the entity must have legal title to that item; in other words, it must own that item, and so it is an asset of the business. Ownership of an item is not simply about payment for and physical possession of the item—it is more complicated than that. While it is easy to determine ownership when an entity has purchased (whether for cash or credit) an item, has actual possession of it, and includes the item in inventory, it is not as easy when the entity has purchased or committed to purchase an item that it does not yet physically possess. In those instances, the entity must undertake further analysis in order to determine whether or not that item should be included in its inventory.

There are four factors that an entity should consider when determining whether an item should be included in its inventory: (i) is the item in transit; (ii) is the item governed by a consignment arrangement; (iii) is the item subject to a financing arrangement; or (iv) is the item eligible for a right of return by the buyer.[15]

a. Items in Transit

At the end of the accounting period, the entity must examine those items that are currently in transit from the entity, as the seller, to the buyer. The party in the transaction that bears the transportation costs of the item and the risk of loss is the party that should reflect the item as part of its inventory. If the transportation costs are paid for by the seller and the title to the item does not pass to the buyer until actual delivery (freight on board (FOB) destination point), then the seller should report that item as a part of its inventory even though it is in transit. On the other hand, if the transportation costs are paid for by the buyer and the title to the item passes to the buyer when it is delivered to the transportation provider (FOB shipping point), then the buyer should report that item as part of its inventory even though it is still in transit. The rationale behind these distinctions is that the party that bears the risk of loss holds title to the item while it is in transit and is the party that has the right to recover money in the event of a loss. As a result, that party should report the item in its inventory.

b. Items Governed by a Consignment Arrangement

A consignment arrangement is an arrangement whereby one party (the owner of the item) has asked a third party (an agent) to undertake the task of selling the item, generally for a commission or fee. The owner of the item is the consignor and the agent selling the item is the consignee. In this type of arrangement, the item is included in the consignor's inventory and not in the consignee's inventory. The reason is that the consignor is still the owner of the item until such time as the consignee sells the item to another party and the title passes to that third party. The consignee is simply the middle person facilitating the sale and so does not take ownership of the item.

c. Items Subject to a Financing Arrangement

A financing arrangement occurs when the party selling the item agrees to sell the item and repurchase the item from the financing company for the original

---

[15]*Id.*

purchase price plus the financing company's fees.[16] This type of arrangement allows the party to finance the cost of purchasing that item for resale—in other words, finance the cost of purchasing inventory for sale rather than pay for it outright all at once. This type of transaction is treated in the same manner as if the selling entity had simply entered into a traditional borrower transaction to secure funding to purchase the item.[17] Even though legal title has passed to the financing company, until such time as the seller pays the financing company in full and repurchases the item, the item is still included in the seller's inventory.

d. Items Eligible for Return

In some transactions, the seller gives buyers of its products the right to return the products under certain circumstances. In addition to addressing whether the item sold is subject to a right of return and should be included in the seller's inventory, the seller must also determine the correct time to recognize the revenue from the sale of that item. When the seller determines that it has met the conditions that allow it to recognize revenue for the sale (generally when the item can no longer be returned), the seller no longer includes the item in its inventory. As a result, until the sale can be recognized, the seller will continue to include the item in its inventory even though it has sold the item subject to the right of return by the buyer and legal title has passed. In this circumstance, the seller should not recognize the revenue until the buyer's right to return has lapsed, and it is at that point that the seller can recognize revenue and remove the item from its inventory.

4. Inventory Accounting Methods

Once an entity determines what it should and should not include in its inventory account on the balance sheet, the entity must next establish the amount of COGS that it should recognize as an expense on its income statement during the accounting period.

In order to determine the amount of COGS that an entity must recognize and reflect as an expense, the entity must determine the amount of inventory it has on hand at the end of the accounting period. The difference between beginning inventory and ending inventory for the accounting period reflects the amount of inventory sold for the period, which the entity should recognize as a COGS expense. As a result, ending inventory and COGS are closely related and both are important aspects of accurate financial statements.

In order to determine the amount of ending inventory on hand, the entity must select an inventory-tracking system. An entity can use either a perpetual or a periodic inventory system.

---

[16]*Id.*
[17]*Id.*

a. Perpetual Inventory System

Under a perpetual inventory system, the entity keeps an accurate count of inventory on a continuous basis. In other words, the inventory account is constantly updated and reflects the actual amount of inventory that the entity has on hand at any given point in time. In the current era where an entity operates its business through the use of barcodes on each item that it sells in conjunction with a software system and point-of-sale terminal, it is easier for an entity to maintain a perpetual inventory system.

Under this type of system, the inventory account reflects the inventory on hand at the beginning of the period, any inventory purchases made during the period, and any sales of inventory during the period. In this way, not only is the inventory account kept current, but the COGS account is also kept current. As a result, at any given point in time, the entity knows the exact amount of inventory on hand and the exact amount of COGS expense associated with the inventory that was sold.

EXAMPLE 4.19 **PERPETUAL INVENTORY**

Assume that an entity purchases $225,000 worth of inventory on March 20 and sells products worth $95,000 on March 26, which originally cost the entity $68,000.

Inventory purchase. In order to keep both its inventory and COGS accounts up to date, the entity would record a journal entry reflecting the purchase of $225,000 worth of additional inventory on March 20 for cash (or on account):

Date	Account	Debit	Credit
3/20	Inventory	$225,000	
	Cash (or Accounts Payable)		$225,000

In a perpetual inventory system, each time an entity purchases additional inventory, it debits (or increases) its inventory account to reflect the purchase and credits cash or accounts payable to reflect the payment of cash for the inventory or the purchase of inventory on account.

Product sale. The entity would next record journal entries on March 26 reflecting the sale of $95,000 worth of products, which originally cost $68,000 when purchased as inventory:

Date	Account	Debit	Credit
3/26	Cash (or Accounts Receivable)	$95,000	
	Revenue		$95,000
3/26	COGS	$68,000	
	Inventory		$68,000

In a perpetual system, each time an entity sells its products, it must record two entries — one to recognize the revenue and one to recognize the COGS expense. In the first entry it debits cash or accounts receivable to reflect that it received cash for the product or that the product was sold on account, and credits revenue to recognize the sale for the period. In the second entry, the entity debits COGS to recognize the expense associated with the products sold, and credits inventory to reflect that it has sold those products and no longer owns that particular inventory. The difference between the amount of money received for the inventory sold to the customer and the actual cost of the inventory is the gross profit on that particular sales transaction.

b. Periodic Inventory System

Under a periodic inventory system, the entity does not keep an accurate count of inventory on a continuous basis. Instead, the entity periodically (generally at the end of an accounting period) conducts a physical count of its inventory to determine the amount of inventory it has on hand at that specific point in time.

Under this type of system, the inventory account does not reflect the actual amount of inventory on hand and so is not kept current. In order to determine the amount of inventory on hand and the amount of COGS expense for the period, the entity must undertake a physical count of its inventory. Once the entity has conducted the physical count, it has the amount of ending inventory, which is the exact amount that should be reflected in its inventory account at the end of the period. In order to determine COGS for the accounting period, the entity must start with beginning inventory for the period (as reflected on its balance sheet), add the amount of inventory purchases made during the period, subtract the amount of any purchase returns of or allowances for inventory during the period, and subtract the amount of ending inventory for the period (based on the physical count). The following formula reflects the calculation of COGS under a periodic inventory system:

$$\text{COGS} = \text{Beginning Inventory} + \text{Purchases} - \text{Purchase Returns}$$
$$\text{and Allowances} - \text{Ending Inventory}$$

Under the periodic system, the entity maintains an account titled "purchases," where it records all purchases of inventory it has made during the accounting period, and an account titled "purchase returns and allowances," where it records all returns of or allowances for inventory during the accounting period. Both of these accounts are linked to the inventory account, with purchase returns and allowances acting as a contra account to purchases. As a part of the inventory reconciliation process at the end of the accounting period, the balances in these accounts will be moved into the inventory account. This is different from what occurs under a perpetual system, where the entity records purchases and purchase returns and allowances directly to the inventory account and does not create these temporary accounts. However, in order to determine COGS for the period, an entity must know the amount of purchases it made and purchase returns and allowances it had during the period and thus track that information in separate accounts.

EXAMPLE 4.20 **PERIODIC INVENTORY**

Assume that an entity purchases $225,000 worth of inventory on March 20 and returns $5,000 worth of that inventory on March 25 because it was damaged.

Inventory purchase. In order to track its inventory purchases and keep that information up to date, the entity would record a journal entry reflecting the purchase of $225,000 worth of additional inventory on March 20 for cash (or on account):

Date	Account	Debit	Credit
3/20	Purchases	$225,000	
	Cash (or Accounts Payable)		$225,000

In a periodic inventory system, each time an entity purchases additional inventory, it debits (or increases) the purchases account to reflect the purchase of inventory, and credits cash or accounts payable to reflect the payment of cash for the purchase of inventory or the purchase of inventory on account.

Return of purchased inventory. In order to track its inventory returns and keep that information up to date, the entity would record a journal entry on March 25 reflecting the return of the inventory purchased on March 20:

Date	Account	Debit	Credit
3/25	Cash (or Accounts Payable)	$5,000	
	Purchase Returns and Allowances		$5,000

In a periodic inventory system, each time the entity returns a purchase of inventory, it debits cash or accounts payable to reflect the receipt of a refund, and credits the purchase returns and allowances account to reflect that the purchased inventory has been returned and is no longer owned.

Due to the fact that the entity is not keeping a continuous record of its exact amount of inventory on hand and COGS expense for the accounting period, the entity must update those accounts at the end of the period so that the inventory account reflects the actual amount of ending inventory on hand and the COGS account reflects the correct expense for the period. It does this through a single (or a series of) inventory reconciliation journal entry (or entries) as follows:

EXAMPLE 4.21   **SINGLE-ENTRY INVENTORY ACCOUNT UPDATE AT END OF ACCOUNTING PERIOD**

Assume the entity had $1,235,000 of beginning inventory, purchased $310,000 worth of inventory during the period, returned $10,000 worth of inventory during the period, and determined that it had $1,115,000 of ending inventory on hand at the end of the period by taking a physical count.

If the entity recorded a single journal entry at the end of the accounting period, March 31, to update its inventory and COGS accounts, it would do so as follows:

Date	Account	Debit	Credit
3/31	Inventory (ending)	$1,115,000	
	Purchase Returns and Allowances	$10,000	
	Cost of Goods Sold	$420,000	
	Inventory (beginning)		$1,235,000
	Purchases		$310,000

Utilizing the COGS calculation formula previously discussed, COGS = $1,235,000 (beginning inventory) + $310,000 (purchases) – $10,000 (purchase returns and allowances) – $1,115,000 (ending inventory), which is $420,000.

The debit of $1,115,000 to the inventory account reflects the exact amount of inventory on hand at the end of the period, which becomes the beginning inventory at the start of the next accounting period. The debit of $10,000 to purchase returns and allowances reflects the zeroing out of the purchase returns and allowances contra account balance. The debit of $420,000 to COGS reflects the expense for the period (as determined with the formula). The credit of $1,235,000 to inventory reflects the removal of what was beginning inventory from the inventory account, because that is no longer the amount of inventory on hand. The credit of $310,000 to purchases reflects the zeroing out of the purchases account balance.

EXAMPLE 4.22   **MULTIPLE-ENTRY INVENTORY ACCOUNT UPDATE AT END OF ACCOUNTING PERIOD**

If the entity recorded a series of journal entries at the end of the accounting period, March 31, to update its inventory and COGS accounts, it would do so as follows, assuming the same facts set forth above in Example 4.21:

Date	Account	Debit	Credit
3/31	Cost of Goods Sold	$1,235,000	
	Inventory (beginning)		$1,235,000

continued

3/31	Cost of Goods Sold	$310,000	
	Purchases		$310,000
3/31	Purchase Returns and Allowances	$10,000	
	Cost of Goods Sold		$10,000
3/31	Inventory (ending)	$1,115,000	
	Cost of Goods Sold		$1,115,000

The first entry moves the beginning inventory balance to COGS. The second entry closes out the purchases during the period to COGS. The third entry closes out the purchase returns and allowances during the period to COGS. As a result of these three entries, the inventory account briefly reflects a zero balance, and the purchases account and purchase returns and allowances account balances are zeroed out for the period. The fourth and final entry records the ending inventory in the inventory account, which results in the inventory account now reflecting the actual ending inventory for the period as determined through a physical count. These four entries result in the same outcome as the single entry—ending inventory of $1,115,000 and COGS of $420,000 (1,235,000 + 310,000 − 10,000 − 1,115,000). However, it is sometimes simpler to work through the process of updating the inventory and COGS accounts by recording separate entries versus combining them into one single entry.

In a periodic system, the entity does not update its inventory and COGS accounts each time it makes a sale of its products. Instead, it updates those accounts at the end of the accounting period through one of the methods set forth above. As a result, the entity only knows the amount of ending inventory it has on hand and the amount of COGS it incurred during the period at the end of the accounting period.

Inventory Accounting Problems 4.6 and 4.7

Problems 4.6 and 4.7 focus on accounting for inventory.

Problem 4.6

Joe's Radio Store (JRS) started the week of June 1 with 120 radios in inventory for which JRS had paid $8.00 each (total of $960), and so the inventory account has a beginning balance of $960 on June 1. Prepare the journal entries for the following transactions and post each to the respective T-accounts using the perpetual inventory system.

June 2: JRS sold 70 radios for a total of $700 for cash.

June 3: JRS sold 30 radios for a total of $300 for cash.

June 4: JRS bought an additional 100 radios for a total cost of $800 for cash.

June 5: JRS sold 65 radios for a total of $650 on account.

> ### Problem 4.7
>
> Ryan's Electronics Shop (RES) has a beginning inventory of $2,400 on July 1 and an ending inventory of $5,600 on July 31. Using the periodic inventory system, prepare the journal entries for the transactions below, post each to the respective T-accounts, calculate the COGS for July, and prepare the month-end inventory entry as both a single entry and a series of entries.
>
> *July 3*: RES sold $500 worth of electronics for cash.
>
> *July 10*: RES purchased $4,200 worth of electronics for resale on account.
>
> *July 15*: RES returned $200 worth of defective electronics purchased on July 10 and received a credit on its account.
>
> *July 22*: RES sold $600 worth of electronics on account.

5. Valuation of Inventory

In order to determine the dollar value of ending inventory, whether the entity utilizes a perpetual or periodic inventory system, the inventory must be assigned a value. In other words, the cost of that ending inventory must be established through some type of inventory valuation methodology. There are two main inventory valuation methodologies: specific identification and cost flow assumptions.

a. Specific Identification

Entities that utilize specific identification assign costs to the specific goods to which those costs relate. In other words, the entity assigns the original cost of the item to that specific item upon its sale because it is able to track inventory specifically or individually. This type of valuation has limited application, as most entities do not operate a business that allows it to track each inventory item specifically, as the entity has thousands, if not hundreds of thousands, of items in inventory. As a result, this valuation methodology is generally only utilized by an entity that maintains a small number of items in inventory that have a high individual value. Examples of businesses that may utilize specific identification include art galleries, custom jewelers, or specialty furniture stores. An entity that utilizes specific identification typically uses a perpetual inventory system, as it can accurately reflect the inventory, revenue, and COGS accounts upon the sale of each individual item due to specific tracking and valuation.

b. Cost Flow Assumptions

As most entities are not in a position to use specific identification to value inventory, the entity chooses a cost flow assumption valuation method. These methods allow the entity to assign a cost to an inventory item through some type of assumption. In other words, upon the sale of an item in inventory the entity makes an assumption about the cost of that item in order to establish the COGS expense for that particular sale. No matter the type of cost flow assumption chosen, the entity can still employ either a perpetual or periodic inventory system based upon that particular assumption.

There are three primary cost flow assumptions: first-in, first-out (FIFO); last-in, first-out (LIFO); and weighted average. The entity should choose the cost flow assumption that best fits with its business model and the industry in which it operates. Keep in mind that cost flow assumptions are a method for tracking and valuing inventory and are not meant to reflect the actual physical flow of inventory into and out of the business.

i. First-In, First-Out (FIFO)

Under the FIFO method, the entity assumes that the goods that it first purchased (or which are the oldest) are the goods that are sold first. This method generally fits with the way in which most entities sell their inventory, oldest on hand sold first, though that is not always the case. The inventory on hand at the end of the period for an entity that utilizes FIFO would be comprised of that inventory the entity most recently purchased. As a result, ending inventory is generally a more accurate reflection of the value of the inventory on hand because it reflects more recent purchase costs. On the flip side, FIFO pairs the oldest costs of inventory with current sales, and so recognizes those oldest costs—which are generally less than current inventory purchase costs—as COGS expense for the period. As a result, the COGS is generally thought to be a less accurate reflection of the actual expense incurred for the period.

EXAMPLE 4.23 **FIFO**

This table represents the beginning inventory as of April 1, as well as two inventory purchases of 275 and 415 units that occurred during the month of April, including the per unit and total cost:

	Number of Units Available for Sale	Cost per Each Unit	Total Cost of Units
Beginning Inventory on 4/1	500	$12.20	$6,100
Purchase on 4/12	275	$12.80	$3,520
Purchase on 4/24	415	$13.20	$5,478
Total	1,190		$15,098

Assuming that the entity sold 370 units on April 14 and 245 units on April 28, it would determine the COGS expense as follows:

	Number of Units Sold	Cost per Each Unit Sold	Total Cost of Units Sold
370 units sold on 4/14 (all from beginning inventory)	370	$12.20	$4,514
245 units sold on 4/28 (130 from remaining beginning inventory and 115 from the 4/12 purchase)	130 115	$12.20 $12.80	$1,586 $1,472
Total	615		$7,572

The 370 units sold on April 14 are valued at the cost of $12.20, which is the cost of the 500 beginning inventory units on hand, which left 130 units of beginning inventory.

The 245 units sold on April 28 are valued at different costs. After taking into account the April 14 sale, there were 130 units of beginning inventory still available for sale at a cost of $12.20, which then left zero units of beginning inventory. The remaining 115 units (245 – 130) are valued at the cost of $12.80, which is the cost of the units purchased on April 12, which then left 160 units from the 4/12 purchase. As a result, the COGS for the period was $7,572.

The ending inventory would be valued as follows:

	Number of Units Remaining	Cost per Each Unit Remaining	Total Cost of Units Remaining
Beginning Inventory	0	$12.20	$0.00
275 Units Purchased on 4/12	160	$12.80	$2,048
415 Units Purchased on 4/24	415	$13.20	$5,478
Total	575		$7,526

The entity sold all 500 units of its beginning inventory and 115 of the 275 units purchased on April 12. As a result, it has 160 (275 – 115) of the April 12 units and 415 of the April 24 units remaining in its ending inventory for an ending inventory value of $7,526.

ii. Last-In, First-Out (LIFO)

Under the LIFO method, the entity assumes that the goods that it purchased last, or most recently, are the goods that are sold first. Unlike FIFO, the LIFO method does not fit the method in which most entities sell their inventory (i.e., oldest on hand sold first), but rather is the method whereby the most recently purchased are sold first. In addition, the inventory on hand at the end of the period for an entity that utilizes LIFO would be comprised of that inventory the entity has owned for the longest period of time. As a result, ending inventory is not generally an accurate reflection of the value of the inventory on hand, as it reflects the value of the inventory that was bought in the past and thus often for less. On the flip side, LIFO pairs the most recent costs of inventory with current sales, and so recognizes these recent costs as COGS expense for the period. As a result, the COGS is generally thought to be a more accurate reflection of the actual expense incurred and thus the income statement provides a more accurate reflection of gross profit, as current expenses are matched with current revenues. An important tax aspect to note about the LIFO method is that if an entity chooses to use LIFO for income tax purposes, it is required to use LIFO for inventory costing (or valuation) purposes.[18]

EXAMPLE 4.24   **LIFO**

This table represents the beginning inventory as of April 1, as well as two inventory purchases of 275 and 415 units that occurred during the month of April, including the per unit and total cost:

	Number of Units Available for Sale	Cost per Each Unit	Total Cost of Units
Beginning Inventory on 4/1	500	$12.20	$6,100
Purchase on 4/12	275	$12.80	$3,520
Purchase on 4/24	415	$13.20	$5,478
Total	**1,190**		**$15,098**

Assuming that the entity sold 370 units on April 14 and 245 units on April 28, it would determine the COGS expense as follows:

	Number of Units Sold	Cost per Each Unit Sold	Total Cost of Units Sold
370 units sold on 4/14 (275 from the 4/12 purchase and 95 from beginning inventory)	275 95	$12.80 $12.20	$3,520 $1,159
245 units sold on 4/28 (245 from the 4/24 purchase)	245	$13.20	$3,234
Total	**615**		**$7,913**

The 370 units sold on April 14 are valued at different costs. Of the total units sold, 275 units were from the April 12 purchase, which cost $12.80 and then left zero units from the 4/12 purchase, and the remaining 95 units were from the beginning inventory, which cost $12.20 and then left 405 units (500 − 95) of beginning inventory. The April 14 sale was made prior to the April 24 inventory purchase, so those units were not yet owned.

The 245 units sold on April 28 are valued at the cost of $13.20, which is the cost of the units purchased on April 24, and left 170 units (415 − 245) from the 4/24 purchase. As a result, the COGS for the period is $7,913.

---

[18]*Id.*

The ending inventory would be valued as follows:

	Number of Units Remaining	Cost per Each Unit Remaining	Total Cost of Units Remaining
Beginning Inventory	405	$12.20	$4,941
275 Units Purchased on 4/12	0	$12.80	$0.00
415 Units Purchased on 4/24	170	$13.20	$2,244
Total	**575**		**$7,185**

The entity sold only 95 units of its beginning inventory, all 275 units from its April 12 purchase, and 245 units from its April 24 purchase. As a result, it has 405 (500 – 95) units of beginning inventory, no (275 – 275) units from the April 12 purchase, and 170 (415 – 245) units from the April 24 purchase remaining in its ending inventory for a total ending inventory value of $7,185.

---

iii. Weighted Average

The final cost flow assumption method for valuing inventory is the weighted average method. Under this method, the entity calculates the weighted average of its inventory and uses that average to value COGS and ending inventory for the accounting period. In order to determine the weighted average per unit cost, the entity must determine the cost of goods available for sale, which includes beginning inventory plus purchases during the period, less any purchase returns and allowances during the period, divided by the total number of units available for sale.

EXAMPLE 4.25 **WEIGHTED AVERAGE**

This table represents the beginning inventory as of April 1, as well as two inventory purchases of 275 and 415 units that occurred during the month of April, including the per unit and total cost:

	Number of Units Available for Sale	Cost per Each Unit	Total Cost of Units
Beginning Inventory on 4/1	500	$12.20	$6,100
Purchase on 4/12	275	$12.80	$3,520
Purchase on 4/24	415	$13.20	$5,478
Total	**1,190**		**$15,098**
Weighted Average = $15,098 (cost of goods available for sale)/1,190 (total units available for sale) or $12.69 per unit			

Assuming that the entity sold 370 units on April 14 and 245 units on April 28, it would determine the COGS expense as follows:

	Number of Units Sold	Weighted Average Cost	Total Cost of Units Sold
370 units sold on 4/14	370	$12.69	$4,695.30
245 units sold on 4/28	245	$12.69	$3,109.05
Total	615		$7,804.35

All 615 units sold during the period are valued at the weighted average cost of $12.69 per unit, for total COGS of $7,804.35

The ending inventory would be valued as follows:

	Number of Units Remaining	Cost per Each Unit Remaining	Total Cost of Units Remaining
Inventory	575	$12.69	$7,296.75

The entity started the period with 1,190 units available for sale and sold 615 units, leaving 575 units in ending inventory. All 575 units of ending inventory are valued at the weighted average cost of $12.69 per unit, for a total ending inventory value of $7,296.75.

---

iv. Comparison of Cost Flow Assumption Methods

As demonstrated by the examples above, each of the cost flow assumption methods results in a different COGS and ending inventory value. This is due to the fact that each method tracks sales of goods in a slightly different manner. As a result, each method has a unique impact on the entity's balance sheet and income statement depending on the value of COGS and ending inventory. However, all methods are equally valid, and an entity should select the method that best fits its business model.

EXAMPLE 4.26   **COMPARISON OF COST FLOW METHODS**

The following table sets forth the COGS and ending inventory for the three cost flow assumption methods as determined in the examples set forth above, which all used the same underlying fact scenario:

	Cost of Goods Sold	Ending Inventory Value
FIFO	$7,572.00	$7,526.00
LIFO	$7,913.00	$7,185.00
Weighted Average	$7,804.35	$7,296.75

Keep in mind that this comparison is limited to the situation in which inventory costs were steadily increasing, thus representing an inflationary situation. In this scenario, the COGS under LIFO is greater than under FIFO and, as noted previously, matches the most recent (and also higher) inventory costs against current revenues, which results in a more accurate reflection of COGS and gross profit for the entity on its income statement. On the other hand, ending inventory under FIFO is greater than under LIFO and, as noted previously, more accurately reflects the value of ending inventory of the entity on its balance sheet because the most recent costs are included. Weighted average falls in between LIFO and FIFO in regard to both COGS and ending inventory, as would be the case since the average cost of inventory is utilized in that methodology.

EXAMPLE 4.27 INVENTORY METHODOLOGY IMPACT TO BALANCE SHEET AND INCOME STATEMENT

The following table sets forth a comparison of how FIFO and LIFO impact the balance sheet and income statement in a period of rising inventory costs and a period of falling inventory costs:

Change in Inventory Cost	Balance Sheet—FIFO	Balance Sheet—LIFO	Income Statement—FIFO	Income Statement—LIFO
Rising Costs (inflation)	Ending inventory has higher value	Ending inventory has lower value	Lower COGS and higher Gross Profit and Net Income	Higher COGS and lower Gross Profit and Net Income
Falling Costs (deflation)	Ending inventory has lower value	Ending inventory has higher value	Higher COGS and lower Gross Profit and Net Income	Lower COGS and higher Gross Profit and Net Income

Cost of inventory is increasing. During inflationary times, the cost of inventory increases, meaning that the entity is paying steadily increasing prices over time to purchase its inventory. In this situation under the FIFO method, the ending inventory balance is higher, as ending inventory consists of those items most recently purchased (or those that cost the entity the most), and COGS is lower, as COGS consists of those items that were purchased in the past (or those that cost the entity the least). As a result of the lower value of COGS, the entity recognizes greater gross profit (sales – COGS) and greater net income during the period. Under the LIFO method, the ending inventory balance is lower, as ending inventory consists of those items that were purchased in the past (or those that cost the entity the least), and COGS is higher, as COGS consists of those items that were most recently purchased (or those that cost the entity the most). As a result of the higher value of COGS, the entity recognizes less gross profit and less net income during the period.

During inflationary times, LIFO results in a more accurate measurement of net income, but not of ending inventory. This is due to the fact that COGS is made up of the inventory that was most recently purchased, and thus matches current inventory costs to revenues, resulting in a more accurate reflection of gross profit and net income but a less accurate reflection of the cost of ending inventory as reflected on the balance sheet.

Cost of inventory is decreasing: During deflationary times, the cost of inventory decreases, meaning the entity is paying steadily decreasing prices over time to purchase its inventory. In this situation under the FIFO method, the ending inventory balance is lower, as ending inventory consists of those items most recently purchased (or those that cost the entity the least), and COGS is higher, as COGS consists of those items that were purchased in the past (or those that cost the entity the most). As a result of the higher value of COGS, the entity recognizes less gross profit and less net income during the period. Under the LIFO method, the ending inventory balance is higher, as ending inventory consists of those items that were purchased in the past (or those that cost the entity the most), and COGS is lower as COGS consists of those items that were most recently purchased (or those that cost the entity the least). As a result of the lower value of COGS, the entity recognizes greater gross profit and greater net income during the period.

During deflationary times, FIFO results in a more accurate measurement of ending inventory, but not of net income. This is due to the fact that ending inventory is made up of the inventory that was most recently purchased, and thus it reflects the current inventory costs on the balance sheet. However, gross profit and net income are a less accurate reflection.

Inventory Valuation Problems 4.8 and 4.9

Problems 4.8 and 4.9 focus on inventory valuation.

Problem 4.8

Bob's Soda Company (BSC) commences the month of January with 500 cases of soda in inventory for which it paid $5.00 per case (total of $2,500). The transactions set forth below occurred during the month of January. Assume that each time BSC sold a case of soda, the case was sold for $10.00. Also assume that BSC uses a perpetual inventory system.

January 4: BSC buys 400 cases of soda for a total cost of $2,400.

January 7: BSC sells 120 cases of soda for a total of $1,200.

January 12: BSC sells 110 cases of soda for a total of $1,100.

January 16: BSC sells 290 cases of soda for a total of $2,900.

January 21: BSC buys 340 cases of soda for a total cost of $1,785.

January 23: BSC sells 150 cases of soda for a total of $1,500.

January 26: BSC sells 320 cases of soda for a total cost of $3,200.

January 29: BSC buys 70 cases of soda for a total of $357.

BSC undertook a physical inventory count on January 31 and determined it held 320 remaining cases of soda in inventory. Calculate the value of COGS, ending inventory, revenues, and gross profit for the month of January under each of the following methods:

Part A: FIFO
Part B: LIFO
Part C: Weighted Average
Part D: Specific Identification (assume that ending inventory includes 90 cases from beginning inventory, 90 cases purchased on January 4, 110 cases purchased on January 21, and 30 cases purchased on January 29).

Problem 4.9

Comic Emporium, Inc.'s (CEI) quarterly inventory record for the last quarter of the fiscal year (October 1 to December 31) is set forth below:

CEI INVENTORY FOR THE OCTOBER 1-DECEMBER 31 QUARTER

	Units	Per Unit Cost
Beginning Inventory, October 1	600	$8.75
Purchases During Quarter:		
October 27	800	$8.50
November 14	1,200	$8.40
November 29	2,000	$8.25
December 4	1,400	$8.35
December 30	1,000	$8.50

CEI COMIC BOOK SALES FOR OCTOBER 1-DECEMBER 31

	Units
Sales During Quarter:	
October 15	600
November 4	600
November 15	800
December 1	1,000
December 6	900
December 28	900

CEI undertook a physical inventory on December 31 and determined it had 2,200 comic books remaining in inventory. Assuming CEI's sales for the quarter were $86,000, calculate the value of COGS and gross profit for the quarter ending December 31 under each of the following methods:

Part A: FIFO
Part B: LIFO
Part C: Weighted Average
Part D: Specific Identification (assume that ending inventory includes 80 comic books from beginning inventory, 160 comic books purchased on October 27, 138 comic books purchased on November 14, 391 comic books purchased on November 29, 491 comic books purchased on December 4, and 940 comic books purchased on December 30).

6. Lower of Cost or Market Method for Inventory

In accordance with GAAP, if an entity's inventory loses value, the entity must revalue that inventory pursuant to the lower of cost or market method (LCM).[19] In other words, if the inventory's original cost falls below the current market value of that inventory, the inventory is written down to reflect the lower market value. An entity's inventory may decrease in value for a number of reasons, such as changes in general market prices for the inventory, damage to or spoilage of the inventory, or obsolescence of the inventory. In those circumstances, the entity must apply LCM as a means of measuring the loss in value of the inventory so that it can be recognized.[20] The concept of LCM aligns with the conservatism principle in that the entity will recognize the loss on the value of inventory, as it is now worth less than what the entity paid for it originally, and thus recognize a lower profit for the accounting period as a result of the loss.

For purposes of LCM, market means the current replacement cost of the inventory, but not to exceed the net realizable value (the upper limit) nor be less than the net realizable value minus an allowance for the normal profit (the lower limit).[21] Net realizable value is equal to the selling price of the inventory less any reasonable costs of completion and disposal that can be estimated by the entity.[22] The entity can apply LCM to each individual inventory item or to all inventory as a group.

In determining the value of the inventory to reflect on its financial statements, the entity determines the current replacement cost and values the inventory as follows: (i) if that cost is between the upper limit and lower limit, the market value is the current replacement cost; (ii) if the cost exceeds the upper limit, the market value is the upper limit or net realizable value; and (iii) if the cost is below the lower limit, the market value is the lower limit or net realizable value minus normal profit. The reason for the upper and lower limits is to prevent the entity from recognizing either excessive profits

---

[19] Accounting Standards Codification, Inventory, ASC §330-10-35 (Fin. Accounting Found. 2017).
[20] *Id.*
[21] *Id.*
[22] *Id.*

or excessive losses in the future as a result of the inventory revaluation.[23] The loss from the write-down in the value of inventory is reflected as a part of the entity's COGS or, if material, as a separate line item on its income statement. In addition, the entity reflects a credit or reduction to its inventory asset account to reflect the adjusted value of the inventory. After the entity reduces the value of its inventory under LCM, it never increases the value even if the value of the inventory rebounds and rises in the future. That increase in value is ultimately reflected in the entity having greater net income for the period due to its ability to sell the inventory for a greater amount as a result of its rebound in value.

EXAMPLE 4.28   **LOWER OF COST OR MARKET METHOD**

In this example, the entity sells three separate products, and the table below reflects the actual or initial cost to purchase each product, the current replacement cost of the product, the estimated sales price of the product, the cost to complete the product and ready it for sale, and the expected normal profit the entity anticipates it will earn on the sale of the product.

Product	Actual Cost	Replacement Cost	Estimated Selling Price	Cost to Complete	Normal Profit %/Amount
1	$30.00	$25.00	$29.00	$3.00	20%/$5.80
2	$26.00	$21.00	$28.00	$2.00	15%/$4.20
3	$33.00	$32.50	$36.00	$4.00	25%/$9.00

The following table sets forth the net realizable value (upper limit) and the net realizable value less normal profit (lower limit).

Product	Estimated Selling Price	Cost to Complete	Net Realizable Value (Upper Limit)	Normal Profit	Net Realizable Value Less Normal Profit (Lower Limit)
1	$29.00	$3.00	$26.00	$5.80	$20.20
2	$28.00	$2.00	$26.00	$4.20	$21.80
3	$36.00	$4.00	$32.00	$9.00	$23.00

The following table sets forth the actual or initial cost of the product, the net realizable value upper limit, which is estimated selling price less cost to complete (NRV upper limit), the net realizable value lower limit, which is NRV upper limit less normal profit (NRV lower limit), the replacement cost, and the lower of cost or market (LCM). The bolded number represents the amount that would be used to revalue the inventory.

---

[23] *Id.*

Product	Actual Cost	NRV Upper Limit	NRV Lower Limit	Replacement Cost	LCM
1	$30.00	$26.00	$20.20	**$25.00**	$25.00
2	$26.00	$26.00	**$21.80**	$21.00	$21.80
3	$33.00	**$32.00**	$23.00	$32.50	$32.00

In the case of product #1, the replacement cost is between the NRV upper and lower limits and so the replacement cost is used to value the inventory. In the case of product #2, the replacement cost is less than the NRV lower limit and so the NRV lower limit is used to value the inventory. In the case of product #3, the replacement cost is greater than the NRV upper limit and so the NRV upper limit is used to value the inventory.

7. Estimating the Value of Inventory

In some instances, an entity chooses not to take a physical count of its inventory at the end of every accounting period and so must engage in some type of method of estimating the value of its ending inventory, as without a physical count the entity cannot calculate the value under FIFO, LIFO, or weighted average. At the end of the quarter or year when the entity takes a physical count of its inventory on hand, it then adjusts the value of its inventory that it has estimated throughout the accounting quarter or year. There are two primary methods for estimating inventory: the gross profit method and the retail method. These are methods for estimating the cost of an entity's inventory on hand, which is different from the cost flow assumption methods discussed above that an entity uses to value its inventory on hand at the end of each accounting period.

a. Gross Profit Method

The gross profit method allows the entity to estimate the value of ending inventory or estimate the amount of inventory lost as a result of fire, theft, or other destruction.[24] Pursuant to GAAP, while the gross profit method may be used for analytical purposes, it is not an acceptable method for financial or tax reporting purposes.[25] The entity utilizes its gross profit percentage ((Sales – COGS)/Sales) × 100) to determine the value of ending inventory. If the entity's gross profit percentage is 10 percent, it assumes that 90 percent of its sales represent COGS for the accounting period. If it takes its ending inventory for the period (beginning inventory plus purchases of inventory less any purchase returns and allowance for inventory) and subtracts COGS for the period, it has the estimated value of its ending inventory.

[24]*Id.*
[25]*Id.*

EXAMPLE 4.29 **GROSS PROFIT METHOD**

As an example, assume that an entity has $370,000 of beginning inventory, purchases an additional $63,000 of inventory during the period, and returns $4,000 worth of its inventory purchases due to defects. As a result it has $429,000 worth of inventory available for sale ($370,000 + $63,000 − $4,000). If the entity had sales of $329,000 for the period and its gross profit percentage is 10 percent, its COGS would be $296,100 ($329,000 × 90%). As a result, the entity would have an estimated value of ending inventory of $132,900 ($429,000 − $296,100).

b. Retail Method

The retail method allows an entity, generally a retailer, to estimate the value of ending inventory. The entity must first determine its cost-to-retail ratio, which measures the relationship between the cost of the goods available for sale and the retail price of those goods.[26] This ratio is then used to convert the ending retail inventory back to cost. An entity can use the retail method under any of the cost flow assumptions: FIFO, LIFO, or weighted average. This method allows an entity to determine the value of its ending inventory without having to determine the original cost for each inventory item through an examination of its invoices.[27]

F. FIXED ASSETS AND DEPRECIATION

One of the largest items reflected in the long-term assets section of an entity's balance sheet is its fixed or long-lived assets, or what is also referred to as "property, plant, and equipment" (PP&E). PP&E is made up of tangible property (other than inventory) that the entity owns and will use over time in the operation of its business. Items that make up an entity's PP&E include property or land used in the entity's primary business operations, buildings and structures, equipment and machinery, and furniture and fixtures. While there are a number of accounting issues that arise in regard to PP&E, this section focuses on the following critical issues: (i) determining the amount at which the entity should initially record the asset upon its purchase, (ii) determining the method of depreciation the entity will utilize to expense the cost of the asset over its useful life, (iii) accounting for post-acquisition costs that relate to the asset, and (iv) accounting for the sale or disposal of the asset.

1. Accounting for the Initial Acquisition of the Asset

As is true for every asset that an entity purchases, it is crucial that the asset be recorded at the correct cost. Determining the cost of PP&E is not as

---

[26]*Id.*
[27]*Id.*

straightforward as it is for other assets that are generally recorded at historical cost or for the amount the entity paid to purchase the asset. In regard to PP&E, the entity must also take into account other costs in determining the initial acquisition amount that should be recorded for the asset. In general, the initial acquisition cost of PP&E includes the cost to purchase the asset, as well as the costs associated with the delivery of the asset to its intended location and the costs associated with getting the asset ready for use.

In regard to personal property, such as machinery or fixtures, the following costs may be added to the initial acquisition cost of the asset: (i) sales, use, and other taxes; (ii) import duties; (iii) finders' fees; (iv) freight costs; (v) shipping insurance costs; (vi) storage and handling costs; (vii) installation and setup costs; (viii) costs of providing proper foundational support; and (ix) costs of fixing up a newly purchased used asset for production.[28] In regard to buildings, the following costs may be added to the initial acquisition cost of the asset: (i) costs to demolish preexisting structures on the land; (ii) costs to excavate, grade, or fill land to prepare it for the new structure; (iii) fees paid to contractors to undertake the work; (iv) architectural and engineering costs; (v) costs of building permits; and (vi) costs of renovating a preexisting building for use.[29]

EXAMPLE 4.30   INITIAL ACQUISITION OF PP&E

Assume that Smith & Sons, Inc. made the following purchases of PP&E:

Machinery purchase. Smith & Sons, Inc. purchases a large piece of machinery that costs $425,000 including sales tax. It will also cost $3,500 to have the machine delivered and $4,000 to have the machine set up and ready for use at the entity's facility. Smith & Sons, Inc. pays $100,000 cash and finances the remainder of the purchase, including all costs, through a short-term loan with its commercial lender.

Property purchase. Smith & Sons, Inc. purchases a new piece of property with a building that will require renovation to make it usable for the entity's business operations. The property, with the building, costs $545,000. It will cost Smith & Sons, Inc. $96,000 to renovate the building for use, including the contractors' fees. In addition, it will cost $2,400 to secure the necessary building permits for the renovation. Smith & Sons, Inc. pays $225,000 cash and finances the remainder of the purchase, including all costs, through a commercial loan.

Journal entries for each. The table below reflects the appropriate journal entries for the two purchases of PP&E:

---

[28] ACCOUNTING STANDARDS CODIFICATION, Property, Plant, and Equipment, ASC §360-10-30 (Fin. Accounting Found. 2017).
[29] *Id.*

Date	Account	Debit	Credit
Machinery Purchase	PP&E	$432,500	
	Cash		$100,000
	Short-Term Debt		$332,500
Property Purchase	PP&E	$643,400	
	Cash		$225,000
	Long-Term Debt		$418,400

For the machinery purchase, Smith & Sons, Inc. debits PP&E for $432,500, which is the actual cost of the machine including sales tax ($425,000) and the costs to have it delivered and readied for use ($7,500). It credits cash to reflect the expenditure of $100,000 and short-term debt to reflect that it owes its commercial lender $332,500.

For the property, Smith & Sons, Inc. debits PP&E for $643,400, which is the actual cost of the property with the building ($545,000), plus the cost to renovate the preexisting building for use ($96,000), and the costs of the necessary building permits ($2,400). It credits cash to reflect the expenditure of $225,000 and long-term debt to reflect that it owes its commercial lender $418,400.

In some instances an entity may purchase PP&E through the exchange of other property as opposed to paying cash or financing the purchase. In particular, an entity may issue shares of its stock in exchange for PP&E. In that situation, the entity should recognize an initial acquisition cost that is equal to the fair market value of the property being exchanged (i.e., the value of the stock).

2. Depreciation Accounting

Most fixed assets that an entity acquires provide benefits over more than a single accounting period and in many cases provide benefits for greater than five or ten years. The number of years that an entity will benefit from a fixed asset is referred to as the asset's useful life. Because fixed assets have a long life, it would not be accurate to recognize an immediate expense of the full cost to the business when the entity purchases the fixed asset, as it will take years to use up the asset and for the entity to reap its benefits. Instead, the entity recognizes a portion of the cost of the asset as an expense of the business for each accounting period over its useful life to reflect the fact that the entity is gradually using up the value of the fixed asset in its business and operations. This allows the entity to spread the cost of the fixed asset over the years in which the asset contributes to the entity's business operations, whether that asset is a piece of machinery, a building, or furniture. The process of allocating the cost of the asset is referred to as depreciation in regard to tangible assets and amortization in regard to intangible assets (discussed later).

Depreciation is not a way for the entity to attempt to reflect the current fair market value of the asset on its financial statements. Instead, depreciation is a systematic and rational way in which the entity allocates the cost of the asset as an expense over the period of time that represents the asset's useful life. The fixed asset of land is an exception to the general rule that tangible long-lived assets are depreciated. Unlike other tangible fixed assets, land is never depreciated even though the structures and equipment on the land are depreciated. The rationale for this is that land generally appreciates in value the longer it is owned and so does not lose value over its life that should be expensed.

The depreciation of a fixed asset impacts both the balance sheet and income statement of the entity. As discussed above, when the entity initially purchases a fixed asset, it recognizes the cost of that purchase as an expenditure of cash or creation of a payable and records the fixed asset on its balance sheet in the long-term assets section. When the entity depreciates the fixed asset, it recognizes an immediate expense to the entity on the income statement and records the balancing entry to an account called accumulated depreciation on the balance sheet. The entity's net income is decreased for the accounting period due to the depreciation expense and, at the same time, the book value of the entity's fixed asset is reduced by the amount of accumulated depreciation. While the entity records the depreciation expense each period, this entry does not impact the entity's cash account, as the recognition of depreciation expense is a noncash transaction. As a result, even though the entity is recognizing depreciation expense and recording an entry to accumulated depreciation each period, it is not actually setting aside or accumulating cash for future use to replace that particular asset. This entry is simply an allocation of the cost of the asset as an expense over accounting periods to recognize the fact that the entity is using up that asset. In other words, it is just a bookkeeping entry and nothing more or nothing less.

The accumulated depreciation account on the entity's balance sheet is tied to the asset that is being depreciated and is referred to as a "contra account," meaning that it is an offset or reduction to the account to which it is tied or related. By maintaining this contra account as opposed to simply recording accumulated depreciation on the credit side of the fixed-asset account, the entity continues to maintain the historical cost of the fixed asset on its balance sheet and at the same time is able to separately track the amount of depreciation the entity has recognized for that particular fixed asset. The difference between the historical cost of the fixed asset and its accumulated depreciation is referred to as the "book value" of the asset and indicates what that asset is valued at on the entity's books and records. As a reminder, this book value is not meant to be a reflection of the current fair market value of the fixed asset.

EXAMPLE 4.31   **BALANCE SHEET DISCLOSURE**

The following table sets forth an example of an entity's long-term assets section on its balance sheet:

Long-Term Assets		
Property		$1,050,000
Equipment	$2,605,000	
Less: Accumulated depreciation	$(550,000)	

continued

Net equipment		$2,055,000
Intangible assets	$1,809,000	
Less: accumulated amortization	$(653,000)	
Net intangible assets		$1,156,000
Other long-term assets		$5,706,000
Total long-term assets		$9,967,000

As noted above, land or property is never depreciated, and so it is reflected at its historical or original purchase price on the balance sheet. Equipment is depreciated, and so the line titled "equipment" reflects the historical cost for that particular equipment, which is offset by the contra account "accumulated depreciation" to reflect the net book value for equipment. Intangible assets are amortized, and so the line titled "intangible assets" reflects the historical cost for that particular asset, which is offset by the contra account "accumulated amortization" to reflect the net book value for the intangible asset.

a. Determining Depreciation Expense

In order to calculate the depreciation expense for a fixed asset, the entity must have three pieces of information: (i) estimated useful life of the asset, (ii) salvage value of the asset, and (iii) method of depreciation.

i. Useful Life

The useful life of the asset is the amount of time the entity believes it will use the asset and that it will be productive in the entity's business operations. An entity must estimate the useful life of the asset upon purchase in order to set the depreciation schedule. However, just because an entity estimates that an asset has a useful life of ten years does not mean that the entity is required to use the asset for that entire amount of time. The entity may choose to sell the asset off in eight years' time and thus will not recognize full depreciation of the asset, or the entity may choose to use the asset for 11 years before it scraps the asset and replaces it and thus use it after the asset is fully depreciated. In other words, useful life is truly an estimate based on the entity's past practice and experience with similar fixed assets.

In determining an appropriate useful life, an entity should take into consideration technological changes, normal deterioration, and physical usage.[30] Entities can also rely on their own experience or industry experience, as well as the useful life tables provided by the Internal Revenue Service, to estimate the number of years the asset will be productive. Additionally, entities often set a standard useful life for different classes of assets for consistency purposes—for instance, all computer equipment has a useful life of five years, and all office furniture and fixtures have a useful life of seven years.

---

[30]*Id.*

No matter what factors an entity takes into consideration in establishing the useful life of a fixed asset, that determination impacts the entity and its net income through the recognition of depreciation expense on the income statement. If the entity overestimates the useful life of the asset, depreciation expense will be reduced each accounting period, and so net income will be higher. However, if the entity underestimates the useful life of an asset, depreciation expense will be increased each accounting period, and so net income will be lower. In either case, the choice of useful life has a direct impact on the entity's net income or loss for the accounting period.

ii. Salvage Value

The salvage value of a fixed asset is an estimate of what the entity believes that asset will be worth at the end of its useful life. In other words, it is the amount the entity believes it can recoup if it sells that fixed asset at the end of its useful life or the asset's residual value. Just like useful life, an entity must estimate the salvage value of the fixed asset upon its purchase in order to set the depreciation schedule. The entity may rely on its past experience or industry knowledge in order to determine the salvage value of a fixed asset, and in some instances, the salvage value of a fixed asset may be zero at the end of its useful life. However, one thing to note is that a fixed asset is never depreciated beyond its established salvage value.

No matter what factors an entity takes into consideration in establishing the salvage value of a fixed asset, similar to the useful life estimate, the determination of salvage value impacts the entity and its net income through the recognition of depreciation expense on the income statement. If the entity overestimates the salvage value of the asset, depreciation expense will be reduced each accounting period, and so net income will be higher. However, if the entity underestimates the salvage value of an asset, depreciation expense will be increased each accounting period, and so net income will be lower. In either scenario, just like useful life, the salvage value has a direct impact on the entity's net income or loss for the accounting period.

iii. Method of Depreciation

The final piece of information that an entity must establish in order to calculate the depreciation schedule is the method of depreciation the entity will utilize. The depreciation method may be either a function of time or a function of physical production.[31] While each of the available methods will ultimately result in the same amount of depreciation expense, the amount of expense recognized each accounting period will vary depending on the methodology selected. The principal methods of depreciation as a function of time are (i) straight-line; (ii) declining balance; and (iii) sum-of-the-years' digits. The principal method of depreciation as a function of physical usage is units of production.

---

[31]*Id.*

(a) Straight-Line Method

The straight-line method of depreciation is the easiest to determine and results in an equal amount of depreciation expense each accounting period. The formula to calculate straight-line depreciation is as follows:

$$\text{Depreciation Expense} = \frac{(\text{Original Cost} - \text{Salvage Value})}{\text{Estimated Useful Life in Years}}$$

EXAMPLE 4.32 **STRAIGHT-LINE DEPRECIATION**

Assume that Smith & Sons, Inc. purchases a new piece of equipment on January 1 for $80,000, which includes all costs. At the time of purchase, Smith & Sons, Inc. estimates the useful life of the piece of equipment to be five years and the salvage value to be $5,000.

$$\text{Depreciation Expense} = \frac{(\$80,000 - \$5,000)}{5}$$

$$= \$15,000 \text{ per year (or } \$1,250 \text{ per month)}$$

(b) Declining Balance Method

The declining balance method of depreciation is an accelerated method, and as a result, the entity recognizes greater depreciation expense in the earlier years of the asset's life. An accelerated method of depreciation is appropriate when an asset loses more value during its early years of use as opposed to its later years.

Under the declining balance method, the entity must choose the percentage at which it wishes to depreciate the asset, generally 150 percent or 200 percent. If the entity chooses 150 percent, it is depreciating its asset at a rate of one and a half times the straight-line rate, and if it chooses 200 percent, it is depreciating its asset at a rate of two times the straight-line rate. In order to calculate the declining balance rate, the entity must first determine the straight-line rate with the following formula:

$$\text{Straight-Line Rate} = 1/\text{Estimated Useful Life}$$

It then multiplies the straight-line rate by the declining balance percentage to determine the declining balance rate. If the declining balance percentage selected is 150 percent and the useful life is five years, the declining balance rate would be calculated as follows:

$$\text{Straight-Line Rate} = 1/5$$
$$= .20$$
$$\text{Declining Balance Rate} = 150\% \times .20$$
$$= 30\% \text{ (or .30)}$$

In order to calculate the amount of depreciation expense for each year, the entity multiplies the declining balance rate by the net book value of the asset at the beginning of the fiscal year. Under the declining balance method, the entity uses the actual cost of the asset (and not actual cost less salvage value) to commence the depreciation calculation.

EXAMPLE 4.33   **DECLINING BALANCE DEPRECIATION**

Utilizing the same facts from Example 4.32 and assuming Smith & Sons, Inc. adopts a 200 percent declining balance depreciation rate (the declining balance rate would be 40 percent or .40, which is the straight-line rate multiplied by 200 percent), the depreciation on the new piece of equipment would be calculated as follows:

Year	Net Book Value (NBV) at Beginning of Fiscal Year	Yearly Depreciation Expense (NBV at beginning of fiscal year × 40% or .40)	Net Book Value at End of Fiscal Year (NBV at beginning of period – depreciation expense)
1	$80,000.00	$32,000.00	$48,000.00
2	$48,000.00	$19,200.00	$28,800.00
3	$28,800.00	$11,520.00	$17,280.00
4	$17,280.00	$6,912.00	$10,368.00
5	$10,368.00	$4,147.20	$6,220.80
6	$6,220.80	$1,220.80[1]	$5,000.00[1]
Total		$75,000.00	

[1] Note that the calculation yields a result of $2,488.32, but the amount of depreciation expense is capped at $1,220.80 in year 6 so that the piece of equipment is not depreciated below its established salvage value of $5,000.

(c) Sum-of-the-Years' Digits Method

The sum-of-the-years' digits (SYD) method of depreciation is another type of accelerated depreciation through which the entity recognizes greater depreciation expense during the earlier years of the asset's life. The formula for calculating depreciation under SYD is as follows:

$$\text{Depreciation} = (\text{Original Cost} - \text{Salvage Value}) \times \text{Applicable Percentage}$$

$$\text{Applicable Percentage} = \frac{\text{\# of Years of Estimated Life Remaining at the Beginning of the Year}}{\text{SYD}}$$

$$\text{SYD} = \frac{n(n+1)}{2}, \text{ where } n = \text{estimated useful life}$$

If the asset had a useful life of five years, the SYD would be calculated as follows:

$$\text{SYD} = \frac{5(5+1)}{2}$$
$$= 15$$

EXAMPLE 4.34   **SUM-OF-THE-YEARS' DEPRECIATION**

Utilizing the same facts from Example 4.32, SYD would be calculated as follows:

Year	Actual Cost – Salvage	Remaining Useful Life at Beginning of Year	SYD	Applicable Percentage (remaining useful life at beginning of year/SYD)	Annual Depreciation Expense
1	$75,000.00	5	15	33.33%	$24,997.50
2	$75,000.00	4	15	26.67%	$20,002.50
3	$75,000.00	3	15	20.00%	$15,000.00
4	$75,000.00	2	15	13.33%	$9,997.50
5	$75,000.00	1	15	6.67%	$5,002.50
Total					**$75,000.00**

EXAMPLE 4.35   **COMPARISON OF RESULTS OF DEPRECIATION METHODOLOGIES**

The following table sets forth a comparison of the annual depreciation expense for each depreciation methodology:

Year	Straight Line	200% Declining Balance	Sum-of-the-Years' Digits
1	$15,000.00	$32,000.00	$24,997.50
2	$15,000.00	$19,200.00	$20,002.50
3	$15,000.00	$11,520.00	$15,000.00
4	$15,000.00	$6,912.00	$9,997.50
5	$15,000.00	$4,147.20	$5,002.50
6	$0.00	$1,220.80	$0.00
Total Depreciation	**$75,000.00**	**$75,000.00**	**$75,000.00**

As is evident from the depreciation calculations, an entity that chooses to use one of the accelerated methods of depreciation will recognize significantly more depreciation expense in the earlier years of the asset's life than in the later years. However, no matter the depreciation method selected, the entity will still depreciate the same amount for the fixed asset, in this case $75,000 (cost – salvage).

EXAMPLE 4.36   **DEPRECIATION EXPENSE JOURNAL ENTRIES**

The following table sets forth the journal entries Smith & Sons, Inc. would record for year 1 for each of the depreciation methods:

Year 1	Account	Debit	Credit
Straight Line	Depreciation Expense	$15,000.00	
	Accumulated Depreciation – Equipment		$15,000.00

Declining Balance	Depreciation Expense	$32,000.00	
	Accumulated Depreciation – Equipment		$32,000.00
Sum-of-the-Years Digits	Depreciation Expense	$24,997.50	
	Accumulated Depreciation – Equipment		$24,997.50

(1) Prorating Depreciation

While the example above with Smith & Sons, Inc. utilized a fact pattern where the entity purchased the fixed asset on January 1 and so was not required to prorate depreciation for the year or for the month, that is generally not how the transaction will occur in the business world. Fixed assets are purchased at any given time during the year and on any given day of the month. As a result, the entity will need to prorate the amount of depreciation expense it recognizes for the first and last year or month, as the case may be, based on the number of days the fixed asset was owned for that year or month.

EXAMPLE 4.37 **PRORATING DEPRECIATION**

If Smith & Sons, Inc. had purchased the new piece of equipment on June 15, under the straight-line method, it would recognize six and a half months of depreciation expense during the first year, a full year's worth of depreciation expense during the next four years, and five and a half months of depreciation expense during the sixth year. The following table sets forth the amount of depreciation Smith & Sons, Inc. would recognize as an expense based on the above facts:

Year	First Month's Depreciation	Full Month's Depreciation	Last Month's Depreciation	Annual Depreciation
1	$625[1]	$1,250[2]	n/a	$8,125
2	n/a	$1,250[3]	n/a	$15,000
3	n/a	$1,250[3]	n/a	$15,000
4	n/a	$1,250[3]	n/a	$15,000
5	n/a	$1,250[3]	n/a	$15,000
6	n/a	$1,250[4]	$625[5]	$6,875
Total				**$75,000**

1: One-half month's depreciation for June; 2: Full month's depreciation for July through December; 3: Full month's depreciation for January through December; 4: Full month's depreciation for January through May; 5: One-half month's depreciation for June.

A similar methodology of prorating would also be applied under the declining balance and SYD methods. The first and last year or first and last month would be prorated to reflect that the fixed asset was purchased part-way through the accounting period.

(d) Units of Production Method

The units of production method of depreciation is the principal method an entity will use if it desires to recognize depreciation expense as a function of physical usage versus time. The formula to calculate units of production is as follows:

$$\text{Depreciation Rate} = \frac{(\text{Original Cost} - \text{Salvage Value})}{\substack{\text{Estimated Number of Units to Be Produced} \\ \text{by the Asset over Its Useful Life}}}$$

$$\text{Depreciation Expense} = \text{Depreciation Rate} \times \text{Number of Units Produced}$$

EXAMPLE 4.38   UNITS OF PRODUCTION DEPRECIATION

Assume Smith & Sons, Inc. purchases a new piece of equipment on January 1 for $80,000, which includes all costs. At the time of the purchase, Smith & Sons, Inc. estimates that the machine will produce 150,000 units over its useful life and the salvage value is $5,000.

$$\text{Depreciation Rate} = \frac{\$80,000 - \$5,000}{150,000}$$
$$= \$0.50 \text{ per unit produced}$$

If Smith & Sons, Inc. produced 32,000 units during the first year it owned the piece of equipment, it would calculate its depreciation expense for the year as follows:

$$\text{Depreciation Expense} = \$0.50 \times 32,000$$
$$= \$16,000$$

An entity that utilizes the units of production depreciation method will recognize a different amount of depreciation expense each period depending upon how many units the fixed asset produces during the accounting period. As is true with all depreciation methodologies, the asset can only be depreciated to its salvage value.

Depreciation Accounting Problems 4.10 and 4.11

Problems 4.10 and 4.11 focus on depreciation accounting.

Problem 4.10

During its first year of operations, United Entertainment Co. (UEC) purchased a piece of equipment for $96,000. It submitted and paid for the purchase via the seller's online purchase order system on January 1, so for purposes of this problem you can assume that UEC has owned the equipment for a full year during year one of operations. UEC estimates that the equipment will have an expected useful life of 12 years and a salvage value of $40,000. In addition, UEC estimates that the equipment will produce 80,000 units over its useful life.

Determine the amount of depreciation expense that UEC should recognize for years one to five using each of the following depreciation methods and assume that UEC produces 6,800, 6,400, 6,600, 6,100, and 5,900 units in years one to five, respectively:

Part A: Straight-Line Method
Part B: Declining Balance Method (for both 150 percent and 200 percent)
Part C: Sum-of-the-Years' Digits Method
Part D: Units of Production Method

Problem 4.11

UEC also purchased office computers worth $112,000 during its first year of operations on June 1. In addition to the cost of the computers, it cost UEC an additional $2,100 in delivery charges, which included the delivery fee and cost of in-transit insurance. Lastly, UEC paid a third-party contractor $900 to install the computers. UEC believes the computers will only last four years, at which point UEC will sell them for parts for $12,400.

Determine the amount of depreciation expense that UEC should recognize for each year under the following depreciation methods:

Part A: Straight-Line Method
Part B: Declining Balance Method (for both 150 percent and 200 percent)
Part C: Sum-of-the-Years' Digits Method

3. Post-Acquisition Costs

In many cases, an entity will incur post-acquisition costs related to a previously purchased fixed asset. In those circumstances, the entity must determine how to account for those post-acquisition costs and whether such costs should be immediately recognized as an expense or whether such costs should be capitalized and depreciated over future periods. If the entity recognizes the post-acquisition cost as an immediate expense of the business, it has a direct impact on the entity's net income for the period, as the expense would be a reduction on the entity's income statement and so would reduce its net income or increase its net loss for the period. If the entity capitalizes the cost and depreciates it over future periods, it will recognize an increase in an asset on the balance sheet and will expense only a portion of that asset's cost each accounting period in the form of depreciation. As a result, a post-acquisition cost recognized as a capital expenditure has less impact to the entity's net income or net loss for the period, as the entity only recognizes a small portion of the cost as an expense each period as opposed to all at once.

Post-acquisition costs may include such things as additions, alterations, improvements, maintenance, refurbishment, repair, replacement, and more. In order to make a determination as to how to classify a post-acquisition cost, the entity must assess whether the cost will provide a future economic benefit. If the cost provides a future economic benefit for the entity, such as increasing the fixed asset's productivity or extending its useful life, it should be capitalized and depreciated. Otherwise, it should be immediately expensed.

If the post-acquisition cost increases the value of the asset, the entity will generally treat this as the acquisition of a new asset and depreciate it over time.[32] However, many entities simply establish a dollar threshold to determine whether a post-acquisition cost should be capitalized or expensed immediately. The rationale for this approach is that the entity views an insignificant post-acquisition cost as immaterial to its business and operations, and thus it makes better sense to simply recognize the cost as an immediate expense.

Post-acquisition costs that increase productivity or extend the useful life of the asset are either added to the recorded value of the asset or are recorded as a separate and new asset of the business. However, if the post-acquisition cost is deemed a repair or maintenance, unless the cost increases productivity or extends the useful life of the asset, the entity will recognize the repair or maintenance cost as an immediate expense of the business.

4. Sale or Disposal of a Fixed Asset

Upon the sale of a fixed asset, the entity will recognize either a gain or loss dependent upon the amount of depreciation it has recognized up to the date of the sale and the amount of money it receives in the sale. When the fixed asset is sold, the entity must remove that asset and the related accumulated depreciation from its balance sheet, as it no longer owns the asset. The entity also recognizes the receipt of cash and the relevant gain or loss on the sale of the asset.

EXAMPLE 4.39   **SALE OF A FIXED ASSET FOR A GAIN**

Assume that Smith & Sons, Inc. determined it wants to sell one of its large machines, as the machine is nearing the end of its useful life and the entity has decided to replace it. The machine originally cost $215,000 and through the date of the sale, March 31, Smith & Sons, Inc. had recorded $144,000 worth of accumulated depreciation. If Smith & Sons, Inc. sold the machine for $75,000, it would record the following entry and recognize a gain on the sale of the machine, as the total of the cash received for the sale and the recorded

---

[32]*Id.*

accumulated depreciation exceed the original cost of the machine, indicating the entity recouped more than the original cost of the machine:

Date	Account	Debit	Credit
3/31	Cash	$75,000	
	Accumulated Depreciation	$144,000	
	PP&E		$215,000
	Gain on Sale of Fixed Asset		$4,000

EXAMPLE 4.40   **SALE OF A FIXED ASSET FOR A LOSS**

Using the basic facts above, assume that Smith & Sons, Inc. sold the machine for $65,000 instead. Then it would record the following entry and recognize a loss on the sale of the machine, as the total of the cash received for the sale and the recorded accumulated depreciation do not exceed the original cost of the machine, indicating the entity did not recoup the original cost of the machine:

Date	Account	Debit	Credit
3/31	Cash	$65,000	
	Accumulated Depreciation	$144,000	
	Loss on Sale of Fixed Asset	$6,000	
	PP&E		$215,000

An entity may also choose to dispose of a fixed asset by abandoning the asset when it is of no further use or has become obsolete, versus selling the asset. The entries to recognize the abandonment of a fixed asset differ depending on whether the asset has been fully depreciated or not.

EXAMPLE 4.41   **DISPOSAL OF A FULLY DEPRECIATED FIXED ASSET**

Assume that Smith & Sons, Inc. decided to abandon one of its machines that originally cost $215,000. In the first scenario, the machine has been fully depreciated and Smith & Sons, Inc. has recorded $180,000 worth of accumulated depreciation (the machine has a salvage value of $35,000). Smith & Sons, Inc. will eliminate the asset and accumulated depreciation from its balance sheet and recognize the salvage value as a loss, as it did not sell the machine and recoup its original estimate of salvage value. Smith & Sons, Inc. would record the following entry to recognize the abandonment of this machine:

Date	Account	Debit	Credit
3/31	Accumulated Depreciation	$180,000	
	Loss on Disposal of Fixed Asset	$35,000	
	PP&E		$215,000

EXAMPLE 4.42 **DISPOSAL OF A NOT FULLY DEPRECIATED FIXED ASSET**

Using the basic facts above, assume that Smith & Sons, Inc. is scrapping the machine six months prior to the end of its useful life, and as a result, it has only recorded $171,000 worth of accumulated depreciation. Smith & Sons, Inc. will eliminate the asset and accumulated depreciation from its balance sheet and recognize the un-depreciated amount and salvage value as a loss. Smith & Sons, Inc. would record the following entry to recognize the abandonment of this machine:

Date	Account	Debit	Credit
3/31	Accumulated Depreciation Loss on Disposal of Fixed Asset	$171,000 $44,000	
	PP&E		$215,000

5. Impairment of a Fixed Asset

In some instances, a fixed asset becomes impaired, meaning that its fair market value is less than its actual value, or carrying value, as reflected on the entity's balance sheet. However, an entity is only required to recognize an impairment loss if the carrying amount of the fixed asset is not recoverable.[33] Recoverability is determined by comparing the carrying amount of the fixed asset to the amount of the undiscounted cash flows the entity expects to result from the continued use and disposal of the asset.[34] Additionally, an entity only has to test for impairment under the recoverability theory in certain circumstances. Those circumstances include situations where (i) there has been a significant reduction in the market price of a fixed asset, (ii) there has been a significant negative change in the way the entity is using the fixed asset or in the asset's condition, (iii) there is a change in overall business economics that affects the value of the fixed asset, or (iv) the entity believes it will sell the fixed asset long before the end of its useful life.[35]

In those circumstances where the entity must test a fixed asset for impairment, if the entity determines that the asset has been impaired under the recoverability test, it must write down the value of the asset to its fair value and recognize an immediate loss to the business on the income statement. In the event of impairment, the entity would debit impairment loss to recognize the expense for the period and credit the fixed asset to reflect the reduction in value.

---

[33]*Id.*
[34]*Id.*
[35]*Id.*

EXAMPLE 4.43 **IMPAIRMENT OF A FIXED ASSET**

Assume that Smith & Sons, Inc. owns a large piece of equipment that it purchased for $215,000 two years ago. The current cost of this particular machine has dropped significantly due to the introduction of a more innovative option. Smith & Sons, Inc. believes its machine is now worth $129,000, a 40 percent decline from the original purchase price. Smith & Sons, Inc. would record the following journal entry to reflect the impairment to this fixed asset:

Date	Account	Debit	Credit
3/31	Impairment Loss	$86,000	
	PP&E		$86,000

6. Other Long-Lived Assets

In addition to tangible fixed assets that undergo depreciation, entities may also own intangible assets that undergo amortization or natural resources that undergo depletion.

a. Intangible Assets and Amortization

Many entities own a variety of intangible assets, with a finite useful life, that are utilized in the business, such as patents, trademarks, copyrights, or licenses. While these are fixed or long-term assets, since they are intangible assets they are amortized as opposed to depreciated over their expected useful economic life.[36] An entity should take into account a number of factors in assessing an intangible asset's useful economic life, such as (i) the entity's expected use of the intangible asset; (ii) limitations established by law (e.g., term of a patent registration); (iii) the entity's past experiences; and (iv) the effects of demand, competition, and other economic factors.[37] In conjunction with assessing its useful economic life, the entity must also assess whether the intangible asset will have residual value at the end of its useful economic life, which is similar to salvage value. An intangible asset only has a residual value if the asset will continue to have a useful life for another entity after the end of its useful life as determined by its current owner.[38] Otherwise, the intangible asset has no residual value to take into consideration in the amortization assessment. The formula to calculate amortization of an intangible asset with a finite life is as follows:

$$\text{Amortization Expense} = \frac{(\text{Original Cost} - \text{Residual Value})}{\text{Estimated Useful Economic Life in Years}}$$

---

[36] ACCOUNTING STANDARDS CODIFICATION, Intangibles — Goodwill and Other, ASC §350-30-35 (Fin. Accounting Found. 2017).
[37] *Id.*
[38] *Id.*

Intangible assets that have an indefinite useful economic life are not amortized, but are instead subjected to impairment testing on an annual basis to determine if the asset has been impaired and the entity should write down the carrying value of the asset and recognize a loss.

i. Goodwill

Goodwill is its own type of intangible asset, with an indefinite life, that an entity acquires as a result of a business combination. Although goodwill is an intangible asset, most entities do not amortize goodwill. Instead, on an annual basis the entity assesses the value of the goodwill to determine whether or not it has been impaired. In the event that the current fair value of the goodwill is less than what is reflected on the entity's balance sheet, the entity must recognize a loss and write down the value of goodwill to its current fair value.[39] While most large or public entities assess the value of goodwill annually, private entities may elect to amortize goodwill on a straight-line basis over ten years to forgo impairment testing, which is often expensive.[40]

EXAMPLE 4.44   **GOODWILL IMPAIRMENT**

Assume an entity undertook its annual assessment (in December) of goodwill and found that the fair value was $50,000 less than the current carrying value of goodwill and so goodwill had been impaired. The entity would record the following journal entry to reflect that impairment of goodwill:

	Account	Debit	Credit
12/31	Impairment Loss	$50,000	
	Goodwill		$50,000

As a result of this entry, the entity recognizes a loss during the accounting period to reflect the fact that its goodwill has been impaired and records a reduction to its goodwill asset. An impairment of goodwill has a direct impact on the entity's income statement, as it is a loss for the period and reduces the entity's net income for the period.

---

b. Natural Resources and Depletion

Many entities own the rights to natural resources, meaning those resources that are mined, extracted, or otherwise removed from the environment for use. The use of natural resources results in the depletion, or consumption, of the asset. Many entities calculate depletion utilizing the units of production method. In

---

[39]*Id.* at §350-20-35.
[40]*Id.*

order to use this method in regard to natural resources, the entity must know the actual cost to purchase the natural resource, an estimate of the resource's salvage value, if any, and the amount of the resource available for recovery (e.g., number of gallons of oil). The formula to calculate the depletion rate is as follows:

$$\text{Depletion Rate} = \frac{(\text{Original Cost} - \text{Salvage Value})}{\text{Estimated Amount of Resource Available for Recovery}}$$

EXAMPLE 4.45   **DEPLETION**

Assume an entity purchased the rights to extract natural gas from a piece of land for a total cost of $3,500,000 and it plans to extract all the natural gas available so there will be no salvage value. The entity also believes it can extract 5,250,000 cubic feet of natural gas from the land. The entity would calculate the depletion rate as follows:

$$\text{Depletion Rate} = \frac{(\$3,500,000 - \$0.00)}{5,250,000}$$
$$= \$0.67 \text{ per cubic foot}$$

If the entity extracted 450,000 cubic feet of natural gas during the first year it owned the land, it would calculate its depletion expense for the year as follows:

$$\text{Depletion Expense} = \$.67 \times 450,000$$
$$= \$301,500$$

The table below sets forth the journal entry the entity would record to recognize depletion expense during the first year:

Year 1	Account	Debit	Credit
Units of Production	Depletion Expense	$301,500	
	Accumulated Depletion		$301,500

Culminating Problems 4.12 and 4.13

Problems 4.12 and 4.13 focus on and integrate the concepts learned throughout this chapter. These two problems build on each other so must be completed in sequence.

Problems 4.12 and 4.13: Background Information

Tom and Janie Patterson, who are brother and sister, decided to open a small custom furniture shop. Tom and Janie incorporated T&J Furniture, Inc. (TJF) on July 1 of year one, and the entity's fiscal year will run from July 1 through June 30. TJF authorized 100,000 shares of common stock, $1.00 par value, and 50,000 shares of preferred stock, $5.00 par value upon incorporation.

TJF uses straight-line depreciation on all of its fixed assets and recognizes depreciation expense for either a full month or half month (i.e., TJF does not count actual days and recognize depreciation expense in that manner). TJF uses a periodic inventory system with first-in, first-out (FIFO) as its inventory valuation method. TJF's effective tax rate is 20 percent, and it rounds taxes to the nearest whole dollar using standard rounding conventions and accrues for taxes on a monthly basis.

Problem 4.12

For the July transactions set forth below, prepare the journal entries for the month of July in a general journal, post the journal entries to the respective T-accounts, prepare any necessary adjusting entries for the month of July and post the adjusting entries to the respective T-accounts, total the T-accounts as of the end of July, close the books for the month of July (i.e., prepare the closing entries, including the tax entries, and post the entries to the respective T-accounts), prepare a balance sheet as of July 31, and prepare an income statement for the month ended July 31.

July 1: TJF issued 2,500 shares of common stock to Tom Patterson for $10,000 and 2,500 shares of common stock to Janie Patterson for $10,000.

July 1: TJF leased warehouse space from Commercial Warehouses Leasing (CWL) for $2,800 per month with a lease commencement date of July 1 and rent due no later than the third of the month. CWL provided TJF with a month of free rent for prepaying two full months of rent at lease signing. TJF immediately prepaid for August and September rent to secure the deal (month of July rent free) and moved into the space. *Due to the free month, must recalculate new monthly lease. Use the new monthly rate for accounting purpose.*

July 2: TJF purchased and paid for one year's worth of commercial liability insurance to cover its new business, property, and rented space for a total cost of $4,800. The insurance coverage had a commencement date of July 1, the date TJF took possession of its space.

July 6: TJF's first customer, Sally Mann, agreed to purchase a custom dining room table and chairs from TJF. TJF required a deposit of $2,800 with the remainder due upon delivery of the furniture in mid-August.

July 9: TJF purchased $3,950 worth of lumber and related supplies from Joe's Lumber Shop for cash, some of which it will use to build Sally Mann's order and some of which it will use to build other furniture pieces for future sale.

July 11: TJF sold two pre-built side tables to Wendy Wills, a friend of Tom and Janie. Wendy purchased the tables for $3,250 in cash.

July 14: Tom and Janie's mother, Nancy Patterson, purchased 5,000 shares of preferred stock for $50,000 and paid cash.

July 16: TJF purchased two pieces of machinery on account for its new business from Machinery Supply Company. The first machine cost $5,000 and has an estimated useful life of eight years, with a salvage value of $200. The second machine cost $7,200 and has an estimated useful life of ten years, with a salvage value of zero.

July 18: TJF sold two pre-built bookcases to Small Book Shop for $2,800, which Small Book Shop will pay for in August.

July 22: TJF purchased $6,300 worth of lumber and related supplies from Joe's Lumber Shop and paid for half in cash and put the other half on account.

July 24: TJF returned $450 worth of lumber purchased on July 22, as it was damaged, and Joe's Lumber Shop issued TJF a credit on its account.

July 26: TJF hired Kate Patterson to work as a part-time assistant in the shop. TJF will pay Kate $1,200 per month, and she will start work on August 1.

July 30: TJF received and paid its July utility bill in the amount of $350.

July 31: TJF took a physical count of its inventory and had $6,775 of inventory on hand.

Problem 4.13

For the August transactions set forth below, prepare the journal entries for the month of August in a general journal, post the journal entries to the respective T-accounts (you should utilize your T-accounts from the month of July and add new T-accounts as needed), prepare any necessary adjusting entries for the month of August and post the adjusting entries to the respective T-accounts, total the T-accounts as of the end of August, close the books for the month of August (i.e., prepare the closing entries, including the tax entries, and post the entries to the respective T-accounts), prepare a balance sheet as of August 31, and prepare an income statement for the month ended August 31.

August 1: TJF took out a three-year $180,000 small business loan from Bank North, with a simple interest rate of 5 percent. TJF is required to make monthly interest payments on the last day of each month (commencing in August) to Bank North with the outstanding principal due at the end of the three years.

August 3: TJF paid $300 in cash to Machinery Supply Company to make a minor repair to one of the pieces of equipment purchased in July.

August 5: TJF delivered the custom dining table and chairs to Sally Mann for a total sales price of $28,000, and Sally Mann paid the remaining balance due upon delivery.

August 8: Jeffrey Han agreed to purchase five pieces of custom furniture from TJF, which will cost $52,750 in total. TJF required an immediate deposit of $5,275, which Jeffrey paid, with a second deposit of $10,500 due on August 25, and the balance due upon delivery of the pieces in early September.

August 10: TJF purchased $14,900 worth of lumber and supplies from Joe's Lumber Shop and paid cash.

August 11: TJF sold two more pre-built bookcases to Small Book Shop for $2,200 in cash.

August 13: Small Book Shop returned one of the bookcases it bought on August 11, as it did not fit in the designated space. TJF issued Small Book Shop a cash refund for the full purchase price of $800, since it can resell the bookcase.

August 14: Small Book Shop paid TJF $2,800 for its July purchase.

August 15: TJF paid Kate Patterson her salary of $600 for the first half of the month.

August 18: TJF paid Joe's Lumber Shop $2,700 that it owed on its account.

August 20: TJF received its August utility bill in the amount of $470, which TJF will pay in September on or before the September 13 due date.

August 23: TJF purchased $6,800 worth of lumber and supplies on account from Mary's Lumber Yard.

August 25: Jeffrey Han made the second payment of $10,500 on his custom furniture order.

August 26: TJF sold a pre-built table for $8,900 to the Better Business Company, which paid in cash.

August 27: TJF sold four pre-built chairs for $11,100 to Conference Room Rentals, which placed the purchase on its account.

August 28: TJF paid $12,200 to Machinery Supply Co. that it owed on its account.

August 29: TJF made its required monthly interest payment to Bank North.

August 31: Since the last day of the month fell on a Sunday, TJF did not pay Kate her salary of $600 for the second half of the month. TJF will pay Kate on September 1, the next business day.

August 31: TJF took a physical count of its inventory and had $18,485 of inventory on hand.

Dividend Distributions

A. INTRODUCTION

Dividends are distributions that entities make to their shareholders as a method of rewarding a class of shareholders for investing in the entity. By issuing a dividend, and in particular a cash dividend, the entity is distributing, or sharing, a portion of its earnings. Dividends result in an immediate return to shareholders on their investment, as opposed to the potential future return shareholders may make upon the sale of their shares.

While an entity may elect to issue a dividend, it may also choose to retain those earnings and reinvest them to fund its continued operations. It is typical for larger and more established entities to issue dividends on a regular basis, quite often even quarterly. However, start-up entities are less likely to pay a dividend because they desire to retain the earnings to reinvest in and continue to expand their business. In either case, an entity may opt to never pay a dividend or to stop paying regular dividends at any time, unless guaranteed.

B. DIVIDEND DISTRIBUTION OVERVIEW

A dividend is a distribution of cash or property by a corporation to a class of its shareholders. The distribution must be made on a pro rata basis based upon each shareholder's percentage ownership in that particular class of stock. This pro rata distribution requirement applies whether it is a cash, property, or stock dividend. The board of directors of the corporate entity is the body with the power to declare and issue the dividend. However, the board can only declare and make a distribution in compliance with relevant state statutory requirements, the corporation's governance documents, and any other contractually imposed limitations.

Prior to declaring the dividend, the board should determine whether the corporation is in compliance with the relevant statutory and other requirements governing the distribution. In making this assessment, the board may rely on information provided by other parties. For instance, the board can rely upon financial statements, reports, and opinions provided by both internal accountants and external auditors, as well as information provided by the executive officers of the corporation, including in-house legal counsel. Lastly, the board can rely on information provided by other third parties such as outside counsel, a consultant, or an other expert adviser. To assess the legality of a dividend declaration and distribution, the board of directors should primarily focus on the corporation's short-term prospects and circumstances unless a contributing factor or event requires the board to look at the longer term.[1] In order to determine the amount of dividend an entity can distribute, the board should examine the entity's financial statements and condition in conjunction with the relevant state statute.

C. UNDERSTANDING THE COMPONENTS OF THE BALANCE SHEET'S EQUITY SECTION

In order to delve into the various types of dividend distributions, as well as the legal restrictions imposed on those distributions through state statutes, it is important to understand the balance sheet, and in particular, the stockholders' equity section. Each of the accounts listed in the stockholders' equity section may play a role in determining whether the board of directors of a corporation can legally declare and issue a distribution, as well as the amount that can be distributed.

The first component of the stockholders' equity section lists the capital stock accounts of the entity (or what are often labeled as common stock and preferred stock). The capital stock accounts may include one or more classes of both common stock and preferred stock. Generally, the corporation will indicate the par value, the number of shares authorized, and the number of shares issued and outstanding for each type and class of stock. The amount stated in the capital stock account reflects the number of shares issued and outstanding multiplied by the par value per share. In the event the corporation has not set a specific par value for the type of stock, the board of directors must apportion a certain amount of the proceeds it receives from the sale of the stock to the capital stock account. The amounts reflected in the capital stock accounts are intended to act as a cushion for the creditors of the corporation. The rationale is that this money is restricted and will remain in the corporation to be available for payments to creditors, if necessary. However, today par value is typically minimal, often $0.01 or $0.001 per share, and therefore does not provide any significant type of financial protection for creditors.

The second component of the equity section lists the additional paid-in-capital (APIC) account of the corporation. If a corporation sells its stock,

---

[1] Model Bus. Corp. Act §6.40 (2010).

whether common or preferred, for more than the stated par value, the additional consideration received above the par value per share is recorded in the APIC account. In a case where the corporation has not set a specific par value, the board of directors will record an amount in the APIC account that reflects the proceeds of the stock sale less the amount the board attributed to the capital stock account.

The third component of the equity section lists the retained earnings or accumulated loss account. This account reflects the accumulation of the corporation's net income or losses over time. If the amount in this account is positive, it is referred to as retained earnings, and if the amount is negative, it is referred to as an accumulated loss or deficit.

The fourth component that may be listed in the equity section is the treasury stock account. This account reflects the shares of its own stock that the corporation has repurchased and not retired. The amount stated in this account represents the cost to purchase the treasury stock and is shown as a negative balance in the corporation's stockholders' equity section.

EXAMPLE 5.1 STOCK ISSUANCE WITH STATED PAR VALUE

The stockholders' equity section below for Zero Company reflects the following information:

- 1,000,000 authorized shares of common stock, par value $0.01 with 500,000 shares issued and outstanding for total consideration of $2,500,000 ($5.00 per share)
- 500,000 authorized shares of preferred stock, par value $1.00 with 100,000 shares issued and outstanding for total consideration of $1,000,000 ($10.00 per share)
- The retained earnings balance of $3,350,000

Common Stock, $0.01 par value; 1,000,000 shares authorized, 500,000 shares issued and outstanding	$5,000
Preferred Stock, $1.00 par value; 500,000 shares authorized, 100,000 shares issued and outstanding	$100,000
Additional Paid-In-Capital	$3,395,000
Retained Earnings	$3,350,000
Total Stockholders' Equity	**$6,850,000**

- The common stock line reflects the par value of the shares issued and outstanding (500,000 shares × $0.01 = $5,000)
- The preferred stock line reflects the par value of the shares issued and outstanding (100,000 shares × $1.00 = $100,000)
- The additional paid-in-capital line reflects the consideration received for the sale of the common and preferred stock that exceeds the par value per share for each class (500,000 shares × $4.99 ($5.00 − $0.01) = $2,495,000 (common

stock APIC) and 100,000 shares × $9.00 ($10.00 − $1.00) = $900,000 (preferred stock APIC))
- The retained earnings line reflects the retained earnings balance of $3,350,000

EXAMPLE 5.2 **STOCK ISSUANCE WITH NO STATED PAR VALUE**

The stockholders' equity section below for Zero Company reflects the following facts:

- 1,000,000 authorized shares of common stock, no par value, with 500,000 shares issued and outstanding for total consideration of $2,500,000 ($5.00 per share), where the board of directors designated that ½ percent (0.005) of the proceeds received reflect the par value of the common stock
- 500,000 authorized shares of preferred stock, no par value with 100,000 shares issued and outstanding for total consideration of $1,000,000 ($10.00 per share), where the board of directors designated that 5 percent (0.05) of the proceeds received reflect the par value of the preferred stock
- The retained earnings balance of $3,350,000

Common Stock, no par value; 1,000,000 shares authorized, 500,000 shares issued and outstanding	$12,500
Preferred Stock, no par value; 500,000 shares authorized, 100,000 shares issued and outstanding	$50,000
Additional Paid-In-Capital	$3,437,500
Retained Earnings	$3,350,000
Total Stockholders' Equity	**$6,850,000**

- The common stock line reflects the board-designated par value of the shares issued and outstanding ($2,500,000 × .005 = $12,500)
- The preferred stock line reflects the board-designated par value of the shares issued and outstanding ($1,000,000 × .05 = $50,000)
- The additional paid-in-capital line reflects the consideration received for the sale of the common and preferred stock that exceeds the designated par value for the sale of each class ($2,500,000 − $12,500 = $2,487,500 (common stock APIC) and $1,000,000 − $50,000 = $950,000 (preferred stock APIC))
- The retained earnings line reflects the retained earnings of $3,350,000

While the total stockholders' equity for Zero Company remains the same in both scenarios, as the common and preferred shares were sold for the same amount of consideration, the apportionment of the proceeds between the capital stock accounts and APIC accounts differ. In the situation where a corporation has no stated par value for its shares, every time the corporation sells shares the board of directors must apportion the proceeds between the capital stock account and the APIC account.

D. TYPES OF DIVIDEND DISTRIBUTIONS

A corporation that chooses to declare and issue a dividend distribution has a number of options. Dividend distributions can take a variety of forms, such as a cash distribution, property distribution, stock dividend, or stock split. However, the most common type of distribution, and generally the type that is most appealing to shareholders of the entity, is a cash dividend. A cash dividend rewards the shareholders of the corporation by providing an immediate return on the shareholders' investments, versus a stock dividend that simply results in the ownership of additional shares with each outstanding share generally having less value as a result of the stock dividend.

As previously noted, a corporation is never obligated to declare and make a dividend distribution, unless otherwise stipulated in its corporate governance documents or a shareholder's agreement (e.g., preferred stock guaranteed dividend). Simply because a corporation chooses to declare and pay a dividend in one period does not obligate it to pay a dividend in subsequent periods. Additionally, a corporation may pay a cash dividend in one period and choose to pay a property or stock dividend in the next. It is solely at the discretion of the board of directors as to when and in what form a dividend distribution is made, provided the board is complying with the relevant law, as well as any other restrictions or requirements.

1. Cash Dividends

A cash dividend is exactly as its name implies — it is a distribution of cash to a class of shareholders of the corporation. Once the board declares a cash dividend, the corporation becomes obligated or indebted to the shareholders to pay such dividend, and if it fails to do so, the shareholders may bring an action against the corporation to recover the amount of the declared cash dividend.[2]

The date on which the board of directors declares the dividend is known as the "declaration date," and it is at this point that the corporation becomes obligated to make the dividend payment. At the time of declaration, the board will stipulate (i) the class of shareholders to receive the dividend, (ii) the total amount and per share amount of the dividend, and (iii) the "record date" for the dividend.[3] The "record date" is used to determine those shareholders who are entitled to receive the dividend payment. Only those shareholders who are the record owner of the shares on the "record date" are entitled to the cash dividend payment. Typically, the date that is two business days prior to the "record date," known as the "ex-dividend date," acts as the cutoff date for new purchasers of the corporation's shares. If an investor purchases shares of stock on or after the "ex-dividend date," that investor is not entitled to receive the cash dividend

---

[2]Barbara Black, Corporate Dividends and Stock Repurchases §1.2 (2011).
[3]Jeffrey J. Haas, Corporate Finance 287-290 (2014).

payment.[4] This is because it generally takes two business days to settle the stock purchase and sale transaction. Therefore, the investor would not be the owner of record on the "record date." Lastly, the day on which the corporation issues the payment, whether electronically or in the form of a check, is known as the "dividend payment date."

The declaration of a cash dividend has an immediate impact on the corporation's financial statements. On the declaration date the entity must recognize a decrease in its retained earnings account and reflect a liability for the total amount of the dividend. When the cash dividend is paid to the shareholders on the dividend payment date, the corporation's cash account is decreased and the liability is eliminated. The net effect of a cash dividend distribution is recorded solely on the balance sheet through a reduction of the corporation's assets (cash) and stockholders' equity (retained earnings). The declaration and payment of the cash dividend has no direct impact on the income statement.

EXAMPLE 5.3   **CASH DIVIDEND JOURNAL ENTRIES**

Assume Zero Company declared a cash dividend of $100,000 on February 1 and paid the dividend on March 15. These transactions would be reflected in journal entries as follows:

Date	Account	Debit	Credit
February 1	Retained Earnings	$100,000	
	Dividend Payable		$100,000
March 15	Dividend Payable	$100,000	
	Cash		$100,000

On February 1 (the declaration date), Zero Company reduces its retained earnings account to reflect the reduction in equity and creates a liability to reflect an obligation to pay the dividend in the future. On March 15 (the dividend payment date), Zero Company reflects the payment of the dividend through a reduction of its cash account and elimination of the payable.

2. Property Dividends

In addition to paying a cash dividend, a corporation may pay a dividend in shares of another entity's stock, whether a wholly owned subsidiary or an unrelated entity. When a corporation declares and issues a dividend in the form of another corporation's stock, that stock dividend is viewed as a property distribution. The distribution must comply with the state statutory requirements, as well as any other relevant restrictions. As with any dividend distribution, the

---

[4]*Id.*

shareholders will receive a pro rata share of the stock dividend based upon their current percentage ownership interest.

3. Stock Dividends

A stock dividend is a distribution of stock, and the most common type is a distribution of the corporation's own stock, which is a type of non-property distribution. Unlike a cash dividend, which results in the transfer of corporate assets (cash) to the shareholders, this type of dividend does not result in such a transfer. Instead, the corporation transfers additional shares of stock to the shareholders rather than deplete its cash reserves and reduce its retained earnings. While a stock dividend does not provide an immediate cash return to the investor, it gives the shareholder additional shares of the corporation's stock that can be sold in the future for a return. However, as a result of a stock dividend, share value is diluted, as there are now a greater number of shares issued and outstanding.

Just as with a cash dividend, the corporation, through the board of directors, may declare and issue a stock dividend. A stock dividend provides the shareholders with additional shares of the corporation's stock at no out-of-pocket cost to the shareholder. In a stock dividend, each shareholder receives a pro rata portion of the distributed stock based on current ownership, and therefore, each shareholder's percentage ownership interest in the corporation remains unchanged.

The relevant state dividend statutes do not apply to a stock dividend distribution of a corporation's own shares, as such distribution is not viewed as a distribution of property but is instead viewed as a dilution of preexisting shares of that class of stock.[5] In other words, by declaring and issuing a stock dividend of its own shares, the corporation is not making a distribution of its assets or property. Instead, it is simply diluting the number of shares it had previously sold and issued.

In order for the board of directors to declare and issue a stock dividend, the entity must have a sufficient number of authorized and unissued shares to cover the stock dividend distribution. In the event the corporation does not have a sufficient amount of authorized but unissued shares, the corporation must seek approval of the shareholders to increase the number of authorized shares of that class of stock before the stock dividend can be declared and issued.

A declaration of a stock dividend of the corporation's own stock does not have the same impact on the corporation's financial statements as a cash dividend. The accounting treatment will differ depending upon whether the corporation declares a small stock dividend (one that is less than 25 percent of the shares currently issued and outstanding) or a large stock dividend (one that is 25 percent or more of the shares currently issued and outstanding).[6] In the

---

[5]Williams v. W. Union Tel. Co., 57 N.Y.S. 446, 453 (N.Y. 1883).
[6]ACCOUNTING STANDARDS CODIFICATION, Equity, ASC §505-10 (Fin. Accounting Found. 2017).

former, the stock dividend is treated as a traditional stock dividend, but in the latter the stock dividend is treated like a stock split for accounting purposes. In addition to having a sufficient number of authorized and unissued shares, the board of directors must ensure that the corporation holds a surplus (or retained earnings) at least equal to the fair market value of the shares distributed if it is a small stock dividend or a surplus at least equal to the par value of the shares distributed if it is a large stock dividend.[7]

EXAMPLE 5.4 **SMALL STOCK DIVIDEND**

Assume that Zero Company currently has 1,000,000 authorized shares of common stock, par value $1.00 with 100,000 shares issued and outstanding, and that its common stock has a fair market value of $10.00 per share. Zero Company declares a stock dividend of 10,000 shares of common stock (or 10 percent of its currently issued and outstanding shares) on February 1 and issues the shares on March 15. The stock dividend transactions would be reflected as journal entries as follows:

Date	Account	Debit	Credit
February 1	Retained Earnings	$100,000	
	Common Stock Dividend Distributable		$10,000
	Additional Paid-In-Capital		$90,000
March 15	Common Stock Dividend Distributable	$10,000	
	Common Stock		$10,000

On February 1, Zero Company reduces its retained earnings account to reflect the reduction in equity of the corporation based on the fair market value or market price of the shares issued as a dividend ($10.00 × 10,000 shares). At the same time, it recognizes an obligation to distribute the stock dividend based upon the par value of the shares, with the difference attributed to its additional paid-in-capital account. On March 15, Zero Company eliminates its obligation to distribute the stock dividend and reflects the issuance and distribution of the stock dividend by increasing its common stock capital account. In essence, Zero Company's total stockholders' equity balance remains the same, but the individual account balances are adjusted to reflect the stock dividend and the fact that there are now additional shares issued and outstanding.

EXAMPLE 5.5 **LARGE STOCK DIVIDEND**

Assume that Zero Company currently has 1,000,000 authorized shares of common stock, par value $1.00 with 100,000 shares issued and outstanding, and that its common stock has a fair market value of $10.00 per share. Zero Company

---

[7]Haas, *supra* note 3, at 290.

declares a stock dividend of 30,000 shares of common stock (or 30 percent of the currently issued and outstanding shares) on February 1 and issues the shares on March 15. The stock dividend transactions would be reflected as journal entries as follows:

Date	Account	Debit	Credit
February 1	Retained Earnings	$30,000	
	Common Stock Dividend Distributable		$30,000
March 15	Common Stock Dividend Distributable	$30,000	
	Common Stock		$30,000

On February 1, Zero Company reduces its retained earnings account to reflect the reduction in the stockholders' equity of the corporation based on the par value of the shares issued as a dividend ($1.00 × 30,000 shares). At the same time, it recognizes an obligation to distribute the stock dividend. On March 15, Zero Company eliminates its obligation to distribute the stock dividend and reflects the distribution of the stock dividend by increasing its common stock capital account. Again, Zero Company's total stockholders' equity balance remains the same, but the individual account balances are adjusted to reflect the stock dividend and the fact that there are now additional shares issued and outstanding.

The rationale for treating a large stock dividend differently than a small stock dividend for accounting purposes is that the large stock dividend is viewed as more similar to a stock split (discussed below) because it may materially impact the market price of the stock.[8] On the other hand, the small stock dividend is viewed as more similar to a cash dividend due to its small nature — less than 25 percent of the current shares issued and outstanding. As a result, the large stock dividend is accounted for in the same manner as a stock split by using the par value of the stock to reflect the value of the dividend, but the small stock dividend is accounted for by using the fair market value or market price of the stock as the value of the dividend.

4. Stock Splits

A corporation may also choose, through its board of directors, to declare a stock split. A stock split may be a forward split or a reverse split. In either case, a stock split, like a stock dividend, does not require the corporation to transfer any of its assets to shareholders and deplete its cash reserves. It simply requires an update to the corporation's balance sheet description of its stock to reflect the forward or reverse split.

A corporation may use a stock split for a variety of reasons. It may declare a forward stock split (increasing the number of shares issued and outstanding) to decrease the per share price of its stock as a way to reduce the stock's market price so that it is more appealing to a greater range of potential investors in the

---

[8]Accounting Standards Codification, *supra* note 6.

marketplace.[9] On the other hand, the corporation may declare a reverse stock split (reducing the number of shares issued and outstanding) in an attempt to raise or bolster its per share stock price. A reverse split may also be used to eliminate minority shareholders of the corporation.[10]

Neither a forward nor a reverse stock split requires the corporation to make any journal entries. Instead, the entity simply updates the description of the class of stock in the stockholders' equity section of its balance sheet.

EXAMPLE 5.6 **STOCK SPLIT**

Assume that the table below is the current description of Zero Company's common stock account on its balance sheet:

Common Stock, par value $1.00; 1,000,000 shares authorized; 15,000 shares issued and outstanding	$15,000

Forward split example. If Zero Company declares a 10-for-1 forward stock split, the par value per share is decreased ($1.00 ÷ 10 = $0.10), the number of authorized shares is increased (1,000,000 × 10 = 10,000,000), and the number of shares issued and outstanding is increased (15,000 × 10 = 150,000), so the disclosure would be changed to the following:

Common Stock, par value $0.10; 10,000,000 shares authorized; 150,000 shares issued and outstanding	$15,000

Reverse split example. If Zero Company declares a 10-for-1 reverse stock split, the par value per share is increased ($1.00 × 10 = $10.00), the number of authorized shares is decreased (1,000,000 ÷ 10 = 100,000), and the number of shares issued and outstanding is decreased (15,000 ÷ 10 = 1,500) so that the disclosure would be changed to the following:

Common Stock, par value $10.00; 100,000 shares authorized; 1,500 shares issued and outstanding	$15,000

E. LEGAL RESTRICTIONS ON DISTRIBUTIONS

A number of factors must be taken into account when determining whether a dividend distribution can be legally declared and issued. Generally, the most important factor is the relevant state dividend statute. Each state has established its own statute regarding when a corporation can declare and issue a dividend distribution to its shareholders. In order for the board of directors to comply

---

[9]JEFFREY J. HAAS, CORPORATE FINANCE 291 (2014).
[10]*Id.* at 292.

with its fiduciary duties, it must meet the requirements of the relevant state statute before it can declare a dividend. It is the statute of the state where the corporation is incorporated that sets out the dividend distribution requirements.

In addition to complying with the relevant state statute, the board of directors must also take into account and comply with the entity's corporate governance documents and any contractual agreements of the corporation that restrict or curtail the issuance of dividends to the shareholders. For instance, a stock purchase agreement with the corporation's preferred shareholders may prevent the corporation from declaring and issuing a dividend to the common shareholders if a guaranteed dividend payment is due, or in arrears, to the preferred shareholders. Additionally, the corporation's credit facility or loan agreement may impose financial covenants that prevent the board from declaring a dividend even if the state statute requirements are satisfied. If the board of directors fails to take into account these types of potential contractual restrictions regarding dividend distributions, the entity may find itself in breach of a contract.

1. Statutory Restrictions

There are two main dividend distribution tests: the traditional surplus test and the modern insolvency test. Seven states utilize a type of surplus test, and 39 states and the District of Columbia utilize a form of the insolvency test.[11] The remaining four states use a combination of the various dividend distribution tests, sometimes utilizing both traditional and modern concepts.

a. Traditional Legal Capital Tests

Many states still operate under a traditional dividend distribution statute, where the board of directors must evaluate the legal capital of the corporation in order to determine if a dividend can be declared and issued. Under the legal capital theory, the amount contained in the corporation's capital stock accounts, including both common stock and preferred stock, represents its legal capital.[12] These funds are intended to act as a financial cushion for the entity in order to satisfy creditors' claims against the corporation, particularly in the event that the entity dissolves, voluntarily or otherwise. As a result, the funds contained in the capital stock accounts cannot be distributed as part of a dividend distribution.

As an example, Delaware still operates under the legal capital test pursuant to Delaware General Corporation Law §170(a), which is set forth below:

§170 Dividends; payment; wasting asset corporations.
   (a) The directors of every corporation, subject to any restrictions contained in its certificate of incorporation, may declare and pay dividends upon the shares of its capital stock either:

---

[11]Barbara Black, Corporate Dividends and Stock Repurchases §6:15 (2011).
[12]Haas, *supra* note 9, at 280.

(1) Out of its surplus, as defined in and computed in accordance with §§154 and 244 of this title; or

(2) In case there shall be no such surplus, out of its net profits for the fiscal year in which the dividend is declared and/or the preceding fiscal year.

If the capital of the corporation, computed in accordance with §§154 and 244 of this title, shall have been diminished by depreciation in the value of its property, or by losses, or otherwise, to an amount less than the aggregate amount of the capital represented by the issued and outstanding stock of all classes having a preference upon the distribution of assets, the directors of such corporation shall not declare and pay out of such net profits any dividends upon any shares of any classes of its capital stock until the deficiency in the amount of capital represented by the issued and outstanding stock of all classes having a preference upon the distribution of assets shall have been repaired. Nothing in this subsection shall invalidate or otherwise affect a note, debenture or other obligation of the corporation paid by it as a dividend on shares of its stock, or any payment made thereon, if at the time such note, debenture or obligation was delivered by the corporation, the corporation had either surplus or net profits as provided in (a)(1) or (2) of this section from which the dividend could lawfully have been paid.[13]

Under Delaware law, the board of directors may declare and pay a dividend (i) out of the corporation's surplus, or (ii) out of the corporation's net profits for the current fiscal year and/or preceding fiscal year, if there is no surplus.[14] In order to determine whether the corporation has a surplus, the board must determine if the entity's net assets exceed its capital stock account balances, taking into account both common and preferred stock. Under the Delaware statute, net assets are equal to the corporation's total assets minus total liabilities. If the board determines that the corporation has a surplus, the board can declare and issue a dividend up to the amount of that surplus.

EXAMPLE 5.7   **LEGAL CAPITAL DIVIDEND TEST**

Example 1: Assume Company X, a Delaware corporation, has total assets of $2,500,000 and total liabilities of $1,750,000. In addition, Company X has $100,000 in its common stock capital account. Also assume that Company X had net income of $350,000 in the current fiscal year and a net loss of $50,000 in the prior fiscal year. In order to determine if Company X has a surplus, the board must first calculate net assets as follows:

$2,500,000 (total assets) $1,750,000 (total liabilities) = $750,000 (net assets)

---

[13]Del. Code Ann. tit. 8, §170 (West 2017).
[14]*Id.* §170(a)

Then Company X can determine the amount of its surplus as follows:

$750,000 (net assets) − $100,000 (capital stock) = $650,000 (surplus)

In this scenario, Company X has a surplus of $650,000; therefore, the board of directors could declare and issue a dividend up to that amount. Because Company X has a surplus, the board of directors does not utilize the second prong of the legal capital test under DGCL §170(a)(2).

Example 2: Assume the facts were changed slightly so that Company X had total liabilities of $2,750,000 (instead of $2,500,000), making its net assets negative:

$2,500,000 (total assets) − $2,750,000 (total liabilities) = ($250,000)

Without a surplus, the board would have to rely on the second prong of the Delaware test (net profits) to determine if a dividend could be declared and issued. In examining Company X's financials, it had net profits of $350,000 in the current fiscal year and a net loss of $50,000 in the prior fiscal year. Even though it did not have a surplus, Company X could still declare and issue a dividend of up to $350,000 based on the current fiscal year's net profits. It is irrelevant that Company X had a net loss in the prior fiscal year, because the second prong of the test is an "and/or" test that allows Company X to look to either the current fiscal year, prior fiscal year, or both fiscal years to determine the amount of dividend it can declare and issue.

b. Modern Legal Capital Tests

In lieu of the traditional test, many states have adopted the modern test that prevents corporations from declaring and issuing a dividend if prior to, or as a result of, the distribution the corporation would become insolvent. A corporation is considered to be insolvent if it is "unable to pay its debts as they become due" in the ordinary course of its operations or business.[15] In other words, in order to be able to declare and issue a dividend, the corporation must have sufficient assets on hand to satisfy its liabilities or obligations as they are owed.

These types of modern statutes are based upon the distribution rule in §6.40 of the Model Business Corporation Act (1984), which is set forth below:

§6.40 DISTRIBUTIONS TO SHAREHOLDERS
(a) A board of directors may authorize and the corporation may make distributions to its shareholders subject to restriction by the articles of incorporation and the limitation in subsection (c). . . .

(c) No distribution may be made if, after giving it effect:

---

[15]*John T. Callahan & Sons, Inc. v Dykeman Elec. Co.,* 266 F. Supp. 2d 208 (D. Mass. 2003).

(1) the corporation would not be able to pay its debts as they become due in the usual course of business; or

(2) the corporation's total assets would be less than the sum of its total liabilities plus (unless the articles of incorporation permit otherwise) the amount that would be needed, if the corporation were to be dissolved at the time of the distribution, to satisfy the preferential rights upon dissolution of shareholders whose preferential rights are superior to those receiving the distribution.

(d) The board of directors may base a determination that a distribution is not prohibited under subsection (c) either on financial statements prepared on the basis of accounting practices and principles that are reasonable in the circumstances or on a fair valuation or other method that is reasonable in the circumstances.[16]

Under the modern test, the board of directors must determine whether the entity is insolvent or would be rendered insolvent by the issuance of the dividend distribution as part of their fiduciary responsibilities. There are two insolvency tests — balance sheet and equity insolvency. While some states choose to employ only one of the two tests, most states require a corporation to meet both insolvency tests before it can declare a dividend.

i. Balance Sheet Insolvency

The balance sheet insolvency test is a bright-line, numbers-based test. Under the balance sheet insolvency test, a corporation cannot make a dividend distribution if its total assets minus its total liabilities are equal to or less than zero. In other words, the corporation must have total assets that exceed total liabilities in order to make any type of distribution. If the corporation's total assets exceed total liabilities, it can distribute up to the amount of the difference as a dividend. In the event the corporation also has preferred stock, the board of directors must take into consideration any preferential rights or superior liquidation preferences in calculating the funds available for distribution. In those circumstances the formula for determining balance sheet insolvency becomes total assets minus total liabilities minus any preferential rights or other superior preferences. If that calculation results in a positive amount, the corporation can distribute up to that amount as a dividend.

EXAMPLE 5.8 **MODERN DIVIDEND TEST**

Example 1: Assume Company X has $2,500,000 in total assets, $1,500,000 in total liabilities, and a preferred stock liquidation preference of $750,000 (a class with preferential rights upon dissolution). The board could legally declare a dividend distribution of up to $250,000:

---

[16]Model Bus. Corp. Act §6.40(a), (c), (d).

$2,500,000 (total assets) − $1,500,000 (total liabilities) − $750,000
(liquidation preference) = $250,000

Example 2: Assume the circumstances were to change and Company X had total liabilities of $2,000,000 (instead of $1,500,000). The board could not legally
declare a dividend because assets are less than liabilities after accounting for
the preference:

$2,500,000 (total assets) − $2,000,000 (total liabilities) − $750,000
(liquidation preference) = ($250,000)

Even in Example 2, where Company X's total assets exceed its total liabilities,
it still cannot legally declare a divided because that difference, $500,000, is not
sufficient to cover the preferred stock liquidation preference.

(a) Valuation of Assets: *Randall v. Bailey* and Introduction of Fair Market Value

In the 1940 case of *Randall v. Bailey*, 23 N.Y.S.2d 173 (Sup. Ct. 1940), Randall, acting
as trustee for the Bush Terminal Company, brought an action against Bailey and
the other directors of the Bush Terminal Company seeking to recover dividends
declared and paid between November 22, 1928, and May 2, 1932, in the total
amount of $4,639,058.06. Randall claimed that at the time of the distributions
the company did not have a surplus, its capital was impaired to an amount that
exceeded the dividends, and as a result the directors were personally liable to
the corporation for the amount of the declared and distributed dividends. On
the other hand, the board of directors, as defendants, claimed that the company
had a surplus at all times during the distributions that was greater than the
actual amounts reflected on the company's books, which ranged from a high of
$4,378,554.83 at the end of 1927 to a low of $2,199,486.77 in April 1932.

By 1918, the company had written up the value of its land by $7,211,791.72
to its actual fair market value of $8,737,949.02 (historical cost was $1,526,157.30).
Randall claimed that this unrealized appreciation on the land should not have been
taken into account in determining whether the dividends could be declared, or in
other words, that the board could only consider the historical cost, and not the fair
market value, of the company's land in its distribution determinations. Randall also
argued that the company should have written down the cost of its investments in
and advances to its subsidiaries to actual value, which was less than historical cost.

At the time of this action, the relevant dividend statute stated that

> "no stock corporation shall declare or pay any dividend which shall impair its capital
> or capital stock, nor while its capital or capital stock is impaired . . . unless the value
> of its assets remaining after the payment of such dividend . . . shall be at least equal
> to the aggregate amount of its debts and liabilities including capital or capital stock
> as the case may be."

After an analysis of the relevant statute and related case law, the court determined that there was not a single case in the State of Delaware that prevented

unrealized appreciation from being taken into consideration in the determination of whether a dividend could be declared and issued. However, the court stated that if unrealized appreciation was to be considered, then unrealized depreciation should also be taken into account in the distribution determination.

The court ultimately determined that the dividend distributions would have been legal after taking into account both the unrealized appreciation on the land and unrealized depreciation on the investments and advances, because the value of the assets exceeded the total liabilities by an amount in excess of the dividends, and thus there was no impairment to the capital or capital stock of the company.

(b) Modern Statutes and Fair Market Value

As a result of the *Randall v. Bailey* case, many states have adopted dividend distribution statutes that allow the board of directors to take into account the fair market value of the corporation's assets in its determination. The Model Business Corporation Act permits the board of directors to base their balance sheet insolvency determination upon financial statements prepared on the basis of reasonable accounting practices and principles, on fair valuation, or on other methods reasonable in the circumstances.[17] In permitting the board to take into account fair market value of the assets, the corporation can distribute true financial gains, and not just book gains, to its shareholders.

EXAMPLE 5.9   **MODERN DIVIDEND TEST — FAIR MARKET VALUE ANALYSIS**

Example 1: Assume Company B, a corporation in a Model Business Corporation Act state, has total assets valued at a historical cost of $2,000,000 and total liabilities of $3,000,000. It would not meet the balance sheet insolvency test, as its total assets do not exceed its total liabilities.

$2,000,000 (total assets) – $3,000,000 (total liabilities) = ($1,000,000)

Example 2: Assume, however, that Company B's total assets have a fair market value of $3,500,000. The board of directors could declare and issue a dividend of up to $500,000, the amount by which total assets based on fair market value exceed total liabilities.

$3,500,000 (total assets @ FMV) – $3,000,000 (total liabilities) = $500,000

As a result, the board of directors in a state that allows for fair market valuation of assets has broader discretion when determining whether a dividend distribution under the balance sheet insolvency test is legal.

---

[17]Model Bus. Corp. Act §6.40(d).

ii. Equity Insolvency

Under the equity insolvency test, a corporation can only make a distribution if it is solvent and will remain solvent after the distribution. In other words, if the entity is insolvent or the distribution would result in the entity becoming insolvent, it cannot make the distribution. When the corporation is unable to pay its debts and meet its ongoing obligations as they come due, it is not solvent under this test.

In order to determine equity insolvency, the board of directors should undertake an investigation of the corporation, its financial condition, and its operations. The corporation's financial condition as reflected on its balance sheet and income statement alone is generally not enough to satisfy this test; however, the fact that a corporation maintains a significant balance in its stockholders' equity accounts and is operating normally is a strong indication that the entity is solvent.[18]

When determining whether the equity insolvency test is met, the board of directors might take into account a variety of factors. One factor that can play an important role in making this determination is the auditor's opinion letter, if the entity's financial statements are audited. If the corporation prepares audited financial statements, the board should review the auditor's opinion and determine if it is unqualified, qualified, or adverse. An unqualified opinion in the most recent fiscal year, meaning the auditor views the entity as a "going concern," and a lack of any other negative events since the issuance of the opinion are strong indications that the corporation has met the equity insolvency test.[19] In the event that the corporation has received a qualified opinion, the board of directors will need to explore the reason for the qualification. It may be due to a small or isolated deviation from GAAP regarding one issue, which does not prevent the financial statements from fairly presenting the results of the corporation as a whole, or it may be due to a lack of conformity to GAAP, incomplete disclosures, or a scope limitation. In the former instance, where the qualification is minor, it may not be a significant cause for concern. On the other hand, if the qualified opinion is a result of something more significant regarding the corporation's financial condition, the board of directors will need to continue their investigation. In the event the corporation has received an adverse opinion, it is an indication to the board that the financial statements are materially lacking, misstated, or misleading and do not fairly present the financial condition of the corporation. An adverse opinion signifies to the board of directors that it should investigate further the reasons for such adverse opinion in its determination of whether the corporation can legally declare and issue a dividend.

In addition to taking into account an auditor's opinion letter, or in the event the corporation does not audit its financial statements, the board could also examine other factors and information to determine whether the equity insolvency test is met. Some of those factors include (i) whether the corporation

---

[18]*Id.* §6.40.
[19]*Id.*

generates sufficient demand for its products or services to fund its obligations as they come due or mature, (ii) whether the corporation is in a position to refinance any indebtedness that comes due in the short term, or (iii) whether the corporation is facing any asserted or unasserted contingent liabilities that might adversely impact its financial condition.[20] The board may calculate various financial ratios to assess these factors, such as the current ratio, quick ratio, and debt-to-equity ratio (see Chapter 6). Lastly, in those circumstances where it is difficult to determine if the corporation has met the equity insolvency test or the entity is facing financial concerns, the board of directors might consider undertaking a cash flow analysis of the business to assist it in reaching a determination.

iii. Combination of Equity and Balance Sheet Insolvency

Under most modern dividend test statutes, a corporation must meet both the equity and balance sheet insolvency tests before the board of directors can legally declare and issue a dividend. In those states, it is not enough to simply meet the balance sheet insolvency test; the corporation's board of directors must also evaluate the entity's circumstances under the equity insolvency test. Therefore, the board must evaluate and determine that the corporation meets both tests prior to declaring the dividend.

iv. Earned Surplus Test

Another example of a modern test is the earned surplus test. Under this test, a corporation can declare and issue a dividend if it has an "earned surplus." Put another way, if the corporation has a positive balance in its retained earnings account, the board can legally declare a dividend distribution. This allows the board of directors of the corporation to declare a dividend up to the full amount of the entity's retained earnings and thus deplete the entire earned surplus of the corporation. However, the corporation must also take into account any superior stock preferences, similar to what is required under the balance sheet insolvency test, in determining the amount that can be distributed as a dividend.

EXAMPLE 5.10: **EARNED SURPLUS TEST**

Assume Company X has retained earnings of $500,000, a preferred stock guaranteed dividend of $50,000 in arrears, and a preferred stock liquidation preference of $100,000. Company X could declare and issue a dividend of up to $350,000:

$500,000 (retained earnings or earned surplus) – $50,000 (preferred stock guaranteed dividend) – $100,000 (preferred stock liquidation) = $350,000

---

[20] *Id.*

c. Other Dividend Distribution Tests

California, one of the more unique states, utilizes a statute that allows for a dividend distribution under (i) a version of the earned surplus test or (ii) the balance sheet insolvency test.[21] Under Cal. Corp. Code § 500, a corporation may make a distribution out of its "retained earnings," and can declare a dividend up to the amount of its entire retained earnings account provided it retains enough to meet any preferential dividends that are in arrears. In the alternative, a California corporation can declare a dividend if, after taking into account the proposed distribution amount, the entity's total assets exceed its total liabilities plus any preferential rights amounts.[22]

2. Other Restrictions

In addition to the statutory restrictions placed upon a corporation regarding a dividend distribution, there may be other restrictions that impact the ability of the board of directors to declare a dividend. The corporation may have created higher standards as a part of its corporate governance documents, or the corporation may be subject to contractual provisions that limit its right to declare a dividend. The most typical contractual limitations arise from provisions or obligations pertaining to a preferred stockholders' rights agreement or loan agreement covenants.

a. Shareholders' Agreement Restrictions

In their corporate governance documents, many corporations create one or more series of preferred stock that the board of directors can issue in their sole discretion. As a part of such issuance, the preferred shareholders' rights agreement often grants a guaranteed or fixed dividend payment, as well as a liquidation preference. As a result, preferred shareholders are entitled to preferential payments prior to the declaration and issuance of a dividend to the common shareholders. Thus, the preferred shareholders' agreement creates an additional restriction on the board of directors' ability to declare and issue a dividend to the common shareholders. In the event the board declares a dividend without meeting these contractual obligations, the corporation will have breached the contract with the preferred shareholders, who may institute a lawsuit. As noted earlier, many state statutes also require the corporation to consider any guaranteed, but unpaid, preferred stock dividends and any preferred stock liquidation preferences in its common stock dividend determination.

The guaranteed dividend to the preferred shareholders may be noncumulative or cumulative. If the guaranteed dividend is noncumulative, the preferred shareholders are only entitled to receive the dividend if it was declared in that

---

[21]Cal. Corp. Code § 500 (West 2017).
[22]*Id.*

given year. If the guaranteed dividend is cumulative, the preferred shareholders are entitled to receive the dividend every year no matter what year it is ultimately paid. As a result, if the corporation is not in a position to legally declare and issue a dividend distribution for a number of years, the preferred shareholders' guaranteed cumulative dividend will accumulate nonetheless and generally must be satisfied in full before a dividend can be declared and issued to the common shareholders.

The preferred shareholders may also have a liquidation preference. The liquidation preference is a guaranteed payment to the preferred shareholders in the event the corporation is liquidated or dissolved, whether voluntarily or otherwise. In that situation, the corporation must ensure that it maintains adequate funds to cover the liquidation preference payment due the preferred shareholders before it can make any distributions to the common shareholders.

EXAMPLE 5.11 **PREFERRED SHAREHOLDER LIMITATIONS**

Example 1: Assume Company Y is incorporated in a state that utilizes the balance sheet insolvency test, and Company Y has $5,350,000 in total assets, $4,200,000 in total liabilities, a guaranteed cumulative preferred stock dividend of $150,000 in arrears, and a preferred stock liquidation preference of $450,000. Also assume that Company Y wants to declare a common stock dividend in October. In order to determine the amount of common stock dividend Company Y could issue in October, it would make the following calculation:

$5,350,000 (total assets) − $4,200,000 (total liabilities) − $150,000
(preferred stock guaranteed dividend in arrears) − $450,000
(liquidation preference) = $550,000

Company Y could declare and issue a common stock dividend of up to $550,000 in October, assuming Company Y also paid the preferred stock dividend in arrears.

Example 2: Assume that Company Y has the same total assets, total liabilities, guaranteed cumulative preferred stock dividend, and preferred stock liquidation preference, but the guaranteed preferred stock dividend of $150,000 is three years in arrears. In order to determine the amount of common stock dividend Company Y could issue in October, it would make the following calculation:

$5,350,000 (total assets) − $4,200,000 (total liabilities) − $450,000 (three years
of the cumulative preferred stock dividend in arrears) − $450,000
(liquidation preference) = $250,000

Company Y could declare and issue a common stock dividend of up to $250,000 in October, assuming Company Y also paid the preferred stock dividends in arrears. In this scenario, Company Y has to take into account all three years of the preferred stock dividend that is in arrears.

b. Loan Agreement Covenants

Loan agreements often present additional restrictions the corporation must meet before the board of directors can legally declare and issue a dividend distribution. When a corporation enters into a commercial loan transaction, it generally agrees to a detailed set of contractual provisions that govern the transaction and relationship. In particular, the contract may contain financial covenants and restrictions that impact the corporation's ability to declare and issue a dividend even when the relevant state statutory test has been met. One of the lender's rationales for such restrictions is to prevent the corporation from depleting its available cash or cash reserves by issuing dividends to its shareholders and thus not having adequate funds available to meet its loan payment obligations (interest or principal).

A typical financial covenant in many loan agreements restricts the corporation from making certain types of payments, and in particular cash dividend distributions. Many times this covenant contains language that specifically prohibits the corporation from distributing cash to its shareholders through a dividend distribution or through a stock repurchase unless certain financial conditions are met.[23] Those conditions might include a requirement that the corporation not be in default under the loan agreement or that the corporation comply with certain financial restrictions, such as not distributing more than a certain percentage of its net income or retained earnings in the cash dividend distribution.[24]

As a result of the requirements or restrictions in a loan agreement, the board of directors must fully understand the impact that a dividend distribution may have on the corporation's compliance with those terms. The board must ensure that a dividend distribution will not result in a breach of a specific term or covenant of an ancillary agreement and thus result in a breach of or default under the agreement.

F. CREDITORS' RIGHTS

Creditors' rights may arise as a result of a legal or illegal dividend distribution. In particular, illegal distributions give creditors claims against the board of directors, who declared the illegal distribution, as well as the shareholders who received the illegal distribution (in limited circumstances). Creditors' rights in regard to dividend distributions primarily arise as a result of a fraudulent conveyance. A fraudulent conveyance or transfer occurs when a debtor, such as a corporation, conveys or transfers assets or monies for the specific purpose of defrauding its creditors. In other words, the debtor is attempting to shift those assets or funds out of reach of the creditors by placing them into another party's possession. In regard to dividend distributions, there may be occasions when

---

[23]Jeffrey J. Haas, Corporate Finance 180 (2014).
[24]*Id.*

the board of directors declares and issues a cash or property dividend in an attempt to defraud the creditors of the corporation by shifting the assets of the corporation into the hands of the shareholders and thus outside the creditors' reach.

Typically, a fraudulent conveyance through a cash or property dividend distribution by the board of directors is done in violation of the relevant state dividend statutory requirements, and is thus an illegal distribution. As a result, it is the board of directors that is at fault and not the shareholders who receive the distribution.[25] However, if the shareholders who received the cash or property dividend distribution were aware that the dividend was in violation of statutory requirements, such shareholders may also face liability for the fraudulent conveyance. This is often the case when it is a closely held company where the shareholders may also be the executive officers, members of the board of directors, or both, and thus are intimately involved in the day-to-day operations and decisions of the corporation.

Every state, through its business corporation statutes, holds the directors of a corporation jointly and severally liable for the declaration and payment of a dividend distribution in violation of the relevant state statute. Many of these state statutes are modeled after § 8.33 of the MBCA, which states "a director who votes for or agrees to a distribution in excess of what is legally authorized is personally liable to the corporation for the amount of the distribution that exceeds what could have been distributed legally."[26] In the event that a director is held liable for an unlawful distribution, the director may seek contribution from every other director who could also be liable for the illegal distribution and recoup from each shareholder, who was aware of the illegality of the distribution, the pro rata portion of the dividend distribution.[27]

While it would appear that this language opens the door to a significant risk of personal director liability, the director will not be held liable if he can establish that he acted in good faith upon the reliance of advice from other experts, such as in-house or outside counsel, public accountants, or officers of the corporation.[28] Additionally, the director can avail himself of the business judgment rule, which assumes that directors act in the best interests of the corporation, and thus provides a director immunity from lawsuits if it is found he acted in good faith, to protect against personal liability for dividend distributions.[29]

1. Fraudulent Conveyance Laws

In addition to state corporation statutes, fraudulent conveyance laws may also come into play in regard to a dividend distribution.

---

[25]James D. Cox & Thomas Lee Hazen, Corporate Counsel Guides: Corporation Law 479 (2013).
[26]Model Bus. Corp. Act §8.33.
[27]*Id.*
[28]*Id.*
[29]*Id.*

Under the Uniform Fraudulent Transfer Act of 1984 (UFTA),

> "any transfer of property by the debtor for any purpose is considered fraudulent if the debtor makes the transfer (i) with the intent to defraud the creditor, or (ii) without receiving reasonably equivalent value and the debtor was engaged in or about to engage in business or a transaction that would leave the debtor with small or insufficient assets in relation to that business or transaction after the transfer."[30]

In other words, if the transfer of the property places the debtor in a position where it has insufficient assets to continue to operate, then the conveyance will be viewed as fraudulent. Under part (ii) of the test, it is irrelevant whether there was an actual intent to defraud the creditor.

While the debtor, or the members of the board of directors in the case of an illegal cash or property dividend distribution, are liable for the fraudulent conveyance, under the UFTA a fraudulent transfer is not voidable against a person who took the transfer in good faith and for reasonably equivalent value.[31] Due to this language, actions against shareholders turn on whether or not the shareholder took the dividend distribution in good faith (was not aware that it was a fraudulent conveyance) and provided reasonably equivalent value.

2. **Federal Bankruptcy Code**

Under the U.S. Bankruptcy Code, a trustee may avoid a voluntary or involuntary fraudulent transfer by a debtor that was made or incurred on or within two years before the date of filing the bankruptcy petition.[32] In order for a transfer to be deemed fraudulent,

> "the debtor must have (i) made the transfer with the intent to hinder, delay, or defraud any entity to which the debtor was or became indebted to; or (ii) received less than a reasonably equivalent value in exchange for such transfer and (a) was insolvent on the date of such transfer or became insolvent as a result of such transfer; (b) was engaged in a business or transaction for which any property remaining with the debtor was an unreasonably small amount of capital; (c) intended to incur or believed the debtor would incur debts that would be beyond the debtor's ability to pay; or (d) made such transfer to or for the benefit of an insider under an employment contract and not in the ordinary course of business."[33]

As a result, a trustee for a corporation in a bankruptcy proceeding has the power to recover a fraudulent transfer for the benefit of the corporation's creditors. Thus, the trustee may recover an illegal cash or property dividend distribution from the shareholders as part of the bankruptcy proceeding.

In the circumstances where the shareholders were not aware that the cash or property dividend was declared and issued illegally by the board of directors and took the distribution in good faith, such shareholders have a lien or may retain any interest transferred to the extent that such shareholder gave value

---

[30]Unif. Fraudulent Transfer Act §4 (West 2017).
[31]*Id.* §8.
[32]11 U.S.C.A. §548 (West 2017).
[33]*Id.*

to the debtor in exchange for such transfer.[34] However, in those circumstances where the shareholder was aware that the dividend distribution was illegal, it is highly likely that the trustee will be able to claw back those funds or property as part of the bankruptcy proceeding.[35]

Dividend Distribution Problem

Problem 5.1

ABC Company was incorporated in 20XX, and at the time of incorporation ABC authorized 1,000,000 shares of common stock, $0.01 par value, and 250,000 shares of preferred stock, $1.00 par value. Upon incorporation, ABC issued 100,000 shares of common stock for total consideration of $10,000. One year after incorporation, ABC issued another 100,000 shares of common stock for total consideration of $25,000. Two years after incorporation, ABC issued 10,000 shares of preferred stock for $50,000. The preferred stock has a guaranteed liquidation preference of $2.00 per share.

ABC Company's balance sheet at the end of the most recent fiscal year reflected the following information:

Assets		Liabilities	
Cash	$35,000	Accounts payable	$35,000
Accounts receivable	$25,000	Note payable	$80,000
Inventory	$15,000	Taxes payable	$20,000
Land	$75,000	**Total liabilities**	**$135,000**
Building	$40,000		
		Stockholders' Equity	
		Common stock	$2,000
		Preferred stock	$10,000
		APIC	$73,000
		Retained earnings or accumulated loss	($30,000)
		Total stockholders' equity	**$55,000**
Total assets	**$190,000**	**Total liabilities & stockholders' equity**	**$190,000**

A. Utilizing Delaware law and the governing dividend distribution statute, determine the amount of cash dividend ABC Company could declare and issue to its common shareholders utilizing the balance sheet set forth above.

---

[34]*Id.*
[35]*Id.*

1. How would your answer change if ABC Company had Total Assets of $145,000 in the current year (versus $190,000) with everything else remaining the same?

2. How would your answer change if ABC Company had Total Assets of $130,000 in the current year (versus $190,000), with the rest of the balance sheet remaining the same, and had a net loss of $12,000 in the current fiscal year and a net income of $57,000 in the prior fiscal year?

B. Utilizing the Model Business Corporation Act and the governing dividend distribution statute, determine the amount of cash dividend ABC Company could declare and issue to its common shareholders utilizing the balance sheet set forth above. You can assume that ABC Company received an unqualified audit opinion for the past three years and that it is operating in the normal course of business and able to meet its ongoing obligations.

1. How would your answer change if the fair market value of ABC Company's Inventory was $20,000 and the fair market value of its Land was $90,000 at the time of the dividend distribution determination?

C. Utilizing your state's law governing dividend distributions, determine the amount of cash dividend ABC Company could declare and issue to its common shareholders using the balance sheet set forth above. Explain your answer in detail.

Analysis of Financial Statements

A. INTRODUCTION

Financial statement analysis is the process of reviewing an entity's financial statements for the purpose of understanding and assessing that entity's performance. This process allows for the analysis of both past and current performance, as well as provides a basis for projecting future performance. Analyzing an entity's financial statements can provide important information regarding not just the strengths of the entity and its financial condition, but also its weaknesses. This type of analysis provides insight into whether an entity can earn a return on capital, generate cash to pursue various opportunities, or generate sufficient cash to meet its obligations.[1]

Various parties may undertake a financial statement analysis. Owners of a small business may use this type of assessment to determine whether the business is profitable and should be continued. Management of a public company may use this type of assessment to assist in the process of business decisions. Potential creditors of an entity, such as a commercial lender will likely employ financial analysis to determine whether or not the entity is creditworthy. Potential purchasers of an entity may undertake this assessment to determine whether or not to move forward with an acquisition. Lastly, potential plaintiffs may assess the financial condition of an entity to determine if it is economically sound to move forward with a lawsuit. In every one of these circumstances, lawyers may be involved in the process as the legal representative of one of the parties and should have an understanding of financial statement analysis, what its results indicate, as well as its limitations.

---

[1] INTERNATIONAL FINANCIAL STATEMENT ANALYSIS 2 (Thomas R. Robinson ed., 2d ed. 2012).

B. ANNUAL REPORT ON FORM 10-K

The Annual Report on Form 10-K (Form 10-K) is a document required to be filed with the U.S. Securities and Exchange Commission on an annual basis by publicly traded companies or companies that are otherwise required to file pursuant to the Securities Exchange Act of 1934 (Exchange Act). Both Regulation S-K and Regulation S-X of the Exchange Act govern the disclosure requirements of Form 10-K. This annual filing, submitted within a set number of days following the end of an entity's fiscal year, contains a significant amount of information regarding the entity's business, potential risks, management, securities, and financial condition. As a result, the Form 10-K can supplement and edify the results of the financial statement analysis.

The Form 10-K, as a whole, is an informative document, but certain sections offer additional insight when undertaking a financial analysis of an entity. In particular, the risk factors, selected financial data, management's discussion and analysis of financial condition and results of operations, and financial statements and supplementary data augment the information learned through the trend and ratio analyses discussed below.

 ### 1. Risk Factors   *— paragraph form*

As a part of the risk factor disclosures, an entity is required to discuss significant factors that it is facing that make it a risky or speculative investment. Risk factors are not meant to be "boilerplate" disclosures, but instead are meant to be specific to that particular entity, its circumstances, and its industry. Each risk factor heading must adequately describe the risk to be discussed so that an evaluator of the entity can read the headings to the risk factors and have an overview of what is included as a part of that particular risk.[2] In particular, an entity should include disclosure regarding those risks that pertain to its lack of operating history, lack of profitability, financial condition, business, and market for its securities.[3]

The information contained in an entity's risk factor disclosure offers insight into those areas that management believes could be detrimental to the entity. For instance, this section may include information regarding (i) the impacts to the entity's financial position if customers fail to pay their outstanding accounts receivable or customers purchase fewer products; (ii) the effects of competition as a whole and certain specific competitors; (iii) suppliers and the costs of inventory; and (iv) the entity's credit facility, including pertinent financial covenants and restrictions. The information garnered from the risk factors can be read in conjunction with the trend analysis and financial ratio results for a deeper understanding of the entity's financial condition.

---

[2] 17 C.F.R. §229.503 (West 2017).
[3] *Id.*

2. Selected Financial Data

An entity is required to provide selected financial data for the past five fiscal years or as long as the entity has been in business in an easy-to-read format so that an evaluator can readily examine trends in the entity's financial condition and operations.[4] The entity must include financial information regarding its revenues, operating income, net income, net income per share, total assets, long-term obligations, and cash dividends.[5] The entity can also include additional information it believes will enhance understanding of the disclosures or prevent them from being misleading.

The information contained in the selected financial data may be culled from examining the entity's financial statements for the various fiscal years covered. However, the selected financial data presentation brings the information together in one table and presents it in such a way as to allow easier comparison across time. One aspect to keep in mind is that this information does not have to conform to GAAP.

3. Management's Discussion and Analysis

Management is required to discuss the financial condition and results of operations of the entity, generally for the three most recent fiscal years, in the management's discussion and analysis of financial condition and results of operations (MD&A) section of the Form 10-K. In particular, management must address material matters relating to the entity's liquidity, capital resources, results of operations, off-balance sheet arrangements, and contractual obligations.[6] The idea behind MD&A is to enhance the understanding of the entity's disclosures regarding its financial condition and related changes, as well as how the various areas discussed in MD&A might impact future operating results of the entity or cause current financial results to not be indicative of future results.[7]

The information contained in the MD&A section can provide context for results presented in the financial statements and found through the trend and financial ratio analyses. For instance, management will often elaborate on their beliefs as to why the entity's results, such as gross profit, increased or decreased over the accounting periods discussed, as well as why the results may differ from other entities operating in the same industry. Another example of information found in MD&A might be an explanation as to why the entity's revenues changed over the periods discussed. Lastly, management will discuss certain forward-looking events that can be useful in assessing the entity's potential future performance. Of all the sections of the Form 10-K, MD&A is most likely to provide background, context, and explanation for the information learned through an examination and analysis of the actual numbers.

---

[4] *Id.* §229.301.
[5] *Id.*
[6] *Id.* §229.303.
[7] *Id.*

4. Financial Statements and Supplementary Data   *SEC* × *FASB*

An entity is required to furnish audited consolidated financial statements for the parent and its subsidiaries, including supplementary financial information, in this section of the Form 10-K. Pursuant to Regulation S-X, the entity must include a consolidated balance sheet, income statement and statement of comprehensive income, statement of cash flows, as well as information in either a footnote or separate financial statement regarding the entity's stockholders' equity.[8] The balance sheet must cover each of the two most recent fiscal years, and the income statement and statement of comprehensive income, statement of cash flows, and stockholders' equity information must cover each of the three most recent fiscal years. In addition to the financial statements, the entity must include detailed and extensive footnotes accompanying the financial statements.[9]

The financial statement footnotes are a critical component of the financial statements and may explain the black-and-white numbers or contain information that cannot be included on the face of the financial statements themselves. Some examples of information the entity will address in its footnotes include (i) significant accounting policies, methods, and estimates and their application; (ii) information regarding acquisitions; (iii) details regarding the entity's goodwill, other intangible assets, and long-term debt; and (iv) potential commitments and contingencies, items often not reflected on the face of the balance sheet. Similar to MD&A, the financial statement footnotes provide background information and context for the results of the trend and ratio analyses. Many of the line items on the entity's balance sheet and income statement are more fully discussed and detailed in the footnotes.

5. Audit Report

In conjunction with audited financial statements, the auditors issue an audit report or opinion. While audit reports vary slightly, each contains the following: (i) information regarding the financial statements that were audited, as well as the auditor's and management's role in the process; (ii) the scope of the audit, which describes the audit process and sets forth the basis for the auditor's opinion, as well as any limitations; and (iii) the actual auditor's opinion regarding whether the financial statements of the entity are fairly presented in accordance with GAAP.

An auditor will generally issue one of the following types of audit opinions: (i) unqualified or clean opinion (with explanatory language in some circumstances), meaning the financial statements are fairly presented in accordance with GAAP (see **Exhibits D** and **E**); (ii) qualified opinion, meaning there is some type of limitation of scope or the auditor is concerned with certain accounting

---

[8] *Id.* §§210.3-01 to 210.3-16.
[9] *Id.* §10.4-08.

principle applications (see **Exhibit F**); (iii) adverse opinion, meaning the financial statements are not fairly presented (see **Exhibit G**); or (iv) disclaimer of opinion, meaning the auditor is unable to issue an opinion for some reason (see **Exhibit H**).[10]

While the audit report or opinion does not provide any insight into the results of the financial statement analysis, it is critical from the standpoint of knowing whether or not the financial statements of the entity are fairly presented or subject to some type of limitation or explanation.

C. HORIZONTAL TREND ANALYSIS

Horizontal trend analysis is a technique for analyzing an entity's financial statements that provides insight into its historical performance over periods of time. There are two primary methods used to examine the horizontal trends of an entity. The first method examines the change from period to period for specific accounts on both the balance sheet and income statement[11] — for example, computing the percentage change in current assets or gross profit from the first quarter in the prior year to first quarter in the current year or from last fiscal year end to the current fiscal year end. The second method of horizontal trend analysis reflects each item on the balance sheet or income statement in relation to the same item in a base year. For example, if the base year is fiscal year 2014, then the balance sheet or income statement item for each of the following fiscal years is reflected relative to that base year and can be expressed as a percentage or fraction of the base year.[12] Analyzing the trends of an entity can underscore changes that have occurred in the business over time, may provide insight into whether those trends will continue, and in some cases may allow for predictions of an entity's future performance.[13]

In addition to using horizontal trend analysis to compare information on either the balance sheet or income statement from period to period, this technique can be used to compare items from the balance sheet to the income statement to see if growth rates are trending comparatively. For example, are inventory and revenues growing at a similar rate or is one outpacing the other? If inventory is growing at a faster rate than revenues, it might be an indication that the entity is maintaining too much inventory on hand or that sales of its products have slowed.

In order to compute percentage growth over periods of time, the following formula is used:

Percentage Growth = [(current value – past value)/past value] × 100

---

[10]INTERNATIONAL FINANCIAL STATEMENT ANALYSIS 25 (Thomas R. Robinson ed., 2d ed. 2012).
[11]Percentage change = (ending value – beginning value)/beginning value × 100.
[12]Base year comparison as a fraction = comparison year/base year; base year comparison as a percentage = (comparison year/base year) × 100.
[13]International Financial Statement Analysis, *supra* note 10, at 315.

If the result is negative, there was a decrease from the prior to the current period, and if the result is positive, there was an increase.

EXAMPLE 6.1   PERCENTAGE CHANGES OF BALANCE SHEET ITEMS

The following table sets forth the percentage changes over the course of three accounting periods for the selected balance sheet line items.[14]

(Numbers are expressed in thousands)

Balance Sheet Category	12/31/13	12/31/14	12/31/15	% Change from 2013 to 2014	% Change from 2014 to 2015
Current Assets	$1,128,811	$1,549,399	$1,498,763	37.3%	(3.3)%
Total Assets	$1,577,741	$2,095,083	$2,868,900	32.8%	36.9%
Current Liabilities	$426,630	$421,627	$478,810	(1.2)%	13.6%
Total Liabilities	$524,387	$744,783	$1,200,678	42.0%	61.2%
Total Stockholders' Equity	$1,053,354	$1,350,300	$1,668,222	28.2%	23.5%

By examining the above trend analysis, one can see that the entity's current assets increased significantly from 2013 to 2014 (37.3 percent), but decreased slightly from 2014 to 2015 (–3.3 percent). By examining the detailed items in the current assets section of the balance sheet, it could be discovered that one of the main reasons for these fluctuations over time was due to the entity's changes in its cash and cash equivalents account.

In order to compute base year trend analysis, the following formula is used:

Percent of Base Year = (amount in current year/amount in base year) × 100

EXAMPLE 6.2   ANALYSIS OF BALANCE SHEET ITEMS IN RELATION TO BASE YEAR

The following table sets forth the relation of fiscal years 2014 and 2015 to the base year of 2013 utilizing the same amounts as reflected in Example 6.1 above.[15]

Balance Sheet Category	12/31/13 (Base Year)	12/31/14	12/31/15
Current Assets	1.00/100%	1.37/137%	1.33/133%
Total Assets	1.00/100%	1.33/133%	1.82/182%

continued

---

[14]*See* Under Armour, Inc.'s Annual Reports on Form 10-K for the periods ended December 31, 2014, and December 31, 2015, filed February 20, 2015, and February 22, 2016, respectively.
[15]*See* Under Armour, Inc.'s Annual Reports on Form 10-K for the periods ended December 31, 2014, and December 31, 2015, filed February 20, 2015, and February 22, 2016, respectively.

Current Liabilities	1.00/100%	0.99/99%	1.12/112%
Total Liabilities	1.00/100%	1.42/142%	2.29/229%
Total Stockholders' Equity	1.00/100%	1.28/128%	1.58/158%

By examining the above trend analysis, one can see that the entity had 99 percent of the amount of current liabilities in 2014 that it had in 2013, indicating that liabilities decreased in relation to the base year, but had 112 percent of the amount of current liabilities in 2015 that it had in 2013, indicating liabilities increased 12 percent over the base year. However, the entity had more than twice as many total liabilities in 2015 as compared to 2013.

D. COMMON-SIZE ANALYSIS

Common-size, or vertical, analysis is another method of analyzing an entity's financial statements. This form of analysis allows an entity to compare its results from year to year, as well as compare its results against other peer companies. The concept of common-size analysis is to reflect each item, or amount, on the financial statement as a percentage of a base item. This type of analysis is most often used with the balance sheet and the income statement. In regard to the balance sheet, total assets are generally used as the base number; and for the income statement, top line revenue is generally used as the base number. Every other number on the financial statement is expressed as a percentage of the selected base number.[16]

Common-size analysis is a particularly useful tool for an entity to compare itself against competitors in the same industry that are different sizes, whether larger or smaller. By reflecting every number on the financial statement as a percentage of a base number, an entity can more easily compare itself to other companies, as this takes the size of the entity or the dollar amount of its financial statement line items out of the equation. For example, an entity can compare its percentage of long-term debt to total assets to other companies in the industry to see if it is maintaining an equal, greater, or lesser percentage of long-term debt, as opposed to attempting to compare or contrast total long-term debt of $1,500,000 for a small entity to $4,750,000 for a larger entity.

EXAMPLE 6.3 **BALANCE SHEET COMMON-SIZE ANALYSIS**

The following table sets forth the percentage of selected balance sheet line items as compared to the base amount of total assets.[17]

---

[16]Common-size formula = (item/base item) × 100.
[17]*See* Under Armour, Inc.'s Annual Report on Form 10-K for the period ended December 31, 2015, filed February 22, 2016.

(Numbers are expressed in thousands)

Balance Sheet Category	12/31/14	% of Total Assets	12/31/15	% of Total Assets
Current Assets	$1,549,399	74.0%	$1,498,763	52.2%
Total Assets	$2,095,083	100.0%	$2,868,900	100.0%
Current Liabilities	$421,627	20.1%	$478,810	16.7%
Long-Term Debt	$284,201	13.6%	$394,000	13.7%
Total Liabilities	$744,783	35.5%	$1,200,678	41.9%
Total Stockholders' Equity	$1,350,300	64.5%	$1,668,222	58.1%

By examining the balance sheet common-size analysis, one can see that current assets as a percentage of total assets fell significantly from 2014 to 2015 (by 21.8 percent). Additionally, current liabilities decreased and long-term debt remained fairly constant as a percentage of total assets from one period to the next. As noted previously, cash and cash equivalents decreased from 2014 to 2015, which explains some of the decrease in current assets as a percentage of total assets.

EXAMPLE 6.4   **INCOME STATEMENT COMMON-SIZE ANALYSIS**

The following table sets forth the percentage of selected income statement line items as compared to the base amount of net revenues.[18]

(Numbers are expressed in thousands)

Income Statement Category	12/31/14	% of Net Revenues	12/31/15	% of Net Revenues
Net Revenues	$3,084,370	100.0%	$3,963,313	100.0%
COGS	$1,572,164	51.0%	$2,057,766	51.9%
Gross Profit	$1,512,206	49.0%	$1,905,547	48.1%
SG&A	$1,158,251	37.6%	$1,497,000	37.8%
Operating Income	$353,955	11.5%	$408,547	10.3%
Net Income	$208,042	6.7%	$232,573	5.9%

By examining the income statement common-size analysis, one can see that cost of goods sold (COGS) increased slightly as a percentage of net revenues from 2014 to 2015 (0.9 percent), which resulted in a corresponding decrease of gross profit as a percentage of net revenues. This change may be as a result of the increased cost in inventory from 2014 to 2015. Additionally, net income decreased as a percentage of net revenues from 2014 to 2015 (-0.8 percent), indicating that the entity is earning less bottom-line profit on sales in the current year than the prior year.

---

[18] See id.

In addition to using common-size analysis to compare results of the entity during various periods of time, the entity could also compare its results to competitors in the industry to determine how it fared against other companies. For example, it might examine whether other competitors were able to maintain their long-term debt as a percentage of total assets, or if competitors also had a decrease in net income as a percentage of net revenues in those same years, possibly indicating an economic or industrywide impact as opposed to just an individual entity concern.

[handwritten: Do not use a verb / doing first meeting with / owning company.]

E. RATIO ANALYSIS

Another type of financial statement analysis involves the calculation of financial ratios that can provide insight into an entity's financial health at a given point in time. Financial ratios fall into the following broad categories: (i) liquidity ratios; (ii) profitability ratios; (iii) leverage ratios; (iv) coverage ratios; and (v) efficiency or activity ratios. While there are many different ratio options within each category, this section focuses on the most commonly used ratios to assess an entity's ability to operate efficiently and meet its ongoing obligations. When analyzing financial ratios, in order to achieve the most value from the analysis, the results should be compared across the entity's periods of time, compared against competitors, and compared against the industry as whole.

In discussing and calculating the various ratios below, numbers (expressed in thousands) will be used from a public company engaged in a retail business.[19]

1. Liquidity Ratios *[handwritten: Combined Number → in relation to what?]*

Liquidity ratios measure an entity's ability to meet its short-term obligations, or those amounts due in the next 12 months. Liquidity measures the ability of an entity to convert its current assets into cash in order to pay its short-term obligations in the ordinary course of its business operations.[20] The level of necessary liquidity varies by industry and within each company, as every entity is unique in its financial situation and needs. *[handwritten: >1 ... good. industry sensitive]*

a. Current Ratio

The current ratio examines the relationship of an entity's current assets to its current liabilities. The higher the current ratio, the greater liquidity an entity has, indicating that it has the ability to meet its short-term obligations. The lower the current ratio, the more likely that an entity may fail to pay its short-term obligations. A current ratio of 1.0 indicates that the entity has $1.00 of current assets for every $1.00 of current liabilities.

---

[19]*See id.*
[20]INTERNATIONAL FINANCIAL STATEMENT ANALYSIS 326 (Thomas R. Robinson ed., 2d ed. 2012).

A general rule is that a current ratio close to or less than 1.0 indicates an unsafe level of liquidity, as the entity has no buffer of current assets over its current liabilities. A ratio of 2.0 is an indication of a safe level of liquidity, indicating the entity has twice as many current assets as current liabilities. However, the current ratio can also be too high, signaling that the entity is maintaining too much cash and other current assets on hand as opposed to utilizing those available assets in its business operations or as a return to shareholders.[21] The formula for calculating the current ratio is as follows:

 Current Ratio = Current Assets ÷ Current Liabilities

EXAMPLE 6.5 **CURRENT RATIO**

(Numbers are expressed in thousands)

	Current Assets	Current Liabilities	Current Ratio
12/31/14	$1,549,399	$421,627	3.67
12/31/15	$1,498,763	$478,810	3.13

An examination of the current ratio shows it decreased from 2014 to 2015; however, it is still greater than 3.0, indicating that the entity has sufficient liquidity to meet its short-term obligations. While in some circumstances a decreasing current ratio may raise concerns, in this situation the entity remains highly liquid even taking into account the decrease. Additionally, this entity reduced its cash and cash equivalent balance from 2014 to 2015, indicating that it has less cash on hand potentially as a result of utilizing that money in its business operations.

b. Quick Ratio or Acid Test

The quick ratio, or acid test, examines the relationship of an entity's quick assets to its current liabilities and is a more conservative test than the current ratio. Quick assets are those that are most easily converted to cash. As a result, inventory is excluded from this calculation, and in some cases prepaid expenses are also excluded if discernible from the entity's balance sheet disclosures. The quick ratio is often viewed as a more realistic assessment of an entity's liquidity than the current ratio.[22] Just like the current ratio, the higher the quick ratio, the greater liquidity an entity has, and the lower the quick ratio, the more likely that an entity may not meet its short-term obligations. A quick ratio of 1.0 indicates that the entity has $1.00 of quick assets for every $1.00 of current liabilities. A general rule of thumb is that a quick ratio of 1.0 or greater implies a safe level of liquidity.

---

[21]Karen Berman, Joe Knight, & John Case, Financial Intelligence: A Manager's Guide to Knowing What the Numbers Really Mean 177 (rev. ed. 2013).
[22]International Financial Statement Analysis, *supra* note 20, at 328.

The formula for calculating the quick ratio is as follows:

Quick Ratio = [(Current Assets − Inventory)/Current Liabilities], or

Quick Ratio = [(Current Assets − Inventory − Prepaid Expenses)/Current Liabilities]

If inv → cash, current ratio →
Quick ↑

EXAMPLE 6.6   **QUICK RATIO**

(Numbers are expressed in thousands)

	Current Assets	Inventory	Current Liabilities	Quick Ratio
12/31/14	$1,549,399	$536,714	$421,627	2.40
12/31/15	$1,498,763	$783,031	$478,810	1.49

An examination of the quick ratio, shows it decreased from 2014 to 2015; however, it is still significantly greater than 1.0, indicating that the entity has sufficient liquidity in the form of quick assets to cover its short-term obligations. A potential reason for the decrease in this ratio is the fact that the entity increased its inventory from 2014 to 2015 (possibly using cash), and thus its quick assets decreased during that period (less cash and greater inventory), resulting in a decline in the quick ratio for 2015.

2. Profitability Ratios

Profitability ratios measure an entity's ability to generate profits from its resources. These ratios assess an entity's ability to generate earnings as compared to its expenses or costs for a given period. Generally, a higher profitability ratio is better, and particularly in comparison to a prior period or to competitors in the industry.

a. Gross Profit Margin

The gross profit margin examines the relationship of gross profit to revenues. This ratio indicates an entity's profitability from the sales of its primary products or services. A higher gross profit margin may indicate that the entity is able to charge more for its products or services or that the entity is able to produce its products for a lower price, both of which may imply that the entity has a competitive advantage in its industry.[23]
    The formula for calculating gross profit margin is as follows:

Gross Profit Margin = (Gross Profit ÷ Revenues) × 100, where gross profit = revenues or net revenues − cost of goods sold or cost of sales

---

[23]International Financial Statement Analysis, *supra* note 20, at 336.

EXAMPLE 6.7   **GROSS PROFIT MARGIN**

(Numbers are expressed in thousands)

	Gross Profit	Revenues	Gross Profit Margin	Gross Profit Margin (as a %)
12/31/14	$1,512,206	$3,084,370	.4903	49.03%
12/31/15	$1,905,547	$3,963,313	.4808	48.08%

An examination of the gross profit margin shows it decreased slightly from 2014 to 2015. The entity used $0.51 and $0.52 of each $1.00 of revenues in the production of its products in 2014 and 2015, respectively, and thus has $0.49 and $0.48 of each revenue dollar remaining to use for its non-direct business expenses. One potential reason for the decrease in gross profit margin is the increase in COGS expense from 2014 to 2015, which may have been impacted by an increase in the cost of inventory.

b. Net Profit Margin

The net profit margin examines the relationship of net profit to revenues. This ratio indicates an entity's bottom-line profitability, or the amount an entity makes as profit from each $1.00 of revenues. A higher net profit margin indicates that the entity achieves a greater bottom-line profit on its sales. However, profit margin is also directly tied to the industry in which the entity operates, as some industries generally have a higher profit margin (e.g., real estate leasing) or lower profit margin (e.g., grocery stores) as compared to other industries.

The formula for calculating net profit margin is as follows:

$$\text{Net Profit Margin} = (\text{Net Income} \div \text{Revenues}) \times 100$$

EXAMPLE 6.8   **NET PROFIT MARGIN**

(Numbers are expressed in thousands)

	Net Income	Revenues	Net Profit Margin	Net Profit Margin (as a %)
12/31/14	$208,042	$3,084,370	.067	6.75%
12/31/15	$232,573	$3,963,313	.058	5.87%

An examination of the net profit margin reveals it decreased slightly from 2014 to 2015, indicating the entity is turning less of each revenue dollar into bottom-line profit. The entity made a profit of $0.067 and $0.058 on each $1.00 of revenues in 2014 and 2015, respectively. As this entity operates in a retail industry, profit margins are typically lower than in other industries. Potential reasons for the decrease in net profit margin are the increases in COGS, interest expense, and income tax expense.

c. Return on Assets

The return on assets ratio examines the relationship of net income to total assets. This ratio indicates the amount or percentage of net income earned on each dollar that was invested in the assets of the entity. It measures how effectively an entity is using its assets. A higher return on assets indicates that more income is generated from each $1.00 of assets. However, return on assets may become too high and indicate that the entity is not investing enough in new assets for future operations and growth.[24] There are a number of different ways to calculate return on assets. While this section examines the basic calculation, in some cases interest expense is added to net income in the numerator, or operating income (or earnings before interest and taxes (EBIT)) is used in the numerator. In other cases average total assets instead of total assets is used in the denominator.[25] Return on assets is also directly tied to the type of industry and its norms.

The basic formula for calculating return on assets is as follows:

$$\text{Return on Assets} = (\text{Net Income} \div \text{Total Assets}) \times 100$$

EXAMPLE 6.9 **RETURN ON ASSETS**

(Numbers are expressed in thousands)

	Net Income	Total Assets	Return on Assets	Return on Assets (as a %)
12/31/14	$208,042	$2,095,083	.099	9.93%
12/31/15	$232,573	$2,868,900	.081	8.11%

An examination of the return on assets shows it decreased slightly from 2014 to 2015. The results indicate that the entity is generating 9.93 percent (or $0.099) and 8.11 percent (or $0.081) bottom-line profit on its investment in total assets in 2014 and 2015, respectively. As with net profit margin, retail entities generally have a lower return on assets than entities in other industries.

d. Return on Equity

The return on equity ratio examines the relationship of net income to total equity and indicates the amount, or percentage, of net income earned on every dollar of equity invested. Return on equity can also examine the relationship of net income—before taking into account dividends paid to common stockholders and after taking into account dividends paid to preferred stockholders—to equity invested only by the common stockholders' of the entity, which is referred to as return on common equity. While return on equity will not indicate

---

[24]Berman, Knight, & Case, *supra* note 21, at 167.
[25]Average total assets = (beginning total assets + ending total assets) ÷ 2.

the amount of cash an investor will receive for an investment, it is an indication of whether the entity is in a position to generate a return sufficient for that particular investor's risk tolerance.[26] A higher return on equity indicates that an investor can expect to receive a higher return on the investment at some point in the future. One thing to note in regard to return on equity is that this ratio includes the impact of an entity's debt situation, meaning that the more debt an entity has, the lower the return on equity ratio result.

The formulas for calculating return on equity and return on common equity are as follows:

Return on Equity = (Net Income ÷ Average Stockholders' Equity) × 100, where average stockholders' equity = [(total equity at beginning of period + total equity at end of period) ÷ 2]

→ stocks with fixed divide

Return on Common Equity = [(Net Income − Preferred Stock Dividends Paid) ÷ Average Common Stockholders' Equity] × 100, where average common stockholders' equity = [(common equity at beginning of period + common equity at end of period) ÷ 2]

EXAMPLE 6.10: RETURN ON EQUITY AND RETURN ON COMMON EQUITY

(Numbers are expressed in thousands)

	Net Income	Average Equity	Return on Equity	Average Common Equity[a]	Return on Common Equity[a]
12/31/14	$208,042	$1,201,827	17.31%	$1,201,827	17.31%
12/31/15	$232,573	$1,509,261	15.41%	$1,509,261	15.41%

[a] This entity does not have a preferred class of stock, so the results for return on equity and return on common equity are identical.

An examination of the results reveals that return on equity decreased from 2014 to 2015. The results indicate that the entity is generating a 17.22 percent (or $0.172) and 15.41 percent (or $0.154) return on each dollar of equity invested for 2014 and 2015, respectively. One potential explanation for the decrease in return on equity from 2014 to 2015 is the entity's increased long-term debt.

e. Earnings per Share

Earnings per share (EPS) reflects the amount of earnings, or net income, attributable to each share of common stock. Generally when EPS is increasing or growing, it is an indication that the stock price is increasing or likely to increase.[27] EPS is directly related to the number of common shares issued and

[26]Berman, Knight, & Case, *supra* note 21, at 169.
[27]*Id.* at 187.

outstanding, meaning that the more common shares issued and outstanding, the lower the EPS result. If examining the financial statements of a public company, both basic EPS and diluted EPS will be reported. The difference between basic and diluted EPS is that diluted EPS takes into account the effect of any securities of the entity that can be converted into or exercised for common stock (e.g., convertible preferred stock, convertible debt, or stock options).

The formula for calculating EPS is as follows:

EPS = (Net Income – Preferred Stock Dividends Paid) ÷ Weighted Average Number of Common Shares, where weighted average number of common shares outstanding = [(common shares outstanding at beginning of period + common shares outstanding at end of period) ÷2]

EXAMPLE 6.11 **EARNINGS PER SHARE**

	Basic EPS	Diluted EPS
12/31/14	$0.98	$0.95
12/31/15	$1.08	$1.05

An examination of EPS shows that both basic and diluted EPS increased from 2014 to 2015. These results indicate that the entity is earning more for each common stockholder in 2015 as compared to 2014. The increase is tied directly to the entity's increase in net income during 2015.

f. Price-to-Earnings Ratio

The price-to-earnings ratio, or P/E ratio, compares an entity's current common stock market price to its EPS. This ratio indicates the amount of money a common stockholder pays per each $1.00 dollar of net income.[28] A higher P/E ratio is generally an indication that an investor expects the entity to have higher earnings growth in the future.

The formula for calculating the P/E ratio is as follows: *lower the better*

P/E Ratio = Market Price per Common Stock Share ÷ EPS

EXAMPLE 6.12 **PRICE-TO-EARNINGS RATIO**

	Closing Price of Common Stock	Basic EPS	P/E Ratio
12/31/14	$67.90	$0.98	69.29
12/31/15	$80.61	$1.08	74.64

---

[28]INTERNATIONAL FINANCIAL STATEMENT ANALYSIS 349 (Thomas R. Robinson ed., 2d ed. 2012).

An examination of the P/E ratios at fiscal year end for 2014 and 2015 shows that the P/E ratio increased significantly. This is an indication that the entity is expected to continue to grow in the future and to increase its earnings or net income. In essence, a potential investor would pay $74.64 per $1.00 of net income in 2015 versus $69.29 in 2014.

3. Leverage Ratios

Leverage ratios focus on the balance sheet and measure an entity's ability to meet its long-term obligations, or those amounts due more than 12 months in the future. Leverage refers to an entity's use of debt, as opposed to equity, to finance purchases of assets or to finance business operations. An entity borrows money, and thus leverages its business, to increase its potential returns.[29] However, leverage creates risk. The greater an entity is leveraged, the higher the risk of that entity not being able to service its long-term obligations. The two main leverage ratios are debt-to-equity and debt-to-assets.

a. Debt-to-Equity Ratio

The debt-to-equity ratio examines the amount of debt versus equity that an entity is using in its business operations. It measures the amount of debt the entity has for each dollar of stockholders' equity. A ratio of 1.0 indicates that an entity is using an equal amount of debt and equity in its business operations, whereas a ratio of 2.0 indicates an entity is using twice as much debt as equity. The debt-to-equity ratio can be calculated in different ways — using total debt in the numerator or only long-term debt. In some cases the ratio may be calculated using total liabilities, particularly if the entity has no long-term debt.

The formula for calculating the debt-to-equity ratio is as follows:

$$\text{Debt-to-Equity} = \text{Total Debt} \div \text{Total Stockholders' Equity}$$

EXAMPLE 6.13   **DEBT-TO-EQUITY**

(Numbers are expressed in thousands)

	Total Debt[a]	Total Stockholders' Equity	Debt-to-Equity Ratio
12/31/14	$284,201	$1,350,300	.21
12/31/15	$669,000	$1,668,222	.40

[a] Includes current maturities of long-term debt and revolving credit facility.

An examination of the debt-to-equity ratio reveals it doubled from 2014 to 2015. However, the entity is still using considerably less debt to finance its business

---

[29] KAREN BERMAN, JOE KNIGHT, & JOHN CASE, FINANCIAL INTELLIGENCE: A MANAGER'S GUIDE TO KNOWING WHAT THE NUMBERS REALLY MEAN 173 (rev. ed. 2013).

operations than equity (less than half), which indicates the entity is not highly leveraged. In 2015, the entity had $0.40 of debt for every $1.00 of equity. The increase in debt-to-equity is due to the entity's increase of long-term debt and entering into its new revolving credit facility during 2015.

b. Debt-to-Assets Ratio

The debt-to-assets ratio measures the amount of an entity's assets that are financed with debt rather than with equity. The higher the ratio, the more leveraged the entity and the greater the risk that the entity will not be able to service its debt obligations. As with debt-to-equity, an entity may use total debt, long-term debt, or total liabilities as the numerator.

The formula for calculating the debt-to-assets ratio is as follows:

$$\text{Debt-to-Assets} = \text{Total Debt} \div \text{Total Assets}$$

EXAMPLE 6.14   **DEBT-TO-ASSETS**

(Numbers are expressed in thousands)

	Total Debt[a]	Total Assets	Debt-to-Assets Ratio
12/31/14	$284,201	$2,095,083	.14
12/31/15	$669,000	$2,868,900	.23

[a] Includes current maturities of long-term debt and revolving credit facility.

An examination of the debt-to-assets ratio shows it increased from 2014 to 2015, indicating the entity is financing more of its total assets with debt in 2015. In 2014, the entity financed 14 percent of its assets through debt as compared to 23 percent in 2015. The increase in the debt-to-assets ratio is due to the entity's increase of long-term debt during 2015. However, the entity is still maintaining a low ratio and utilizing a low amount of debt to finance assets, indicating it is not highly leveraged.

4. Coverage Ratios

Coverage ratios focus on the income statement and measure an entity's ability to cover payments related to its debt obligations. Like leverage ratios, coverage ratios provide insight into whether the entity can meet its debt obligations. The primary coverage ratio is interest coverage.

a. Interest Coverage Ratio

The interest coverage ratio measures an entity's ability to cover its interest payments with its EBIT (earnings before interest and taxes) and indicates how many times the entity could meet its interest obligations on its outstanding debt with EBIT. A higher interest coverage ratio indicates that the entity is solvent and that it is able to service its debt obligations, meaning make its required interest payments, from its earnings.[30]

The formula for calculating the interest coverage ratio is as follows:

Interest Coverage = EBIT ÷ Interest Expense, where interest expense includes the amounts due on debt obligations

EXAMPLE 6.15   **INTEREST COVERAGE**

(Numbers are expressed in thousands)

	EBIT[a]	Interest Expense	Interest Coverage
12/31/14	$353,955	$5,335	66.4
12/31/15	$408,547	$14,628	27.9

[a] For purposes of this example, income from operations was used as EBIT.

An examination of the interest coverage ratio reveals it decreased significantly from 2014 to 2015 as a result of the entity's increased interest expense due to the increase in its long-term debt obligations. However, the entity could cover its interest expense from EBIT 66.4 and 27.9 times over in 2014 and 2015, respectively. This indicates the entity is extremely solvent and has a low risk of defaulting on its interest expense obligations under its long-term debt.

b. Other Coverage Ratios

Other coverage ratios that can be used to assess whether an entity can cover its obligations are the debt service coverage ratio and asset coverage ratio. The debt service coverage ratio measures an entity's ability to pay its entire debt obligation (principal plus interest) from its bottom line net income. Whereas, the asset coverage ratio measures an entity's ability to meet its entire debt obligation with its tangible assets.

5. Efficiency or Activity Ratios

Efficiency or activity ratios measure how efficiently an entity operates, and in particular, how well it utilizes certain of its assets.[31] Because these ratios use information from the income statement, which covers a period of time, and the balance sheet, which speaks as of a specific point in time, average balance sheet data is used to create consistency and a more accurate analysis.[32]

---

[30]INTERNATIONAL FINANCIAL STATEMENT ANALYSIS, *supra* note 28, at 649.
[31]*Id.* at 320.
[32]*Id.* at 321.

a. Asset Turnover

Asset turnover examines the entity's ability to generate revenues with its total assets. It is an indication of how well management is using all of the assets of the entity to create revenues. A higher ratio indicates that the entity is using its total assets more efficiently or generating higher revenues with every $1.00 of assets.

The formula for calculating asset turnover is as follows:

Asset Turnover = Revenues ÷ Average Total Assets, where average total assets = [(total assets at beginning of period + total assets at end of period) ÷ 2]

EXAMPLE 6.16   **ASSET TURNOVER**

(Numbers are expressed in thousands)

	Revenues	Average Total Assets	Asset Turnover
12/31/14	$3,084,370	$1,836,412	1.68
12/31/15	$3,963,313	$2,481,992	1.60

An examination of asset turnover shows it decreased from 2014 to 2015. The entity is generating $1.68 and $1.60 worth of revenues from each dollar of total average assets for 2014 and 2015, respectively. One potential reason for the decrease could be due to the increase in assets, and in particular, inventory.

b. Accounts Receivable Turnover

Accounts receivable turnover measures the relationship between accounts receivable and revenues. It indicates the amount of time it takes for the entity to collect an accounts receivable as a result of a sale, or how fast the entity collects cash from its customers to which it has extended credit.[33] The higher the result, the more frequently the entity turns its accounts receivable. However, a result that is too high may be an indication that the entity's collection policies are too strict, and a result that is too low could be an indication that the entity is not efficient at collecting on its receivables.[34] In the ideal calculation, only sales made on credit would be used in the numerator, but it is difficult to access that information so, in the alternative, this ratio is calculated using total revenues in the numerator, which includes cash and credit sales.

The formula for calculating accounts receivable turnover is as follows:

Accounts Receivable Turnover = Revenues ÷ Average Accounts Receivable, where average accounts receivable = [(accounts receivable at beginning of period + accounts receivable at end of period) ÷ 2]

---

[33]*Id.* at 323.
[34]*Id.*

Once accounts receivable turnover is calculated, the number of days that sales are outstanding can be determined, meaning how many days it takes, on average, for a customer to pay an outstanding accounts receivable. The formula to calculate the number of days sales are outstanding is as follows:

Days Sales Outstanding = 365 ÷ Accounts Receivable Turnover

EXAMPLE 6.17 **ACCOUNTS RECEIVABLE TURNOVER**

(Numbers are expressed in thousands)

	Revenues	Average Accounts Receivable	Accounts Receivable Turnover	Days Sales Outstanding
12/31/14	$3,084,370	$244,894	12.59	28.99
12/31/15	$3,963,313	$356,737	11.11	32.85

An examination of accounts receivable turnover reveals it decreased from 2014 to 2015, indicating that the entity has turned its accounts receivable a bit slower in 2015 than in 2014. The entity turned its receivables 12.59 and 11.11 times during the year for 2014 and 2015, respectively. This means that the entity collected its accounts receivable an average of every 29 days in 2014 and every 33 days in 2015. One potential explanation for the slower collection time is the increase in the amount of total accounts receivable, meaning potentially more sales on credit.

c. Inventory Turnover

Inventory turnover measures the relationship between inventory and COGS (cost of goods sold), or in other words the ratio of cost of inventory to COGS. It indicates the number of times that an entity sells, or turns over, its inventory over the course of the accounting period, or how effectively the entity uses its inventory. Generally, a higher result indicates that management is effective at managing and utilizing inventory, provided that the entity is retaining enough inventory on hand to meet the demands of its business.[35] A lower result indicates that inventory is moving or selling more slowly, and may be due to inventory that is obsolete.

The formula for calculating inventory turnover is as follows:

Inventory Turnover = Cost of Goods Sold ÷ Average Inventory, where average inventory = [(inventory at beginning of period + inventory at end of period) ÷ 2]

---

[35]KAREN BERMAN, JOE KNIGHT, & JOHN CASE, FINANCIAL INTELLIGENCE: A MANAGER'S GUIDE TO KNOWING WHAT THE NUMBERS REALLY MEAN 180 (rev. ed. 2013).

Once inventory turnover is calculated, the number of days that inventory is on hand can be determined, meaning how many days it takes, on average, to sell or turn over inventory. The formula to calculate the number of days inventory is on hand is as follows:

Days Inventory on Hand = 365 ÷ Inventory Turnover

EXAMPLE 6.18   **INVENTORY TURNOVER**

(Numbers are expressed in thousands)

	COGS	Average Inventory	Inventory Turnover	Days Inventory on Hand
12/31/14	$1,572,370	$502,860	3.13	116.6
12/31/15	$2,057,766	$659,873	3.12	117.0

An examination of inventory turnover shows it decreased slightly from 2014 to 2015. The entity turned over its inventory 3.13 times in 2014 and 3.12 times in 2015. This turnover translates to the entity holding its inventory on average for 117 days each year.

F. OVERVIEW OF ANALYST'S REPORTS

Financial analysts are professionals with expertise in evaluating securities or other types of investment vehicles. The majority of analysts specialize in a particular area of the economy or an industry. There are three main types of analysts: (i) sell-side, (ii) buy-side, and (iii) independent. A sell-side analyst works for a broker-dealer or brokerage firm and makes recommendations regarding the securities those broker-dealers cover.[36] A buy-side analyst works for mutual funds, hedge funds, or investment advisers that purchase securities for their own accounts for funds that they manage.[37] Independent analysts are just that — they are independent and prepare and sell their research reports to third parties, whether a broker-dealer, money manager, investor, or others.

No matter what category an analyst falls in, they are paid to utilize their expertise to prepare a report that makes a recommendation regarding whether to buy, sell, or hold a particular security. Because many analysts are affiliated with broker-dealers or mutual funds, or are selling their reports for a fee, there is an inherent conflict of interest in the information an analyst

---

[36]SEC Investor Publications: Analyzing Analyst Recommendations (Aug. 30, 2010), *available at* https://www.sec.gov/tm/reportspubs/investor-publications/investorpubsanalystshtm.html.
[37]*Id.*

supplies in the report. While analysts are required to disclose any potential conflicts of interest when making a recommendation as to whether a security should be bought or sold, it is wise to approach analyst reports with a degree of caution in any assessment of the entity covered by the report. Some potential conflicts that may arise are the analyst's relationship with the investment bank, various economic and compensation-based pressures to prepare a positive report, and an ownership interest in the entity covered by the report.[38]

Most analyst reports contain the same information and have a similar structure. Generally, the recommendation will appear on the first page of the report and ranges from sell to hold to buy, with different levels of sell or buy (e.g., strong buy or buy). Additionally, there will be key stock statistics, risk assessment, specific financial data (e.g., revenues or earnings per share), and other highlighted information. Most analyst reports also contain an overview of the entity, including information about the market or industry, competition, and financial and economic trends, as well as basic corporate information (i.e., contacts, website, number of employees, number of stockholders, and recent press releases). The report will have a wealth of financial information and analyses, including the results of many of the ratios discussed in the prior sections, as well as other financial ratios and analyses. The report will also analyze the stock price of the entity over time, assess the entity's position within the industry, and highlight other news and related industry information. Lastly, the report will contain information describing its various terminology and ratings, and its required disclosures and disclaimers.

First and foremost, an analyst report offers insight into how those with an expertise view the entity and the value of its stock. For instance, is it an entity that has the potential for significant future success and is rated a "strong buy," or is it an entity that is viewed as having little future value or underperforming and is rated a "sell"? The analyst report provides an assessment of a particular entity and where it fits in its related industry, as well as a significant number of financial ratios regarding the entity over the course of time — often up to five to ten years. This alone can assist an evaluator of the entity in examining financial trends.

While an analyst report should not be the sole source of information that a potential evaluator of an entity relies upon for information, it is a useful tool and one that provides a significant amount of insight. Provided the user of the analyst report keeps in mind whether it is a buy-side, sell-side, or independent analyst report, as well as any potential conflicts the analyst may have in regard to this particular entity, examining the report should be a component of any evaluation of an entity's financial condition.

---

[38]*Id.*

Financial Statement Analysis Problems 6.1 to 6.3

Problem 6.1

Locate the most recent Annual Report on Form 10-K for Nike (Symbol: NKE—May 31 fiscal year end). You can find the Form 10-K a number of ways: Nike's website, the SEC EDGAR database, or Bloomberg Law. Undertake the following analyses of Nike's financial statements:

Part A: Horizontal trend analysis from the prior year to the current year on the following balance sheet items: total assets, long-term debt, and total liabilities.

Part B: Vertical or common-size trend analysis for the prior year and current year on the following income statement items: net revenues, COGS, gross profit, SG&A, operating income, and net income.

Part C: Calculate the following ratios for the prior year and the current year: current ratio, quick ratio, debt-to-equity, interest coverage, and inventory turnover.

In conjunction with the above analyses, briefly examine the business overview and MD&A overview for the entity in its Form 10-K, as well as any relevant financial statement footnote disclosures and the auditor's report.

Problem 6.2

Locate the most recent Annual Report on Form 10-K for Under Armour (Symbol: UAA—December 31 fiscal year end). Undertake the following analyses of Under Armour's financial statements:

Part A: Horizontal trend analysis from the prior year to the current year on the following balance sheet items: total assets, long-term debt, and total liabilities.

Part B: Vertical or common-size trend analysis for the prior year and current year on the following income statement items: net revenues, COGS, gross profit, SG&A, operating income, and net income.

Part C: Calculate the following ratios for the prior year and the current year: current ratio, quick ratio, debt-to-equity, interest coverage, and inventory turnover.

Problem 6.3

Part A: Once the above analyses for Nike and Under Amour are complete, compare, contrast, and assess the results of the two companies.

Part B: Locate an industry analyst report for the sporting goods industry (NAICS: 339920 or SIC: 3949) and use the overall industry information to assess how Nike and Under Armour are performing in relation to the industry as a whole.

Commitments and Contingencies

A. INTRODUCTION

Commitments and contingencies, which are potential future liabilities of an entity, are critical pieces of information for any person assessing or examining an entity's financial condition. Both have the ability to obligate the entity to expend a significant amount of money at some point in the future, but are generally only reflected as a line item on the balance sheet titled "commitments and contingencies," with no associated dollar amount.

A commitment is an actual obligation to a third party created pursuant to a contract that requires the entity to engage in a specific activity in the future, such as purchasing a set amount of raw materials. In contrast, a contingency is only a potential obligation of the entity depending on the outcome of a future event, such as a covered loss under a product warranty claim. In either circumstance, the disclosures regarding commitments and contingencies, whether set forth as a dollar amount on the face of the balance sheet or described in the footnotes to the financial statements, provide insight into future cash expenditures that the entity may be obligated to make.

B. COMMITMENTS

Commitments are obligations pursuant to contractual arrangements between the entity and a third party, and are governed by Accounting Standards Codification 440: Commitments (ASC 440).[1] While the contractual obligation is typically binding on the parties, no goods or services have yet to be received by the buyer in the contract. As a result, the entity cannot reflect the contractual commitment as a liability on its balance sheet (or reflect the purchased goods

---

[1] ACCOUNTING STANDARDS CODIFICATION, Commitments, ASC §440-10 (Fin. Accounting Found. 2017).

as an asset). However, pursuant to ASC 440, an entity should disclose all significant contractual commitments in the footnotes to its financial statements.[2] This type of information warrants disclosure, as once the commitment or contractual obligation is fulfilled, the entity will recognize a liability: the obligation to pay for the goods or services. The footnote disclosure puts third parties on notice that the entity has a future obligation that will impact its financial statements.

In particular, ASC 440 requires disclosure regarding take-or-pay contracts and through-put contracts, which are considered unconditional purchase obligations.[3] These types of contracts provide a means of financing new facilities, machines, or other expenditures.[4] Unconditional purchase contracts require a party to pay specified amounts on a date in the future in return for products or services, even if the products or services have not yet been received or provided.

A take-or-pay or through-put contract is often used in the energy industries. A take-or-pay contract typically requires the purchaser to pay for the amount of the natural resource to which it has committed, whether or not it takes delivery of the resource. A take-or-pay contract allows the purchaser and supplier to manage the risks associated with transactions involving resources that often fluctuate in availability and value. The purchaser is guaranteed delivery of the natural resource at specific times, and the supplier is guaranteed payment for the natural resource. A through-put contract requires the purchaser to use a product or service for a certain amount of time and, like a take-or-pay contract, allows the parties to manage the risks associated with the needed product or services. A through-put contract guarantees the purchaser the right to that product or service for the contracted period of time and the supplier a guaranteed payment for the product or service.

EXAMPLE 7.1   **TAKE-OR-PAY CONTRACT**

Assume Western Corporation enters into a take-or-pay contract with Natural Resources, Inc. to purchase 500,000 cubic feet of natural gas each month for the next 12 months at a price of $13.10 per one thousand cubic feet. Each month, Western Corporation must pay Natural Resources, Inc. $6,550 (500 × $13.10) for the quantity of natural gas it has committed to whether or not it takes physical delivery of the natural gas.

EXAMPLE 7.2   **THROUGH-PUT CONTRACT**

Assume Eastern Corporation enters into a through-put contract with Gas Processing, Inc. to pass 50,000 barrels of oil to be refined into gasoline through Gas Processing each month for the next 12 months at a price of $3.50 per barrel. Each month, Eastern Corporation must pay Gas Processing, Inc. $175,000

---

[2]*Id.* §440-10-50.
[3]*Id.* §440-10-50.
[4]*Id.*

(50,000 × $3.50) for the quantity of crude oil it has committed to process at Gas Processing, Inc. whether or not it processes the oil.

Additionally, other types of commitments that require disclosure include commitments in regard to unused letters of credit, long-term leases, construction of a new facility, pension plan obligations, cumulative preferred stock dividends that are in arrears, and employee stock-based compensation plans.[5]

 An unconditional purchase obligation that is not recognized on the face of the entity's balance sheet must be disclosed in the financial statement footnotes if it meets the following criteria: (i) it cannot be canceled (except in very limited circumstances such as permission of the other party or payment of a penalty); (ii) it pertains to an arrangement for the financing of a facility; and (iii) it has more than one year left in its term.[6] The disclosure regarding the obligation should include the following information: (i) its nature; (ii) the term; (iii) the amount of the fixed and determinable portion; (iv) the nature of variable components, if any; and (v) amounts already purchased.[7]

Airlines are a prime example of entities that often have significant contractual obligations and commitments that are discussed in the financial statement footnotes and management's discussion and analysis (MD&A) of a public entity. For example, in its Annual Report on Form 10-K for the period ended December 31, 2017, Southwest Airlines Co. indicated that it had the following commitments: interest, operating leases, capital leases, aircraft purchases, as well as other commitments. In particular, Southwest had commitments in the total amount of $874 million in 2018, $666 million in 2019, $1.1 billion in 2020, and $7.4 billion commencing in 2021 and extending into the future. However, that future liability, which is quite significant, is not reflected on the face of the entity's balance sheet, as it represents future obligations pursuant to contracts that have not yet been executed or completed. The detailed disclosure regarding these significant commitments is found in the footnotes to the financial statements and in the MD&A discussion.

C. CONTINGENCIES

A contingency, in general, is an event that has occurred but that poses an uncertain outcome for the entity from a financial perspective. Contingencies and the related disclosure requirements are governed by Accounting Standards Codification 450: Contingencies (ASC 450), which replaced and updated the Statement of Financial Accounting Standards 5 (SFAS 5), which previously covered the disclosure of contingent obligations under GAAP. While ASC 450 is the authoritative standard for contingency reporting, SFAS 5 still provides supplemental information that can be utilized to interpret and apply ASC 450.

---

[5] *Id.* §440-10-50.
[6] *Id.*
[7] *Id.*

Pursuant to ASC 450, a contingency is "an existing condition, situation, or set of circumstances involving uncertainty as to possible gain or loss to an entity that will ultimately be resolved when one or more future events occur or fail to occur."[8] One thing to note is that a contingency can result in either a gain or a loss for an entity. While a contingency may result in a gain, such as receipt of a potential damages award for an infringement action brought by the entity, the general rule is that an entity should not recognize the gain before it is actually realized (i.e., payment of the damages award).[9] However, the entity should include disclosure regarding the potential gain contingency, but should ensure that such disclosure is not misleading regarding the entity's ability to receive the gain or award.[10] As a result of the limitations on disclosure of gain contingencies due to the conservatism principle, this section focuses on the various types of loss contingencies that an entity may encounter. Examples of potential loss contingencies include pending or threatened litigation, product warranty or defect obligations, risk of loss from potential catastrophes, environmental claims, and guarantees of indebtedness.

Before examining in detail those items that are contingencies of an entity and subject to disclosure analysis, it is first important to understand that not every uncertainty is a contingency. An entity encounters many uncertainties in its daily business operations that do not fall within the definition of contingency. For example, an entity often estimates the amount of depreciation it should recognize in regard to tangible assets (e.g., equipment) and the amount of amortization to recognize in regard to intangible assets (e.g., patents); however, neither of these, which are only estimates and thus inherently uncertain, is considered a contingency. Additionally, an entity engaged in a manufacturing business generally purchases an abundance of raw materials that it will use in the production of its goods. At the time of purchase, it is highly likely that some of the raw materials will be damaged and thus returned by the entity. However, that uncertainty is not recognized as a contingency of the entity, and instead is reflected as a purchase return or discount. As a result, the first assessment an entity must make is whether or not the uncertainty is a contingency, and in particular a loss contingency, and subject to ASC 450.

1. Loss Contingencies   *recognize estimable and probable losses*

According to ASC 450, a loss contingency can only be recognized if an asset has been impaired or a liability incurred as of the date of the most recent financial statements or financial period.[11] Once an entity has determined that a loss contingency exists, the next step is to go through the process of deciding whether the entity (i) must accrue for the loss; (ii) must disclose the loss, but not accrue; or (iii) must not accrue for nor disclose the loss.

---

[8] Accounting Standards Codification, Contingencies, ASC §450-10-20 (Fin. Accounting Found. 2017).
[9] *Id.* §450-30-25.
[10] *Id.* §450-30-50.
[11] *Id.* §450-20-25.

An entity must reflect an accrual or recognize the potential liability for the loss contingency if (i) the entity determines that it is probable that an asset has been impaired or a liability incurred on or before the date of the financial statements, and (ii) the amount of the loss can be reasonably estimated.[12] While the loss contingency will not be resolved until some point in the future (e.g., a court issues a decision on a lawsuit or an entity pays out on a product warranty claim), the entity must still accrue for and recognize the potential loss or liability in order to provide accurate (and not misleading) information in its financial statements.[13]

a. Probability Determination

probable.
reasonably possible
remote

Under the two-part test set forth above, the first determination that the entity must make is whether the loss rises to the level of probable, which is a matter of opinion. There are three levels of potential probability in regard to loss contingencies: (i) probable, which means the odds of the future event occurring are likely; (ii) reasonably possible, which means the odds of the future event occurring are greater than remote but less than likely; and (iii) remote, which means the odds of the future event occurring are slight.[14] What should be evident from these limited definitions and guidelines regarding probability is that the entity (and its advisers) must make a judgment call as to the loss contingency's level of probability. Only if the loss contingency rises to the level of probable and falls within the financial statement timing limitations (discussed below) can the entity proceed to the next step of determining if that loss can be reasonably estimated and thus accrued for or reflected on the current financial statements. If the contingency reaches one of the lesser probability thresholds—reasonably possible or remote—the entity should still assess if it should make any type of disclosure in its footnotes, but the entity will not be in a position to accrue for the potential loss in its financial statements since it failed part one of the test, meaning the loss was not deemed probable.

b. Timing Determination

The next piece of the assessment, once the entity has determined the probability level, is to verify whether the loss contingency was incurred on or before the date of the financial statements, as well as when the loss contingency was known. If the loss contingency resulted from an action or impairment that predated the financial statements, the entity should include the proper accrual or disclosure in those financial statements, assuming the entity had knowledge of the loss contingency prior to the filing or issuance of those financial statements.

If the potential loss contingency resulted from an action that occurred after the date of the financial statements, and the entity had knowledge of the loss contingency prior to the filing or issuance of those financial statements,

---

[12]*Id.*
[13]*Id.*
[14]*Id.*

the entity should not reflect an accrual, as that event did not occur during the accounting period. However, depending on the nature of the loss contingency (probability level and reasonably estimable), the entity may choose to disclose the potential loss contingency in its footnotes to prevent its financial statements from being misleading.[15]

If the loss contingency resulted from an action or impairment that pre-dated the financial statements, but was not known prior to the issuance or filing date of the financial statements, the entity is not in a position to make any accrual or disclosure regarding the contingency, as the financial statements have already been issued or filed. In that event, the entity should appropriately assess and address the loss contingency in its next set of financial statements or determine if the issued financial statements should be amended and restated.

EXAMPLE 7.3   **TIMING AND KNOWLEDGE OF LOSS CONTINGENCY**

This diagram sets forth the timeline for a loss contingency event that occurred during the current fiscal quarter, and for purposes of this example assume the entity determined that the loss contingency is probable, meaning it is "likely" to occur.

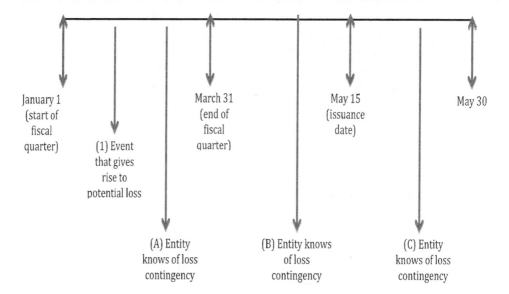

For this discussion, the event that gave rise to the loss contingency (1) occurred during the current fiscal quarter, sometime between January 1 and March 31. If the entity is aware of the loss contingency event (1) during the fiscal quarter (A), the entity must disclose and accrue, if a reasonable estimate can be made. If the entity becomes aware of the loss contingency event (1) after

---

[15]*Id.* §450-20-55.

the end of the fiscal quarter, but prior to the financial statements issuance date (B), the entity must disclose and accrue, if a reasonable estimate can be made. If the entity becomes aware of the loss contingency event (1) after the financial statements issuance date (C), the entity will neither disclose nor accrue as those financial statements have already been issued and will address the contingency in the next set of quarterly financial statements.

EXAMPLE 7.4   TIMING AND KNOWLEDGE OF LOSS CONTINGENCY

This diagram sets forth the timeline for a loss contingency event that occurred after the close of the current fiscal quarter, and for purposes of this example assume the entity determined that the loss contingency is probable, meaning it is "likely" to occur.

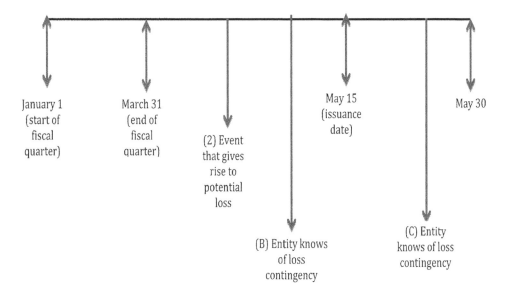

For this discussion, the event that gave rise to the loss contingency (2) occurred after the end of the current fiscal quarter, sometime between March 31 and May 15, but prior to the issuance date of May 15. If the entity becomes aware of the loss contingency event (2) after the end of the fiscal quarter, but prior to the financial statements issuance date (B), the entity should consider whether to disclose, but cannot accrue, as the event did not pertain to the current fiscal quarter. If the entity becomes aware of the loss contingency event (2) after the financial statements issuance date (C), the entity will neither disclose nor accrue, as those financial statements have already been issued and the loss contingency does not pertain to the current fiscal quarter. Instead, the entity will address the contingency in the next set of quarterly financial statements.

EXAMPLE 7.5 **TIMING AND KNOWLEDGE OF LOSS CONTINGENCY**

This diagram sets forth the timeline for a loss contingency event that occurred after the close of the current fiscal quarter, as well as after the issuance of the quarterly financial statements, and for purposes of this example assume the entity determined the loss contingency is probable, meaning it is "likely" to occur.

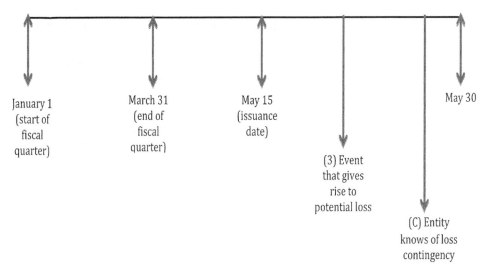

For this discussion, the event that gave rise to the loss contingency (3) occurred after the current fiscal quarter, sometime between May 16 and May 30, and after the financial statements issuance date of May 15. If the entity becomes aware of the loss contingency (3) after the financial statements issuance date (C), the entity will do nothing, as those financial statements have already been issued and the loss contingency does not pertain to the current fiscal quarter. Instead, the entity will address the contingency in the next set of quarterly financial statements.

c. Reasonably Estimable Determination

The second part of the test under ASC 450 deals with whether the loss can be reasonably estimated. An entity must assess whether the dollar value of the loss associated with the contingency can be reasonably estimated, and similar to the level of probability assessment, this is a judgment that must be made by the entity and its advisers. An entity need not determine a fixed or specific amount of the potential loss for it to be considered reasonably estimable. Instead, if the entity can specify a range in value for the loss it might suffer, the loss contingency is reasonably estimable and the entity can make an accrual for that potential future loss.[16] The identification of a range provides sufficient evidence

---

[16]*Id.* §450-20-25.

Rule of Consorvatism.

that the entity may incur a loss, and so the entity must then determine the most appropriate amount to accrue.[17] In the event that the entity is not able to identify the most appropriate amount in the range, the entity should accrue the low end of the range and make adequate disclosure in its financial statement footnotes regarding the potential maximum exposure for such loss contingency.[18] As the loss contingency matter progresses, the entity should update both its accrual and disclosure to accurately reflect the current status of the contingency.

In the event that the entity cannot make a reasonable estimate of the loss, whether a specified dollar value or range, it does not meet the two-part test and cannot accrue for the loss on its balance sheet. However, if the loss contingency is probable and thus meets the probability requirement, the entity must still provide adequate disclosure in its financial statement footnotes regarding the loss contingency. If the loss is only reasonably possible, the entity may still provide disclosure in its financial statements depending on its overall assessment of the loss contingency and its potential impact on the entity and its financial position.

2. Type of Disclosures

Once an entity has analyzed the loss contingency under the two-part test and assessed the probability and timing, as well as whether the loss can be reasonably estimated, it must next determine the information it should disclose in conjunction with its financial statements and footnotes. The choice of whether to reflect no information, to only disclose in a footnote, or to both accrue and disclose hinges on the results of the two-part test.

a. Loss Contingency Is Probable and Timing Is Met

In the case where the entity has determined that the loss contingency is probable and falls within the timing limitations, the entity must do the following: (i) if the loss can be reasonably estimated, the entity must reflect an accrual for the loss and include additional disclosure in the financial statement footnotes, including listing the estimated maximum amount of the loss if a best estimate within the range or the low end of the range is used for determining the accrual, and (ii) if the loss cannot be reasonably estimated, the entity should include disclosure in the financial statement footnotes regarding the potential loss contingency and that a reasonable estimate of the loss is not yet feasible, and the entity should reflect an accrual once the loss becomes reasonably estimable.[19]

b. Loss Contingency Is Reasonably Possible and Timing Is Met

In the scenario where the entity has determined that the loss contingency is reasonably possible and falls within the timing limitations, the entity should

---

[17]*Id.* §450-20-30.
[18]*Id.*
[19]*Id.* §450-20-50.

likely include disclosure in its financial statement footnotes regarding the potential loss and an estimate of the amount, whether a specified value or range of values, if one can be determined.[20] However, since the loss is not probable, the entity cannot reflect an accrual.

c. Loss Contingency Is Remote and Timing Is Met

In the case where the entity has determined that the loss contingency is remote and falls within the timing limitations, the entity is not required to accrue or make disclosures regarding that remote loss contingency.[21]

d. Loss Contingency Is Unasserted

Lastly, in the event that the claim or assessment is not yet asserted, the entity is not required to make any disclosure regarding the potential loss contingency unless the entity determines it is probable that the claim will be asserted and that the outcome has a reasonable chance of being unfavorable.[22]

i. Disclosure Generally

In the case of publicly reporting companies, the SEC suggests that the entity should pay particular attention to its disclosure obligations pursuant to Items 301 (Selected Financial Data) and 303 (MD&A) of Regulation S-K.[23] The disclosures should allow a reader to sufficiently understand the scope of the potential loss contingencies and management's rationale for its estimates.[24] Additionally, the disclosure should include discussion of potential legal fees and costs; exposure to additional losses; availability of insurance, indemnification, or other contributions; and other relevant information.[25]

3. Types of Potential Loss Contingencies

As noted at the start of this chapter, there are many different types of loss contingencies. These loss contingencies range from the potential loss or damage due to a catastrophic event such as a fire or flood, a guarantee of indebtedness of a third party, an obligation pursuant to a standby letter of credit, a product warranty claim, pending or threatened litigation, or a potential environmental liability. This section addresses several specific types of potential loss contingencies — those that may arise as a result of pending or threatened litigation, a guarantee, a product warranty claim, or an environmental liability.

---

[20] *Id.*
[21] *Id.* §450-20-25.
[22] *Id.* §450-20-50.
[23] SEC Staff Accounting Bull. No. 5, S.E.C. Rel. No. SAB-5 (Nov. 18, 2014).
[24] *Id.*
[25] *Id.*

a. Litigation

Pending or threatened litigation is a potential loss contingency that many entities face at some point in their existence, if not regularly. As a result, it is crucial for lawyers to understand the circumstances that may require an entity, as a client, to recognize a liability or provide disclosure in their financial statements and footnotes regarding such events. Like all potential loss contingencies, and as previously discussed, the entity must assess the probability level of the litigation, whether the event that gave rise to the litigation occurred within the designated timing limitations, and whether a reasonable estimate of the potential loss can be determined. In addition, the entity must also determine if the potential litigation matter will result in a material or immaterial loss to the entity.[26]

In the circumstance where the two-part test is met, if the potential litigation results from an event that occurred during the most recent financial statement period and the entity knows about it prior to the issuance or filing of the financial statements, it will have to make the appropriate accrual and disclosure. On the other hand, if the litigation is as a result of an event that occurred after the most recent financial statement period and the entity knows about it prior to the issuance or filing of the financial statements, the entity cannot make an accrual, as that would result in misleading financial statements. However, in this circumstance the entity should provide adequate disclosure in the financial statement footnotes. Generally, unless the probability of the potential litigation is remote, or unless the potential loss is immaterial, the entity will likely make some type of disclosure and/or accrual in its financial statements for the period.[27]

i. Probability Assessment in Litigation Context

In assessing probability in regard to litigation, the entity should take into account all relevant facts and circumstances, including the following information, if available or relevant:

(i) the type of litigation or claim (i.e., a small claim by a single plaintiff versus a large claim by a single plaintiff versus a class action suit);

(ii) the progress and status of the case (i.e., threatened, action filed, discovery under way, motion to dismiss denied, trial date set, etc.);

(iii) the opinion of the entity's lawyers, both outside and inside legal counsel;

(iv) the opinion of the entity's other advisers (e.g., executive officers, board of directors, and other experts);

(v) the entity's experiences with similar matters (i.e., whether the entity has faced similar actions and, if so, what the outcomes and the entity's approach were in those matters);

---

[26]ACCOUNTING STANDARDS CODIFICATION, Contingencies, ASC §450-20-55 (Fin. Accounting Found. 2017).
[27]Id. §450-20.

[handwritten: ⋈ ✦]

(vi) other entities' experiences with similar matters (i.e., whether other similarly situated entities have faced these types of actions and, if so, what the outcomes and the entities' approaches were); and

(vii) management's intended course of action (i.e., try to settle the matter, engage in full-blown litigation of the matter, etc.).[28] → *discuss internally but no need to lay out full strategy*

[handwritten margin: *In real world, disclosure of litigation may impact the outcome of the outcome of litigation.*]

The assessment of whether to disclose threatened litigation or unasserted claims is even more complicated. In that situation, the entity must determine the probability of whether the lawsuit will be filed and initiated or the claim asserted, as well as whether it will bring about an unfavorable outcome.[29] If the entity determines it is probable that the lawsuit will be filed or claim asserted, it must then assess whether the outcome of such lawsuit or the claim will be negative, or unfavorable, to the entity.[30] If the outcome is deemed to be potentially unfavorable, the entity must reasonably estimate the potential loss, if it can do so. If the loss can be estimated, the entity should accrue for the potential loss, and if the loss cannot be estimated, the entity should provide disclosure regarding the potential loss.

In many instances when a loss contingency concerns pending or threatened litigation, even if the entity concludes a loss is probable, it often cannot make a reasonable estimate of the potential loss. This is especially true in regard to a matter that has yet to be filed, is in the early stages of litigation, or is complex litigation. As a result, even though the entity cannot accrue for the potential litigation loss contingency, it should make adequate disclosure in its financial statement footnotes (as well as in other areas of the Form 10-K if a publicly reporting company). Additionally, as the litigation matter progresses, the entity should update its disclosure, and at the point in time it can make a reasonable estimate of the loss, it should record the appropriate accrual.

EXAMPLE 7.6 **POTENTIAL LITIGATION LOSS CONTINGENCY SCENARIOS**

For purposes of the following examples, assume that Acme & Company is a small hardware store that has an obligation to prepare audited financial statements. Acme's fiscal year end is June 30, and it must issue its quarterly financial statements no later than one month after quarter end (i.e., by October 31, January 31, and April 30) and its year-end financial statements no later than August 31. Acme owns the building and land where it operates its store, including the adjacent parking lot.

Scenario 1: Acme is currently preparing its second quarter financial statements (for the period ended December 31). A customer slipped and fell in Acme's parking lot on November 15, and Acme is aware of the incident. The customer has not contacted Acme regarding the fall. In this scenario, Acme is dealing with an unasserted claim, as the customer has simply fallen and Acme is aware of the

[28]*Id.* §450-20-55.
[29]*Id.*
[30]*Id.*

accident, but there is no threatened or pending lawsuit. In order to determine the appropriate course of action, Acme must first assess whether it is probable that the customer will make a claim or file a lawsuit against it for the accident. In this case, Acme believes it is probable that the customer will file a lawsuit, as something similar has happened to Acme on three previous occasions. Next, Acme must assess the likelihood of an unfavorable outcome. Acme is unable to assess whether the outcome will be unfavorable, as prior lawsuits for similar accidents have resulted in both favorable and unfavorable outcomes for Acme, so Acme believes it is only reasonably possible that the outcome will be unfavorable at this point. As a result, Acme cannot accrue for this potential loss, as it is only reasonably possible (not probable), but it should include disclosure in its financial statement footnotes regarding the potential unasserted claim or lawsuit.

Scenario 2: Acme is currently preparing its third quarter financial statements (for the period ended March 31). On February 14 the customer filed a lawsuit, and discovery is under way. In order to determine the appropriate course of action, Acme must assess whether it is probable that a liability has been incurred. Based upon what Acme has learned through the discovery phase, what its outside counsel has indicated, and what happened in similar lawsuits faced previously, Acme believes it is probable that it will incur a loss as a result of this matter. Since Acme has determined a loss is probable, it must now assess whether it can make a reasonable estimate of the loss. Acme indicates it is not able to make a reasonable estimate at this point in time, as it is too early in the litigation; this matter differs from previous lawsuits, as this customer suffered more extreme and long-term injuries; and its outside counsel is not able to provide a range of potential damages. As a result, Acme cannot accrue for this potential loss, even though it rises to the level of probable, because no reasonable estimate can be made. Instead, Acme should update the disclosure in its financial statement footnotes regarding the fact that the unasserted claim is now a pending lawsuit, including the fact that it is not yet able to estimate the potential loss.

Scenario 3: Acme is currently preparing its year-end financial statements (for the year ended June 30). On June 15, Acme's outside counsel suggested that Acme offer a settlement in the amount of $185,000 to the customer. Acme extended the settlement offer on June 23, but the customer indicated he will not accept a settlement for less than $295,000. Acme is currently considering whether to increase its settlement offer. Acme already determined (Scenario 2) that it is probable that it will incur a loss as a result of this matter, but could not previously make a reasonable estimate. However, now Acme has offered a proposed settlement of $185,000 and the customer has indicated he will settle for $295,000. As a result, Acme has a range of the potential loss ($185,000 to $295,000) and can make a reasonable estimate. Acme should now accrue for this potential loss on its financial statements, and if Acme cannot pinpoint the exact amount of the loss within the range, it should accrue the low end of the range ($185,000) as a liability and recognize that amount as an expense. Acme should also update the disclosure in its financial statement footnotes regarding the reasonable estimate and the fact that the loss may go higher.

Other gains and losses

 JOURNAL ENTRY REFLECTING ACCRUAL OF CONTINGENT LIABILITY

Date	Account	Debit	Credit
June 23	Legal Expense	$185,000	
	Accrued Liability (Contingency)		$185,000

Scenario 4: Acme is currently preparing its first quarter financial statements (for the period ended September 30). On September 9, Acme and the customer came to an agreement and the matter was settled for $240,000, the customer signed a release of liability, and Acme sent the settlement funds. As a result, the pending litigation has concluded, and Acme should reflect the payment of $240,000, including the elimination of the prior accrued liability of $185,000, and the recognition of the additional $55,000 expense to Acme: the amount paid of $240,000 less the previously recognized legal expense of $185,000. Acme should also update the disclosure in its financial statement footnotes to reflect that the case was settled and the amount of the final settlement.

 JOURNAL ENTRY REFLECTING PAYMENT OF CONTINGENT LIABILITY

Date	Account	Debit	Credit
September 9	Legal Expense	$55,000	
	Accrued Liability (Contingency)	$185,000	
	Cash		$240,000

b. Guarantees

A contractual guarantee requires the guarantor to make some type of payment to the party that is provided with the guarantee in the event of certain circumstances. The circumstances that might give rise to the obligation range from a change in a foreign currency exchange rate, to another party's failure to perform an obligation, to a specific event that triggers a payment.[31]

Pursuant to GAAP, an entity previously had to provide disclosure regarding both direct and indirect guarantees of the indebtedness of another party in its financial statements, but did not have to recognize a liability. However, ASC 460: Guarantees provided clarification about reporting guarantees, which resulted in changes to the disclosure and recognition requirements. According to ASC 460, a guarantee has two distinct obligations: (i) the potential obligation to make a future payment if the third party does not perform (the contingent obligation), and (ii) the obligation to be ready to perform during the entire time frame of the guarantee (the noncontingent obligation).[32] The entity must recognize a liability for the fair value of the noncontingent portion of the guarantee upon its commencement (e.g., execution of the contract), and in some cases, the entity must also recognize a liability for the contingent portion of

[31] ACCOUNTING STANDARDS CODIFICATION, Guarantees, ASC §460-10-15 (Fin. Accounting Found. 2017).
[32] *Id.* §460-10-25.

the guarantee.[33] The contingent portion is analyzed under the same guidelines as other potential loss contingencies. If the contingent portion of the guarantee is determined to have a probability level of reasonably possible or remote, the guarantor will not reflect a liability. However, if the contingent portion is probable and can be reasonably estimated, the guarantor must recognize a liability.[34] In that instance, the entity will recognize the greater of the fair value of the contingent portion of the guarantee or the estimate reached under the guidance of ASC §450-20.[35]

EXAMPLE 7.7 **GUARANTEE**

Assume that Alpha Corporation agrees to act as a guarantor for a loan in the amount of $250,000 to its 51 percent owned subsidiary, Sub Corporation, on June 15. Alpha Corporation undertook a loss contingency analysis and as of June 15 does not believe that Sub Corporation will fail to make any required payments pursuant to its commercial loan. As a result, Alpha Corporation cannot accrue, as the loss contingency is not probable and Alpha Corporation may or may not choose to make disclosure in its financial statement footnotes.

c. Product Warranties

Product warranties are a distinct type of guarantee. In general, a warranty is an obligation created as a result of the sale of goods or services that may require some type of additional performance by the seller of the warranty after the sale of the good or completion of the service.[36] The product warranty may be included in the sales price of the good or service or may be sold as a separate stand-alone product. Because it is uncertain whether a buyer of the good or service will make a claim pursuant to the product warranty, it is considered a contingency and is thus evaluated under the guidance of ASC §450-20 in the same manner that other loss contingencies are evaluated.[37] In other words, the entity must assess the level of probability of a future claim under the warranty and if that future claim is reasonably estimable. When assessing whether disclosure and/or an accrual should be made for a product warranty, the entity may make the assessment for each individual product warranty or for groups of similar product warranties.[38]

If an entity determines it is probable that a future claim will arise under the warranty, it must then make a determination of a reasonable estimate for that claim. The entity can use its own past experiences in reaching an estimate or may rely on experiences and estimates of other companies in the same or similar type

---

[33]*Id.*
[34]*Id.* §460-10-30.
[35]*Id.*
[36]*Id.* §460-10-20.
[37]*Id.* §460-10-25.
[38]*Id.*

of business.[39] If the entity finds itself in a position where it cannot reasonably estimate the potential loss, or future warranty claim, or if it cannot adequately narrow the range of the loss, the entity should consider whether it is in a position to recognize the sale as revenue.[40] The rationale is that if the entity cannot estimate the potential loss it may incur as a result of the sale of the good or service that comes with a warranty, it may ultimately lose the entire value of the sale; thus it would be misleading to recognize the revenue for that sale. In this scenario, the entity should refrain from recognizing the revenue for the sale until a point in time where it can reasonably estimate the potential loss under the warranty.[41]

EXAMPLE 7.8 **PRODUCT WARRANTY**

Assume that Southern Corporation sells 5,000 microwave ovens per year at a cost of $150 each, every microwave is sold with a one-year warranty, and Southern Corporation requires that warranty claims must be submitted within 90 days of the claim event. Based on past experience, Southern Corporation believes that 1 percent of the microwaves sold result in a product warranty claim during year 1 at an average cost of $15.00. Since this contingent liability is probable and can be reasonably estimated, Southern Corporation should accrue for the potential liability and recognize the expense.

Southern Corporation would calculate the potential warranty expense for year 1 as follows: 5,000 microwaves × 1% = 50 microwaves that are estimated to require repairs, and 50 microwaves × $15.00 = $750 in estimated repairs during year 1. Based on this information, Southern Corporation would record the following journal entry during year 1 to recognize the loss contingency:

Date	Account	Debit	Credit
Year 1	Warranty Expense	$750	
	Accrued Liability Payable (Warranty)		$750

Assume Southern Corporation pays all warranty claims submitted during year 1 in the amount of $825 in April of year 2, meaning the requisite time period for all potential claims has passed. Southern Corporation would record the following journal entry to reflect those payments:

In a way like unearned revenue

Date	Account	Debit	Credit
March, Year 2	Accrued Liability Payable (Warranty)	$750	
	Warranty Expense	$75	
	Cash		$825

---

[39] ACCOUNTING STANDARDS CODIFICATION, Contingencies, ASC §450-20-55 (Fin. Accounting Found. 2017).
[40] ACCOUNTING FOR CONTINGENCIES, Statement of Financial Accounting Standards No. 5 (Fin. Accounting Standards Bd. 1975).
[41] *Id.*

Since Southern Corporation underestimated its potential liability, it must recognize the difference between what it actually paid and its initial estimate ($825 – $750) as an additional warranty expense in year 2 to update its financial records.

d. Environmental Liabilities

Environmental liabilities, meaning damages resulting from the polluting party, are often one of the largest and most complicated loss contingencies an entity may face. When an entity is named as a potentially responsible party (PRP) in an environmental action, meaning the entity has been determined to have played a role in or caused the environmental pollution, the entity is likely to face future liability and thus has a potential loss contingency.[42] Just as it does with any other loss contingency, the entity must assess the level of probability and whether it can reasonably estimate the potential loss in order to determine its disclosure requirements. Generally, once an entity is named as a PRP and an environmental action has commenced, it is assumed that it is probable that the entity will suffer some type of future loss as a result of the action, so it must disclose and may also have to accrue.[43]

The amount that an entity must accrue for an environmental liability is highly complex, is difficult to determine, and can be impacted by a number of factors. Those factors include (i) the type of hazardous substance and the extent of the contamination; (ii) the various technologies that may be used as a part of the remediation process; (iii) the standards that govern remediation of that particular hazardous substance; (iv) the number of other PRPs, as well as the financial condition of those PRPs; and (v) the entity's share of the responsibility versus that of the other PRPs.[44] The costs reflected in the accrual for this type of potential loss contingency include the direct costs of the remediation, as well as the costs associated with employees directly involved in the remediation (e.g., salaries and benefits).[45] These direct costs of remediation may include (i) fees for consultants, such as lawyers and engineers; (ii) actual amounts paid for the remediation; (iii) costs of persons performing the remediation work; (iv) costs for the machinery used to perform the remediation; (v) costs associated with governmental entities overseeing the remediation; and (vi) costs associated with monitoring the site post remediation.[46]

In addition, ASC 410: Asset Retirement and Environmental Obligations indicates that the entity cannot discount the costs of the remediation to present value dollars, but instead must estimate the costs based on the current laws addressing the remediation and the technologies available to undertake the remediation.[47] Lastly, the entity cannot offset the accrual for an environmental liability with potential recoveries it expects to receive from other parties in the future.[48]

---

[42] ACCOUNTING STANDARDS CODIFICATION, Asset Retirement and Environmental Obligations, ASC § 410-30-25 (Fin. Accounting Found. 2017).
[43] *Id.*
[44] *Id.*
[45] *Id.* §410-30-30.
[46] *Id.*
[47] *Id.*
[48] *Id.*

Loss Contingency Problems 7.1 to 7.3

The following three problems address various types of loss contingencies. For purposes of these three problems assume that Jones, Inc. is a local entity with strong ties to its business community. Jones, Inc. prepares audited financial statements and its fiscal year ends on December 31. Jones, Inc. issues its financial statements on March 31 of the following year.

For each problem, assess the potential loss contingency for each period and address whether it (i) requires no disclosure and no accrual, (ii) requires only disclosure but no accrual, or (iii) requires both disclosure and accrual. Discuss and explain your analysis in detail and include any identified journal entries that Jones, Inc. should make during the relevant periods. Address each problem individually without taking into account or incorporating information from the other problems.

Problem 7.1: Guarantee

Jones, Inc. agreed to act as a guarantor to a $1,000,000, five-year commercial loan of Beta Company, a local company that is an unrelated entity. Jones, Inc. provided the guarantee in exchange for a fee of $25,000, as well as to help out another local business owner. The loan closed on July 15 in year 1 and Beta Company paid the fee to Jones, Inc. Prior to agreeing to guarantee the loan, Jones, Inc. assessed the risk and determined that it was highly unlikely that Beta Company would default on any payments pursuant to its loan agreement. During the remainder of year 1, Beta Company met all of its loan obligations. However, in August of year 2, Beta Company missed an interest payment in the amount of $2,500 that was due, and Jones, Inc. made the payment on Beta Company's behalf. Beta Company also missed another interest payment in the amount of $2,500 in October of year 2. Jones, Inc. has grown more concerned regarding Beta Company's ability to meet its loan obligations, and in particular the monthly interest payments of $2,500 remaining in year 2 as well as an upcoming principal payment in the amount of $50,000 due at the end of year 2. Based on a thorough analysis of Beta Company's current financial condition, Jones, Inc. believes Beta Company will ultimately get back on track in year 3 and will once again meets its loan obligations based on its forecasted revenues.

Undertake an assessment and analysis for the first three years of the loan.

Problem 7.2: Product Warranty

Jones, Inc. recently started selling a new lawn mower model, called the Ultimate Lawn Machine, which includes a one-year product warranty that requires that all warranty claims must be filed within 30 days after the end of the one year warranty period. The Ultimate Lawn Machine sells for $950. Jones, Inc. had not previously included a product warranty with any of its products, but based on an industry analysis it believes that approximately 3 percent of the mowers sold will result in a warranty claim during the one-year warranty period.

Jones, Inc. sold 15,000 mowers during fiscal year 20X1, the first year of sales. Jones, Inc. paid $4,500 worth of product warranty claims on the mowers during fiscal year 20X1 and $10,250 worth of product warranty claims during fiscal year 20X2 on those 15,000 mowers sold. The one-year warranty period lapsed on all sales during fiscal year 20X2.

Undertake an assessment and analysis for the fiscal years 20X1 and 20X2 regarding the Ultimate Lawn Machine product warranties.

Problem 7.3: Litigation Claim

In November of year 1, Jones, Inc.'s in-house legal counsel, Stanley Wright, who follows social media and blog sites about the entity, saw a posting on a blog that a person who bought one of the Ultimate Lawn Machines was injured while mowing his lawn. The injured customer had posted a detailed account about the injury, which resulted in severe cuts to the purchaser's feet and legs. At this point in time, that is all the information available. Jones, Inc. has been involved in claims regarding injuries from its other brands of lawn mowers in the past, but those injuries have all been relatively minor and Jones, Inc. was able to settle most of those claims for a minimal amount of money.

In January of year 2, Stanley Wright received a demand letter from legal counsel for John Smith (the customer who was injured and wrote the blog post) demanding that Jones, Inc. pay her client $675,000 for the injuries he sustained. At this point, Stanley consulted Jones, Inc.'s outside law firm, Wonder & Full Law Offices, LLC, and also spoke to the entity's executive officers. Everyone, including Stanley, thought the demand was outrageous and so Stanley responded to John Smith's lawyer telling her that without further information Jones, Inc. would not make any payment to John Smith. Stanley and John Smith's lawyer engaged in further correspondence and phone conversations through the early months of year 2 but were unable to reach any type of agreement.

In May of year 2, John Smith's lawyer filed a lawsuit against Jones, Inc. on Smith's behalf for the injuries sustained from the lawn mower and sought damages of $1,200,000 and requested a jury trial. Stanley, Wonder & Full Law Offices, LLC, and the Jones, Inc. executives still felt that the damages sought were outlandish and way outside any amount the entity might actually pay as a result of litigation. The matter progressed throughout year 2, and in late October of year 2 Jones, Inc. offered a settlement of $145,000 to John Smith, which Jones, Inc. believed was more than fair based on the information learned during the discovery process about how the injuries occurred and the extent of the injuries. In late November of year 2, John Smith's attorney indicated the settlement was not acceptable to her client and stated they would continue to trial. Jones,

Inc. decided to move forward with the trial versus making another settlement offer at that point in time.

In February of year 3, the jury trial was scheduled and was set to start in mid-March. Jones, Inc. decided to make one more settlement offer in order to mitigate the potential costs of the trial as well as the risk of losing at trial. In late February of year 3, Jones, Inc. offered John Smith a settlement of $180,000, which Jones, Inc. still believed was more than fair. John Smith had until March 10 of year 3 (just prior to the start of the trial) to accept or reject the offer. On March 9, John Smith rejected the offer but indicated he would be willing to settle for $195,000. Jones, Inc. requested that the trial be postponed so it could continue settlement negotiations, and the court granted the postponement. On March 28, Jones, Inc. agreed to pay John Smith the requested $195,000 provided he signed a release of all future claims against Jones, Inc. for this injury. On April 5 of year 3, John Smith signed the release, and on April 8 of year 3, Jones, Inc. wired the settlement funds of $195,000.

Undertake an assessment and analysis for the first three years of this litigation matter.

Interest and Time Value of Money Principles

A. INTRODUCTION

Time value of money encompasses the idea that a dollar received today is worth more than a dollar received at some point in the future, as the recipient of that dollar can invest it today and begin to make an immediate return. As a result, the dollar received today will increase in value and be worth more than the future dollar. The time value of money finance concepts and principles of interest rate calculations are essential for lawyers to understand, because they arise in many contexts.

There are many situations in which a practicing attorney must understand and assess the principles of interest and time value of money, whether the attorney is in-house counsel, a litigator, or a transactional lawyer. For example, in-house counsel may be evaluating various commercial loan options, and one of the components of that assessment is the interest payment calculation on each loan and how it will impact the entity in future accounting periods. A litigation attorney may have a client who has been offered three different settlement options, and the client would like to discuss the value of each option in today's dollars, or in present value, so that the client can make a decision regarding which offer to accept. Lastly, a trusts and estates attorney may be working with a client to set up a perpetual annuity for a beneficiary of the client, and needs to understand how to meet the client's bequest.

B. OVERVIEW OF THE U.S. FEDERAL RESERVE SYSTEM AND INTEREST RATES

In the United States, the Federal Reserve and interest rates are linked. By setting the federal funds rate and discount rate, the Federal Reserve impacts the rate of interest charged by commercial lenders, whether for a line of credit, mortgage, or car loan. When the Federal Reserve raises its interest rates, it becomes more expensive to borrow money, which costs are passed on to the consumers of money. As a result, understanding how the Federal Reserve operates lends perspective to how interest rates are set.

1. The Federal Reserve

— Open Market Operation { int ↑, sell T / int ↓, but T-

The U.S. Federal Reserve System, or the Fed, is the central bank of the United States. The Fed was created in 1913 with the passage of the Federal Reserve Act and is made up of the Federal Reserve Board, which consists of seven members nominated by the President and confirmed by Congress, as well as 12 regional Federal Reserve Banks, and other financial institution members.[1] While the Fed is subject to congressional oversight, it is considered an independent central bank.[2] Pursuant to the Federal Reserve Act, the Fed seeks to "promote effectively the goals of maximum employment, stable prices, and moderate long-term interest rates."[3] As a result, the Fed is responsible for monetary policy in the United States and exercises the responsibility by influencing the cost of money and credit.[4] Two ways in which the Fed can impact monetary policy in the United States are through the federal funds rate and the discount rate.

Fed Reserve Rate (FRR)

The federal funds rate is the rate of interest at which a depository institution — a financial institution that obtains funds through deposits primarily from the public — lends funds to other depository institutions on an overnight basis.[5] By influencing the federal funds rate, the Fed can impact economic growth and price stability.[6] A decrease in the federal funds rate generally encourages economic growth, and an increase in the federal funds rate generally slows economic growth.[7]

risk free rate

Banks overnight lending rate

In addition to its role in influencing the federal funds rate, the Federal Reserve Board sets the discount rate, which is the interest rate a Federal Reserve bank charges a depository institution to borrow money directly from the Federal Reserve.[8] This rate is typically slightly less than the federal funds rate, but borrowings directly from the Federal Reserve are limited.[9]

After 2008, Fed bought FM² MBS. Now muni bonds

2. Prime Rate and LIBOR

↳ rate at which banks willing to lend.

In addition to the federal funds rate and the discount rate, there are two other critical interest rates that a lawyer is likely to encounter: the prime rate and the London Interbank Offered Rate (LIBOR). These interest rates are expressed

---

[1]12 U.S.C. §226 .
[2]JEFFREY J. HAAS, CORPORATE FINANCE 41 (2014).
[3]12 U.S.C. §226.
[4]Haas, *supra* note 2, at 42.
[5]*Id.*
[6]*Id.*
[7]*Id.*
[8]*Id.* at 44.
[9]*Id.*

as a percentage or as basis points. A basis point is the equivalent of 1/100th of one percent, so if the interest rate is 7.5 percent, it is the equivalent of 750 basis points.

The prime rate of interest is the rate that banks charge their most stable and creditworthy customers or borrowers, meaning those borrowers that are highly unlikely to default on the repayment of a commercial loan. The prime rate is an indication of how all interest rates will trend, meaning whether interest rates will rise or decrease. As a result, the financial community and commercial borrowers follow the prime rate closely.[10] The actions of the Federal Reserve directly impact interest rates charged by commercial lenders. When the Federal Reserve raises its rates, the United States market generally follows suit with increases in the prime rate.

LIBOR is the short-term interest rate that the world's major banks charge each other for a short-term loan, and is similar to the United States federal funds rate. Many commercial loans are tied to current LIBOR plus an additional percentage or number of basis points. As a result, LIBOR also impacts commercial lenders and borrowers.

3. Interest

Interest is the fee paid to use another party's money, whether that party is a family member, friend, or commercial lender. In other words, it is the cost to the borrower of accessing and using money loaned from a third party. There are a number of components that make up an actual interest rate charged by a lender to a borrower, including (i) the real rate of interest; (ii) the inflation premium; (iii) the default risk premium; and (iv) the opportunity cost premium.[11]

The real rate of interest is the rate that a lender would charge in a world where there was no risk, and reflects the return the lender wants to receive in exchange for lending the money. In essence, it is the nominal rate of interest (the actual amount the lender charges the borrower) less the inflation, default risk, and opportunity cost premiums.

The inflation premium is meant to compensate the lender for the anticipated rate of inflation over the term of the loan.[12] As a result of inflation, the same amount of money in the future will allow for the purchase of fewer goods. Or, in other words, it will take more money in the future to purchase the same amount of goods as it would today. In order to compensate for that potential loss of purchasing power, the lender includes an inflation premium as a part of the interest rate it charges the borrower. This puts the lender in a position to be able to buy the same amount of goods in the future when the loan is repaid as it could have bought today.[13] If the lender anticipates that the rate of inflation over the term of the loan will be 5 percent, meaning that an item that costs $10.00

haircuts to collaterals when borrower defaults

---

[10]*Id.* at 48.
[11]Jeffrey J. Haas, Corporate finance 40 (2014).
[12]*Id.*
[13]*Id.*

today will cost $10.50 at the end of the term of the loan, then the lender will add that premium to compensate for the inflation.

The default risk premium is meant to compensate the lender in the event that the borrower fails to repay the loan.[14] In order to determine the amount of default risk premium, the lender must assess the likelihood that the borrower will default on its loan repayment obligations. If a lender believes that a borrower is more likely to default, it will charge that borrower a higher default risk premium than it would a borrower who is less likely to default. As a result, the default risk premium fluctuates depending on the borrower and its risk of nonpayment. One way in which a lender mitigates its default risk is to require the borrower to provide collateral to secure the loan.

The opportunity cost premium is meant to compensate the lender for lending money to a particular borrower and thus forgoing the opportunity to use the money for another purpose or loan.[15] This is the idea that by making this particular loan, the lender is giving up the opportunity to make another loan, which could be on better terms for the lender, such as a lower default risk or a higher interest rate. As a result, the lender includes an opportunity cost premium in the actual interest rate it charges.

The total of the real interest rate, the inflation premium, the default risk premium, and the opportunity cost premium results in the actual interest rate charged by the lender to the borrower. Because every borrower is unique, two borrowers could request the same amount as a commercial loan on the same day from the same lender and receive two entirely different interest rates for that loan.

C. CALCULATING INTEREST

There are two ways to calculate interest due on borrowed money or interest earned on invested money: simple interest and compound interest. Simple interest is a set rate calculated solely on the principal loaned, and compound interest is a set compounding rate calculated on the principal loaned plus accrued interest.

1. Simple Interest

When interest is calculated using the simple method, interest is only calculated on the principal due or the amount invested over the term of the loan or investment. In other words, the accrued or earned interest itself is not added to the principal or investment each time interest is calculated. As a result, the amount of simple interest remains the same for each year. The formula to calculate simple interest is as follows:

Simple Interest = P x I, where P = principal and I = the simple interest rate

[14]*Id.*
[15]*Id.*

EXAMPLE 8.1   **SIMPLE INTEREST**

The following example illustrates the concept of simple interest on a three-year loan of $50,000 with a 6 percent annual interest rate:

Year	Interest @ 6%	Amount Due (Principal + Interest)
1	$3,000	
2	$3,000	
3	$3,000	
Total Due	**$9,000**	**$59,000**

Each year, simple interest is calculated on the principal. At the end of three years, the borrower would owe $59,000, which is the amount of the principal, $50,000, plus the total of the three years of simple interest, $9,000.

2. Compound Interest

When interest is calculated using the compound method, interest is calculated on the principal plus any accrued interest over the term of the loan, or the amount invested plus interest earned over the term of the investment. In other words, the accrued or earned interest itself also accrues or earns interest. As a result, the amount of compound interest will change each year. The formula to calculate compound interest and determine the amount of principal and interest due at the end of the term of the loan or the amount of investment and interest earned is as follows:

$$P_n = P(1 + I)^n, \text{ where } P_n = \text{principal} + \text{interest due at the end of the term,}$$
$$P = \text{original principal, } I = \text{compound interest rate,}$$
$$\text{and } n = \text{the number of periods}$$

EXAMPLE 8.2   **COMPOUND INTEREST**

The following example illustrates the concept of compound interest on a three-year loan of $50,000 with a 6 percent annual compound interest rate:

Year	Principal + Accrued Interest	Interest @ 6%	Amount Due
1	$50,000	$3,000.00	
2	$53,000	$3,180.00	
3	$56,180	$3,370.80	
Total Due		**$9,550.80**	**$59,550.80**

Each year, compound interest is calculated on the principal plus the accrued interest from the prior year. At the end of three years, the borrower would owe $59,550.80, which is the amount of the principal, $50,000, plus the total of three years of compound interest, $9,550.80.

As you can see from the two examples, when interest is compounded, the borrower will owe more at the end of the term of the loan. In this example, the borrower owes an additional $550.80 at the end of three years. As a result of these differences, borrowers would always prefer simple interest, as it costs the borrower less money over the term of the loan. On the other hand, lenders would always prefer compound interest as it results in a greater amount due at the end of the term of the loan, meaning the lender makes more on the loan.

In many cases, interest compounds more than annually, such as monthly, quarterly, or semi-annually. In those cases, calculating the compound interest manually is burdensome and is much more easily accomplished with a financial calculator, Excel formula, or future value of a lump sum table (see **Exhibit I**).

When interest compounds more than annually, two adjustments must be made in order to determine the amount of the interest payment. The first adjustment is to the interest rate (I). If interest compounds semi-annually, quarterly, or monthly, the interest rate must be divided by 2, 4, or 12, respectively, to determine the interest rate for each compounding period.

EXAMPLE 8.3   **COMPOUNDING RATE DETERMINATION**

For example, if interest on the loan is 6 percent per annum, the following table sets forth the interest rate applicable to each compounding period:

	Annual Interest Rate	Number of Compounding Periods	Interest Rate per Compounding Period
Semi-Annually	6%	2	3%
Quarterly	6%	4	1.5%
Monthly	6%	12	0.5%

The second adjustment is to the number of periods (n). If interest compounds semi-annually, quarterly, or monthly, the number of periods must be multiplied by 2, 4, or 12, respectively, to determine the number of compounding periods over the term of the loan.

EXAMPLE 8.4   **COMPOUNDING PERIODS DETERMINATION**

The following table sets forth the number of periods over which interest must be calculated:

Compounding Schedule	Total Number of Compounding Periods per Year
Semi-Annually	2
Quarterly	4
Monthly	12
Bi-Monthly	24
Daily	365

Once these two adjustments have been made, the compound interest rate formula can be used to calculate the amount of interest due at the end of the term of the loan. That amount of interest would be added to the initial principal to determine the total principal and interest due at the end of the term of the loan.

EXAMPLE 8.5   **SEMI-ANNUAL COMPOUND INTEREST**

The following example illustrates the concept of interest that compounds semi-annually on a three-year loan of $50,000 with a 6 percent semi-annual compound interest rate:

Year	Principal + Accrued Interest	Interest @ 3% (period 1)	Principal + Accrued Interest	Interest @ 3% (period 2)	Principal & Interest
1	$50,000.00	$1,500.00	$51,500.00	$1,545.00	
2	$53,045.00	$1,591.35	$54,636.35	$1,639.09	
3	$56,275.44	$1,688.26	$57,963.70	$1,738.91	
Total Due		$4,779.61		$4,923.00	$59,702.61

Each year there are two compounding periods (3 years × 2), and so over the term of the loan, interest compounds a total of six times. The compound interest rate is 6 percent, or 3 percent per each compounding period (6% ÷ 2). At the end of three years, the borrower would owe $59,702.61, which is the amount of the principal, $50,000, plus the total of three years of semi-annual compound interest, $9,702.61.

As demonstrated from the two compound interest examples, if interest is compounded semi-annually, the borrower will owe more at the end of the term of the loan than if interest was compounded annually. In this example, the borrower owes an additional $151.81 if interest compounds semi-annually ($59,702.61 – $59,550.80).

Interest Calculation Problems 8.1 to 8.4

The following problems deal with the calculation of simple and compound interest.

Problem 8.1: Simple Interest

Assume that Fox Corporation secures a $650,000 five-year loan with a simple interest rate of 3.5 percent:

Part A: Calculate the annual interest on the loan for each year.
Part B: Calculate the total due at the end of the five-year loan.

Problem 8.2: Compound Interest

Assume that Fox Corporation secures an $800,000 three-year loan with a compound interest rate of 4.6 percent:

Part A: Calculate the interest and principal for each period of the loan with a 4.6 percent interest rate that compounds annually.
Part B: Calculate the interest and principal for each period of the loan with a 4.6 percent interest rate that compounds semi-annually.

Problem 8.3: Simple versus Compound Interest

Assume a person makes an investment of $60,000. Would the investor benefit more from a 4 percent simple interest rate or a 3.5 percent interest rate that compounds annually?

Calculate the value of the principal plus interest for both options at the end of each of the following periods:

Part A: Five years
Part B: Seven years

Problem 8.4: Effects of Interest on Value in the Future

Assume a person makes a $50,000 investment:

Part A: What is the investment worth at the end of two years under the following three scenarios: (i) a 10 percent simple interest rate, (ii) a 7 percent interest rate that compounds annually plus a $2,000 bonus paid at the end of year 2, or (iii) an 8 percent interest rate that compounds quarterly?
Part B: What is the increase to principal at the end of year 1 for each option in Part A?
Part C: Explain how the starting value of the principal, the rate of compounding, the length of time of the investment, and the amount or timing of the bonus would affect the investor's decision.

D. OVERVIEW OF THE TIME VALUE OF MONEY

The time value of money concept provides methods for the determination of both the future value of money and the present value of money, whether that money is a lump sum or a series of payments over time (an annuity). As discussed in the simple and compound interest sections above, what was actually being determined with those interest calculations was the future value of the amount of money that would be due as a result of a loan with a set interest rate. In other words, the calculations determined the amount of money the borrower would have to repay in the future at the end of the term of the loan at the specified interest rate, as well as the amount of money the lender would receive in the future as a result of making the loan today at the specified interest rate. While the examples above dealt with a loan scenario, those examples could have just as easily dealt with a determination of how much the sum of $50,000 would grow to if invested over a period of time at a specific simple or compound interest rate.

The following four time value of money concepts are used in varying ways and circumstances by practicing lawyers.

1. Future Value of a Lump Sum

The future value of a lump sum calculation is used to determine how much a set amount or lump sum of money will grow to at some point in the future at a specified interest rate. The future value calculation is often used to determine how much an investment or sum of money will grow to over the course of time if it is invested and earns a certain amount of interest (or rate of return), or to determine the amount of principal and interest due at the end of the loan. In order to determine the future value of a lump sum, four pieces of information must be known: (i) the initial lump sum amount, (ii) the period of time, (iii) the interest rate or rate of return, and (iv) the rate of compound interest and compounding frequency. The formula for determining the future value of a lump sum of money is as follows:

$$FV_n = PV(1 + I)^n$$, where FV_n = the future value in "n" periods, PV = the initial sum of money, I = the interest rate, and n = number of periods

Just as discussed above in regard to interest that compounds more than annually, the same two adjustments must be made to the rate of interest and number of periods in order for the above formula to work for a calculation of the future value of a sum of money with an interest rate or rate of return that compounds more than annually (i.e., semi-annually, quarterly, or monthly).

The formula or the future value of a lump sum table (see **Exhibit I**) can be used to make the calculation. The table sets forth the relevant future value factor for the specified interest rate for the number of periods, or the "$(1 + I)^n$" portion of the equation. In order to utilize **Exhibit I** and find the relevant future value of a lump sum factor, locate the number of periods in the left-hand column and the interest rate along the top. The intersection of the number of periods and interest rate provides the correct future value factor to use in the calculation.

EXAMPLE 8.6   FUTURE VALUE OF A LUMP SUM

Assume a client desires to form a trust for the benefit of her children and wants to determine how much the sum of money she is going to invest today will grow to in ten years. The client indicates that she currently has $150,000 and believes that a reasonable rate of return is 5 percent compounded annually. In order to determine the future value of this lump sum utilizing the formula, the calculation would be as follows:

$$FV_n = \$150,000(1 + .05)^{10}$$
$$= \$150,000(1.62889)$$
$$= \$244,333.50$$

Utilizing the future value calculation, the attorney could advise the client that her investment of $150,000 today at a rate of return of 5 percent compounded annually would grow to $244,333.50 in ten years.

The same calculation could be made utilizing the future value table by locating the correct number of periods in the left column, which is ten periods, and locating the specified interest rate along the top row, which is 5 percent. The intersection of those two numbers would provide the future value factor of 1.6289. Determining the future value of the sum requires the multiplication of the sum of money by the future value factor as follows:

$$FV_n = \$150,000 \times 1.6289$$
$$= \$244,335.00$$

Note that there is a slight difference in the future value obtained using the formula versus using the future value table factor due to rounding, which will occur in each of the examples of time value of money calculations.

Keep in mind that the future value of a lump sum table factor takes into account the initial lump sum amount, in this case the $150,000, and that initial investment is not added to the calculated result.

Future Value of a Lump Sum: Problems 8.5 and 8.6

The following two problems address future value of a lump sum calculations.

Problem 8.5: Value of a Settlement Offer

You represent a client who is unable to work due to a workplace injury caused by her employer's negligence. She thinks that starting today and continuing over the next five years, her lost wages and medical bills will total $200,000. Her employer has offered a settlement in the form of a lump sum of $150,000 paid today. Your client believes she can invest the lump sum and receive a rate of return of 7 percent.

Part A: What formula or table would you use to determine the value of the settlement offer in five years?
Part B: What is the value of the settlement offer?
Part C: Based on the value of the settlement offer, how would you advise your client?

Problem 8.6: Value of a Book of Business

You recently joined a large firm as a junior partner. Your partnership agreement requires that for the first 12 years as partner, you achieve 5 percent annual growth in the dollar value of client billables, and requires that you start by bringing on at least $500,000 worth of billables.

Part A: If your current book of business is $500,000, how much business will you have to be generating at the end of year 12 in order to fulfill your obligation under the partnership agreement?
Part B: If your current book of business is $750,000 and grows at the required 5 percent, how much business will you have at the end of year 12?

2. Present Value of a Lump Sum

The present value of a lump sum calculation is used to determine how much a set amount or lump sum of money to be received or paid in the future is worth in today's dollars. In order to determine the present value of a lump sum, the sum is discounted to reflect what that amount would be worth if it were received or paid today. The present value calculation is often used to determine how much a payment that is to be received, such as a payment from a trust fund, or a payment to be made, such as a lawsuit settlement, in the future is worth today. This can allow a party to know how much money it must invest today to have it grow to that amount in the future. It also allows a party to compare and contrast various future payment options by discounting each option to its present value. In order to determine the present value, four pieces of information must be known: (i) the amount of the future payment; (ii) the point in time when such payment will be received or made; (iii) the interest rate or rate of return expected to be earned from the present day to a future date; and (iv) the compounding frequency. The formula for determining the present value of a lump sum of money is as follows:

$$PV = FV/(1 + I)^n, \text{ where } PV = \text{the present value, } FV = \text{the future}$$
$$\text{value or the sum of money paid or received, } I = \text{the interest rate,}$$
$$\text{and } n = \text{number of periods}$$

The formula or the present value of a lump sum table (see **Exhibit J**) can be used to make the calculation. The table sets forth the relevant present value factor for the specified interest rate at the number of periods until payment, or the "$(1 + I)^n$" portion of the equation.

EXAMPLE 8.7   **PRESENT VALUE OF LUMP SUM**

Assume your client knows that she must pay off a $75,000 loan in full in five years and is attempting to determine the sum of money she must put away now to have it grow to $75,000 in that time frame. Your client indicates that she believes that a reasonable rate of return over those five years is 5 percent compounded annually. In order to determine the present value of this lump sum utilizing the formula, the calculation would be as follows:

$$PV = \$75,000/(1 + .05)^5$$
$$= \$75,000/(1.27628)$$
$$= \$58,764.53$$

Utilizing the present value calculation, the attorney could advise her client that if she were to invest $58,764.53 today at a rate of return of 5 percent compounded annually, it would grow to the required $75,000 in five years.

The same calculation could be made utilizing the present value table by locating the intersection of five periods and 5 percent interest, which provides a present value factor of 0.78353. Determining the present value of the lump sum requires the multiplication of the future amount by the present value factor as follows:

$$PV = \$75,000 \times .7835$$
$$= \$58,762.50$$

Present Value of a Lump Sum: Problems 8.7 and 8.8

The following two problems address the present value of a lump sum calculations.

Problem 8.7: Value of a Future Promise

A friend, confident in her future but short on cash today, offers you $10,000 to be paid in 30 years, $5,000 to be paid in 20 years, or $3,000 to paid in 10 years to let her stay rent free in your house for one month. If you expect an 8 percent interest rate, what is each promise worth to you today?

Problem 8.8: Value of Future Earnings

Sally Smith is assessing the following three options and believes a reasonable rate of return is 7 percent:

Part A: Sally can go to graduate school and her parents will pay her $50,000 three years from today as a graduation gift. What is the gift worth today?
Part B: Sally can take a job offer today that pays an immediate signing bonus of $20,000, a bonus of $5,000 at the end of year 1, and a bonus of $10,000 at the end of year 2. What are the bonus payments worth today?
Part C: Sally can take care of her grandparents, who will pay her $5,000 at the end of the first year, $10,000 at the end of the second year, $15,000 at the end of the third year, and $20,000 at the end of the fourth year. What are these payments worth today?

3. Annuities

There are two types of annuities: an ordinary annuity, or annuity in arrears, and an annuity due, or annuity in advance. In either case, an annuity is a series of equal payments made at regularized time intervals.

An ordinary annuity is a series of equal payments made at the same time at the end of each period (such as end of the week, month, quarter, or year). An annuity due is a series of equal payments made at the same time at the beginning of each period (first day of the week, month, quarter, or year).

In comparing an ordinary annuity and an annuity due, the annuity due will reflect a higher return as the payments are made sooner (at the beginning of the period), versus later as is the case with the ordinary annuity (at the end of the period). As a result of the earlier payment, the annuity due accrues interest over a longer period of time than an ordinary annuity does.

EXAMPLE 8.8 INTEREST ACCRUED ON AN ORDINARY ANNUITY

Assume an individual decided to invest $25,000 at the end of each year for three years starting in 2017: under an ordinary annuity, the investor would only accrue interest on the investment over the course of two years, from the end of the first year to the end of the third year.

	Payments on 12/31	12/31/17	12/31/18	12/31/19
First Payment	$25,000	0 months' interest	12 months' interest	24 months' interest
Second Payment	$25,000	n/a	0 months' interest	12 months' interest
Third Payment	$25,000	n/a	n/a	0 months' interest

EXAMPLE 8.9 INTEREST ACCRUED ON AN ANNUITY DUE

Assume an individual decided to invest $25,000 at the beginning of each year for three years starting in 2017: under an annuity due, the investor would accrue interest on the investment over the course of three years, from the start of the first year to the end of the third year.

	Payments on 1/1	12/31/17	12/31/18	12/31/19
First Payment	$25,000	12 months' interest	24 months' interest	36 months' interest
Second Payment	$25,000	n/a	12 months' interest	24 months' interest
Third Payment	$25,000	n/a	n/a	12 months' interest

a. Future Value of an Annuity

The future value calculation is also used to determine how much an ordinary annuity or annuity due will grow to at some point in the future at a specified interest rate or rate of return. In order to determine the future value of the annuity, five pieces of information must be known: (i) the amount of the annuity payment; (ii) whether the annuity payment is made at the beginning or end of period; (iii) the period of time; (iv) the interest rate or rate of return; and (v) the compounding frequency.

i. Future Value of an Ordinary Annuity

The formula for determining the future value of an ordinary annuity is as follows:

$$FV_n = X[(1 + I)^n - 1]/I, \text{ where } FV_n = \text{the future value in "n" periods,}$$
$$X = \text{the fixed amount of the annuity payment, } I = \text{the interest rate,}$$
$$\text{and } n = \text{number of periods}$$

The formula or the future value of an ordinary annuity table (see **Exhibit K**) can be used to make the calculation. The table sets forth the relevant future value of an ordinary annuity factor for the specified interest rate at the specified number of periods, or the "$[(1 + I)^n - 1]/I$" portion of the equation.

EXAMPLE 8.10   **FUTURE VALUE OF ORDINARY ANNUITY**

Assume your client desires to form a trust for the benefit of his children and wants to determine how much an ordinary annuity of $15,000 per year will grow to in ten years. Your client indicates that he believes that a reasonable rate of return is 5 percent compounded annually. In order to determine the future value of this ordinary annuity utilizing the formula, the calculation would be as follows:

$$FV_n = \$15,000[(1 + .05)^{10} - 1]/.05$$
$$= \$15,000[(1.62889 - 1)/.05]$$
$$= \$15,000(12.5778)$$
$$= \$188,667.00$$

Utilizing the future value calculation, the attorney could advise his client that an ordinary annuity investment of $15,000 yearly at a rate of return of 5 percent compounded annually would grow to $188,667.00 at the end of ten years.

The same calculation can be made utilizing the future value of an ordinary annuity table by locating the future value of an ordinary annuity factor of 12.5779 (intersection of ten periods at 5 percent). Determining the future value of the annuity payments requires the multiplication of the annuity payment by the future value of an ordinary annuity factor as follows:

$$FV_n = \$15,000 \times 12.5779$$
$$= \$188,668.50$$

When using the future value of an ordinary annuity table, the future value factor takes into account the annuity payments, in this case $15,000 at the end of each year (for a total of $150,000 over ten years), so those annuity payments are not added to the calculated result.

---

ii. Future Value of an Annuity Due

The formula for determining the future value of an annuity due is as follows:

$$FV_n = X[(1 + I)^n - 1]/I](1 + I), \text{ where } FV_n = \text{the future value in "n" periods,}$$
$$X = \text{the fixed amount of the annuity payment, } I = \text{the interest rate,}$$
$$\text{and } n = \text{number of periods}$$

The formula or the future value of an ordinary annuity table can be used to make the calculation. However, the table requires some minor adjustments. In order to find the correct factor for an annuity due, maintain the same interest rate but add one time period (or one "n"). Once that factor is located from the table, subtract one from the factor and the result will be the correct factor to use in calculating the annuity due.

EXAMPLE 8.11   **FUTURE VALUE OF ANNUITY DUE**

Assume your client desires to form a trust for the benefit of his children and wants to know how much an annuity due of $15,000 per year will grow to at the end of ten years. Your client indicates that he believes that a reasonable rate of return is 5 percent compounded annually. In order to determine the future value of this annuity due utilizing the formula, the calculation would be as follows:

$$FV_n = \$15,000[(1 + .05)^{10} - 1]/.05](1 + .05)$$
$$= \$15,000[(1.62889 - 1)/.05](1.05)$$
$$= \$15,000(12.5778)(1.05)$$
$$= \$15,000(13.20669)$$
$$= \$198,100.35$$

Utilizing the future value of an ordinary annuity table, locate the number of periods plus one period in the left column, which is 11 periods, and locate the specified interest rate along the top row, which is 5 percent. The intersection of those two numbers would provide the future value of an ordinary annuity factor of 14.2068. Now subtract one (14.2068 − 1) to determine the correct factor of 13.2608 to use to calculate the annuity due. Determining the future value of the annuity due requires the multiplication of the annuity payment by the adjusted future value of an ordinary annuity factor as follows:

$$FV_n = \$15,000 \times 13.2068$$
$$= \$198,102.00$$

As previously discussed, an annuity due accrues interest over one additional period of time and results in a larger value at the end of the term. In this case, utilizing the results obtained from the future value table, the client would have earned an additional $9,433.50 with an annuity due versus an ordinary annuity.

Future Value of an Annuity Problems 8.9 to 8.11

The following three problems address the future value of an annuity calculations.

Problem 8.9: What Will an Annuity Grow To?

Your clients are a couple who just adopted a baby. They have come to you, as their estate lawyer, to discuss creating a college fund for their new child. The couple will contribute $21,000 at the end of each year starting today and anticipates a rate of return of 4 percent compounded annually. What will be the balance of these contributions at the end of 18 years when their child is ready to attend college?

Problem 8.10: How Much Is a Settlement Worth?

Your client, the plaintiff, is an avid jogger and was struck by a vehicle during one of her early morning runs. As a part of the settlement offer, opposing counsel indicated that the defendant, who was driving the vehicle, would be willing to pay the avid jogger $3,500 per year for the next 30 years with the payments made on the last day of each 12-month period from the settlement date. The avid jogger thinks that her costs for recovery from her injuries will be in excess of $120,000 over the course of her remaining life. If she can earn a rate of return of 5 percent, will this settlement offer satisfy her estimated costs for recovery?

Problem 8.11: What Is the Difference Between the Future Value of an Ordinary Annuity and the Future Value of an Annuity Due?

Your client desires to open a brokerage account and intends to deposit $11,500 in the account each year for the next ten years. He believes that he can earn a rate of return of 6 percent compounded annually. What will these deposits grow to if the client makes the deposit on January 1 of each year (annuity due), and what will these deposits grow to if the client makes the deposit on December 31 of each year (ordinary annuity)?

b. Present Value of an Annuity

The present value of an ordinary annuity calculation is used to determine how much an annuity that will be received in the future is worth in today's dollars. In order to determine the present value of an annuity, the annuity payments are discounted to reflect what they would be worth today. The present value calculation is often used to compare two potential offers—for instance, a lump sum paid today or an annuity paid over the course of five years. By reflecting both offers in today's dollars, the party can assess which is the better offer, taking into account all other facts and circumstances. In order to determine the present value of an annuity, five pieces of information must be known: (i) the amount of the annuity payment; (ii) when the annuity payment is made, beginning or end of period; (iii) the period of time; (iv) the interest rate or rate of return; and (v) the compounding frequency.

i. Present Value of an Ordinary Annuity

The formula for determining the present value of an ordinary annuity is as follows:

$$PV = X[(1 - (1 + I)^{-n})/I],$$ where PV = the present value, X = the fixed amount of the annuity payment, I = the interest rate compounded annually, and -n = number of periods to a negative power

The formula or the present value of an ordinary annuity table (see **Exhibit L**) can be used to make the calculation. The table sets forth the relevant present value of an ordinary annuity factor for the specified interest rate at the specified number of periods, or the "$[(1 - (1 + I)^{-n})/I]$" portion of the equation.

EXAMPLE 8.12 **PRESENT VALUE OF ORDINARY ANNUITY**

Assume your client is attempting to determine the present value of an ordinary annuity of $150,000 per year for ten years so that she can compare it to the lump sum offer that is also available. Your client indicates that she believes that a reasonable rate of return is 5 percent compounded annually. In order to determine the present value of this ordinary annuity utilizing the formula, the calculation would be as follows:

$$
\begin{aligned}
PV &= \$150{,}000[(1 - (1 + .05)^{-10})/.05] \\
&= \$150{,}000[(1 - .6139)/.05] \\
&= \$150{,}000(.3861)/.05) \\
&= \$150{,}000(7.722) \\
&= \$1{,}158{,}300.00
\end{aligned}
$$

In order to determine the present value of this ordinary annuity using the table, locate the present value of an ordinary annuity factor of 7.7217 (intersection of ten years at 5 percent). Determining the present value of the annuity payments requires the multiplication of the annuity payment by the present value of an ordinary annuity factor as follows:

$$PV = \$150{,}000 \times 7.7217$$
$$= \$1{,}158{,}255.00$$

If the client was considering a lump sum payment today of $1,000,000 or a ten-year ordinary annuity of $150,000, she would now know that the ordinary annuity is worth more in today's dollars, $158,255.00 more, and could take that into account in making her decision.

Keep in mind when using the present value of an ordinary annuity table that the present value of an ordinary annuity factor takes into account the annuity payments, in this case $150,000 at the end of each year for ten years, and so those annuity payments should not be added to the calculated result.

ii. Present Value of an Annuity Due

The formula for determining the present value of an annuity due is as follows:

$PV = X[(1 - (1 + I)^{-n})/I] \times (1 + I)$, where PV = the present value, X = the fixed amount of the annuity payment, I = the interest rate compounded annually, and -n = number of periods to a negative power.

In essence, the present value of an annuity due uses the same formula as the present value of an ordinary annuity, except that it adds an extra payment (1 + I) to account for the fact that each payment occurs one period sooner, since the payment is made at the beginning of the period instead of the end.

In this instance, it is quicker to use the present value of an annuity due formula versus the table. In order to calculate the present value of an annuity due using the present value of a lump sum table, calculate the present value of each individual annuity due payment and add the total together to determine the present value of the annuity due.

EXAMPLE 8.13 **PRESENT VALUE OF ANNUITY DUE**

Assume your client is attempting to determine the present value of an annuity due of $150,000 per year for ten years so that she can compare it to the lump sum offer of $1,000,000 that is also available. Your client indicates that she believes that a reasonable rate of return is 5 percent compounded annually. In order to determine the present value of this annuity due utilizing the formula, the calculation would be as follows:

$$PV = \$150,000[(1 - (1 + .05)^{-10})/.05](1 + .05)$$
$$= \$150,000[(1 - .6139)/.05](1.05)$$
$$= \$150,000(7.722) \times (1.05)$$
$$= \$150,000(8.1081)$$
$$= \$1,216,215.00$$

In order to determine the present value of this annuity due using the present value of a lump sum table, locate the present value of a lump sum factor for each annuity payment. The first annuity payment happens at the beginning of the period, or today, and so it is not discounted as it is present value; the second annuity payment happens one year from today's date, and so it is discounted for a period of one year to determine its present value; the third annuity payment happens two years from today's date, and so it is discounted for a period of two years; and so on. The following table sets forth the calculations for this annuity due utilizing the present value of a lump sum table:

Annuity Payment	Number of Periods to Discount	Interest Rate	Annuity Due Factor	Amount of Annuity Due
$150,000	0	5%	1.00	$150,000
$150,000	1	5%	.9524	$142,860
$150,000	2	5%	.9070	$136,050
$150,000	3	5%	.8638	$129,570
$150,000	4	5%	.8227	$123,405
$150,000	5	5%	.7835	$117,525
$150,000	6	5%	.7462	$111,930
$150,000	7	5%	.7107	$106,605
$150,000	8	5%	.6768	$101,520
$150,000	9	5%	.6446	$96,690
Total				**$1,216,155**

Utilizing the result from the above table, the present value of the annuity due yields $216,155 more than the lump sum payment of $1,000,000.

Present Value of an Annuity Problems 8.12 and 8.13

The following two problems address the present value of an annuity calculations.

Problem 8.12: Value of a Lump Sum versus an Annuity

Your client, the plaintiff, desires to settle a personal injury lawsuit that resulted from a car accident. He has been offered the following two settlement choices: (i) a lump sum payment of $120,000 today, or (ii) regular payments of $12,000 per year for 15 years paid on the last day of each 12-month period from the settlement date. Your client believes he can earn a 6 percent rate of return. Which is the better option?

Problem 8.13: Comparing an Ordinary Annuity and Annuity Due

Your client, the testator, desires to set up an annuity payment stream for her only nephew, but she is also considering a one-time lump sum gift instead. The proposed annuity amount is $12,500 every 12 months for the next five years. She believes her nephew can earn an 8 percent return.

Part A: If your client creates an ordinary annuity, what would that equate to in today's dollars?
Part B: If your client creates an annuity due, what would that equate to in today's dollars?

c. Amount of an Annuity Payment

In some situations, the annuity payment amount is unknown, but the present value of the annuity is known. In that scenario it is possible to determine the annuity payment by rearranging and utilizing the equation for the present value of an ordinary annuity. The equation for the present value of an ordinary annuity is as follows:

$$PV = \text{Annuity Payment} \times \text{Present Value of an Ordinary Annuity Factor}$$

If the present value and the present value of an ordinary annuity factor are known, the equation can be rearranged as follows:

$$\text{Annuity Payment} = PV \div \text{Present Value of an Ordinary Annuity Factor}$$

EXAMPLE 8.14 CALCULATING ANNUITY PAYMENT AMOUNT

Assume your client borrows $250,000 from his parents to purchase a new home. The terms of the loan require the client to repay the loan over the course of 15 years in equal installments with the loan accruing interest at the rate of

3 percent compounded annually. The annual payment amount can be determined by utilizing the equation above as follows:

Annuity Payment = $250,000 ÷ 11.9379 (PV of an ordinary annuity factor for 15
periods at 3%)
Annuity Payment = $20,941.71

In this scenario, the client would make a payment of $20,941.71 at the end of each year for 15 years to repay his parents for the loan in full at the prescribed interest rate.

---

d. Perpetual Annuity

A perpetual annuity is a type of annuity that has no end, or in other words, the stream of annuity payments continues into perpetuity. In order to calculate the amount that must be deposited today to establish an annuity in perpetuity, two pieces of information must be known: (i) the interest rate or expected rate of return, and (ii) the amount of the perpetual annuity payment. In order to determine the amount of money to fund the perpetual annuity, the following equation is used:

Amount of Money = Perpetual Annuity Payment ÷ Interest Rate or Rate
of Return

EXAMPLE 8.15 **PERPETUAL ANNUITY**

Assume a client wants to establish a perpetual annuity whereby the client can receive a set payment each year for the client's life, at which time the annuity will pass to the client's only child. The client indicates that she desires to receive a payment of $175,000 per year and believes that a reasonable rate of return is 4 percent compounded annually. Utilizing the above equation, the amount the client would need to deposit today to ensure that perpetual annuity stream is determined as follows:

Amount = $175,000 ÷ .04
Amount = $4,375,000

In order for the client to receive a payment of $175,000 per year in perpetuity, the client must deposit $4,375,000 today at a rate of return of 4 percent.

Perpetual Annuity Problem 8.14

The following problem addresses perpetual annuity calculations.

Problem 8.14: Funding a Scholarship

You have a successful client who would like to give back to her alma mater, which was instrumental in her success. She attributes her success to receiving an education through a scholarship. She would like to establish a scholarship fund that provides two annual scholarships of $42,000 each.

Part A: How much would she need to invest today in order to create this perpetual scholarship fund assuming a 3 percent rate of return?
Part B: How much would she need to invest today in order to create this perpetual scholarship fund if she could achieve a 6 percent rate of return?

4. Rules of 72 and 110

These two rules, the Rule of 72 and the Rule of 110, are useful rules to be aware of in regard to time value of money calculations. By utilizing the Rule of 72, a party can determine the approximate number of years it would take for a lump sum to double in value, assuming it is earning interest that is compounded annually. In order to determine this information, the following formula is used:

    Years to Double = 72 ÷ I, where I = the interest rate compounded annually

By utilizing the Rule of 110, a party can determine the approximate number of years it would take for a lump sum to triple in value, assuming it is earning interest that is compounded annually. In order to determine this information, the following formula is used:

    Years to Triple = 110 ÷ I, where I = the interest rate compounded annually

EXAMPLE 8.16   **RULES OF 72 AND 110**

Assume a client is discussing various estate planning options with his lawyer and is trying to determine how long it would take to grow $150,000 to $300,000 or $450,000 in order to fund a trust in the future. The client believes he could earn 6 percent interest compounded annually. Using the formulas above, the attorney could advise the client as follows:

$$72 \div 6 = 12 \text{ years for the investment to double; and}$$
$$110 \div 6 = 18.33 \text{ years for the investment to triple}$$

5. Time Value of Money Limitations

While the use of present value and future value is a critical tool in many areas of the practice of law, it also has limitations. In order to make a present value or future value calculation, certain assumptions are made, whether an assumption about the actual lump sum payment or annuity payment, or an assumption about the effective interest or discount rate, or anticipated rate of return. In either scenario, if the assumptions are incorrect, the results will be inaccurate, meaning that a client may not receive the correct amount of damages or the client may not fund a trust in the manner desired. Therefore, when undertaking these analyses, careful thought and consideration should be given to making the most accurate assumptions possible so that the results are reflective of the client's established goals.

E. BONDS AND BOND VALUATION

A bond is a type of debt instrument that is predominantly used by a corporation or the government to finance a project or activity. Bonds are often issued in lieu of seeking a traditional commercial loan. The investor in a bond loans money to the corporation or the governmental entity for the stated period of time at the stated interest rate and, in return, receives the interest payment (whether annually or semi-annually) for the term of the bond and repayment of the face amount of the bond on its maturity date. Most bonds are issued in increments of $1,000, but can be issued in any increment.

There are three main types of bonds: corporate bonds, municipal bonds, and treasuries. Corporate bonds are issued by corporations, municipal bonds are issued by states and municipalities, and treasuries are issued by the U.S. government. Treasuries include the following: (i) U.S. Treasury bonds, which have a maturity of greater than ten years; (ii) U.S. Treasury notes, which have a maturity of one to ten years; and (iii) U.S. Treasury bills, which have a maturity of less than one year.

There are a number of relevant terms to know and understand in regard to bonds. The *issue price* is the price at which the bond is originally sold, and the *face value* is the amount the bond is worth at maturity. The *coupon rate* is the rate of interest the issuer will pay the bond holder, and the *coupon dates* are the dates on which the interest payments are made. Lastly, the *maturity date* is the date on which the bond matures and the date when the issuer pays the *face value* to the bond holder.

The bond holder may choose to hold the bond until it matures or may sell it before maturity. However, when a bond is sold, the current purchaser is entitled to the remaining interest payments and face value payment. When an investor chooses to hold a bond to maturity, that investor receives each interest payment and the face value at maturity. If an investor chooses to sell the bond prior to maturity, the investor may do so at a premium or a discount. In some cases, bonds are listed on an exchange and thus easily traded. In other cases, bonds trade in an over-the-counter market, meaning not on a formal exchange.[16]

In the event a bond holder desires to sell a bond, the bond holder must determine the present value of the bond, both its face value and its interest payments, in order to understand what the bond is currently worth so as to determine an acceptable sales price.

EXAMPLE 8.17   **PRESENT VALUE OF A BOND DETERMINATION**

Assume your client holds $140,000 worth of 15-year corporate bonds with a coupon rate of 7 percent compounded annually and the client has now held the bonds for four full years. In order to determine the present value of the bond, the present value of the face value and the interest payments must be calculated using the present value of a lump sum table (see **Exhibit J**) and present value of an ordinary annuity table (see **Exhibit L**) or the relevant formulas, respectively. Knowing that there are 11 years or periods remaining in the term of the bond (15 years – 4 years) and the interest rate is 7 percent compounded annually, which equates to $9,800 per year ($140,000 x .07), the calculations are as follows:

$$\text{PV of Face Value} = \$140,000 \times .4751$$
$$= \$66,514.00$$
$$\text{PV of Interest Payments} = \$9,800 \times 7.4987$$
$$= \$73,487.26$$
$$\text{PV of Bond} = \$66,514.00 + \$73,487.26$$
$$= \$140,001.26$$

In this example, the present value of the bond is $140,001.26, which is the total of the present value of the face amount (a lump sum) and present value of the interest payments (an ordinary annuity). If this client were to sell the bond at this point in time with the assumption that the market interest rate remained at 7 percent, the client now knows the bond's present value to use as a benchmark.

However, in most cases when an investor decides to sell a bond, she will not receive the present value of the bond due to the fact that the current market interest rate has likely fluctuated. There is an inverse relationship between the value of a bond in the secondary market and the current interest rate.[17] If the

---

[16]JEFFREY J. HAAS, CORPORATE FINANCE 61 (2014).
[17]*Id.*

current interest rate is higher than the bond's coupon rate, the bond is worth less in the secondary market. On the other hand, if the current interest rate is lower than the bond's coupon rate, the bond is worth more in the secondary market.

1. Increased Market Interest Rates

As noted above, when new bonds are being issued at an interest rate that is higher than the coupon rate on a previously issued bond, then the value of the preexisting bond decreases and it is sold at a discount on the secondary market. This is a result of the fact that an investor could purchase a new bond with a higher coupon rate and thus receive a higher interest payment and rate of return than it could through a purchase of the preexisting bond at the lower interest rate. However, the selling bond holder may be willing to sell at a discount in order to reinvest and earn a higher rate of return.

EXAMPLE 8.18   **PV OF BOND IN INCREASED MARKET INTEREST RATES**

Utilizing the same facts above, assume that new bonds are being issued with a 9 percent coupon rate compounded annually. In order to determine the value of the previously issued bond, calculate the present value of the face value and interest payments at the current market interest rate of 9 percent for the remaining life of the bond, which is 11 years. That calculation would be as follows:

$$PV \text{ of Face Value} = \$140,000 \times .3875$$
$$= \$54,250.00$$
$$PV \text{ of Interest Payments} = \$9,800 \times 6.8052$$
$$= \$66,690.96$$
$$PV \text{ of Bond} - \text{Discounted} = \$54,250.00 + \$66,690.96$$
$$= \$120,940.96$$

As a result of the increased interest rates, the preexisting bond is now worth $19,059.04 less than its face value and would sell at a discount on the secondary market.

---

2. Decreased Market Interest Rates

When new bonds are being issued at an interest rate that is lower than the coupon rate on a previously issued bond, then the value of the preexisting bond increases and it is sold at a premium on the secondary market. This is a result of the fact that an investor can only purchase a new bond at a lower coupon rate, and thus receives a lower interest payment and rate of return than it could through a purchase of the preexisting bond with the higher interest rate.

EXAMPLE 8.19   **PV OF BOND IN DECREASED MARKET INTEREST RATES**

Utilizing the same facts above, assume that new bonds are being issued with a 5 percent coupon rate compounded annually. In order to determine the value of the previously issued bond, calculate the present value of the face value and interest payments at the current market interest rate of 5 percent for the remaining life of the bond, which is 11 years. That calculation would be as follows:

$$PV \text{ of Face Value} = \$140,000 \times .5847$$
$$= \$81,858.00$$
$$PV \text{ of Interest Payments} = \$9,800 \times 8.3064$$
$$= \$81,402.72$$
$$PV \text{ of Bond} - \text{Premium} = \$81,858.00 + \$81,402.72$$
$$= \$163,260.72$$

As a result of the decreased interest rates, the preexisting bond is now worth $23,260.72 more than its face value and would sell at a premium on the secondary market.

EXAMPLE 8.20   **BOND VALUATION COMPARISONS**

The following table compares the actual present value of the bond, the present value of the bond in an increased interest rate market, and the present value of the bond in a decreased interest rate market.

	PV—Actual (@ 7%)	PV—Discounted (@ 9%)	PV—Premium (@ 5%)
Face Amount	$66,514.00	$54,250.00	$81,858.00
Interest Payments	$73,487.26	$66,690.96	$81,402.72
Total	$140,001.26	$120,940.96	$163,260.72

3. Other Bond Features

The discussion above focused on a traditional bond, one that is issued for a long term at a set interest rate or coupon rate and where the issuer will make all the interest payments on the coupon dates and repay the face value on the maturity date. However, there are other types and features of bonds.

A zero coupon bond is a type of bond that pays no annual interest, but due to this feature, it is sold at a discount from its face value. At maturity, the investor in this type of bond receives the full face value, and so the difference between the face value and the discounted sales price represents the return to the investor. One negative feature of the zero coupon bond is that the investor must pay taxes on the imputed income from the investment even though not receiving an actual interest payment.[18] As a result, many individuals choose not to invest in this type of bond, though tax-exempt entities often take advantage of it.

In some instances, an issuer issues a convertible bond, which means that the bond has a conversion option that allows the investor to convert that bond into some type of equity interest, whether common or preferred stock. There are generally triggers that allow for this type of bond to be converted. In other instances, an issuer issues a callable bond. This type of bond gives the issuer of the bond the right to call the bond and buy it back from the investor prior to its maturity date. Lastly, an issuer may issue a bond with a put option that gives the investor the right to put the bond back to the issuer and receive payment prior to maturity.

4. Bond Ratings

Bonds are generally given a rating by a credit rating agency that indicates the creditworthiness of the bond. These ratings are assessed and adjusted periodically based on current facts and circumstances regarding that particular bond issuer. This rating assists an investor in assessing how likely it is that the bond issuer, whether a corporation or the government, will make the interest payments and repay the face value of the bond at maturity. There are two primary credit rating agencies: Standard & Poor's Corp. (S&P) and Moody's Investors Service, Inc. (Moody's).

EXAMPLE 8.21   **S&P AND MOODY'S CREDIT RATINGS**[19]

The following table sets forth the credit ratings used by S&P and Moody's to rate the creditworthiness of bonds, or long-term debt:

Rating Description		S&P Rating	Moody's Rating
Investment Grade	Prime	AAA	Aaa
	High Grade	AA+, AA, AA-	Aa1, Aa2, Aa3
	Upper Medium Grade	A+, A, A-	A1, A2, A3
	Lower Medium Grade	BBB+, BBB, BBB-	Baa1, Baa2, Baa3

---

[18]Jeffrey J. Haas, Corporate Finance 66 (2014).
[19]S&P Global Ratings, Understanding Ratings, *available at* http://www.spratings.com/en_US/understanding-ratings#firstPage; Moody's Inv'rs Serv., Rating Symbols and Definitions (July 2017), *available at* https://www.moodys.com/researchdocumentcontentpage.aspx?docid=PBC_79004.

Non-Investment Grade	Speculative	BB+, BB, BB-	Ba1, Ba2, Ba3
	Highly Speculative	B+, B, B-	B1, B2, B3
	Substantial Risks	CCC+	Caa1
	Extremely Speculative	CCC, CCC-	Caa2, Caa3
	Default Imminent	CC, C	Ca
	In Default	D	C

EXAMPLE 8.22 RATING DESCRIPTION EXPLANATIONS[20]

The following table sets forth a brief explanation of each of the rating descriptions:

Rating Description		Explanation
Investment Grade	Prime	Extremely strong capacity to meet financial commitments; highest quality and lowest level of credit risk
	High Grade	Very strong capacity to meet financial commitments; high quality and low credit risk
	Upper Medium Grade	Strong capacity to meet financial commitments, but somewhat susceptible to adverse economic conditions and changes; upper medium quality and low credit risk
	Lower Medium Grade	Adequate capacity to meet financial commitments, but susceptible to adverse economic conditions; medium quality and moderate credit risk
Non-Investment Grade	Speculative	Less vulnerable in the near-term but faces major ongoing uncertainties related to business, financial, and economic conditions; speculative and subject to substantial credit risk
	Highly Speculative	Currently has capacity to meet financial commitments, but more vulnerable to adverse business, financial, and economic conditions; speculative and subject to high credit risk
	Substantial Risks	Currently vulnerable and dependent on favorable business, financial, and economic conditions to meet financial commitments; speculative, poor standing, and very high credit risk
	Extremely Speculative	
	Default Imminent	Highly vulnerable and while default has not yet occurred it is virtually certain; highly speculative and likely in or near default with slight prospect of principal and interest recovery
	In Default	Payment default on a financial commitment; bankruptcy petition has been filed; typically in default with little prospect of principal and interest recovery

[20]S&P Global Ratings, Understanding Ratings, *available at* http://www.spratings.com/en_US/understanding-ratings#firstPage; Moody's Inv'rs Serv., Rating Symbols and Definitions (July 2017), *available at* https://www.moodys.com/researchdocumentcontentpage.aspx?docid=PBC_79004.

Bond Valuation Problem 8.15

The following problem addresses bond valuation calculations.

Problem 8.15

Exactly seven years ago, Zinc Corporation issued 20-year convertible bonds with an 8 percent coupon rate and annual payments. Sam Jones purchased $100,000 worth of Zinc Corporation's bonds upon their original issuance.

Part A: What are Sam's bonds worth today if the current 20-year bond rate is still 8 percent?

Part B: What are Sam's bonds worth today if the current 20-year bond rate is 6 percent?

Part C: What are Sam's bonds worth today if the current 20-year bond rate is 9 percent?

Financial Terms and Covenants in Contracts

A. INTRODUCTION

While understanding basic accounting concepts is a necessary knowledge base for any lawyer, it is also important for lawyers to understand financial terms and covenants and their implications in the context of various contractual agreements. Finance-related provisions arise in many contracts, such as a commercial loan agreement, indenture agreement, promissory note, or merger and acquisition agreement. These financial terms and covenants require an understanding of how the term or covenant is applied or calculated, as well as how it may impact the client.

B. COMMERCIAL LOAN AGREEMENT

Many entities, whether private or public, enter into various types of commercial loan transactions with single lenders or syndicates of lenders to obtain financing for some aspect of the entity's business and operations. These commercial loans may fund the entity's day-to-day operations, the ongoing purchase and replacement of equipment, or a business expansion. Commercial loans take many forms, such as a traditional term loan (a lump sum amount) or revolving credit facility (access to funds as needed), and may be secured or unsecured. Additionally, many commercial loan transactions include letters of credit, or a bank letter guaranteeing an entity's payment. As a part of any commercial loan transaction, the borrower and lenders will enter into a loan agreement that explicitly sets forth the terms and conditions of the commercial loan.

1. Financial Covenants

One of the main components of the commercial loan agreement is the financial covenants provisions. These types of covenants monitor certain financial aspects of the borrower, such as its net worth, liquidity, cash flow, and leverage. One of the primary reasons for financial covenants in this context is to protect the lenders during the term of the loan by monitoring the borrower's financial condition, as well as ensuring the repayment of the loan by the borrower. As a result of the significance of these covenants to the borrower, the entity's lawyers should have a clear understanding of financial covenants so that they are in a position to advise their client regarding those contract terms, as well as the risks, impacts, and ongoing obligations to the entity as a result.

Financial covenants can be either affirmative or negative, meaning the borrower either promises to take a certain action or promises not to take a certain action. Affirmative covenants may be viewed as "housekeeping" type covenants and require the borrower to do such things as keep accurate financial records, provide financial statements to the lenders, or permit the lenders to inspect the borrower's books and records.[1] Negative covenants, generally the more stringent of the two types, require the borrower to refrain from taking certain actions, such as not incurring additional long-term debt, or require the borrower to meet certain financial levels, such as maintaining a certain level of earnings before interest, taxes, depreciation, and amortization (EBITDA). A critical component of all financial covenants, but in particular negative covenants, is the definitions of the relevant terms. In order to fully understand the covenant, its requirements, and its impact, the lawyer must carefully read and decipher the definitions of the terms that play a key role in the covenant's requirements.[2] There are two main types of negative financial covenants in a commercial loan agreement: incurrence and maintenance.

a. Incurrence Covenants

Incurrence covenants prevent the borrower from taking certain actions unless it remains in compliance with the financial conditions specified in that particular covenant. An incurrence covenant is tested when the borrower desires to take the action, such as declaring and issuing a dividend to its common stockholders or incurring additional debt. As a result, only the borrower can trigger, or trip, the incurrence covenant and cause a breach under the terms of the loan agreement by taking an action that violates the specified conditions.

---

[1]Carolyn E. C. Paris, Drafting for Corporate Finance: Concepts, Deals, and Documents 162-180 (2d ed. 2014).
[2]Id.

b. Maintenance Covenants

Maintenance covenants require the borrower to maintain certain financial thresholds over the term of the loan, and on many occasions are subject to adjustment as the loan term progresses; typically becoming more restrictive. Maintenance covenants are tested at a set point in time or on a recurring basis (e.g., quarterly) and the borrower must be in compliance with the covenants on each testing date or for each testing period. Otherwise, the borrower will be in breach of the loan agreement, and failure to meet a maintenance covenant often results in an immediate default. Maintenance covenants are often thought of as either balance sheet or cash flow driven.

i. Balance Sheet Covenants

A balance sheet covenant examines the borrower's condition at a specific point in time, such as at quarter end.[3] Balance sheet covenants are more typical for a borrower that is deemed "investment grade," meaning a borrower with greater financial stability.[4] The two most common balance sheet covenants are minimum net worth and debt-to-equity.

(a) Minimum Net Worth

The minimum net worth covenant requires the borrower to maintain a certain amount or level of stockholders' equity or net worth, or in essence a certain amount of assets in excess of liabilities. The critical definition for this covenant is stockholders' equity and, in particular, what is included or what is deducted as a part of the calculation. In addition, the definition of intangible assets and what is or is not included is relevant if a tangible net worth calculation derivation is utilized to calculate net worth.

In the traditional minimum net worth covenant, stockholders' equity can be calculated in two ways, and the borrower is required to maintain a minimum level of equity or greater utilizing that calculation. Net worth can be calculated in the following ways:

Method One: In this traditional calculation, the entity's net worth is simply the value of total assets less total liabilities (or its total stockholders' equity):

$$\text{Net Worth} = \text{Total Assets} - \text{Total Liabilities}$$

Method Two: In this alternative calculation, the entity does not have to decrease its stockholders' equity by the amount of its treasury stock (if any exists):

Net Worth = Capital Stock + Capital Surplus + Retained Earnings, where capital stock includes common stock and preferred stock and capital surplus is the equivalent of additional paid-in-capital

---

[3]*Id.* at 207-216.
[4]Eric Klar, Marius Griskonis, & Hazem Derhalli, *Understanding and Negotiating Financial Covenants,* Practical Law Finance (July 23, 2014), *available at* Practical Law Co.

Method Three: In a derivation of this covenant, called tangible net worth, the value of intangible assets such as intellectual property and goodwill is deducted from stockholders' equity or net worth:[5]

$$\text{Tangible Net Worth} = \text{Capital Stock} + \text{Capital Surplus} +$$
$$\text{Retained Earnings} - \text{Intangible Assets}$$

← less liquid. e.g copy

No matter the calculation of net worth, the loan agreement will establish a minimum threshold that the borrower cannot fall below without being in breach of the covenant. It is also common for the minimum net worth requirement to escalate over the course of the term of the loan, meaning the threshold amount increases periodically and thus requires the borrower to maintain increasing levels of minimum net worth.

(b) Debt-to-Equity or Debt-to-Total-Capital

The debt-to-equity or debt-to-total-capital covenant examines the amount of debt the borrower carries as compared to its stockholders' equity or total capital (stockholders' equity plus total debt), and curtails the amount of debt the borrower can carry during the term of the loan agreement.[6] The critical definition for this covenant is what is included in the determination of total debt. Total debt will generally include indebtedness for all borrowed money, as well as obligations pursuant to (i) bonds, debentures, and notes; (ii) mandatorily redeemable equity interests; (iii) letters of credit; (iv) guarantees; and (v) some types of deferred purchases. This covenant is calculated as follows:

$$\text{Debt-to-Equity} = \text{Total Debt} \div \text{Stockholders' Equity}$$
$$\text{Debt-to-Total-Capital} = \text{Total Debt} \div (\text{Stockholders' Equity} + \text{Total Debt})$$

No matter which calculation is utilized, the loan agreement will establish a maximum ratio or percentage that the borrower cannot exceed without being in breach of the covenant, as the higher the ratio, the greater amount of debt the borrower carries. In some loan agreements, it is common for the maximum ratio or percentage to decrease periodically, thus requiring the borrower to either decrease its total debt or increase its stockholders' equity (e.g., through increases in retained earnings) to meet the more restrictive threshold.

ii. Cash Flow Covenants — *based on income statement*

A cash flow covenant tests the borrower's financial condition over a period of time, whether a full fiscal quarter, four fiscal quarters, or four rolling fiscal quarters.[7] Cash flow covenants are more typical for a borrower that is deemed "non-investment grade," meaning the borrower has greater financial risk and so its

---

[5]Paris, *supra* note 1, at 207-216.
[6]*Id.*
[7]*Id.*

cash flow is crucial in meeting its debt obligations.[8] Some of the most common cash flow covenants are minimum EBITDA, Debt-to-EBITA, and coverage ratios.

(a) Minimum EBITDA

The minimum EBITDA covenant requires the borrower to maintain a minimum level of EBITDA or in essence a certain amount of earnings. The idea is that earnings generate cash flow, which is used to repay debt obligations. The critical definition for this covenant is EBITDA and, in particular, what is added back to EBITDA to arrive at its final determination. Some common adjustments to EBITDA include the addition of extraordinary losses or expenses and discontinued operation losses, and the subtraction of extraordinary or unusual gains and discontinued operation gains (i.e., those amounts that are not considered to be losses or gains in the ordinary course of operations).[9] While GAAP no longer requires an entity to separately report extraordinary losses or gains on the income statement, those items that are extraordinary or unusual in nature are still detailed in the entity's financial statement footnotes.

The loan agreement will establish a minimum or floor for EBITDA that the borrower cannot fall below without being in breach of the covenant. As it is with the minimum net worth covenant, it is common for the minimum EBITDA requirement to escalate over the course of the term of the loan, meaning the threshold amount increases periodically and thus requires the borrower to maintain increasing levels of earnings.

(b) Debt-to-EBITDA

The debt-to-EBITDA covenant is a leverage ratio and requires the borrower to not exceed a certain amount of indebtedness as compared to its earnings attributed to its primary business operations. The covenant attempts to ensure that the borrower can meet its loan obligations from its cash flows. The critical definitions for this covenant are total debt and EBITDA. This covenant is calculated as follows:

$$\text{Debt-to-EBITDA} = \text{Total Debt} \div \text{EBITDA}$$

The loan agreement will establish a maximum ratio or ceiling that the borrower cannot exceed without being in breach of the covenant, as the greater amount of debt a borrower carries, the greater the possibility it cannot meet its obligations. It is common for the maximum ratio or ceiling to decrease periodically, thus requiring the borrower to either decrease its total debt obligations or increase its earnings.

(c) Interest Coverage

The interest coverage covenant requires the borrower to maintain a certain level of earnings from its primary business operations as compared to its

---

[8]Klar, Griskonis, & Derhalli, *supra* note 4.
[9]*Id.*

interest expense. This covenant is meant to ensure that the borrower can meet its interest expense obligations on the loan through its cash flows. The critical definitions for this covenant are EBITDA and interest expense. The definition of interest expense typically includes any interest due on traditional debt, as well as interest attributable to letters of credit, capital leases, and sales-leaseback transactions. In addition, the borrower is generally not permitted to offset its interest expense with any interest income it earns. This covenant is calculated as follows:

$$\text{Interest Coverage} = \text{EBITDA} \div \text{Interest Expense}$$

The loan agreement will set a minimum or floor for the interest coverage ratio that the borrower cannot fall below without being in breach of the covenant, as the higher this ratio, the greater the ability of the borrower to meet its interest expense obligations through its earnings. It is common for the minimum ratio to escalate over the course of the loan, thus requiring the borrower to either increase its earnings or decrease its interest expense obligations.

(d) Fixed Charge Coverage

The fixed charge coverage covenant requires the borrower to maintain a certain level of earnings from its primary business operations as compared to its fixed charges. This covenant is meant to ensure that the borrower can meet its regular and ongoing fixed expenses. The critical definitions for this covenant are EBITDA and fixed charges. The definition of fixed charges typically includes any cash interest expense, principal payments due on debt obligations, certain lease and capital expenditures, mandatory or cash dividend payments, and taxes paid in cash.[10] This covenant is calculated as follows:

$$\text{Fixed Charge Coverage} = \text{EBITDA} \div \text{Fixed Charges}$$

The loan agreement will set a minimum or floor for the fixed charge coverage ratio that the borrower cannot fall below without being in breach of the covenant, as the higher this ratio, the greater the ability of the borrower to meet its fixed charge expenses. In many circumstances the minimum fixed charge coverage ratio will remain static over the course of the loan.

C. INDENTURES, BONDS, AND NOTES

There are three main types of debt instruments that an entity may issue as a means to raise additional capital: debentures, bonds, and notes. These debt instruments result in a loan to the entity with an agreement to repay that amount plus interest at some point in the future. All of these debt instruments

---

[10] *Id.*

are contractually governed by a promissory note that sets forth the terms of the relationship between the parties, meaning the borrower (the corporate entity borrowing the money) and the bond holder or note holder (the party lending the money). The contract that governs a debenture and a bond is called an indenture and is typically between the borrower and the trustee, who acts as the agent for the holders of the debentures or the bonds. The contract that governs a note is a note agreement and is generally a direct contract between the borrower and the note holders.

While bonds and notes are often secured debt obligations, a debenture is usually unsecured. Additionally, these debt instruments may contain other interesting terms and features, such as fixed versus floating interest, a set term versus a revolving loan, a senior versus a subordinated obligation, and a convertible right versus non-conversion.[11]

1. Financial Covenants

As they are in a commercial loan agreement, the financial covenants are one of the main components of an indenture or note agreement. The financial covenants protect the debt holders by imposing restrictions on the borrower's conduct of its business during the term of the obligation so as to ensure repayment by the borrower at the end of the term. The covenants contained in the governing contract will vary depending on a number of factors, including the borrower's credit rating or riskiness, the borrower's industry and related market conditions, and the type of debt obligation issued, secured or unsecured.[12]

Contracts governing debt obligations often contain similar financial covenants as those discussed above in the context of a commercial loan agreement, including minimum net worth, debt-to-equity, and fixed charge coverage.[13] In addition, these agreements contain a number of other negative financial covenants that prevent the borrower from engaging in certain acts, of which the main ones will be discussed below. As is the case with commercial loan agreements, the definitions tied to financial covenants in debt instruments are also critical to understanding the scope of the covenant and its implications for and requirements of the borrower.

a. Limitation on Incurrence of Indebtedness

One of the most important covenants is the restriction on the borrower from incurring additional debt. By limiting the borrower's ability to incur additional debt, it protects the debt holders by preventing the borrower from increasing its default risk, creating additional claims against its assets, and decreasing the

---

[11]BNA, In Practice: Finance, Document Description – Notes & Debentures, Bloomberg Law Reports (Bloomberg Law, Banking & Finance, 2017).
[12]BNA, In Practice: Finance, Drafting Guide – Indenture: Financial Covenants (Unsecured Debt), Bloomberg Law Reports (Bloomberg Law, Banking & Finance, 2016).
[13]Jeffrey J. Haas, Corporate Finance 184-185 (2014).

value of the debt securities.[14] This covenant prevents the borrower from incurring additional debt unless it meets the established consolidated coverage ratio after giving effect to the additional indebtedness. Meeting this covenant is an indication that the borrower is generating sufficient cash flow to meet its ongoing fixed obligations.[15] The consolidated coverage ratio is calculated as follows:

$$\text{Consolidated Coverage Ratio} = \text{EBITDA} \div \text{Fixed Charges}$$

In addition to being able to incur additional indebtedness if the consolidated coverage ratio is met, the borrower often seeks other exceptions to this covenant. Those may include exceptions for (i) debt that existed prior to or at the time of the issuance of the current debt securities; (ii) bank debt via a credit facility up to a certain dollar limit; (iii) intra-company debt; and (iv) debt as a result of the refinancing or restructuring of existing debt, provided there is no increase in the principal.[16] In some circumstances, the consolidated coverage ratio may increase over the course of the debt obligation and thus allow the borrower to incur a greater amount of debt if the ratio is met.

b. Limitation on Restricted Payments

This restricted payments covenant limits the borrower's ability to expend cash on certain restricted items in an effort to keep money within the entity so that the borrower is able to meet its debt obligation.[17] Restricted payments typically include payments of cash dividends, payments to repurchase stock, payments to redeem subordinated debt, investments in or loans to third parties, and guarantees of indebtedness of third parties.[18] The borrower will seek exceptions that allow it to make (i) restricted payments if a specified financial ratio is met or if the restricted payments do not exceed a set dollar threshold; (ii) payments for capital expenditures; (iii) payments on intra-company loans and guarantees; and (iv) investments in or acquisitions of restricted subsidiaries, meaning subsidiaries that are included with the parent and governed by the indenture or note agreement.[19]

c. Limitation on Liens

This lien covenant, which is generally included in an agreement for the issuance of secured debt obligations, prevents the borrower from creating or allowing

---

[14]*Id.* at 178-179.
[15]*Id.*
[16]*Id.*
[17]Gerald T. Nowak, *Negotiating the High-Yield Indenture,* USA (Nat'l/Fed.) (Feb. 17, 2009), *available at* Practical Law Co. 6-384-6814.
[18]*Id.*
[19]BNA, In Practice: Finance, Drafting Guide – Indenture: Financial Covenants (Unsecured Debt), Bloomberg Law Reports (Bloomberg Law, Banking & Finance, 2016).

additional liens on its assets unless certain conditions are met.[20] The idea behind this covenant is to protect the seniority rights of the debt holders so that their rights are not subordinated or diluted. The borrower will seek exceptions that allow (i) liens that existed prior to the issuance of the current debt obligations; (ii) liens that occur in the ordinary course of business, such as for workers' compensation, unemployment insurance, mechanics, and taxes; (iii) liens securing additional indebtedness permitted pursuant to that particular covenant; and (iv) liens on acquired assets.[21] It is common that the definition of permitted liens in this covenant matches the definition of permitted liens in the borrower's credit facility, if it has one in place, in order to prevent conflict and confusion.[22]

d. Limitation on the Sale of Assets

This asset sale covenant limits or prohibits the borrower from selling off substantially all of its assets except in certain circumstances such as (i) where the borrower receives consideration for the assets sold at least equal to their fair market value and the consideration is predominately (greater than 70 percent) in the form of cash or cash equivalents; (ii) where the assets are sold and replaced with other income-producing assets within a set time frame; or (iii) where the asset sale proceeds are used to repay the debt obligation.[23] The idea is that the borrower generates income from its assets and so those assets should be protected for the benefit of the business to ensure it can repay the debt holders. Additionally, the borrower's assets often act as collateral securing the debt obligation. The borrower will seek an exception that allows it to make de minimis sales of assets in the ordinary course of business.[24]

e. Limitation on Transactions with Affiliates

This affiliate transaction covenant imposes restrictions on transactions between the borrower and its affiliates. The idea of this covenant is to prevent the borrower from circumventing the restricted payments covenant by disguising a payment, such as a cash dividend, as a business transaction with an affiliate and thus draining cash from the borrower's business that should be utilized to meets its obligations.[25] Generally, the covenant will allow the borrower to engage in arm's-length transactions with affiliates, in affiliate transactions that do not exceed a specified dollar threshold, or in affiliate transactions approved by the borrower's board of directors.[26]

---

[20]Jeffrey J. Haas, Corporate Finance 183 (2014).
[21]Bloomberg Law Reports, *supra* note 19.
[22]Bloomberg Law Reports, *supra* note 19.
[23]Haas, *supra* note 20, at 180-181.
[24]Bloomberg Law Reports, *supra* note 19.
[25]Haas, *supra* note 20, at 183.
[26]BNA, In Practice: Finance, Drafting Guide – Indenture: Financial Covenants (Unsecured Debt), Bloomberg Law Reports (Bloomberg Law, Banking & Finance, 2016).

f. Limitation on Sale and Leaseback Transactions

This sale-leaseback covenant, which is typically only included in a debt offering for senior notes, imposes restrictions on the type of sale-leaseback transactions into which the borrower can enter.[27] Similar to the sale of assets covenant, this covenant is attempting to protect the borrower's assets for the benefit of the debt holders, since in a sale-leaseback the borrower will sell the asset and lease it back with the obligation to make lease payments. So, while the borrower can still utilize the asset to generate income, it no longer owns that asset. Generally, the covenant will allow the borrower to enter into a sale-leaseback transaction provided (i) it does not violate the limitation on indebtedness or restrictions on lien covenants, (ii) the proceeds received at least equal the fair market value of the assets sold, and (iii) the proceeds are used to purchase replacement assets or to pay off the debt obligation.[28] The borrower will typically seek exceptions that allow it to enter into a sale-leaseback with a restricted subsidiary or if the term is for a short period of time.[29]

g. Limitation on Dividends

This dividend covenant, which is included in a debt offering where the borrower is an entity with restricted subsidiaries (a subsidiary subject to the covenants in the governing debt instrument), prevents the borrower and the restricted subsidiaries from creating limitations on the ability of the restricted subsidiaries to declare and pay dividends, or stream cash to or transfer assets to the borrower (the holding or parent company).[30] The idea is that the borrower should use the cash generated by its subsidiaries to meet its obligations to its debt holders. Typical exceptions to this covenant exist for restrictions that were already in place at the time of the issuance of the debt obligation or limitations that are imposed by law (e.g., limits on the amount of cash dividend the restricted subsidiary can declare and issue to the parent company).

D. MERGER AND ACQUISITION AGREEMENT

In the merger and acquisition context, covenants play a significant role in the acquisition agreement, many of which are financially oriented, such as requiring the target to continue to use the same accounting principles and practices it has always used, requiring the target to not accelerate the collection of accounts receivable or delay the payment of accounts payable, or requiring the target to not incur additional debt.

---

[27]Jeffrey J. Haas, Corporate finance 183-184 (2014).
[28]*Id.*, at 183-184.
[29]Bloomberg Law Reports, *supra* note 26.
[30]Gerald T. Nowak, *Negotiating the High-Yield Indenture*, USA (Nat'l/Fed.), (Feb. 17, 2009), *available at* Practical Law Co.

However, there are two other provisions that arise in the context of a merger and acquisition that have direct implications for the entity's lawyer (whether representing the buyer or the seller): purchase price adjustments and earn-outs. While the businesspeople generally determine the terms of the purchase price adjustment or earn-out provision, the lawyers are tasked with drafting that provision in the merger and acquisition agreement to reflect the parties' intent. As a result, not only must transactional lawyers understand the concepts of a purchase price adjustment and earn-out, but also they must be able to draft language that reflects those two accounting-driven concepts.

1. Purchase Price Adjustments

A purchase price adjustment, which is generally only found in a private merger transaction, is a provision that provides for an adjustment to the closing purchase price at some point in the future, or post-closing. The underlying concept of the purchase price adjustment is that the agreed upon purchase price between the buyer and target's selling shareholders is determined based on financial statements of the target provided at some point prior to closing (maybe even a month or more prior to closing) when the merger and acquisition agreement is executed. The purchase price adjustment ensures that the parties receive the agreed upon value of the target based on its financial position as of the actual closing date.[31]

Depending on the terms of the merger and acquisition agreement, there may be one or two purchase price adjustments. In the simplest scenario, there is one purchase price adjustment that is determined once the financial statements of the target as of the closing date are finalized—often 30 to 60 days after closing. In the more typical scenario, there are two purchase price adjustments—one based on the financial statements of the target prepared a few business days prior to closing and the second based on the finalized financial statements of the target as of the closing date—30 to 60 days after closing. In the two-adjustment scenario, the purchase price agreed upon at the date of the merger and acquisition agreement is adjusted a few business days prior to closing based upon the parties' mutually agreed upon financial metrics applied to the target's estimated closing date financial statement numbers. Then the second adjustment is made 30 to 60 days after closing using the target's final financial statement numbers as of closing. By using this two-adjustment method, the difference between the agreed upon financial metric and the actual financial metric as of closing is less likely to have significantly fluctuated and thus requires less of a purchase price adjustment payment between the parties post closing of the transaction.

The purchase price adjustment is most often based on a calculation involving the target's net working capital, meaning current assets less current

---

[31]BNA, In Practice: M&A, Clause Description – Description of Transaction: Purchase Price Adjustment, Bloomberg Law Reports (Bloomberg Law, Corporate, 2016).

liabilities, but other financial metrics such as inventory or accounts receivable may be used depending on the nature of the transaction, the target, and the target's industry.[32] Net working capital is the most common metric, as the buyer generally anticipates having a certain amount of working capital upon closing of the merger transaction that it will require for the smooth continuation of the target's business operations. The difference between the agreed upon net working capital that was established prior to closing and the actual net working capital as of the closing date forms the basis for the purchase price adjustment. As a result, the purchase price adjustment can be either negative or positive. If the net working capital on the closing date is determined to be below the agreed upon net working capital, then the target's selling shareholders owe the buyer a refund on the purchase price. On the other hand, if the net working capital on the closing date is determined to be above the agreed upon net working capital, then the buyer owes the target's selling shareholders additional money as part of the purchase price. An example of a net working capital purchase price adjustment provision is set forth in **Exhibit M**.

A critical component of the purchase price adjustment is accurately setting forth the financial metrics and formula to be used, and the definitions of the pertinent terms. For example, if the purchase price is based on net working capital, the terms current assets and current liabilities should be specifically defined so there is no confusion between the parties as to what amounts are included or excluded in the calculation. In addition, the purchase price adjustment provision must address such issues as (i) whether there is a cap on the amount of the adjustment payment; (ii) whether a de minimis difference requires no payment, and if so, what is de minimis; (iii) whether just a negative result, or if both a negative and a positive result, requires a payment by a party; and (iv) how disputes regarding the final calculation will be handled if, or when, they arise.

2. Earn-Outs

An earn-out, which is more prevalent in a private merger transaction, is a provision stipulating that a portion of the purchase price may be paid to the target's selling shareholders after the transaction has closed and based upon certain financial metrics to be achieved by the target post-closing. An earn-out is often included when the buyer and target's selling shareholders are unable to agree on the purchase price or have differing perspectives on the value of the target, with the target's selling shareholders typically believing the target's value is greater than the buyer's valuation.[33] The earn-out is a contingent purchase price payment, as it is only paid if the established metrics are achieved, and so

---

[32]*Id.*
[33]George M. Taylor, Robert T. Harper, & Scott Whittaker, Portfolio 61-3rd: Negotiated Acquisitions, VII. Purchase Price (Bloomberg Law, Corporate Practice Portfolio Series: Forms of Business Portfolios).

the target's selling shareholders may or may not earn this additional purchase price consideration.

The financial metrics that determine whether or not the earn-out is paid are deal specific, but the most common metrics include the target achieving a certain level of (i) net revenues; (ii) earnings before interest and taxes (EBIT); (iii) earnings before interest, taxes, depreciation, and amortization (EBITDA); or (iv) net income.[34] An earn-out may be structured as a single payment if the set financial metric is achieved as of the specified date, though it is more often structured as a tiered payment based upon the percentage of the financial metric met by the target on the specified date or on multiple dates. While an earn-out may seem simple at first glance, the drafted provision must set out the earn-out formula with clarity and precision so that it does not result in a potential dispute regarding the earn-out calculation. An example of an earn-out provision is set forth in **Exhibit N**.

All of the parties to the merger transaction will have their own set of apprehensions regarding an earn-out provision. The target's selling shareholders will be concerned (i) with how the target will be managed and operated by the buyer post-closing, (ii) that the target's books and records remain separate so the earn-out can be determined, and (iii) that accounting practices and procedures remain consistent post-closing, all so the buyer does not manipulate the target's financial results in such a way as to prevent the target's selling shareholders from achieving the earn-out payment.[35] On the other hand, the buyer will be concerned with restrictions regarding its operation of the target post-closing, ranging from (i) the requirement to operate the target in a specified manner; (ii) the requirement to maintain separate books and records; (iii) the rights of the target's selling shareholders to veto certain target post-closing actions; and (iv) the ability to integrate the target into its overall business enterprise.[36]

As a result of the plethora of issues that surround an earn-out, this merger and acquisition agreement provision must be scrutinized by both sides to ensure that it is an accurate reflection of the agreed upon terms. In addition, the earn-out provisions must address how disputes regarding the earn-out calculation will be handled if, or more likely when, they arise.

Financial Terms and Covenants Problems 9.1 to 9.3

The following problems require the review, assessment, and analysis of various financial terms and covenants in transactional documents.

---

[34]Maryann A. Waryjas, Acquiring or Selling the Privately Held Company 2003: Corporate Law and Practice Course Handbook Series 937-942 (2008).
[35]Id.
[36]Id.

Problem 9.1: Financial Covenants in Loan Agreements

Access the following documents through a database (e.g., Westlaw, Lexis, Bloomberg Law, or the SEC's EDGAR system):

1. RetailMeNot, Inc.'s (as the borrower) Second Amended and Restated Revolving Credit and Term Loan Agreement Dated as of December 23, 2014, filed as Exhibit 1.1 to its Form 8-K dated and filed on December 29, 2014.
2. RetailMeNot, Inc.'s Form 10-K for the period ended December 31, 2015, filed on February 19, 2016.
3. RetailMeNot, Inc.'s Form 10-K for the period ended December 31, 2016, filed on February 17, 2017.

Part A: Review Section 7 (affirmative covenants) and Section 8 (negative covenants) of the Loan Agreement in conjunction with the relevant definitions to gain a clear understanding of the entity's financial covenant obligations.

Part B: Using the entity's financial statements and footnotes filed with its Form 10-Ks for December 31, 2015 and 2016, for each year calculate and assess whether the entity met its requirements under Section 7.9(a) — Minimum EBITDA, Section 7.9(b) — Maximum Consolidated Total Debt to EBITDA Ratio, Section 7.9(c) — Minimum Fixed Charge Coverage Ratio, and Section 7.9(d) — Consolidated Senior Secured Debt to EBITDA Ratio.

Problem 9.2: Indenture

Access the following document through a database (e.g., Westlaw, Lexis, Bloomberg Law, or the SEC's EDGAR system):

1. Lithia Motors, Inc.'s Senior Notes Indenture dated as of July 24, 2017, and filed as Exhibit 4.1 to its Form 8-K dated and filed on July 24, 2017.

Review the Indenture to gain a clear understanding of the terms of the senior notes, and in particular, review and analyze the financial covenants set forth in Article 4, Sections 4.07-4.13, to understand the entity's obligations pursuant to the Indenture.

Problem 9.3: Net Working Capital Adjustment

Access the following document through a database (e.g., Westlaw, Lexis, Bloomberg Law, or the SEC's EDGAR system):

1. Intercontinental Exchange, Inc.'s Agreement and Plan of Merger dated as of September 5, 2014, and filed as Exhibit 2.1 to its Form 8-K dated and filed on September 11, 2014.

Part A: Review and analyze the net working capital adjustment set forth in Section 1.8, including the relevant defined terms, to gain a clear understanding of the calculation of net working capital and the process for the payment of the potential purchase price adjustment.

Part B: Calculate the net working capital adjustments using the following information:

Scenario 1: E-NWC = $23,560,000 and F-NWC = $24,180,000
Scenario 2: E-NWC = $28,180,000 and F-NWC = $26,340,000

Business Valuation

A. INTRODUCTION

Business valuation is the process used to establish an estimate of the economic value of a business. There are many circumstances that may require a valuation of a business entity, such as a merger and acquisition, an asset sale, a restructuring or divestiture, a shareholder buy-sell arrangement, shareholder litigation, divorce proceedings, a reorganization, or bankruptcy liquidation. Business valuations can run the gambit from a simple model to a complex computer driven model.

There are many valuation professionals and experts who are trained to undertake a business valuation. These experts may be business valuation analysts, certified public accountants, investment bankers, business brokers, or others. Lawyers will often work with these professionals in circumstances where their client requires a valuation. So, while lawyers are not retained to undertake a business valuation, it is critical for lawyers to understand why and when a client may require a business valuation and who would be the most appropriate expert. Additionally, the lawyer will often assist in the valuation process by providing information regarding the client and its business to the valuation expert. Lastly, the lawyer must be able to read and understand the valuation report as it is generally used in the context of a legal scenario, such as establishing a purchase price in a merger transaction or establishing the value of stock in a shareholder buy-sell agreement.

B. BUSINESS VALUATION METHODS

There are three primary methods used to value a business: the income, market, or asset approach. Each method approaches the valuation from a different perspective with its own set of pros and cons. The valuation expert should select the approaches that make sense in the given circumstances, including taking into account the type of entity and valuation requested. While the valuation expert may believe that one approach will provide a more accurate result than another, in most situations the expert should utilize more than one methodology to establish the valuation. By using multiple approaches, the valuation expert can cross-check assumptions and results, and provide a more accurate valuation.

1. Income Approach

One method for business valuation utilizes an income approach and culls information from the entity's income statement regarding its future cash flows or future earnings to establish a valuation. In the income approach, the entity's future cash flows or earnings are used to estimate the value of the entity through either a capitalization or discounting process.[1] The underlying concept is that the value of the entity or an investment in an entity is equivalent to the present value of the future benefits the entity is expected to generate or produce into perpetuity, where the present value factor takes into account both the desired rate of return and the degree of risk.[2]

An income valuation method is often used to value a closely held entity, as it is typically difficult to find comparable companies for these types of entities and establish appropriate multiples, which measure an aspect of the entity's financial condition by dividing one financial metric by another.[3] The valuation expert must first determine the appropriate future benefit stream to use — earnings or cash flows — and should consider the nature and size of the entity and its business, the capital structure of the entity, and what is being valued (an entire business or simply a controlling interest), as well as the risk of investing in this entity as compared to other alternatives.[4] Once that decision is made, the valuation expert must determine whether to use a capitalization or discounting method. As many income valuations rely on cash flows as the chosen benefit stream, the methods will be discussed from that perspective.

a. Determining Cash Flows

The first step in the process of valuing an entity using a capitalized or discounted cash flow method is to determine the entity's cash flows. There are two

---

[1]Gary R. Trugman, Understanding Business Valuation: A Practical Guide to Valuing Small to Medium-Sized Businesses 308 (3d ed. 2008).
[2]Jeffrey M. Risius, Business Valuation: A Primer for the Legal Professional 65 (2007).
[3]Trugman, *supra* note 1, at 309.
[4]*Id.* at 310-311.

methods of establishing cash flows: (i) direct equity application or basic net cash flow, and (ii) total invested capital application or net cash flow for invested capital.[5] The valuation expert will select the cash flow application that is most appropriate in the given circumstances.

Basic net cash flow is the amount of cash that is available to distribute to the common stockholders of the entity and starts with the entity's normalized net income, meaning net income adjusted for such things as non-recurring events or transactions that are not arm's length.[6] In order to determine basic net cash flow, the expert starts with normalized net income and (i) adds depreciation and amortization expense, (ii) subtracts anticipated capital expenditures, (iii) adds an increase in amount of necessary working capital or subtracts a decrease in amount of necessary working capital, and (iv) adds debt borrowings or subtracts debt repayments.[7]

Net cash flow for invested capital represents the value of the entity on a "debt-free" basis.[8] In order to determine net cash flow for invested capital, the expert starts with normalized net income (as discussed above) and (i) adds interest expense, net of taxes; (ii) adds depreciation and amortization expense; (iii) subtracts anticipated capital expenditures; and (iv) adds an increase in the amount of necessary working capital or subtracts a decrease in the amount of necessary working capital.[9]

i. Capitalized Cash Flow Method

The capitalized cash flow method requires the valuation expert to determine the value of the expected benefit stream in perpetuity, in this case cash flow.[10] This method is often called a "single-period model," as it is used in those situations where the entity is assumed to have stable growth into the future, and thus uses a single benefit stream growing at a steady rate to determine the entity's valuation.[11] In order to determine the value of the entity with this method, the valuation expert must know the following: (i) cash flow (whether basic net cash flow or net cash flow for invested capital); (ii) the desired rate of return; and (iii) the projected long-term growth rate for cash flow.[12] Once this information is established, cash flow is projected forward one year based on the expected growth rate, and the projected cash flow is divided by the capitalization rate to determine the value of the entity. The capitalization rate is the difference between the desired rate of return and the projected growth rate.

---

[5]Risius, *supra* note 2, at 66; Trugman, *supra* note 1, at 312-313.
[6]Risius, *supra* note 2, at 68-70.
[7]Jeffrey J. Haas, Corporate Finance 80 (2014).
[8]Jeffrey M. Risius, Business Valuation: A Primer for the Legal Professional 67 (2007).
[9]Gary R. Trugman, Understanding Business Valuation: A Practical Guide to Valuing Small to Medium-Sized Businesses 312-313 (3d ed. 2008).
[10]Risius, *supra* note 8, at 67-68.
[11]*Id.* at 68.
[12]*Id.*

EXAMPLE 10.1   **CAPITALIZED CASH FLOW**

Assume that an entity has $250,000 in basic net cash flow, a projected steady growth rate of 4 percent, and the desired rate of return is 12 percent. The value of cash flow one year in the future is $260,000 ($250,000 × 1.04, which is the value of current net cash flow times the projected growth rate). The capitalization rate is 8 percent (12% – 4%, which is the desired return less the projected growth rate). The value of the entity is $3,250,000 ($260,000 ÷ .08, which is cash flow in one year divided by the capitalization rate).

---

ii. Discounted Cash Flow Method

The discounted cash flow method is very similar to the capitalized cash flow method, in that it requires the valuation expert to determine the value of the expected benefit stream in perpetuity and discount that benefit to present value. This method is often called a "multiple-period model," as it is used in those situations where the entity is not expected to have stable growth (whether it is accelerated, decelerated, or fluctuating growth), and thus requires two discrete calculations to determine the entity's valuation.[13] The first calculation projects the entity's cash flow over a projected discrete time period (e.g., number of years until cash flow stabilizes) and discounts that stream to present value.[14] The second calculation determines the present value of the "terminal value" of the entity, or the expected stabilized cash flow stream beyond the projected discrete time period, and discounts that to present value.[15]

In order to determine the value of the entity with this method, the valuation expert must know the following: (i) cash flow: (ii) length of time until cash flow stabilizes; (iii) the desired rate of return; (iv) the projected growth rate for the projected discrete time period; and (v) the projected growth rate for the "terminal value period" or once cash flow has stabilized.[16] Once this information is established, the first step is to project cash flow for each year during the discrete time period and discount each result to present value using the desired rate of return.[17] The second step is to determine the "terminal value" or "residual cash flow" for the period post-stabilization into perpetuity, divide by the capitalization rate, and discount to present value using the desired rate of return.[18] The last step is to add the two results together to establish the value of the entity.

---

[13]Risius, *supra* note 8, at 72-73.
[14]JEFFREY J. HAAS, CORPORATE FINANCE 79-80 (2014).
[15]*Id.* at 79-81.
[16]JEFFREY M. RISIUS, BUSINESS VALUATION: A PRIMER FOR THE LEGAL PROFESSIONAL 72-77 (2007).
[17]*Id.* at 74-76.
[18]*Id.* at 76-77.

EXAMPLE 10.2 **DISCOUNTED CASH FLOW**

Assume that an entity has (i) $35,000 in basic net cash flow in the current year; (ii) projected net cash flow for the following three years—the projected discrete time period—of $38,000, $42,000, and $46,000; (iii) projected net cash flow of $50,600 in year 5; and (iv) a projected steady growth rate of 6 percent starting in year 5. Also assume the desired rate of return is 15 percent.

The first step is to determine the present value of the unstable cash flow for the first four years using the 15 percent rate of return to determine the correct present value factor:

	Year 1	Year 2	Year 3	Year 4
Net Cash Flow	$35,000	$38,000	$42,000	$46,000
PV Factor	.8696	.7561	.6575	.5718
PV of Net Cash Flow	$30,436	$28,732	$27,615	$26,303
Total				**$113,086**

The second step is to determine the residual cash flow for the period post-stabilization (starting in year 5 into perpetuity). Utilizing the capitalization rate of 9 percent (15% – 6%), this results in residual cash flow of $562,222 ($50,600 ÷ .09.). Next, the residual cash flow is discounted to present value using the 15 percent rate of return, which is $321,479 ($562,222 × .5718).

The third step is to add the two results — present value of cash flow during unstable period plus present value of terminal value — to determine the value of the entity, which is $434,565 ($113,086 + $321,479).

Determining the correct capitalization rate, whether using a capitalized or discounted cash flow method, is crucial for establishing an accurate valuation. A slight adjustment can result in a significant impact to the entity's established value. There are a number of resources available to business valuation experts to use in determining or providing guidance in establishing the correct rate.[19]

2. Market Approach

Another method for business valuation utilizes a market approach, and thus information about publicly traded companies is generally gathered to establish the valuation. In a market valuation, data is gathered regarding the stock prices or transactions of comparable business entities to create valuation multiples

---

[19]GARY R. TRUGMAN, UNDERSTANDING BUSINESS VALUATION: A PRACTICAL GUIDE TO VALUING SMALL TO MEDIUM-SIZED BUSINESSES 30-31 (3d ed. 2008).

that are then utilized to value the purchase price for the entity.[20] In some cases, public companies that are comparable to the entity being valued are selected, and the price of that public company's stock in conjunction with another financial variable, such as sales or earnings, are used to establish a pricing multiple.[21] In other cases, the merger and acquisition purchase price of a company comparable to the entity being valued is used to create a pricing multiple.[22] A market valuation is best used when the entity being valued operates in an industry where there are a fair number of publicly traded companies that are competitors, or operates in an industry where there have been a significant number of acquisitions.[23] If the business operates in a specialized or unique industry or market with few competitors or few publicly traded companies, the market approach would not be the best valuation method to utilize due to lack of comparable data.[24]

a. Guideline Method

The guideline method requires the valuation expert to first identify a number of publicly traded companies that are similar or comparable to the entity being valued. Some of the factors that may be taken into consideration in identifying the comparable companies include (i) operation in the same market or channel within the industry; (ii) sales of similar goods and services; (iii) amount of investment in inventory, plant, and equipment; (iv) years in operation; (v) financial position and liquidity; (vi) capital structure; (vii) quality, stability, and growth of earnings; and (viii) competitive position within the industry.[25] Once the comparable companies are identified, the valuation expert will undertake an analysis of key financial metrics and determine the most relevant and appropriate pricing multiples to utilize for the current valuation. These pricing multiples should be adjusted for the differences between the selected comparable companies and the entity being valued, including adjustments for risk levels and growth potential.[26] After the appropriate pricing multiples are selected and adjusted, they are applied to the relevant financial variable of the entity being valued to establish the valuation price.[27] In some circumstances, more than one pricing multiple may be used to value the entity, and the values are then averaged to establish the final valuation.[28]

---

[20]Risius, *supra* note 16, at 97.
[21]Trugman, *supra* note 19, at 199-200.
[22]Jeffrey M. Risius, Business Valuation: A Primer for the Legal Professional 97-98 (2007).
[23]*Id.* at 120-121.
[24]Risius, *supra* note 22, at 97-98.
[25]Gary R. Trugman, Understanding Business Valuation: A Practical Guide to Valuing Small to Medium-Sized Businesses 200-210 (3d ed. 2008).
[26]*Id.* at 228.
[27]*Id.* at 228-231.
[28]Jeffrey M. Risius, Business Valuation: A Primer for the Legal Professional 97-98 (2007).

EXAMPLE 10.3   **GUIDELINE METHOD**

Assume that the selected pricing multiple is total invested capital (market value of equity plus interest-bearing debt) to EBITDA, and that multiple is 5.5. If the entity being valued had EBITDA of $25 million, the entity would be valued at $137.5 million ($25 million × 5.5, which is EBITDA multiplied by the selected multiple).

What should be evident from this brief discussion is that selecting comparable companies, performing the financial analysis of those companies, determining the correct pricing multiples to use, and adjusting those pricing multiples for the entity being valued is not a quick nor an easy process. While gathering information for this model relies on the publicly available data, the valuation is only as good as the comparable data that is used to undertake the valuation, meaning that if incorrect comparable companies or pricing multiples are used, the valuation result will be distorted, whether too low or too high.[29]

b. Transaction Method

The transaction method requires the valuation expert to identify acquisitions of comparable companies and to use the data from the transaction to determine the appropriate pricing multiples.[30] The comparable companies may be either publicly traded or private companies, with the deciding factor often being those acquisitions where information regarding the purchase price specifics can be obtained. Some of the factors that may be taken into consideration in identifying the comparable companies include (i) operation in the same market or channel, (ii) similar size and revenues, (iii) operation in the same region, and (iv) timing of the acquisition.[31] Once the comparable transactions are identified, the valuation expert gathers and verifies the data to the extent possible. Next, in a manner similar to that used with the guideline method, the valuation expert will undertake an analysis of key financial metrics and determine the most relevant and appropriate pricing multiples to utilize for the current valuation. In an ideal scenario, these pricing multiples should be adjusted for the differences between the selected comparable companies in the identified transactions and the entity being valued, but that is often impossible, as historic financial data on the comparable companies is often unavailable.[32] After the appropriate pricing multiples are selected, they are applied to the relevant financial variable of the entity being valued to establish the valuation price.[33]

---

[29]Trugman, *supra* note 25, at 242-243.
[30]Risius, *supra* note 28, at 116.
[31]*Id.*
[32]*Id.* at 117.
[33]GARY R. TRUGMAN, UNDERSTANDING BUSINESS VALUATION: A PRACTICAL GUIDE TO VALUING SMALL TO MEDIUM-SIZED BUSINESSES 245-246 (3d ed. 2008).

EXAMPLE 10.4 **TRANSACTION METHOD**

Assume that the selected pricing multiple is total invested capital (market value of equity plus interest-bearing debt) to revenue, and that multiple is 1.25. If the entity being valued had revenue of $134 million, the entity would be valued at $167.5 million ($134 million × 1.25, which is total revenue multiplied by the selected multiple).

One of the major shortcomings of the transaction method is the lack of complete information regarding the selected comparable transactions. Oftentimes there is little current or historical financial information regarding the comparable target company, and it is difficult to discern the assumptions underlying the purchase price of the target company.[34] Additionally, unless the relevant industry is undergoing consolidation, it is probable that there will not be enough transactions to analyze in order to select and set the appropriate pricing model.[35] As a result, while this method sets an objective standard for valuing the entity, it is not always easy to find enough data to effectively use it.

3. Asset Approach

A third method for business valuation utilizes an asset approach, and thus the entity's balance sheet. In an asset valuation, a select list of the entity's assets is valued using a specific methodology (book, adjusted book, liquidation, or cost to create), and the purchase price for the entity is based upon the value of those assets. In some asset valuations, only the tangible assets of the entity are valued, and in other cases both the tangible and intangible assets are valued.[36]

An asset valuation method is often a common choice, as all entities prepare and present a balance sheet on a regular basis, meaning the information that underlies this valuation methodology is generally more readily available and accessible even for small private businesses.[37] This approach is best used when establishing the value of a holding company, an asset intensive company, or an operating company with little intangible asset value.[38] If a business is service oriented, is asset light, or has significant intangible asset value, one of the previously discussed valuation methods would present a better model.

a. Book Value Method

The book value method is one of the easiest methods for valuing an entity. Book value is simply total assets less total liabilities, which is known as stockholders'

---

[34]Jeffrey M. Risius, Business Valuation: A Primer for the Legal Professional 117 (2007).
[35]Trugman, *supra* note 33, at 278-279.
[36]*Id.* at 281.
[37]Risius, *supra* note 34, at 129.
[38]*Id.*

equity. In this methodology, the assets and liabilities are valued based on the amount reflected on the entity's balance sheet, which means all are valued at their historic cost. In order to determine the book value per share, the book value is divided by the number of shares of common stock issued and outstanding.

A derivation of the book value method is net tangible book value. Under this method, intangible assets (meaning those that are not easily converted to cash, such as intellectual property or goodwill) are removed from total assets prior to the calculation.[39] Net tangible book value is total assets less intangible assets less total liabilities. In order to determine the net tangible book value per share, the net tangible book value is divided by the number of shares of common stock issued and outstanding.

EXAMPLE 10.5 **BOOK VALUE METHOD**

Assume an entity had (i) $4,329,000 in total assets, (ii) $2,115,000 in total liabilities, and (iii) 500,000 shares of common stock issued and outstanding.

The book value per share would be $4.43 [($4,329,000 – $2,115,000)/500,000, which is total assets less total liabilities divided by common stock issued and outstanding].

There are a number of shortcomings with using the book value or net tangible book value method. The most significant shortcoming is that an entity's assets and liabilities are reflected on the entity's balance sheet at their historic costs, which often differs from the fair market value of those same assets and liabilities. As a result, this methodology may overvalue (in limited cases), but more likely will undervalue the entity, as in most instances the entity's assets, particularly its long-term assets, are currently worth more than their reflected historic cost. The other significant shortcoming is that this valuation methodology assumes that the entity is not going to continue to operate as a "going concern," meaning it is not going to continue its business into the future. In other words, the book value does not take into account that the entity utilizes its assets to generate income and will continue to do so in the future, thus increasing the entity's value.[40] It ignores the concept that the entity and its assets are worth more as a whole than as individual parts and pieces.[41] As a result, the book value methodology has limited use in the majority of valuation scenarios.[42]

b. Adjusted Book Value Method

The adjusted book value method is similar to the book value method, except that all the assets and liabilities (or those that are being purchased and assumed)

[39]JEFFREY J. HAAS, CORPORATE FINANCE 70-71 (2014).
[40]Id.
[41]In re Watt & Shand, 304 A.2d 694, 700 (Pa. 1973).
[42]GARY R. TRUGMAN, UNDERSTANDING BUSINESS VALUATION: A PRACTICAL GUIDE TO VALUING SMALL TO MEDIUM-SIZED BUSINESSES 282-283 (3d ed. 2008).

are adjusted to reflect their fair market value instead of their historic cost.[43] As a result, this method eliminates one of the significant shortcomings of the book value method—the fact that most balance sheet amounts reflect historic cost.[44] However, this method does not eliminate the "going concern" shortcoming.[45] Once the assets and liabilities are adjusted, the adjusted book value is the adjusted value of total assets less the adjusted value of total liabilities. In order to determine the adjusted book value per share, the adjusted book value is divided by the number of shares of common stock issued and outstanding. This valuation method is often used to assess the value of a controlling interest in an asset-heavy entity.[46]

EXAMPLE 10.6   **ADJUSTED BOOK VALUE METHOD**

Using the information from Example 10.5, assume the entity's total assets had a fair market value of $5,619,000 and its total liabilities had a fair market value of $2,001,000.

The adjusted book value per share would be $7.24 [($5,619,000 − $2,001,000)/500,000, which is total assets at FMV less total liabilities at FMV divided by common shares issued and outstanding].

---

c. Liquidation Value Method

The liquidation value method is also similar to the book value method, except that the value of the assets is adjusted to reflect the price that would be paid for similar assets in an orderly or forced liquidation proceeding.[47] In an orderly liquidation the assets are valued as if they were available for sale in the marketplace for a reasonable period of time, such as three to six months.[48] Thus, the assets will generally be valued slightly higher, as the seller has time to search or wait for the best offer. In a forced liquidation, the assets are valued as if they must be sold immediately or in a "fire sale."[49] As a result, the assets will generally be valued lower, as the seller has to sell them immediately and cannot wait or search for a higher offer. In addition to the adjustment to the value of the assets, the costs of the liquidation process should also be deducted from the final valuation.[50] The most common use of this valuation methodology is as part of an actual liquidation of an entity.

---

[43]*Id.* at 283.
[44]*Id.*
[45]Jeffrey J. Haas, Corporate Finance 71-72 (2014).
[46]Trugman, *supra* note 42, at 283.
[47]Jeffrey M. Risius, Business Valuation: A Primer for the Legal Professional 130-131 (2007).
[48]*Id.*
[49]*Id.* at 131.
[50]Gary R. Trugman, Understanding Business Valuation: A Practical Guide to Valuing Small to Medium-Sized Businesses 299 (3d ed. 2008).

EXAMPLE 10.7   **LIQUIDATION VALUE METHOD**

Using the information from Example 10.5, assume the entity's total assets had a fire sale value of $2,597,400 and the liquidation costs are estimated to be $80,000.

The fire sale liquidation value per share would be $0.80 [($2,597,400 − $2,115,000 − $80,000)/500,000, which is total assets at fire sale value less total liabilities less liquidation costs divided by common shares issued and outstanding].

d. Cost to Create Method

The cost to create method is similar to the adjusted book value method, but goes a step further and attempts to value the entity as if it is a "going concern," and thus values not only the tangible assets but also the intangible assets.[51] The idea is that the business is valued by assessing the cost to create or duplicate the business, including taking into consideration intangibles such as brand and name recognition, attracting and training employees, and customer base and loyalty, or in other words, the goodwill value of the entity.[52]

C. VALUATION REPORT

The valuation report is the final work product prepared by the valuation expert that sets forth the findings from the valuation engagement. There are three types of valuation reports: detailed report, summary report, and calculation report.[53] The detailed report and summary report are used to present the results of a traditional valuation engagement, whereas the calculation report results in a conclusion of value.[54] The calculation report, which is less in scope than the detailed or summary report, is used to present the results of a calculation engagement where the engagement results in a value, whether a single amount or a range.[55] All valuation reports are required to be presented in a manner that is not misleading to the user, and the user should be able to understand the report's contents, as well as the sources of information used and the basis for the stated conclusions.[56]

[51]*Id.* at 303.
[52]Jeffrey J. Haas, Corporate Finance 72-73 (2014).
[53]Statements on Standards for Valuation Services, Statement on Standards for Valuation Services No. 1: Valuation of a Business, Business Ownership Interest, Security, or Intangible, VS §100 (Am. Inst. of Certified Pub. Accountants 2007).
[54]*Id.*
[55]*Id.*
[56]Gary R. Trugman, Understanding Business Valuation: A Practical Guide to Valuing Small to Medium-Sized Businesses 451 (3d ed. 2008).

The components of a detailed valuation report should include the following:

"(i) letter of transmittal; (ii) table of contents; (iii) introduction; (iv) sources of information; (v) analysis of the subject entity and related nonfinancial information; (vi) financial statement or financial information analysis; (vii) valuation approaches and methods considered; (viii) valuation approaches and methods used; (ix) valuation adjustments; (x) non-operating assets, non-operating liabilities, and excess or deficient operating assets (if any); (xi) representations of the valuation analyst; (xii) reconciliation of estimates and conclusion of value; (xiii) qualifications of the valuation analyst; and (xiv) appendixes and exhibits."[57]

A detailed valuation report is often lengthy and may be anywhere from 40 pages to 80 pages long or more.[58]

D. VALUATION IN PRACTICE

Business valuations and valuation reports are used in many different contexts, often legal in nature, and as a result require that a lawyer understand the report and its contents in order to assist the client. Those contexts may range from a simple valuation of an entity's assets, to a valuation for IRS purposes, to a valuation of a controlling shareholder's interest, to a complex valuation of economic damages such as lost profits. While valuations are often thought of in the traditional transactional context — as a result of a merger or acquisition or sale of substantially all of a business's assets — the need for valuations arises in many other situations. Each situation is unique and may include additional information or regulations that must be taken into consideration.

For example, an entity may require a valuation of an intangible asset such as goodwill, so it can adjust the value on the balance sheet, if necessary, and present an accurate reflection of the value of goodwill and the entity's financial position, or so it knows the value of goodwill as a part of the sale of a segment of its business. Another example may arise in the area of trusts and estates law. A lawyer may represent the beneficiary who just received an interest in a partnership as part of an inheritance, and that interest must be valued for estate and gift tax purposes. Divorce proceedings often give rise to the need for a valuation, such as a valuation of the divorcing couple's closely held business that is one of the marital assets. Shareholder disputes frequently result in the need for a valuation. For instance, a minority shareholder may exercise her rights to dissent, and so her interest in the entity as a dissenting shareholder must be valued. Lastly, businesses often suffer damages or are sued by plaintiffs who claim they have suffered some type of damages as a result of the entity's actions or inactions, and may also suffer damages such as lost profits or lost value, or may be sued under contract or tort actions, such as a breach of a contract or product defect. Each of these scenarios may require a valuation.

---

[57]Statements on Standards for Valuation Services, *supra* note 53.
[58]Trugman, *supra* note 56, at 452.

What should be evident is that the need for a business valuation can arise in many different legally oriented circumstances. No matter the reason for a business valuation, the client's lawyer must be able to read, understand, and assess the provided report and results. This may be so the lawyer can assist the client or so the lawyer can use the information as part of a negotiation strategy or litigation matter.

Business Valuation Report Problem 10.1

The following problem requires the review, assessment, and analysis of a business valuation report.

Problem 10.1

Access one of the following documents through a database (e.g., Westlaw, Lexis, Bloomberg Law, or the SEC's EDGAR system):

1. *Common Stock Valuation:* Ameri Metro, Inc.'s Valuation Report dated November 1, 2016, and filed as Exhibit 99.1 to its Form S-1/A Registration Statement filed on June 23, 2017.
2. *Minority Interest Valuation:* Vivid Learning Systems, Inc.'s Business Valuation Report dated March 31, 2009, and attached as Annex G to its Schedule 13E-3, Amendment No. 3 filed November 16, 2009.
3. *Asset Valuation:* BRF-Brasil Foods S.A.'s Business Valuation Report dated May 2, 2012, and included in its Form 6-K dated and filed on May 9, 2012.

Review the selected business valuation report to gain an understanding of the procedures and methodologies used by the valuation expert in preparation of the final report.

Other Accounting and Corporate Finance Concepts

A. INTRODUCTION

Although a wide variety of accounting concepts and finance principles that are essential for a practicing lawyer in today's world were covered in the first ten chapters of this book, it is impossible to cover everything that might be considered critical knowledge. This final chapter attempts to cover some of those principles that were not addressed elsewhere, but nonetheless deserve attention, including the concepts of operating versus capital leases, the financial markets, and the many ways in which an entity can raise capital, such as through commercial loans, equity, and debt.

B. LEASES   *Op Lease vs. Capital Lease.*

At its most basic, a lease is a contractual arrangement between the lessor and the lessee in which the lessor grants the lessee the right to use an asset, such as a piece of property, a building, or a piece of equipment, for a set period of time for specified lease payments. Entities frequently enter into lease transactions as an alternative to purchasing the property, plant, or equipment. The terms and conditions of the lease transaction will dictate the classification of the lease and the manner in which it must be accounted for by both entities — the lessee and lessor.

There are two primary classifications of leases from a lessee's perspective—operating and capital—and each requires its own accounting treatment. Since leases must be classified at their inception, the lessee must undertake an analysis and determine whether the lease is an operating lease or a capital lease in order to accurately reflect the transaction in its books and records. The following sections discuss the classification of the lease from the lessee's perspective and focus on the accounting treatment by the lessee.

1. Capital Leases from the Lessee's Perspective

A capital lease is a type of lease that transfers most of the benefits and risks of leasing that particular asset to the lessee. As a result, the accounting treatment requires the lessee to reflect the capital lease as an asset of its business, as well as to include a corresponding liability (or obligation) to pay for the leased asset.

If any one of the following criteria is met, the lessee classifies and records the transaction as a capital lease:

   (i) ownership of the leased asset is transferred to the lessee at the end of the lease term;

  (ii) the lease provides the lessee with a bargain purchase option;

 (iii) the term of the lease equals 75 percent or more of the estimated economic life of the leased asset, provided that the lease term is not during the period of time that represents the last 25 percent of the leased asset's estimated economic life; or

 (iv) the present value of the minimum lease payments, as calculated at the start of the lease, equals or exceeds 90 percent of the fair value of the leased asset to the lessor less any investment tax credit that the lessor retains, provided that the lease term is not starting during the period of time that represents the last 25 percent of the leased asset's estimated economic life.[1]

a. Transfer of Ownership

The concept of transfer of ownership is straightforward. If the lease agreement contains a provision that transfers the title, or ownership, of the asset to the lessee at or just after conclusion of the lease term for a payment of a nominal amount, then there is a transfer of ownership.[2]

EXAMPLE 11.1   **TRANSFER OF OWNERSHIP**

Assume that Smith & Sons, Inc. enters into a lease agreement with Equipment Suppliers, Inc. to lease a piece of equipment starting on June 1 for four years at a monthly rental of $2,200. The lease contains a provision that transfers title in the piece of equipment to Smith & Sons, Inc. for a fee of $500.00 paid on or before 30 days after the lease expires.

This constitutes a transfer of ownership and would result in Smith & Sons, Inc. classifying this lease as a capital lease, because they can purchase the

---

[1] Accounting Standards Codification, Leases, ASC §840-10-25 (Fin. Accounting Found. 2017).
[2] *Id.*

leased asset at the end of the lease term for an insignificant amount (approximately ½ percent of the total lease payments), essentially the cost to transfer the title.

b. Bargain Purchase Option

A bargain purchase option is a provision in the lease that gives the lessee the right to purchase the leased asset at the end of the lease term, in its sole discretion, for an amount that is significantly less than the asset's fair market value at that point in time.[3]

EXAMPLE 11.2   **BARGAIN PURCHASE OPTION**

Assume that Smith & Sons, Inc. enters into a lease agreement with Equipment Suppliers, Inc. to lease a piece of equipment starting on June 1 for four years at a monthly rental of $2,200. The equipment has an estimated salvage value of $10,000 at the end of the lease term. The lease contains a provision that allows Smith & Sons, Inc. to purchase the piece of equipment for $2,000, provided that Smith & Sons, Inc. exercises the purchase option on or before 30 days after the lease term ends.

    This constitutes a bargain purchase option and would result in Smith & Sons, Inc. classifying this lease as a capital lease. Smith & Sons, Inc. can purchase the piece of equipment for a cost that is 20 percent ($2,000/$10,000) of, or significantly less than, its fair market value at the end of the lease term.

c. Lease Term

The lease term requirement assesses the amount of time the lessee will lease the asset in comparison to the asset's estimated economic life. The concept is that if the lessee is leasing the asset for 75 percent or more of its economic life, then in essence the lessee is assuming most of the benefits and risks associated with the asset and thus owns it. However, if the lease terms start during the final 25 percent of the asset's estimated economic life, this criteria cannot be met, such as when the lessee leases previously used equipment that is nearing the end of its economic life.

    The lease term includes the following periods of time: (i) term of the initial lease, (ii) terms of any standard renewal options up to the bargain purchase option date, (iii) terms of any bargain renewal options, (iv) terms imposed as

---

[3]*Id.* §840-10-20.

a result of a penalty for a failure to renew by the lessee, and (v) terms of any renewals or extensions at the lessor's option.[4]

EXAMPLE 11.3 **LEASE TERM**

Assume that Smith & Sons, Inc. enters into a lease agreement with Equipment Suppliers, Inc. to lease a piece of equipment starting on June 1 for four years at a monthly rental of $2,200. The lease only provides for the one four-year term and contains no renewals, extensions, or penalties for failing to renew or extend. The piece of equipment has an estimated economic life of five years.

This constitutes a lease term of greater than 75 percent of the asset's estimated economic life, and would result in Smith & Sons, Inc. classifying this lease as a capital lease. Smith & Sons, Inc. is leasing the piece of equipment for 80 percent of its economic life (four years/five years, which is the lease term divided by the asset's economic life).

d. Present Value of Minimum Lease Payments

The present value of the minimum lease payments assesses the present value of the lease payments in comparison to the fair market value of the leased asset. As with the concept of the lease term, if the lessee is paying 90 percent or more of the asset's fair market value in lease payment obligations, the lessee is assuming most of the benefits and risks associated with the asset and thus, in essence, owns it. However, if the lease term starts during the final 25 percent of the asset's estimated economic life, this criteria cannot be met.

Minimum lease payments include the following amounts: (i) the lessee's rental payments over the term of the lease; (ii) a guaranteed residual value at the end of the lease term, even if it constitutes a payment to purchase the asset; (iii) any payment the lessee must make if it fails to renew or extend the lease at the end of the term; and (iv) the amount of the bargain purchase option, if the lease includes one.[5] A guaranteed residual value means the lessee guarantees the lessor that the asset will be worth a stipulated amount, or value, at the end of the lease. If the actual residual value at the end of the lease term is less than the guaranteed residual value, the lessee must pay the difference to the lessor.

In order to calculate the present value of the minimum lease payments, the lessee should determine the current rate at which it could borrow funds pursuant to a term loan for the equivalent lease term if it were to purchase the asset and use that rate to make the present value calculations.[6]

---

[4]*Id.*
[5]*Id.*
[6]Accounting Standards Codification, Leases, ASC §840-10-25 (Fin. Accounting Found. 2017).

EXAMPLE 11.4   **MINIMUM LEASE PAYMENTS**

Assume that Smith & Sons, Inc. enters into a lease agreement with Equipment Suppliers, Inc. to lease a piece of equipment starting on June 1 for four years at a monthly rental of $2,200, which rent is paid on an annual basis at the end of each lease year ($26,400 on each May 31). The lease only provides for the one four-year term and contains no renewals, extensions, or penalties for failing to renew or extend. The lease does not have a guaranteed residual value, but Smith & Sons, Inc. has a bargain purchase option of $2,000 at lease end. The piece of equipment has a current fair market value of $105,000. Smith & Sons, Inc. believes it could currently enter into a four-year term loan at an interest rate of 4 percent.

In order to determine the minimum lease payments, Smith & Sons, Inc. must discount the rent payment stream and bargain purchase option to present value dollars using the Present Value of an Ordinary Annuity Table (**Exhibit L**) and Present Value of a Lump Sum Table (**Exhibit J**) or the respective formulas.

$$\text{PV of Annual Rent Payments} = \$26,400 \times 3.6299$$
$$= \$95,829.36$$
$$\text{PV of Bargain Purchase Option} = \$2,000 \times .8548$$
$$= \$1,709.60$$
$$\text{PV of Lease Obligation} = \$95,829.36 + \$1,709.60$$
$$= \$97,538.96$$
$$90\% \text{ of FMV} = \$105,000 \times .9$$
$$= \$94,500.00$$

This results in lease payments, discounted to present value, greater than 90 percent of the piece of equipment's fair market value, and would require Smith & Sons, Inc. to classify this lease as a capital lease. Smith & Sons, Inc. is making minimum lease payments discounted to present value of $97,538.96, and 90 percent of the equipment's fair market value is $94,500, and so the lease payments exceed 90 percent of the equipment's fair market value.

2. Accounting for Capital Leases by the Lessee

Once an entity determines that a lease must be classified as a capital lease, it will account for that lease in accordance with ASC 840: Leases. The leased asset must be recorded at the lesser of the present value of the minimum lease payments or its fair market value.[7] The lessee will reflect the capital lease as an asset on its balance sheet, with a corresponding liability for the lease payments. The lessee will depreciate the lease on a monthly basis and recognize depreciation expense with an offset to the accumulated depreciation account for the

---

[7]*Id.* §840-30-30.

capital lease. If the lease is classified as a capital lease because there is a transfer of ownership at the end of the term or the lease contains a bargain purchase option, the lessee will depreciate the lease over its estimated useful life because the asset becomes the property of and is owned by the lessee at the end of the term or upon the bargain purchase option exercise.[8] On the other hand, if the lease is classified as a capital lease because it meets the 75 percent of the lease term or 90 percent of the present value of the minimum lease payments tests, the lessee will depreciate the lease over the term of the lease, or the period of time that the lessee is using the leased asset.[9]

EXAMPLE 11.5 **LESSEE'S JOURNAL ENTRIES FOR A CAPITAL LEASE**

Using the same fact pattern as set forth in Example 11.4, Smith & Sons, Inc. would record the following journal entry upon inception of the capital lease on June 1 to recognize the capital lease as an asset of the business at its present value of minimum lease payments, which was less than its fair market value, and the corresponding obligation to make the lease payments.

Date	Account	Debit	Credit
June 1	Capital Lease (Equipment)	$97,538.96	
	Capital Lease Payable		$97,538.96

Each year Smith & Sons, Inc. would record journal entries to recognize the capital lease payment and the depreciation expense associated with the fixed asset under the capital lease. Assume the annual lease payment is due on the first day of each lease year and is $24,384.74, and the annual depreciation expense is $23,034.24 with the equipment having a $5,400 salvage value. Smith & Sons, Inc. would record the following journal entries during the first year of this capital lease to recognize the lease payment and depreciation expense:

Date	Account	Debit	Credit
June 1, first day of year 1	Capital Lease Payable	$24,384.74	
	Cash		$24,384.74
May 31, last day of year 1	Depreciation Expense	$23,034.24	
	Accumulated Depreciation		$23,034.24

3. Operating Leases from the Lessee's Perspective

An operating lease is a traditional lease in the sense that the contract grants the lessee the right to use the asset for the term of the lease, which is less than the useful life of the asset, and does not convey or transfer any type of ownership

---

[8]*Id.* §840-30-35.
[9]*Id.*

rights in the asset upon lease termination. In essence, if a lease does not meet the criteria for classification as a capital lease, it is an operating lease.

The accounting treatment for operating leases is relatively simple. The lessee recognizes the payment of rent and rent expense in the accounting period the rent payment is due, and the lessor recognizes rent revenues in the accounting period the rent payment is due.[10] It is the lessor who records the ownership of the leased asset and reflects it on its balance sheet with a title such as "investment in leased equipment" and recognizes the associated depreciation expense and maintenance costs as the owner of the asset.[11] The lessee does not record the asset or recognize depreciation expense, as it does not have any ownership interest in the asset, neither during nor at the end of the lease; it is simply a rental arrangement.

EXAMPLE 11.6 **LESSEE'S JOURNAL ENTRY FOR AN OPERATING LEASE**

Assume that Smith & Sons, Inc. enters into an operating lease for a piece of equipment with Equipment Suppliers, Inc. Smith & Sons, Inc. agrees to lease the piece of equipment starting on June 1 for four years at a monthly rental of $2,200. Smith & Sons, Inc. would record the following journal entry on the first day of each month of the lease term to recognize the payment of its lease rent and the corresponding expense to the business.

Date	Account	Debit	Credit
1st of Month	Equipment Lease Expense	$2,200	
	Cash		$2,200

4. Leases from the Lessor's Perspective

Similar to the lessee, the lessor must assess the lease at its inception to determine how it should be classified and accounted for in its books and records. There are four types of lease classifications: (i) operating, (ii) sales-type, (iii) direct financing, and (iv) leveraged.[12] In order to be classified as a sales-type, direct financing, or leveraged lease by the lessor, the lease must meet at least one of the four criteria that require a lessee to classify a lease as a capital lease, and also both of the following criteria: (i) the collection of the minimum lease payments is reasonably assured, and (ii) no important uncertainties exist about unreimbursable costs to be included as part of the lease.[13] If a lease does not meet those requirements, it is an operating lease. Accounting for non-operating leases from the lessor's perspective is complicated and outside the scope of this discussion.

---

[10] ACCOUNTING STANDARDS CODIFICATION, Leases, ASC §840-20-25 (Fin. Accounting Found. 2017).
[11] *Id.*
[12] *Id.* §840-10-25.
[13] *Id.*

a. Operating Lease

If the lease does not meet the criteria set forth above to be classified into one of the categories of capital leases from the lessor's perspective, it is an operating lease. As noted above, the lessor accounts for the ownership of the leased asset and reflects it on its balance sheet with a title such as "investment in leased equipment" and recognizes the associated depreciation expense and maintenance costs as the owner of the asset.[14] In return, the lessor receives rental income that it records in the period it is due.

EXAMPLE 11.7   **LESSOR'S JOURNAL ENTRY FOR AN OPERATING LEASE**

Utilizing the same facts as set forth in Example 11.6, Equipment Suppliers, Inc. would record the following journal entry on the first day of each month to recognize the receipt of the lease payment from Smith & Sons, Inc.:

Date	Account	Debit	Credit
1st of Month	Cash	$2,200	
	Rental Income		$2,200

b. Sales-Type Lease

A sales-type lease transaction is one that is structured in a manner that permits the lessor, who is usually the manufacturer or dealer of the leased asset, to recognize interest income, as well as either a profit or loss as a result of the lease transaction.[15] An example of a sales-type lease is a car lease, as when the customer returns the car at the end of the lease term, the dealer may make a profit or suffer a loss upon the returned car's resale.

c. Direct Financing Lease

A direct financing lease transaction is one that is structured in a manner that only allows the lessor to recognize interest income as a result of the lease and no other profit or loss.[16] In this type of lease, a financial institution purchases an asset, such as a piece of equipment, for the benefit of the lessee, and then leases it to the lessee.[17] This creates a transaction similar to a traditional loan transaction where the lender (or the lessor) makes a return based on the interest paid over the course of the loan (or the lease).

---

[14] ACCOUNTING STANDARDS CODIFICATION, Leases, ASC §840-20-25 (Fin. Accounting Found. 2017).
[15] Id. §840-10-25.
[16] Id.
[17] Id.

d. Leveraged Lease

A leveraged lease is a distinct type of direct financing lease, but it involves three parties to the lease contract: the lessee, the lessor, and the long-term creditor.[18] In this scenario, the lessor obtains financing from the long-term creditor for at least 50 percent of the purchase price of the asset to buy the asset that it then leases to the lessee, with the asset acting as collateral for the long-term creditor.[19]

Operating versus Capital Lease
Problems 11.1 and 11.2

The following two problems address the assessment of whether a lease is an operating lease or capital lease from the lessee's perspective.

Problem 11.1

Assume that Omega, Inc. requires a new piece of equipment for its business and while it could take out a term loan at a rate of 5 percent to purchase the equipment, it has decided it would rather lease it. The terms of the lease are as follows:

Lease Term (no extensions or renewals):	6 years
Annual Lease Payments (in arrears):	$29,000
Purchase Option for Equipment (at lease end):	$30,000
Guaranteed Residual Value:	None
Fair Market Value of Equipment:	$235,000
Economic Life of Equipment:	10 years

Part A: Using the information provided, determine whether this is an operating lease or capital lease and explain your answer in detail.
Part B: Prepare the journal entry that Omega, Inc. would record upon entering into this equipment lease.

Problem 11.2

Assume that Omega, Inc. thought the leasing experience was a better business strategy than buying based on its prior experience, and so it decides to lease a new machine for its business operations. At this point in time, Omega, Inc.

---

[18]*Id.*
[19]*Id.*

believes it could secure a term loan at a rate of 6 percent if it were to purchase. The terms of the machine lease are as follows:

Lease Term (no extensions or renewals):	4 years
Annual Lease Payments (in arrears):	$225,000
Purchase Option for Equipment (at lease end):	None
Guaranteed Residual Value:	$42,000
Fair Market Value of Equipment:	$895,000
Economic Life of Equipment:	6 years

Part A: Using the information provided, determine whether this is an operating lease or capital lease and explain your answer in detail.
Part B: Prepare the journal entry that Omega, Inc. would record upon entering into this machine lease.

C. FINANCIAL MARKETS

There are two primary financial marketplaces: the capital markets and the money market. The capital markets are comprised of the primary market and the secondary market and are the marketplace for the purchase and sale of long-term investments. On the other hand, the money market is the market-place for the purchase and sale of short-term investments. Both marketplaces are vital to the economy and provide avenues for entities to raise capital to fund new and ongoing business operations.

1. Capital Markets

The capital markets are marketplaces where financial instruments, both debt and equity, can be purchased and sold by willing participants. Financial instru-ments sold through the capital markets are long-term obligations, meaning the investments are for a year or more.[20] The capital markets allow entities to raise money (or capital) through the sale of various financial instruments to third-party participants, such as individuals or institutional investors, who desire to invest their money for the prospect of a future return.

The capital markets consist of two distinct markets: the primary market and the secondary market. In the primary market, the entity issues or sells the financial instruments directly to the investors (or through an underwriter) and thus reaps the monetary reward of those sales less any potential fees or commissions owed to the underwriter. This is the market where new financial instruments are purchased and sold and requires an issuer and a purchaser.[21] In the secondary market, other investors sell financial instruments, which may

---

[20] ALAN N. RECHTSCHAFFEN, CAPITAL MARKETS, DERIVATIVES AND THE LAW 46 (2009).
[21] Id.

have been purchased directly from the issuer in the primary market or purchased from another investor in the secondary market. This is the market where financial instruments are resold, and requires a seller and a purchaser.[22] The secondary market provides a method for investors to liquidate their holdings and cash out—meaning the issuer does not receive any portion of the proceeds from sales in the secondary market.

EXAMPLE 11.8 **PRIMARY AND SECONDARY MARKET**

Primary Market: Assume that Smith & Sons, Inc. determines that it is going to raise capital through a private offering of its common stock. When Smith & Sons, Inc. issues the common stock in the private offering, those shares are sold directly by Smith & Sons, Inc. to the purchasers (or investors) and thus represent a primary market transaction. Smith & Sons, Inc. will receive the cash proceeds from the sales of the common stock.

   Secondary Market: Assume that one of the investors from the primary market transaction decides to sell its Smith & Sons, Inc. common stock a year later. Those shares are sold by the original investor to the purchaser (new investor) and thus represent a secondary market transaction. The selling investor will receive the cash proceeds from the sale of Smith & Sons, Inc.'s common stock.

---

2. Money Market

The money market is also a marketplace where financial instruments are purchased and sold by willing participants. The types of financial instruments sold on the money market include Treasury bills, certificates of deposit (CDs), commercial paper, and other short-term instruments. However, the money market differs from the capital markets in one significant respect — this is the marketplace for financial instruments with a maturity or obligation of less than one year. As a result, entities generally use the money market to fulfill short-term or temporary capital needs.

D. METHODS OF RAISING CAPITAL

There are two primary methods by which an entity can raise capital to fund its business and operations: equity or debt. Both methods of raising capital have advantages as well as disadvantages. Once the entity has determined it is in need of a capital influx, the board of directors and executive officers of the entity should undertake an assessment as to which method of raising capital is most suitable in the circumstances. In the ideal scenario, the entity is in a position to determine the best method of raising capital, taking into account

---

[22]*Id.* at 47-48.

its current financial and shareholder considerations. However, in other scenarios the entity may be limited in its options. In some circumstances, the entity may not have the requisite level of creditworthiness to qualify for certain debt instruments, and so may be limited to raising capital through the issuance of equity. Yet, in other circumstances, current equity holders (e.g., a venture capitalist investor) may dictate that no further shares of stock can be sold and so the entity may be limited to raising capital only through debt borrowings.

1. Equity

When an entity issues equity (whether through a private offering or a public offering), it is selling an ownership interest in the entity (whether in the form of shares, membership interests, or partnership interests) in exchange for cash. There are some circumstances where an entity may issue equity in exchange for an asset other than cash, such as for a piece of property or a building, especially if the entity is a closely held, private entity. However, in most circumstances the entity issues equity for cash. In either circumstance, the ownership interests of the current equity holders, if not the first equity issuance by the entity, are diluted.

There are a number of aspects of raising capital through equity that are considered advantageous. One advantage is that the entity does not have to repay the equity investor at some point in the future, unlike a loan that must be repaid. The main way in which an equity investor earns a return is through the entity's issuance of dividends, particularly for common shareholders, or through the sale of the equity investment. However, in some circumstances, the equity investor (e.g., preferred shareholder) may be entitled to a guaranteed dividend or liquidation preference. Another advantage is that the entity does not have to make periodic interest payments as it would be required to do on a loan, resulting in an ongoing outflow of cash, nor pay the principal payment at the end of the term.

There are also disadvantages to raising capital through equity. An entity that issues equity must comply with the state and federal securities laws, which can be costly. Additionally, the entity is selling an ownership interest and as a result it is giving up a level of control by expanding its shareholder base. This diminution of control is even more critical in a closely held entity. Another disadvantage is that common shareholders have a right to vote on material transactions and so the larger—or more diluted—the shareholder base, the harder it may be for the entity to achieve the requisite approval.

2. Debt

When an entity incurs debt, it is borrowing money from a third party that must be repaid at some point in the future. This is the aspect that sets debt apart from equity—the requirement that the debt obligation be repaid. There are a number of forms that debt financing can take, such as loans, debt securities, or promissory notes.

As with equity, there are advantages and disadvantages to raising capital through debt financing. One advantage is that the entity is not selling or giving up an ownership stake, and so the lender does not have a right to vote on material transactions. Another advantage is that once the entity has repaid the lender, the relationship comes to an end and there are no further obligations. Lastly, while debt must be repaid, the periodic interest payments and principal amounts are known quantities, and the entity can budget for those expenses.

The biggest disadvantage of debt financing is that the debt (or loan) must be repaid at some given point in the future. Another disadvantage is that entity must make periodic interest payments on the debt obligation, which can often be quite high and, as a result, impact the entity's cash flow. Additionally, many debt obligations come with strings attached, such as requiring collateral (generally in the form of the entity's hard assets) and placing restrictions on how the entity operates its business and spends money during the term of the obligation.

E. TYPES OF EQUITY FINANCING

As noted above, equity is one of the primary methods that an entity can utilize to raise capital for its business needs, whether the entity is raising funds to start a new business or for its ongoing business operations, and whether for its short-term or long-term needs. There are a number of vehicles that allow an entity to raise capital through equity: the sale and issuance of common stock, preferred stock, or convertible securities.

1. Common Stock

Common stock is one of the predominate equity financing vehicles that an entity can use. When a corporate entity is formed, it establishes the types and amounts of stock that it is authorized to issue (or sell). Many entities only establish one type of stock for issuance, and in that case it will be common stock, whether a single class of common stock or multiple classes of common stock. However, it is common for an entity to establish both common and preferred stock.

When an entity sells and issues common stock for capital, it is selling an ownership interest in the entity itself, and that common stock is referred to as issued and outstanding, meaning it is owned by a third party that is not the corporate entity. By selling the common stock, the entity receives cash (less any applicable fees it may owe an underwriter or other third party) that it can immediately use for its business operations. While an investor who purchases common stock does not have the right to be repaid for that equity investment, the investor does obtain other specific rights. Common shareholders have the right to vote on the election or reappointment of the members of the board of directors and on fundamental corporate matters (e.g., a merger or sale of substantially all of the entity's assets).

Common shareholders may be rewarded for their investment through the entity's declaration and payment of a dividend, most often in the form of a cash dividend. While the entity may choose to declare and pay a dividend to its common shareholders, it is not under an obligation to do so, and such dividend is at the discretion of the entity's board of directors. Additionally, the entity can only declare and pay a dividend in compliance with the pertinent state dividend statute, its corporate governance documents, as well as any other contractual restrictions (e.g., a commercial loan agreement restriction). If the entity does declare a dividend, the common shareholders are entitled to share in that dividend on a pro rata basis, which is based upon the number of shares owned in relation to all shares of the class that are issued and outstanding.

The other way in which a shareholder can recoup its initial equity investment is to sell the shares. If the entity is a publicly traded company, the shareholder can sell the shares (assuming they are unrestricted shares) via the exchange where the entity is listed (e.g., NYSE or NASDAQ). If the entity is a privately owned company, the shareholder will have to locate a willing buyer for its shares of common stock and comply with the relevant securities laws as a part of the sale. In either scenario, the shareholder receives the proceeds from the sale of its shares and not the entity. The only impact to the entity is that a new shareholder now owns those issued and outstanding shares.

2. Preferred Stock

Preferred stock is another equity financing vehicle. When the entity issues and sells preferred stock, it is also selling an ownership interest in the entity, but the ownership interest differs from that of the common shareholders. Preferred shareholders are generally granted preferences, meaning they are entitled to benefits that the common shareholders do not receive. These preferences, which reward preferred shareholders for their investment in the entity, may include a guaranteed dividend, a liquidation preference, or both.

The guaranteed dividend may be a set amount or a percentage of the par value per preferred share. The entity must pay the guaranteed dividend to the preferred shareholders before it can declare and pay a dividend to the common shareholders. However, the entity is not required to pay the preferred stock dividend and, just like a common stock dividend, can only declare and pay the dividend in compliance with the pertinent state dividend statute and any other restrictions in place. In some cases, the guaranteed dividend may be cumulative, meaning that if the entity chooses not to or cannot pay the guaranteed dividend in a given year, it accumulates from year to year. This differs from a noncumulative guaranteed dividend that "disappears" if not paid in any given year. If there are cumulative dividends in arrears, the entity must pay all of those dividends to the preferred shareholders before it can pay a dividend to the common shareholders.

Preferred shareholders may also receive a liquidation preference. This liquidation preference means that the entity must pay the preferred shareholders their preference upon a liquidation event before it can pay the common shareholders. The liquidation preference is generally a specified dollar amount per share, often par value per share or the initial purchase price per share, plus any accrued and unpaid or cumulative dividends in arrears. In other words, the preferred shareholders have priority over the common shareholders; thus, they are more likely to be paid in a liquidation event. Due to this, an equity investment in preferred stock is viewed as having less risk than an equity investment in common stock.

However, in exchange for these investment preferences, preferred shareholders often have no voting rights or very limited voting rights. Additionally, their shares may be callable at the entity's discretion or convertible at the entity is or shareholder's discretion. These various rights will be set forth in the preferred shareholders' agreement that describes the contractual relationship between the entity and the preferred shareholders.

It is often the case that preferred shareholders have no rights to vote on any corporate matter, with the exception of a matter that would change the preferred shareholders' rights as a class. In some cases the preferred shareholders may have limited rights to elect directors if the entity misses a set number of guaranteed dividend payments. Additionally, the entity often has the right to call the preferred shares. When the entity calls the preferred shares, it repurchases or redeems those shares from the preferred shareholders at a specified price, and those preferred shareholders no longer own their shares. The entity or preferred shareholders may also have the right to cause the conversion or convert the preferred shares to common shares at a set conversion price or conversion ratio, which typically involves a premium payment. Upon conversion, the preferred shareholder becomes a common shareholder and thus forfeits any guaranteed dividend or liquidation preference.

3. Convertible Securities

Convertible securities are a third method that an entity can use to raise capital through equity. Convertible securities, generally preferred stock (discussed above) or bonds (discussed below), are securities that can be converted into the entity's common stock at the discretion of the convertible security holder. In essence a convertible security is a dual financial instrument — it is preferred stock combined with a conversion right or a bond combined with a conversion right. In the case of preferred stock, the shareholder has an ownership interest in the entity upon the purchase of the preferred stock, as well as upon the conversion of the preferred stock to common stock. In the case of a bond holder, the investor does not have an ownership interest in the entity upon the purchase of the bond, but does obtain an ownership interest if the bond is converted to common stock. The rationale for labeling a convertible security as equity financing is that upon conversion the investor has an equity ownership interest in the entity through the ownership of its common stock.

The conversion right, which cannot be separated from the underlying instrument, permits the investor to convert the preferred stock or bond into common stock of the entity, and most times at the investor's discretion. The contract between the entity and the investor—the preferred shareholders' agreement or indenture—will set forth the terms of the conversion right, including the conversion price or ratio. The conversion right may be at a stipulated price or may fluctuate based on the market price of the common stock, generally only when the entity's common stock is publicly traded. Upon conversion, the entity issues shares of common stock to the preferred shareholder or bond holder, and that investor relinquishes the originally purchased preferred stock or bond and all of the rights and privileges of that instrument. In exchange, the investor receives common stock of the entity and its rights and privileges. An important concept to note in regard to convertible securities is that upon issuance of the shares of common stock, all of the common shareholders of the entity will undergo dilution, as there are now more shares of common stock issued and outstanding. Similar to straight preferred stock or a bond, this type of investment is viewed as less risky than common stock upon its sale and issuance, but bears the same risk of a common stock investment upon conversion.

F. TYPES OF DEBT FINANCING

Debt is the second primary type of financing that an entity can use to raise capital. Debt financing may be either secured with collateral of the entity or unsecured, depending on the nature of the debt and the status of the entity. There are a variety of methods an entity can use to raise debt for its needs, including taking out a commercial or bank loan or issuing debt securities. Unlike an equity investment, debt financing does not give the debt holder an ownership interest in the entity; however, the debt holder generally receives periodic interest payments and must also be repaid in full at some point in the future.

1. Commercial Loans

A commercial loan is a debt financing arrangement between the entity and a financial institution or a syndicate of financial institutions, the lender. Commercial loans come in many forms, and often an entity will enter into an overarching commercial loan arrangement that contains multiple facilities. The most common types of loan facilities are discussed below.

a. Term Loan Facility

A term loan facility is a set amount of money loaned by the financial institution to the entity that must be repaid over the term, which is usually in the range of six to eight years. Most term loans are fully funded on the closing of the loan, meaning that the entity receives the full amount of the loan upon closing. As a result, the entity often uses the term loan to fund a major event such as a business expansion or acquisition. Generally once the term loan is paid in full, the entity cannot re-borrow those funds, or in other words it is a one-time loan transaction.[23]

Many term loans require the entity to repay a portion of the loan principal each year so that it is paid down over time versus all at once at the end of the term. Additionally, the term loan will have an interest rate component and the entity must make the required periodic interest payments. Those interest payments may be at a fixed rate, meaning the interest percentage does not change and the entity pays the same amount of interest each time it makes a payment. In the alternative, the interest payments may be at a floating rate, meaning the interest percentage changes based on underlying market factors, such as the prime rate or LIBOR, and the entity pays a different amount of interest each time it makes a payment. Lastly, some term loans include a prepayment or early payment penalty, meaning the entity must pay an extra fee or penalty to the lender in the event it pays the term loan in full at an earlier than contractually negotiated date.

b. Revolving Credit Facility

A revolving credit facility is a commitment by the financial institution to permit the entity to borrow a maximum amount of money at any given time over a specified term. Revolving credit facilities differ from term loans in that the entity is not required to draw the full amount all at once or to ever borrow any of the available funds. A revolving credit facility allows the entity to draw (or borrow) funds as needed throughout the term of the facility, and so the outstanding balance increases and decreases as the entity borrows and repays funds. Also, once an amount has been repaid, the entity can borrow those funds again or multiple times. Revolving credit facilities are generally utilized to meet an entity's short-term cash needs, such as to meet its payroll obligations, to purchase a new piece of equipment, or pay an unexpected expense.[24]

A revolving credit facility requires that the entity give a set number of days of advance notice to the financial institution when it desires to borrow funds. The facility may require the entity to pay portions of the outstanding principal balance on specified dates throughout the term or simply to pay the outstanding principal balance in full at the end of the term. The revolving credit facility will have an interest rate component that is generally a floating interest rate tied to underlying market factors such as the prime rate or LIBOR. As a result, the interest rate and interest payments due will fluctuate based on what is occurring with the underlying market trigger and the amount of funds the entity has borrowed and not repaid.

---

[23]CAROLYN E. C. PARIS, DRAFTING FOR CORPORATE FINANCE: CONCEPTS, DEALS, AND DOCUMENTS 55 (2d ed. 2014).
[24]*Id.* at 51.

c. Swingline Loan Facility

A swingline loan facility is a type of short-term revolving credit facility. The swingline loan is very much like a revolving credit facility, in that it is a commitment by the financial institution to permit the entity to borrow a maximum amount of money at any given time over the term. Also, as with a revolving credit facility, the entity can draw funds as or when needed, and once repaid can re-borrow the funds. However, it differs from a revolving credit facility in two aspects: generally funds can be requested and borrowed on the same day, or in other words immediately, and any funds borrowed must be repaid quickly, often in one to two weeks. As a result, an entity uses this type of loan for its immediate cash needs or shortfalls. However, there is a consequence to using a swingline loan — it comes with a higher interest rate and contains restrictions on how the borrowed funds can be used, which are often just for debt repayment.

d. Letter of Credit Facility

A letter of credit facility is generally a part of a commercial loan package, and allows the entity to engage in business transactions with third parties seeking assurances that the entity will be able to pay for the assets or goods purchased upon their delivery. A letter of credit is issued by the bank to a third party on behalf of the entity, and can either obligate the financial institution to make the payment on behalf of the entity (standard letter of credit) or act as a guarantee or backup in the event that the entity does not make the payment to the third party (standby letter of credit). In the scenario where the bank pays or must step in and pay the third party on behalf of the entity, the entity must repay the amount of funds drawn (paid by the bank) on the letter of credit.

In many circumstances the letter of credit amount is treated as a draw under the entity's revolving credit facility until such time as the entity repays the financial institution or pays the third party in full, or else the letter of credit is terminated. Additionally, when the financial institution makes the payment on behalf of the entity, the entity must generally repay the amount quickly, and if it does not, the payment may be treated as a draw of funds under the revolving credit facility. Since the risk associated with a letter of credit is high, as the financial institution is in essence acting as a guarantor, the interest rate associated with letters of credit is typically greater than on a revolving credit facility or term loan.[25]

2. Debt Securities

An entity may choose to issue debt securities as an alternative to issuing equity or entering into a commercial loan arrangement for capital purposes. A debt

---

[25]*Id.* at 53.

security creates an obligation on the part of the issuing entity to repay that debt in the future. In essence, a debt security is just another way for the entity to borrow money. The most common types of debt securities are bonds, debentures, notes, and commercial paper.

a. Bonds and Debentures

A corporate bond or debenture is a debt instrument issued by the entity to third-party investors and is a type of promissory note. The third-party investors are lending the entity money that must be repaid when the bond or debenture matures or becomes due. The issuing entity and the investors enter into a contractual agreement — an indenture — that sets forth the terms and conditions of the particular bond or debenture. While the term "bond" is often used to refer to either a bond or a debenture, there are some differences between the two debt instruments. A bond is a secured obligation with the entity's assets acting as the collateral, whereas an indenture is typically an unsecured obligation.[26] Bonds are classified in relation to their time to maturity and are deemed short-term (less than five years), medium-term (five to 12 years), or long-term (greater than 12 years).[27]

As with a commercial loan, the bond investor does not receive an ownership interest in the entity, but instead receives the right to periodic interest payments, based on the bond's coupon or interest rate, and principal repayment of the face amount of the bond upon its maturity. Like any investment, bonds are subject to a certain level of risk. However, bonds are rated according to the creditworthiness of the issuing entity, which is more fully discussed in Chapter 8, and so the investor has a means to assess the risk of a particular bond.

Bonds may also contain additional features beyond the interest payment and principal payment upon maturity. A bond may be redeemable prior to its maturity, meaning the entity may have the option, or in some cases the obligation, to call the bond prior to its maturity and pay the principal amount or face value at the time of the call. In many circumstances, the entity will pay a premium for calling a bond prior to its maturity. The investor may also have the right to force the entity to redeem the bond (a put) and repay its face value in certain circumstance. Also, bonds may be convertible into common stock of the entity (see Convertible Securities in E.3 above).

b. Notes and Commercial Paper

Notes and commercial paper are other types of debt instruments issued by an entity to a third party to raise capital. Notes and commercial paper often have a shorter term, or time to maturity, than do bonds or debentures, and

---

[26]Jeffrey J. Haas, Corporate Finance 161-162 (2014).
[27]Alan N. Rechtschaffen, Capital Markets, Derivatives and the Law 128-129 (2009).

are considered a type of short-term promissory note.[28] The issuing entity and investor enter into a contractual agreement that sets forth the terms and conditions of the issuance, which is referred to as a promissory note instrument or agreement. Notes, which may be secured or unsecured, can have a maturity of anywhere from one to ten years. On the other hand, commercial paper is unsecured and generally matures in nine months or less. As a result of the shorter terms, both of these types of debt obligations are used to meet an entity's short-term cash needs, particularly commercial paper due to its quick maturity.

As is true with other debt securities, the investor does not receive an ownership interest in the entity, but instead simply the right to an interest payment and the repayment of the note on a set date in the future. Unsecured notes and commercial paper bear a higher level of risk, as neither is secured with the collateral of the entity. As a result, the interest rate on those instruments is often higher than on secured notes or bonds.

G. COST OF CAPITAL

Capital encompasses the total amount of cash (and other consideration) invested in the entity by investors who have an expectation of a return, whether the investment is in the form of equity or debt. The cost of capital refers to the return that an entity must promise to these potential investors to convince them to make an equity or debt investment in that particular entity.[29] Put another way, it is the return that the investor, whether an individual, venture capital firm, or lender, requires to make a specific investment and forgo another potential investment opportunity. The required rate of return is tied to the potential risk of the investment, meaning the greater the risk, the higher the required rate of return.[30] Risk is also impacted by the entity's industry and as a result, a higher-risk industry, or one with greater volatility, requires a higher rate of return.[31] There are two distinct pieces to valuing the overall cost of capital: the cost of equity and the cost of debt.

From the entity's perspective, the cost of equity is "the cost of the next dollar of equity to be raised by the issuer," and reflects the minimum that the investor is willing to accept in return for making that investment.[32] A private entity has a higher cost of equity versus a public company, because equity in a private entity is less liquid, as the market for selling the equity investment is limited and so that illiquidity requires a greater return.[33] There are two primary methods of

---

[28]Haas, *supra* note 26, at 162.
[29]Shannon P. Pratt & Roger J. Grabowski, Cost of Capital: Applications and Examples 3 (5th ed. 2014).
[30]Jeffrey M. Risius, Business Valuation: A Primer for the Legal Professional 87 (2007).
[31]Robert B. Dickie, Financial Statement Analysis and Business Valuation for the Practical Lawyer 237-238 (2d 2006).
[32]*Id.* at 237.
[33]*Id.*

estimating the cost of equity: the build-up method and the capital asset pricing model.[34]

From the entity's perspective, the cost of debt is the amount that the entity must pay to borrow money (i.e., the interest rate) and reflects the rate of return the investor or lender requires over the term of the debt financing for making that investment.[35] An entity's cost of debt is impacted by the risk and volatility of the industry in which it operates, its credit rating, its financial condition, and its available collateral.[36] In most circumstances, an entity can calculate or estimate the cost of debt by using (i) its preexisting interest rates, (ii) interest rates of comparable companies, or (iii) information provided by rating agencies.[37]

In order to determine an entity's overall cost of capital, the entity can use the weighted average cost of capital method. This method takes into account the costs of all of the entity's capital in whatever form — equity, bonds, and other debt instruments — and weighs those costs proportionately.[38] An entity can use this method to estimate the expense of funding its business operations or projects so that it can pinpoint the best financing alternative.

H. DERIVATIVE INSTRUMENTS

A derivative instrument is a contract in which the value or price is derived from one or more underlying assets, or from a financial or economic variable, such as an interest rate, market index, or foreign currency (referred to as the "underlying item").[39] Due to the nature of a derivative, its value is driven by or linked to the underlying item, which fluctuates in value. While an investor in a derivative commits to purchasing the underlying item at the specified price in the future, many derivative contracts are settled for cash versus the investor taking actual delivery of the underlying item.[40]

Derivatives are utilized to hedge against risks or speculate on future profit.[41] An investor seeking to hedge invests in a derivative with the goal of offsetting or counterbalancing against a perceived risk associated with another transaction, or in other terms, reducing exposure on that other transaction.[42] An investor seeking to speculate invests in a derivative with the goal of correctly anticipating the direction in which the price of the underlying asset will move in the future—higher or lower—and profiting as a result of anticipating correctly.[43]

---

[34]For further information on these two methods of estimating the cost of equity, see SHANNON P. PRATT & ROGER J. GRABOWSKI, COST OF CAPITAL: APPLICATIONS AND EXAMPLES 91 (5th ed. 2014).
[35]Dickie, *supra* note 31, at 229-231.
[36]Risius, *supra* note 30, at 87.
[37]Dickie, *supra* note 31, at 229-231.
[38]Pratt & Grabowski, *supra* note 34, at 544-545.
[39]JEFFREY J. HAAS, CORPORATE FINANCE 119 (2014).
[40]ALAN N. RECHTSCHAFFEN, CAPITAL MARKETS, DERIVATIVES AND THE LAW 157 (2009).
[41]CHARLES A. BOREK, CHRISTIAN JOHNSON, & MARY GROSSMAN, PORTFOLIO 5112-3RD: ACCOUNTING AND DISCLOSURE FOR DERIVATIVE INSTRUMENTS, II. INTRODUCTION TO DERIVATIVES (Bloomberg Law, Accounting Policy & Practice Portfolios: Accounting Rules and Disclosures).
[42]Haas, *supra* note 39, at 119.
[43]*Id.*

Determining a fair price for a derivatives contract is a complicated endeavor, and one that is beyond the scope of this text. Unlike the equity market for publicly traded instruments, the derivatives market is often less liquid, and as a result, it is more difficult to establish a market price. There are many factors that play a role in the pricing of the derivative and should be taken into account in determining a fair price for both parties. There are a number of formulas and modeling techniques available to price a derivative depending upon the type of instrument, as well as software programs to assist in the calculations.

There are two methods of entering into a derivatives contract: over-the-counter or exchange-traded.[44] An over-the-counter derivative is a privately negotiated or traded derivative, which allows for the contract to be tailored by the parties to meet their specific needs.[45] However, over-the-counter derivatives are less liquid and often have greater risk of default.[46] An exchange-traded derivative utilizes a standard agreement and is entered into or traded through an organized exchange.[47] As a result, exchange-traded derivatives are liquid investments with a lower degree of risk, as the organized exchange imposes margin requirements, or collateral, which reduces risk by regulating market participants.[48]

There are four primary types of derivative instruments: options, forwards, futures, and swaps. Each has its own unique characteristics as well as risks.

1. Options

An option is an agreement between two parties that gives the option holder the right, but not the obligation, to engage in the specified transaction (either a purchase or sale of the underlying asset) with the option writer, or counterparty, at a predetermined price on or before a specified date in the future.[49] An option can be either a call option or a put option. A call option gives the option holder the right to purchase the underlying item in the future, whereas a put option gives the option holder the right to sell the underlying item in the future. A significant component of any option, whether a call or a put option, is that the option holder is not required to exercise the option, meaning it does not have to purchase or sell the underlying item. However, that right, but not obligation, comes at a cost. The option holder pays the counterparty a fee, or an option premium, to enter into an option contract, which fee is paid whether or not the option holder chooses to exercise the option.[50] In essence, by entering into an option contract the option holder is betting on the price or value of the underlying asset in the future.

---

[44]ALAN N. RECHTSCHAFFEN, CAPITAL MARKETS, DERIVATIVES AND THE LAW 151 (2009).
[45]Haas, *supra* note 39, at 120.
[46]*Id.*
[47]Rechtschaffen, *supra* note 44, at 152.
[48]*Id.*
[49]CHARLES A. BOREK, CHRISTIAN JOHNSON, & MARY GROSSMAN, PORTFOLIO 5112—3RD: ACCOUNTING AND DISCLOSURE FOR DERIVATIVE INSTRUMENTS, II. INTRODUCTION TO DERIVATIVES, A. Nature of a Derivative (Bloomberg Law, Accounting Policy & Practice Portfolios: Accounting Rules and Disclosures).
[50]JEFFREY J. HAAS, CORPORATE FINANCE 120 (2014).

There are five terms required for an option contract: (i) specification of the underlying asset; (ii) whether the option is a call or a put; (iii) the exercise price (or strike price) of the option; (iv) the maturity date of the option; and (v) the way in which the option can be exercised.[51]

The underlying asset can be just about any item, ranging from real estate to common stock to a particular type of good. In addition to indicating whether the option is a call or a put, the contract must also specify the exercise or strike price of the option — meaning the price that must be paid for the underlying asset (whether paid by the option holder to the counterparty — a call — or paid by the counterparty to the option holder — a put) if the option holder chooses to exercise the option. Option contracts also contain a maturity date, which establishes the term of the option contract and acts as the expiration date for the option. The parties can negotiate the length or term of an over-the-counter option, which is generally one year or less, whereas an exchange-traded option has a set term, typically one or three months.[52] The option contract also stipulates the method by which the option can be exercised: (i) at any time on or before the maturity date, which is known as the *American Style*; (ii) only on the maturity date, which is known as the *European Style*; and (iii) only on specified dates set forth in the option contract, which is known as the *Asian Style*.[53] All exchange-traded options utilize the American Style, as do many over-the-counter options.[54]

While an option contemplates that the option holder may purchase or sell the underlying asset in the future, in the case of over-the-counter options, the settlement is generally in cash and not with the sale and delivery of or purchase and receipt of the underlying asset.[55] Even though that is generally true, the counterparty must still be prepared to either sell (call option) or purchase (put option) the underlying asset for the specified price.[56] Whereas, with exchange-traded options, the settlement is generally physical and the option holder must purchase or sell the underlying asset, particularly if it is "in-the-money" when exercised, meaning the strike price is below the market price if a call or above the market price if a put.[57] When an option is cash settled versus physically settled, the cash payment is the difference between the market price and the exercise price on the date of exercise.

In the case of a call option, if the market price is above the option's exercise price, then the option holder will make a return on its exercise (the delta between the exercise price and the market price) and the option is deemed to be "in-the-money." If the market price is below the option's exercise price, then the option holder will lose money on its exercise (the delta between the market price and the exercise price) and the option is deemed to be "out-of-the-money." If the market price and option's exercise price are equal, the option holder will

---

[51]*Id.*
[52]*Id.*
[53]*Id.* at 123.
[54]*Id.*
[55]ALAN N. RECHTSCHAFFEN, CAPITAL MARKETS, DERIVATIVES AND THE LAW 161 (2009).
[56]JEFFREY J. HAAS, CORPORATE FINANCE 123 (2014).
[57]*Id.*

neither make a return nor lose money and the option is deemed to be "at-the-money." This concept is often referred to as the intrinsic value of the option.[58]

EXAMPLE 11.9   **CALL OPTION**

Assume that the option holder has a call option to purchase a real estate parcel for an exercise or strike price of $25,000. If the market value of the real estate on the maturity date is $30,000, the option holder will make $5,000 because he can purchase the real estate for less than market price. If the market value of the real estate on the maturity date is $20,000, the option holder will lose $5,000 because he will pay more than the market price for the real estate.

In the case of a put option, if the market price is below the option's strike price, then the option holder will make a return on its exercise (the delta between the strike price and the market price) and the option is deemed to be "in-the-money." On the other hand, if the market price is above the option's strike price, then the option holder will lose money on its exercise (the delta between the market price and the strike price) and the option is deemed to be "out-of-the-money." If the market price and option's strike price are equal, the option holder will neither make a return nor lose money and the option is deemed to be "at-the-money."

EXAMPLE 11.10   **PUT OPTION**

Assume that the option holder has a put option to sell a real estate parcel for an exercise or strike price of $25,000. If the market value of the real estate on the maturity date is $30,000, the option holder will lose $5,000 as he must sell for less than market price. If the market value of the real estate on the maturity date is $20,000, the option holder will make $5,000 as he can sell the real estate for more than market price.

---

2. Forward Contract

A forward contract is a privately negotiated contract, meaning an over-the-counter derivative, that requires the option holder to sell the underlying asset and the counterparty to purchase the underlying asset at an agreed upon price, or forward price, on a specified future date, the settlement date.[59] Parties enter into a forward contract with the intent of limiting exposure to price fluctuations

---

[58]*Id.* at 121.
[59]CHARLES A. BOREK, CHRISTIAN JOHNSON, & MARY GROSSMAN, PORTFOLIO 5112-3RD: ACCOUNTING AND DISCLOSURE FOR DERIVATIVE INSTRUMENTS, II. INTRODUCTION TO DERIVATIVES, A. Nature of a Derivative (Bloomberg Law, Accounting Policy & Practice Portfolios: Accounting Rules and Disclosures).

of the underlying asset.[60] Forward contracts often involve the purchase and sale of commodities, such as wheat, corn, or coffee, financial instruments, or foreign currency, all of which fluctuate in value. Both parties to a forward contract are subject to risk — the risk that the other party will not perform on the settlement date — and so each party must assess and account for that potential risk during the negotiation of the contract.[61]

EXAMPLE 11.11 **FORWARD CONTRACT**

Assume that a coffee farmer enters into a forward contract with a coffee manufacturer to sell 10,000 pounds of coffee in three months at a forward price of $1.30 per pound. On the settlement date, the coffee farmer is obligated to sell the 10,000 pounds of coffee to the manufacturer at that set or forward price of $13,000. If the market price of coffee is $1.25 per pound, which is below the forward price on the settlement date, then the forward has value for the coffee farmer because it is selling the coffee for more than the current market value of $12,500 (meaning the manufacturer is paying more than market, so has lost money on the forward). On the other hand, if the market price of coffee is $1.35 per pound, which is above the forward price on the settlement date, then the forward has value for the coffee manufacturer, as it is purchasing the coffee for less than the current market value of $13,500 (meaning the farmer is selling below market, so has lost money on the forward).

Forward contracts differ from an option in distinct ways. A forward contract is not discretionary like an option, where the option holder has the right, but is not obligated, to exercise the option. In a forward contract, the option holder must sell the underlying asset and the counterparty must buy it on the settlement date. Another difference is that there is no fee associated with a forward contract, meaning the option holder does not pay a premium to the counterparty at the time the forward is entered into. Lastly, forward contracts are typically settled with physical delivery of the underlying asset unlike an option, which is often settled in cash.[62]

3. Futures Contract

A futures contract is an exchange-traded forward contract, meaning that it utilizes a standard contract but is traded on one of the public exchanges.[63] Similar to a forward, a futures contract is an agreement, pursuant to a standardized contract, that requires the option holder to sell the underlying asset to the counterparty at a specified price—the futures price—on a specific date—the

---

[60]JEFFREY J. HAAS, CORPORATE FINANCE 131 (2014).
[61]*Id.* at 133.
[62]ALAN N. RECHTSCHAFFEN, CAPITAL MARKETS, DERIVATIVES AND THE LAW 156 (2009).
[63]*Id.* at 157.

settlement date. However, unlike a forward contract, a futures contract is almost always settled in cash.[64] Just like forward contracts, futures are often for commodities, financial instruments, or foreign currency.

A futures contract differs from a forward contract in that the counterparty's risk is greatly reduced as a result of the following factors: (i) the option holder must deposit a performance bond with a clearinghouse, the party that settles futures transactions; (ii) futures are settled on a daily basis, meaning gains or losses are recognized daily, a concept called "marked-to-market"; and (iii) only exchange members can be a counterparty to a futures contract.[65] Additionally, futures can only be traded on recognized exchanges, which are regulated by and subject to the rules and regulations of the Commodity Futures Trading Commission (CFTC).

4. Swaps

A swap is a privately negotiated contract between two parties who "agree to exchange 'cash flows' on a 'notional amount' over a period of time in the future."[66] The contract establishes a set payment schedule whereby each party will make a payment on one or more payment dates based on the "notional amount" or the underlying principal balance.[67] Similar to a forward contract, swaps are an over-the-counter derivative and so can be tailored by the parties for their specific needs, and as a result they have the same type of risks for the parties as a forward.[68] The most common type of swap is an interest rate swap, but other types include currency swaps, commodity swaps, and credit default swaps.[69]

EXAMPLE 11.12 **SWAP**

Assume that Alpha Company has a fixed interest rate commercial loan and Beta Company has a variable interest rate commercial loan; however, each entity would prefer the opposite type of interest. Alpha Company and Beta Company enter into an interest rate swap whereby Alpha Company will pay Beta Company's variable interest on the interest payment due dates and Beta Company will pay Alpha Company's fixed interest on the interest payment due dates. Both Alpha Company and Beta Company are responsible for the "notional amount" or the loan principal; however, they have swapped the interest payments.

A swap arrangement allows an entity to manage its exposure to market fluctuations in interest rates or foreign currency prices. In essence, the parties can hedge against or profit upon perceived risks.

---

[64]Haas, *supra* note 60, at 133.
[65]Rechtschaffen, *supra* note 62, at 157.
[66]Rechtschaffen, *supra* note 62, at 162.
[67]*Id.* at 162-163.
[68]Jeffrey J. Haas, Corporate Finance 136 (2014).
[69]*Id.*

Exhibit A

Retailers, Inc. Sample Financial Statements

1. Sample Consolidated Balance Sheet for Retailers, Inc.
2. Sample Consolidated Income Statement for Retailers, Inc.
3. Sample Consolidated Statement of Cash Flows for Retailers, Inc.
4. Sample Consolidated Statement of Changes in Stockholders' Equity for Retailers, Inc.

RETAILERS, INC.
CONSOLIDATED BALANCE SHEET
(IN THOUSANDS, EXCEPT SHARE DATA)

	December 31 Current Year	December 31 Prior Year
Assets		
Current Assets		
Cash and cash equivalents	$6,850	$3,474
Accounts receivable	2,798	2,099
Inventory	5,367	4,690
Prepaid expenses and other current assets	8,717	6,398
Total current assets	23,732	16,661
Property	1,050	975
Equipment	2,605	2,533
Less: Depreciation	(550)	(520)
Net equipment	2,055	2,013
Goodwill	1,232	1,222
Intangible assets	1,809	1,809
Less: Amortization	(653)	(600)
Net intangible assets	1,156	1,209
Other long-term assets	5,706	4,754
Total assets	$34,931	$26,834
Liabilities and Stockholders' Equity		
Current Liabilities		
Revolving credit facility	--	$750
Accounts payable	2,104	1,654
Accrued expenses	1,476	1,337
Current portion of long-term debt	1,951	497
Other current liabilities	3,456	2,247
Total current liabilities	8,987	6,485
Long-term debt, net of current maturities	6,295	4,795
Other long-term liabilities	679	498
Total liabilities	$15,961	$11,778
Stockholders' equity		
Common stock, $0.01; 40,000,000 shares authorized; 7,295,988 issued and outstanding as of December 31 Current Year and 6,628,708 issued and outstanding as of December 31 Prior Year	$73	$66
Additional paid-in-capital	6,687	4,842
Retained earnings	12,210	10,148
Total stockholders' equity	$18,970	$15,056
Total liabilities and stockholders' equity	$34,931	$26,834

RETAILERS, INC.
CONSOLIDATED INCOME STATEMENT
(IN THOUSANDS)

	December 31 Current Year	December 31 Prior Year
Revenues	$31,151	$23,553
Less: returns and allowances	(308)	(233)
Net revenues	30,843	23,320
Cost of goods sold	15,721	11,953
Gross profit	15,122	11,367
Selling, general, and administrative expenses	11,582	8,715
Operating income	3,540	2,652
Interest expense	53	29
Other expenses	64	11
Income before income taxes	3,423	2,612
Provision for income taxes	1,361	986
Net income	$2,062	$1,626

RETAILERS, INC.
CONSOLIDATED STATEMENT OF CASH FLOWS
(IN THOUSANDS)

	December 31 Current Year
Cash Flows from Operating Activities	
Net income	$2,062
Adjustments to reconcile net income to net cash used in operating activities:	
Depreciation and amortization	83
Changes in operating assets and liabilities, net of effects of acquisitions:	
Accounts receivable	(699)
Inventory	(677)
Prepaid expenses and other current assets	(3,271)
Accounts payable	450
Accrued expenses and other current liabilities	1,529
Net cash used in operating activities	($523)
Cash Flows from Investing Activities	
Purchases of property and equipment	(147)
Purchase of business	(10)
Net cash used in investing activities	($157)
Cash Flows from Financing Activities	
Proceeds from revolving credit facility	--
Payments on revolving credit facility	(750)
Proceeds from long-term debt	3,931
Payments on long-term debt	(870)
Proceeds from exercise of stock options and other stock issuances	1,852
Payments of debt financing costs	(107)
Net cash provided by financing activities	$4,056
Net increase in cash and cash equivalents	$3,376
Cash and Cash Equivalents	
Beginning of period	$3,474
End of period	$6,850

Retailers, Inc.
Consolidated Statement of Changes in Stockholders' Equity
(In thousands)

	Common Stock		Additional Paid-in Capital	Retained Earnings	Total Stockholders' Equity
	Shares	Amount			
Balance as a of End of Prior Fiscal Year	6,628	$66	$4,842	$10,148	$15,056
Exercise of stock options	600	6	1,550	-	1,556
Issuance of common stock	67	1	295	-	296
Net income (loss)				2,062	2,062
Balance as of End of Current Fiscal Year	7,295	$73	$6,687	$12,210	$18,970

Exhibit B[1]

Sample Audit Inquiry Letter for Fictitious Company

Alpha, Inc.
1234 Fifth Lane
City, State, Zip

January 15, 20X3

Outside Counsel, PC
5678 Sixth Lane
City, State, Zip

      Re: Audit Inquiry Letter for Alpha, Inc.

To Whom It May Concern:

In connection with an audit of our financial statements at December 31, 20X2, and for the year then ended, management of the Company has prepared, and furnished to our auditors, Audit Firm, PC, 9012 Seventh Lane, City, State, Zip, a description and evaluation of certain contingencies, including those set forth below involving matters with respect to which you have been engaged and to which you have devoted substantive attention on behalf of the Company in the form of legal consultation or representation. These contingencies are regarded by management of the Company as material for this purpose. Your response should include matters that existed at December 31, 20X2, and during the period from that date to the date of your response.

Pending or Threatened Litigation (Excluding Unasserted Claims)

[This section will include the following types of information: (i) nature of the litigation; (ii) progress of the case; (iii) how management is responding or intends to respond to the litigation; and (iv) an evaluation of the likelihood of an unfavorable outcome and an estimate, if one can be made, of the amount or range of potential loss.]

---

1 *See generally* Auditing Standards, Inquiry of a Client's Lawyer Concerning Litigation, Claims, and Assessments, AS §2505 (Am. Inst. of Certified Pub. Accountants 2016).

Please furnish to our auditors such explanation, if any, that you consider necessary to supplement the foregoing information, including an explanation of those matters as to which your views may differ from those stated and an identification of the omission of any pending or threatened litigation, claims, and assessments or a statement that the list of such matters is complete.

Unasserted Claims and Assessments (Considered by Management to Be Probable of Assertion, and That, If Asserted, Would Have at Least a Reasonable Possibility of an Unfavorable Outcome)

[This section would ordinarily include the following: (i) nature of the matter; (ii) how management intends to respond if the claim is asserted; and (iii) an evaluation of the likelihood of an unfavorable outcome and an estimate, if one can be made, of the amount or range of potential loss.]

Please furnish to our auditors such explanation, if any, that you consider necessary to supplement the foregoing information, including an explanation of those matters as to which your views may differ from those we stated.

We understand that whenever, in the course of performing legal services for us with respect to a matter recognized to involve an unasserted possible claim or assessment that may call for financial statement disclosure, if you have formed a professional conclusion that we should disclose or consider disclosure concerning such possible claim or assessment, as a matter of professional responsibility to us, you will so advise us and will consult with us concerning the question of such disclosure and the applicable requirements of Accounting Standards Codification 450, Contingencies. Please specifically confirm to our auditors that our understanding is correct.

[The auditor may request the client to inquire about additional matters, for example, unpaid or unbilled charges or specified information on certain contractually assumed obligations of the Company, such as guarantees of indebtedness of others.]

Please specifically identify the nature of and reasons for any limitation on your response. Our auditors expect to have the audit completed around March 1, 20X3, and would appreciate your reply by that date with a specified effective date no earlier than February 15, 20X3.

Sincerely,

Jane Doe, Chief Executive Officer
Alpha, Inc.

Exhibit C[1]

Audit Response Letter for Fictitious Company

Outside Counsel
5678 Sixth Lane
City, State, Zip

February 13, 20X3

Audit Firm, PC,
9012 Seventh Lane
City, State, Zip

      Re: Audit Inquiry Letter Response for Alpha, Inc.

To Whom It May Concern:

By a letter dated January 15, 20X3, Ms. Jane Doe, Chief Executive Officer of Alpha, Inc. (Company) requested us to furnish you with certain information in connection with your examination of the accounts of the Company as of December 31, 20X2.

While this firm represents the Company on a regular basis, our engagement has been limited to the specific matters as to which we were consulted by the Company. Subject to the foregoing and the last paragraph of this letter, we advise you that since January 1, 20X2, we have not been engaged to give substantive attention to, or represent the Company in connection with, material loss contingencies coming within the scope of Clause (a) of Paragraph 5 of the Statement of Policy referred to in the last paragraph of this letter, except as follows:

[Law firm would insert the description of litigation and claims that fit the foregoing criteria here.]

With respect to the matters specifically identified in the Company's letter and upon which comment has been specifically requested, as contemplated by Clauses (b) and

---

1 *See generally* AUDITING STANDARDS, Inquiry of a Client's Lawyer Concerning Litigation, Claims, and Assessments, AS §2505 (Am. Inst. of Certified Pub. Accountants 2016).

(c) of Paragraph 5 of the Statement of Policy referred to in the last paragraph of this letter, we advise you as follows:

[Law firm would insert appropriate information here.]

The information set forth herein is as of the date of this letter *[or other appropriate date]*, except as otherwise noted, and we disclaim any undertaking to advise you of changes that thereafter may be brought to our attention.

[Law firm would insert information regarding outstanding bills for services and disbursements here.]

This response is limited by, and in accordance with, the ABA Statement of Policy Regarding Lawyers' Responses to Auditors' Requests for Information (December 1975). Without limiting the generality of the foregoing, the limitations set forth in such Statement of Policy on the scope and use of this response (Paragraphs 2 and 7) are specifically herein incorporated by reference, and any description herein of any "loss contingencies" is qualified in its entirety by Paragraph 5 of the Statement of Policy and the accompanying Commentary (which is an integral part of the Statement of Policy). Consistent with the last sentence of Paragraph 6 of the Statement of Policy and pursuant to the Company's request, this will confirm as correct the Company's understanding as set forth in its audit inquiry letter to us that whenever, in the course of performing legal services for the Company with respect to a matter recognized to involve an unasserted possible claim or assessment that may call for financial statement disclosure, we have formed a professional conclusion that the Company must disclose or consider disclosure concerning such possible claim or assessment, we, as a matter of professional responsibility to the Company, will so advise the Company and will consult with the Company concerning the questions of such disclosure and the applicable requirements of Accounting Standards Codification 450, Contingencies.

[Law firm should describe any other additional limitations as indicated by Paragraph 4 of the Statement of Policy here.]

Sincerely,

Lawyer Name, Partner
Outside Counsel, PC

Exhibit D[1]

Unqualified Audit Opinion for Fictitious Company

a private

REPORT OF AUDIT FIRM, PC,
INDEPENDENT REGISTERED PUBLIC ACCOUNTING FIRM

(actual will be longer)

The Board of Directors and Stockholders of Alpha, Inc.

We have audited the accompanying balance sheets of Alpha, Inc. as of December 31, 20X2 and 20X1, and the related statements of income, comprehensive income, cash flows, and stockholders' equity for the years then ended. These financial statements are the responsibility of the Company's management. Our responsibility is to express an opinion on these financial statements based on our audit.

We conducted our audits in accordance with the standards of the Public Company Accounting Oversight Board (United States). Those standards require that we plan and perform the audit to obtain reasonable assurance about whether the financial statements are free of material misstatement. An audit includes examining, on a test basis, evidence supporting the amounts and disclosures in the financial statements. An audit also includes assessing the accounting principles used and significant estimates made by management, as well as evaluating the overall financial statement presentation. We believe that our audits provide a reasonable basis for our opinion.

In our opinion, the financial statements referred to above present fairly, in all material respects, the financial position of Alpha, Inc. as of December 31, 20X2 and 20X1, and the results of its operations and its cash flows for the years then ended in conformity with accounting principles generally accepted in the United States of America.

usually GAAP

1 *See generally* Auditing Standards, Reports on Audited Financial Statements, AS §3101 (Am. Inst. of Certified Pub. Accountants 2016).

We have also audited, in accordance with the standards of the Public Company Accounting Oversight Board (United States), the effectiveness of Alpha, Inc.'s internal control over financial reporting as of December 31, 20X2, based on criteria established in *[insert applicable control criteria]*, and our report dated February X, 20X3, expressed an unqualified opinion thereon.

Audit Firm, PC
[Address]
[Date]

Exhibit E[1]

Unqualified Audit Opinion with Explanatory Language for Fictitious Company

(Elective Change in Accounting Principle)

**REPORT OF AUDIT FIRM, PC,
INDEPENDENT REGISTERED PUBLIC ACCOUNTING FIRM**

The Board of Directors and Stockholders of Alpha, Inc.

We have audited the accompanying balance sheets of Alpha, Inc. as of December 31, 20X2 and 20X1, and the related statements of income, comprehensive income, cash flows, and stockholders' equity for the years then ended. These financial statements are the responsibility of the Company's management. Our responsibility is to express an opinion on these financial statements based on our audit. As discussed in Note 18 to the financial statements, the Company has elected to change its method of accounting for [describe accounting method change] in 20X2.

We conducted our audits in accordance with the standards of the Public Company Accounting Oversight Board (United States). Those standards require that we plan and perform the audit to obtain reasonable assurance about whether the financial statements are free of material misstatement. An audit includes examining, on a test basis, evidence supporting the amounts and disclosures in the financial statements. An audit also includes assessing the accounting principles used and significant estimates made by management, as well as evaluating the overall financial statement presentation. We believe that our audits provide a reasonable basis for our opinion.

In our opinion, the financial statements referred to above present fairly, in all material respects, the financial position of Alpha, Inc. as of December 31, 20X2 and 20X1, and the results of its operations and its cash flows for the years then ended in conformity with accounting principles generally accepted in the United States of America.

We have also audited, in accordance with the standards of the Public Company Accounting Oversight Board (United States), the effectiveness of Alpha, Inc.'s internal

PCAOB

---

1 *See generally* AUDITING STANDARDS, Reports on Audited Financial Statements, AS §3101 (Am. Inst. of Certified Pub. Accountants 2016).

Two situations that lead to qualification:
① Asked for something but cannot get it.
② Impasse on "incorrect practice"

control over financial reporting as of December 31, 20X2, based on criteria established in [insert applicable control criteria], and our report dated February X, 20X3, expressed an unqualified opinion thereon.

Audit Firm, PC
[Address]
[Date]

Adverse : able to audit but findings are

Exhibit F[1]

Qualified Audit Opinion for Fictitious Company

REPORT OF AUDIT FIRM, PC,
INDEPENDENT REGISTERED PUBLIC ACCOUNTING FIRM

The Board of Directors and Stockholders of Alpha, Inc.

We have audited the accompanying balance sheets of Alpha, Inc. as of December 31, 20X2 and 20X1, and the related statements of income, comprehensive income, cash flows, and stockholders' equity for the years then ended. These financial statements are the responsibility of the Company's management. Our responsibility is to express an opinion on these financial statements based on our audit.

Except as discussed in the following paragraph, we conducted our audits in accordance with the standards of the Public Company Accounting Oversight Board (United States). Those standards require that we plan and perform the audit to obtain reasonable assurance about whether the financial statements are free of material misstatement. An audit includes examining, on a test basis, evidence supporting the amounts and disclosures in the financial statements. An audit also includes assessing the accounting principles used and significant estimates made by management, as well as evaluating the overall financial statement presentation. We believe that our audits provide a reasonable basis for our opinion.

We were unable to obtain audited financial statements supporting the Company's investment in an affiliate stated at $1,500,000 and $1,100,000 at December 31, 20X2 and 20X1, respectively, or its equity in earnings of that affiliate of $150,000 and $110,000, which is included in net income for the years then ended as described in Note 16 to the financial statements; nor were we able to satisfy ourselves as to the carrying value of the investment in the affiliate or the equity in its earnings by other auditing procedures.

In our opinion, except for the effects of such adjustments, if any, as might have been determined necessary had we been able to examine evidence regarding the affiliate investment and earnings, the financial statements referred to in the first paragraph

---

1 *See generally* AUDITING STANDARDS, Reports on Audited Financial Statements, AS §3101 (Am. Inst. of Certified Pub. Accountants 2016).

above present fairly, in all material respects, the financial position of Alpha, Inc. as of December 31, 20X2 and 20X1, and the results of its operations and its cash flows for the years then ended in conformity with accounting principles generally accepted in the United States of America.

We have also audited, in accordance with the standards of the Public Company Accounting Oversight Board (United States), the effectiveness of Alpha, Inc.'s internal control over financial reporting as of December 31, 20X2, based on criteria established in [insert applicable control criteria], and our report dated February X, 20X3, expressed an unqualified opinion thereon.

Audit Firm, PC
[Address]
[Date]

Exhibit G[1]

Adverse Audit Opinion
for Fictitious Company

REPORT OF AUDIT FIRM, PC,
INDEPENDENT REGISTERED PUBLIC ACCOUNTING FIRM

The Board of Directors and Stockholders of Alpha, Inc.

We have audited the accompanying balance sheets of Alpha, Inc. as of December 31, 20X2 and 20X1, and the related statements of income, comprehensive income, cash flows, and stockholders' equity for the years then ended. These financial statements are the responsibility of the Company's management. Our responsibility is to express an opinion on these financial statements based on our audit.

We conducted our audits in accordance with the standards of the Public Company Accounting Oversight Board (United States). Those standards require that we plan and perform the audit to obtain reasonable assurance about whether the financial statements are free of material misstatement. An audit includes examining, on a test basis, evidence supporting the amounts and disclosures in the financial statements. An audit also includes assessing the accounting principles used and significant estimates made by management, as well as evaluating the overall financial statement presentation. We believe that our audits provide a reasonable basis for our opinion.

As discussed in Note 10 to the financial statements, the Company carries its equipment at appraisal values and provides depreciation on the basis of such values. Accounting principles generally accepted in the United States of America require that equipment be stated at an amount not in excess of cost, reduced by depreciation based on such amount.

Because of the departures from accounting principles generally accepted in the United States of America identified above, as of December 31, 20X2 and 20X1, equipment, less accumulated depreciation, is carried at $793,000 and $687,000 in excess of an amount based on the cost to the Company.

---

1 *See generally* AUDITING STANDARDS, Reports on Audited Financial Statements, AS §3101 (Am. Inst. of Certified Pub. Accountants 2016).

In our opinion because of the effects of the matters discussed in the preceding paragraphs, the financial statements referred to above do not present fairly, in conformity with accounting principles generally accepted in the United States of America, the financial position of Alpha, Inc. as of December 31, 20X2 and 20X1, or the results of its operations or its cash flows for the years then ended.

Audit Firm, PC
[Address]
[Date]

Disclaimer of Opinion for Fictitious Company

REPORT OF AUDIT FIRM, PC,
INDEPENDENT REGISTERED PUBLIC ACCOUNTING FIRM

The Board of Directors and Stockholders of Alpha, Inc.

We have audited the accompanying balance sheets of Alpha, Inc. as of December 31, 20X2 and 20X1, and the related statements of income, comprehensive income, cash flows, and stockholders' equity for the years then ended. These financial statements are the responsibility of the Company's management.

The Company did not make a count of its physical inventory in 20X2 or 20X1, stated in the accompanying financial statements at $2,643,000 as of December 31, 20X2, and $2,147,000 as of December 31, 20X1. The Company's records do not permit the application of other auditing procedures to inventories.

Since the Company did not take physical inventories and we were not able to apply other auditing procedures to satisfy ourselves as to inventory quantities, the scope of our work was not sufficient to enable us to express, and we do not express, an opinion on these financial statements.

Audit Firm, PC
[Address]
[Date]

Not allowed to conduct audit properly

---

1 *See generally* AUDITING STANDARDS, Reports on Audited Financial Statements, AS §3101 (Am. Inst. of Certified Pub. Accountants 2016).

EXHIBIT I

Future Value of a Lump Sum Table

Periods	1%	2%	3%	4%	5%	6%	7%
1	1.0100	1.0200	1.0300	1.0400	1.0500	1.0600	1.0700
2	1.0201	1.0404	1.0609	1.0816	1.1025	1.1236	1.1449
3	1.0303	1.0612	1.0927	1.1249	1.1576	1.1910	1.2250
4	1.0406	1.0824	1.1255	1.1699	1.2155	1.2625	1.3108
5	1.0510	1.1041	1.1593	1.2167	1.2763	1.3382	1.4026
6	1.0615	1.1262	1.1941	1.2653	1.3401	1.4185	1.5007
7	1.0721	1.1487	1.2299	1.3159	1.4071	1.5036	1.6058
8	1.0829	1.1717	1.2668	1.3686	1.4775	1.5938	1.7182
9	1.0937	1.1951	1.3048	1.4233	1.5513	1.6895	1.8385
10	1.1046	1.2190	1.3439	1.4802	1.6289	1.7908	1.9672
11	1.1157	1.2434	1.3842	1.5395	1.7103	1.8983	2.1049
12	1.1268	1.2682	1.4258	1.6010	1.7959	2.0122	2.2522
13	1.1381	1.2936	1.4685	1.6651	1.8856	2.1329	2.4098
14	1.1495	1.3195	1.5126	1.7317	1.9799	2.2609	2.5785
15	1.1610	1.3459	1.5580	1.8009	2.0789	2.3966	2.7590
16	1.1726	1.3728	1.6047	1.8730	2.1829	2.5404	2.9522
17	1.1843	1.4002	1.6528	1.9479	2.2920	2.6928	3.1588
18	1.1961	1.4282	1.7024	2.0258	2.4066	2.8543	3.3799
19	1.2081	1.4568	1.7535	2.1068	2.5270	3.0256	3.6165
20	1.2202	1.4859	1.8061	2.1911	2.6533	3.2071	3.8697
21	1.2324	1.5157	1.8603	2.2788	2.7860	3.3996	4.1406
22	1.2447	1.5460	1.9161	2.3699	2.9253	3.6035	4.4304
23	1.2572	1.5769	1.9736	2.4647	3.0715	3.8197	4.7405
24	1.2697	1.6084	2.0328	2.5633	3.2251	4.0489	5.0724
25	1.2824	1.6406	2.0938	2.6658	3.3864	4.2919	5.4274
26	1.2953	1.6734	2.1566	2.7725	3.5557	4.5494	5.8074
27	1.3082	1.7069	2.2213	2.8834	3.7335	4.8223	6.2139
28	1.3213	1.7410	2.2879	2.9987	3.9201	5.1117	6.6488
29	1.3345	1.7758	2.3566	3.1187	4.1161	5.4184	7.1143
30	1.3478	1.8114	2.4273	3.2434	4.3219	5.7435	7.6123
31	1.3613	1.8476	2.5001	3.3731	4.5380	6.0881	8.1451

Periods	1%	2%	3%	4%	5%	6%	7%
32	1.3749	1.8845	2.5751	3.5081	4.7649	6.4534	8.7153
33	1.3887	1.9222	2.6523	3.6484	5.0032	6.8406	9.3253
34	1.4026	1.9607	2.7319	3.7943	5.2533	7.2510	9.9781
35	1.4166	1.9999	2.8139	3.9461	5.5160	7.6861	10.6766
36	1.4308	2.0399	2.8983	4.1039	5.7918	8.1473	11.4239
37	1.4451	2.0807	2.9852	4.2681	6.0814	8.6361	12.2236
38	1.4595	2.1223	3.0748	4.4388	6.3855	9.1543	13.0793
39	1.4741	2.1647	3.1670	4.6164	6.7048	9.7035	13.9948
40	1.4889	2.2080	3.2620	4.8010	7.0400	10.2857	14.9745
41	1.5038	2.2522	3.3599	4.9931	7.3920	10.9029	16.0227
42	1.5188	2.2972	3.4607	5.1928	7.7616	11.5570	17.1443
43	1.5340	2.3432	3.5645	5.4005	8.1497	12.2505	18.3444
44	1.5493	2.3901	3.6715	5.6165	8.5572	12.9855	19.6285
45	1.5648	2.4379	3.7816	5.8412	8.9850	13.7646	21.0025
46	1.5805	2.4866	3.8950	6.0748	9.4343	14.5905	22.4726
47	1.5963	2.5363	4.0119	6.3178	9.9060	15.4659	24.0457
48	1.6122	2.5871	4.1323	6.5705	10.4013	16.3939	25.7289
49	1.6283	2.6388	4.2562	6.8333	10.9213	17.3775	27.5299
50	1.6446	2.6916	4.3839	7.1067	11.4674	18.4302	29.4570

Periods	8%	9%	10%	11%	12%	13%	14%
1	1.0800	1.0900	1.1000	1.1100	1.1200	1.1300	1.1400
2	1.1664	1.1881	1.2100	1.2321	1.2544	1.2769	1.2996
3	1.2597	1.2950	1.3310	1.3676	1.4049	1.4429	1.4815
4	1.3605	1.4116	1.4641	1.5181	1.5735	1.6305	1.6890
5	1.4693	1.5386	1.6105	1.6851	1.7623	1.8424	1.9254
6	1.5869	1.6771	1.7716	1.8704	1.9738	2.0820	2.1950
7	1.7138	1.8280	1.9487	2.0762	2.2107	2.3526	2.5023
8	1.8509	1.9926	2.1436	2.3045	2.4760	2.6584	2.8526
9	1.9990	2.1719	2.3579	2.5580	2.7731	3.0040	3.2519
10	2.1589	2.3674	2.5937	2.8394	3.1058	3.3946	3.7072
11	2.3316	2.5804	2.8531	3.1518	3.4786	3.8359	4.2263
12	2.5182	2.8127	3.1384	3.4985	3.8960	4.3345	4.8179
13	2.7196	3.0658	3.4523	3.8833	4.3635	4.8981	5.4924
14	2.9372	3.3417	3.7975	4.3104	4.8871	5.5348	6.2613
15	3.1722	3.6425	4.1772	4.7846	5.4736	6.2543	7.1379
16	3.4259	3.9703	4.5950	5.3109	6.1304	7.0673	8.1372
17	3.7000	4.3276	5.0545	5.8951	6.8660	7.9861	9.2765
18	3.9960	4.7171	5.5599	6.5436	7.6900	9.0243	10.5752
19	4.3157	5.1417	6.1159	7.2633	8.6128	10.1974	12.0557
20	4.6610	5.6044	6.7275	8.0623	9.6463	11.5231	13.7435

Exhibit I. Future Value of a Lump Sum Table   **339**

Periods	8%	9%	10%	11%	12%	13%	14%
21	5.0338	6.1088	7.4003	8.9492	10.8038	13.0211	15.6676
22	5.4365	6.6586	8.1403	9.9336	12.1003	14.7138	17.8610
23	5.8715	7.2579	8.9543	11.0263	13.5523	16.6266	20.3616
24	6.3412	7.9111	9.8497	12.2392	15.1786	18.7881	23.2122
25	6.8485	8.6231	10.8347	13.5855	17.0001	21.2305	26.4619
26	7.3964	9.3992	11.9182	15.0799	19.0401	23.9905	30.1666
27	7.9881	10.2451	13.1100	16.7387	21.3249	27.1093	34.3899
28	8.6271	11.1671	14.4210	18.5799	23.8839	30.6335	39.2045
29	9.3173	12.1722	15.8631	20.6237	26.7499	34.6158	44.6931
30	10.0627	13.2677	17.4494	22.8923	29.9599	39.1159	50.9502
31	10.8677	14.4618	19.1943	25.4104	33.5551	44.2010	58.0832
32	11.7371	15.7633	21.1138	28.2056	37.5817	49.9471	66.2148
33	12.6761	17.1820	23.2252	31.3082	42.0915	56.4402	75.4849
34	13.6901	18.7284	25.5477	34.7521	47.1425	63.7774	86.0528
35	14.7853	20.4140	28.1024	38.5749	52.7996	72.0685	98.1002
36	15.9682	22.2512	30.9128	42.8181	59.1356	81.4374	111.8342
37	17.2456	24.2538	34.0039	47.5281	66.2318	92.0243	127.4910
38	18.6253	26.4367	37.4043	52.7562	74.1797	103.9874	145.3397
39	20.1153	28.8160	41.1448	58.5593	83.0812	117.5058	165.6873
40	21.7245	31.4094	45.2593	65.0009	93.0510	132.7816	188.8835
41	23.4625	34.2363	49.7852	72.1510	104.2171	150.0432	215.3272
42	25.3395	37.3175	54.7637	80.0876	116.7231	169.5488	245.4730
43	27.3666	40.6761	60.2401	88.8972	130.7299	191.5901	279.8392
44	29.5560	44.3370	66.2641	98.6759	146.4175	216.4968	319.0167
45	31.9204	48.3273	72.8905	109.5302	163.9876	244.6414	363.6791
46	34.4741	52.6767	80.1795	121.5786	183.6661	276.4448	414.5941
47	37.2320	57.4176	88.1975	134.9522	205.7061	312.3826	472.6373
48	40.2106	62.5852	97.0172	149.7970	230.3908	352.9923	538.8065
49	43.4274	68.2179	106.7190	166.2746	258.0377	398.8814	614.2395
50	46.9016	74.3575	117.3909	184.5648	289.0022	450.7359	700.2330

Periods	15%	16%	17%	18%	19%
1	1.1500	1.1600	1.1700	1.1800	1.1900
2	1.3225	1.3456	1.3689	1.3924	1.4161
3	1.5209	1.5609	1.6016	1.6430	1.6852
4	1.7490	1.8106	1.8739	1.9388	2.0053
5	2.0114	2.1003	2.1924	2.2878	2.3864
6	2.3131	2.4364	2.5652	2.6996	2.8398
7	2.6600	2.8262	3.0012	3.1855	3.3793
8	3.0590	3.2784	3.5115	3.7589	4.0214
9	3.5179	3.8030	4.1084	4.4355	4.7854
10	4.0456	4.4114	4.8068	5.2338	5.6947
11	4.6524	5.1173	5.6240	6.1759	6.7767
12	5.3503	5.9360	6.5801	7.2876	8.0642
13	6.1528	6.8858	7.6987	8.5994	9.5964
14	7.0757	7.9875	9.0075	10.1472	11.4198
15	8.1371	9.2655	10.5387	11.9737	13.5895
16	9.3576	10.7480	12.3303	14.1290	16.1715
17	10.7613	12.4677	14.4264	16.6722	19.2441
18	12.3755	14.4625	16.8790	19.6733	22.9005
19	14.2318	16.7765	19.7484	23.2144	27.2516
20	16.3665	19.4608	23.1056	27.3930	32.4294
21	18.8215	22.5745	27.0336	32.3238	38.5910
22	21.6447	26.1864	31.6293	38.1421	45.9233
23	24.8915	30.3762	37.0062	45.0076	54.6487
24	28.6252	35.2364	43.2973	53.1090	65.0320
25	32.9190	40.8742	50.6578	62.6686	77.3881
26	37.8568	47.4141	59.2697	73.9490	92.0918
27	43.5353	55.0004	69.3455	87.2598	109.5893
28	50.0656	63.8004	81.1342	102.9666	130.4112
29	57.5755	74.0085	94.9271	121.5005	155.1893
30	66.2118	85.8499	111.0647	143.3706	184.6753
31	76.1435	99.5859	129.9456	169.1774	219.7636
32	87.5651	115.5196	152.0364	199.6293	261.5187
33	100.6998	134.0027	177.8826	235.5625	311.2073
34	115.8048	155.4432	208.1226	277.9638	370.3366
35	133.1755	180.3141	243.5035	327.9973	440.7006
36	153.1519	209.1643	284.8990	387.0368	524.4337
37	176.1246	242.6306	333.3319	456.7034	624.0761
38	202.5433	281.4515	389.9983	538.9100	742.6506
39	232.9248	326.4838	456.2980	635.9139	883.7542
40	267.8635	378.7212	533.8687	750.3783	1051.6675
41	308.0431	439.3165	624.6264	885.4464	1251.4843
42	354.2495	509.6072	730.8129	1044.8268	1489.2664

Exhibit I. Future Value of a Lump Sum Table **341**

Periods	15%	16%	17%	18%	19%
43	407.3870	591.1443	855.0511	1232.8956	1772.2270
44	468.4950	685.7274	1000.4098	1454.8168	2108.9501
45	538.7693	795.4438	1170.4794	1716.6839	2509.6506
46	619.5847	922.7148	1369.4609	2025.6870	2986.4842
47	712.5224	1070.3492	1602.2693	2390.3106	3553.9162
48	819.4007	1241.6051	1874.6550	2820.5665	4229.1603
49	942.3108	1440.2619	2193.3464	3328.2685	5032.7008
50	1083.6574	1670.7038	2566.2153	3927.3569	5988.9139

EXHIBIT J

Present Value of a Lump Sum Table

Periods	1%	2%	3%	4%	5%	6%	7%
1	.9901	.9804	.9709	.9615	.9524	.9434	.9346
2	.9803	.9612	.9426	.9246	.9070	.8900	.8734
3	.9707	.9423	.9151	.8890	.8638	.8396	.8163
4	.9610	.9238	.8885	.8548	.8227	.7921	.7629
5	.9515	.9057	.8626	.8219	.7835	.7473	.7130
6	.9420	.8880	.8375	.7903	.7462	.7050	.6663
7	.9327	.8706	.8131	.7599	.7107	.6651	.6228
8	.9235	.8535	.7894	.7307	.6768	.6274	.5820
9	.9143	.8368	.7664	.7026	.6446	.5919	.5439
10	.9053	.8203	.7441	.6756	.6139	.5584	.5083
11	.8963	.8043	.7224	.6496	.5847	.5268	.4751
12	.8874	.7885	.7014	.6246	.5568	.4970	.4440
13	.8787	.7730	.6810	.6006	.5303	.4688	.4150
14	.8700	.7579	.6611	.5775	.5051	.4423	.3878
15	.8613	.7430	.6419	.5553	.4810	.4173	.3624
16	.8528	.7284	.6232	.5339	.4581	.3936	.3387
17	.8444	.7142	.6050	.5134	.4363	.3714	.3166
18	.8360	.7002	.5874	.4936	.4155	.3503	.2959
19	.8277	.6864	.5703	.4746	.3957	.3305	.2765
20	.8195	.6730	.5537	.4564	.3769	.3118	.2584
21	.8114	.6598	.5375	.4388	.3589	.2942	.2415
22	.8034	.6468	.5219	.4220	.3419	.2775	.2257
23	.7954	.6342	.5067	.4057	.3256	.2618	.2109
24	.7876	.6217	.4919	.3901	.3101	.2470	.1971
25	.7798	.6095	.4776	.3751	.2953	.2330	.1842
26	.7720	.5976	.4637	.3607	.2812	.2198	.1722
27	.7644	.5859	.4502	.3468	.2678	.2074	.1609
28	.7568	.5744	.4371	.3335	.2551	.1956	.1504
29	.7493	.5631	.4243	.3207	.2429	.1846	.1406
30	.7419	.5521	.4120	.3083	.2314	.1741	.1314
31	.7346	.5412	.4000	.2965	.2204	.1643	.1228
32	.7273	.5306	.3883	.2851	.2099	.1550	.1147

Exhibit J. Present Value of a Lump Sum Table

Periods	1%	2%	3%	4%	5%	6%	7%
33	.7201	.5202	.3770	.2741	.1999	.1462	.1072
34	.7130	.5100	.3660	.2636	.1904	.1379	.1002
35	.7059	.5000	.3554	.2534	.1813	.1301	.0937
36	.6989	.4902	.3450	.2437	.1727	.1227	.0875
37	.6920	.4806	.3350	.2343	.1644	.1158	.0818
38	.6858	.4712	.3252	.2253	.1566	.1092	.0765
39	.6784	.4619	.3158	.2166	.1491	.1031	.0715
40	.6717	.4529	.3066	.2083	.1420	.0972	.0668
41	.6650	.4440	.2976	.2003	.1353	.0917	.0624
42	.6584	.4353	.2890	.1926	.1288	.0865	.0583
43	.6520	.4268	.2805	.1852	.1227	.0816	.0545
44	.6454	.4184	.2724	.1780	.1169	.0770	.0509
45	.6391	.4102	.2644	.1712	.1113	.0727	.0476
46	.6327	.4022	.2567	.1646	.1060	.0685	.0445
47	.6265	.3943	.2493	.1583	.1009	.0647	.0416
48	.6203	.3865	.2420	.1522	.0961	.0610	.0389
49	.6141	.3790	.2350	.1463	.0916	.0575	.0363
50	.6080	.3715	.2281	.1407	.0872	.0543	.0339

Periods	8%	9%	10%	11%	12%	13%	14%
1	.9259	.9174	.9091	.9009	.8929	.8850	.8772
2	.8573	.8417	.8264	.8116	.7972	.7831	.7695
3	.7938	.7722	.7513	.7312	.7118	.6931	.6750
4	.7350	.7084	.6830	.6587	.6355	.6133	.5921
5	.6806	.6499	.6209	.5935	.5674	.5428	.5194
6	.6302	.5963	.5645	.5346	.5066	.4803	.4556
7	.5835	.5470	.5132	.4817	.4523	.4251	.3996
8	.5403	.5019	.4665	.4339	.4039	.3762	.3506
9	.5002	.4604	.4241	.3909	.3606	.3329	.3075
10	.4632	.4224	.3855	.3522	.3220	.2946	.2697
11	.4289	.3875	.3505	.3173	.2875	.2607	.2366
12	.3971	.3555	.3186	.2858	.2567	.2307	.2076
13	.3677	.3262	.2897	.2575	.2292	.2042	.1821
14	.3405	.2992	.2633	.2320	.2046	.1807	.1597
15	.3152	.2745	.2394	.2090	.1827	.1599	.1401
16	.2919	.2519	.2176	.1883	.1631	.1415	.1229
17	.2703	.2311	.1978	.1696	.1456	.1252	.1078
18	.2502	.2120	.1799	.1528	.1300	.1108	.0946
19	.2317	.1945	.1635	.1377	.1161	.0981	.0829
20	.2145	.1784	.1486	.1240	.1037	.0868	.0728
21	.1987	.1637	.1351	.1117	.0926	.0768	.0638

Periods	8%	9%	10%	11%	12%	13%	14%
22	.1839	.1502	.1228	.1007	.0826	.0680	.0560
23	.1703	.1378	.1117	.0907	.0738	.0601	.0491
24	.1577	.1264	.1015	.0817	.0659	.0532	.0431
25	.1460	.1160	.0923	.0736	.0588	.0471	.0378
26	.1352	.1064	.0839	.0663	.0525	.0417	.0331
27	.1252	.0976	.0763	.0597	.0469	.0369	.0291
28	.1159	.0895	.0693	.0538	.0419	.0326	.0255
29	.1073	.0822	.0630	.0485	.0374	.0289	.0224
30	.0994	.0754	.0573	.0437	.0334	.0256	.0196
31	.0920	.0691	.0521	.0394	.0298	.0226	.0172
32	.0852	.0634	.0474	.0355	.0266	.0200	.0151
33	.0789	.0582	.0431	.0319	.0238	.0177	.0132
34	.0730	.0534	.0391	.0288	.0212	.0157	.0116
35	.0676	.0490	.0356	.0259	.0189	.0139	.0102
36	.0626	.0449	.0323	.0234	.0169	.0123	.0089
37	.0580	.0412	.0294	.0210	.0151	.0109	.0078
38	.0537	.0378	.0267	.0190	.0135	.0096	.0069
39	.0497	.0347	.0243	.0171	.0120	.0085	.0060
40	.0460	.0318	.0221	.0154	.0107	.0075	.0053
41	.0426	.0292	.0201	.0139	.0096	.0067	.0046
42	.0395	.0268	.0183	.0125	.0086	.0059	.0041
43	.0365	.0246	.0166	.0112	.0076	.0052	.0036
44	.0338	.0226	.0151	.0101	.0068	.0046	.0031
45	.0313	.0207	.0137	.0091	.0061	.0041	.0028
46	.0290	.0190	.0125	.0082	.0054	.0036	.0024
47	.0269	.0174	.0113	.0074	.0059	.0032	.0021
48	.0249	.0160	.0103	.0067	.0043	.0028	.0019
49	.0230	.0147	.0094	.0060	.0039	.0025	.0016
50	.0213	.0134	.0085	.0054	.0035	.0022	.0014

Periods	15%	16%	17%	18%	19%
1	.8696	.8621	.8547	.8475	.8403
2	.7561	.7432	.7305	.7182	.7062
3	.6575	.6407	.6244	.6086	.5934
4	.5718	.5523	.5337	.5158	.4987
5	.4972	.4761	.4561	.4371	.4190
6	.4323	.4104	.3898	.3704	.3521
7	.3759	.3538	.3332	.3139	.2959
8	.3269	.3050	.2848	.2660	.2487
9	.2843	.2630	.2434	.2255	.2090
10	.2472	.2267	.2080	.1911	.1756

Periods	15%	16%	17%	18%	19%
11	.2149	.1954	.1778	.1619	.1476
12	.1869	.1685	.1520	.1372	.1240
13	.1625	.1452	.1299	.1163	.1042
14	.1413	.1252	.1110	.0985	.0876
15	.1229	.1079	.0949	.0835	.0736
16	.1069	.0930	.0811	.0708	.0618
17	.0929	.0802	.0693	.0600	.0520
18	.0808	.0691	.0592	.0508	.0437
19	.0703	.0596	.0506	.0431	.0367
20	.0611	.0514	.0433	.0365	.0308
21	.0531	.0443	.0370	.0309	.0259
22	.0462	.0382	.0316	.0262	.0218
23	.0402	.0329	.0270	.0222	.0183
24	.0349	.0284	.0231	.0188	.0154
25	.0304	.0245	.0197	.0160	.0129
26	.0264	.0211	.0169	.0135	.0109
27	.0230	.0182	.0144	.0115	.0091
28	.0200	.0157	.0123	.0097	.0077
29	.0174	.0135	.0105	.0082	.0064
30	.0151	.0116	.0090	.0070	.0054
31	.0131	.0100	.0077	.0059	.0046
32	.0114	.0087	.0066	.0050	.0038
33	.0099	.0075	.0056	.0042	.0032
34	.0086	.0064	.0048	.0036	.0027
35	.0075	.0055	.0041	.0030	.0023
36	.0065	.0048	.0035	.0026	.0019
37	.0057	.0041	.0030	.0022	.0016
38	.0049	.0036	.0026	.0019	.0013
39	.0043	.0031	.0022	.0016	.0011
40	.0037	.0026	.0019	.0013	.0010
41	.0032	.0023	.0016	.0011	.0008
42	.0028	.0020	.0014	.0010	.0007
43	.0025	.0017	.0012	.0008	.0006
44	.0021	.0015	.0010	.0007	.0005
45	.0019	.0013	.0009	.0006	.0004
46	.0016	.0011	.0007	.0005	.0003
47	.0014	.0009	.0006	.0004	.0003
48	.0012	.0008	.0005	.0004	.0002
49	.0011	.0007	.0005	.0003	.0002
50	.0009	.0006	.0004	.0003	.0002

EXHIBIT K

Future Value of an Ordinary Annuity Table

Periods	1%	2%	3%	4%	5%	6%	7%
1	1.0000	1.0000	1.0000	1.0000	1.0000	1.0000	1.0000
2	2.0100	2.0200	2.0300	2.0400	2.0500	2.0600	2.0700
3	3.0301	3.0604	3.0909	3.1216	3.1525	3.1836	3.2149
4	4.0604	4.1216	4.1836	4.2465	4.3101	4.3746	4.4399
5	5.1010	5.2040	5.3091	5.4163	5.5256	5.6371	5.7507
6	6.1520	6.3081	6.4684	6.6330	6.8019	6.9753	7.1533
7	7.2135	7.4343	7.6625	7.8983	8.1420	8.3938	8.6540
8	8.2857	8.5830	8.8923	9.2142	9.5491	9.8975	10.2598
9	9.3685	9.7546	10.1591	10.5828	11.0266	11.4913	11.9780
10	10.4622	10.9497	11.4639	12.0061	12.5779	13.1808	13.8164
11	11.5668	12.1687	12.8078	13.4864	14.2068	14.9716	15.7836
12	12.6825	13.4121	14.1920	15.0258	15.9171	16.8699	17.8885
13	13.8093	14.6803	15.6178	16.6268	17.7130	18.8821	20.1406
14	14.9474	15.9739	17.0863	18.2919	19.598	21.0151	22.5505
15	16.0969	17.2934	18.5989	20.0236	21.5786	23.2760	25.1290
16	17.2579	18.6393	20.1569	21.8245	23.6575	25.6725	27.8881
17	18.4304	20.0121	21.7616	23.6975	25.8404	28.2129	30.8402
18	19.6147	21.4123	23.4144	25.6454	28.1324	30.9057	33.9990
19	20.8109	22.8406	25.1169	27.6712	30.5390	33.7600	37.3790
20	22.0190	24.2974	26.8704	29.7781	33.0660	36.7856	40.9955
21	23.2392	25.7833	28.6765	31.9692	35.7193	39.9927	44.8652
22	24.4716	27.2990	30.5368	34.2480	38.5052	43.3923	49.0057
23	25.7163	28.8450	32.4529	36.6179	41.4305	46.9958	53.4361
24	26.9735	30.4219	34.4265	39.0826	44.5020	50.8156	58.1767
25	28.2432	32.0303	36.4593	41.6459	47.7271	54.8645	63.2490
26	29.5256	33.6709	38.5530	44.3117	51.1135	59.1564	68.6765
27	30.8209	35.3443	40.7096	47.0842	54.6691	63.7058	74.4838
28	32.1291	37.0512	42.9309	49.9676	58.4026	68.5281	80.6977
29	33.4504	38.7922	45.2189	52.9663	62.3227	73.6398	87.3465
30	34.7849	40.5681	47.5754	56.0849	66.4388	79.0582	94.4608
31	36.1327	42.3794	50.0027	59.3283	70.7608	84.8017	102.0730
32	37.4941	44.2270	52.5028	62.7015	75.2988	90.8898	110.2182

Periods	1%	2%	3%	4%	5%	6%	7%
33	38.8690	46.1116	55.0778	66.2095	80.0638	97.3432	118.9334
34	40.2577	48.0338	57.7302	69.8579	85.0670	104.1838	128.2588
35	41.6603	49.9945	60.4621	73.6522	90.3203	111.4348	138.2369
36	43.0769	51.9949	63.2759	77.5983	95.8363	119.1209	148.9135
37	44.5076	54.0343	66.1742	81.7022	101.6281	127.2681	160.3374
38	45.9527	56.1149	69.1594	85.9703	107.7095	135.9042	172.5610
39	47.4123	58.2372	72.2342	90.4092	114.0950	145.0585	185.6403
40	48.8864	60.4020	75.4013	95.0255	120.7998	154.7620	199.6351
41	50.3752	62.6100	78.6633	99.8265	127.8398	165.0477	214.6096
42	51.8790	64.8622	82.0232	104.8196	135.2318	175.9505	230.6322
43	53.3978	67.1595	85.4839	110.0124	142.9933	187.5076	247.7765
44	54.9318	69.5027	89.0484	115.4129	151.1430	199.7580	266.1209
45	56.4811	71.8927	92.7199	121.0294	159.7002	212.7435	285.7493
46	58.0459	74.3306	96.5015	126.8706	168.6852	226.5081	306.7518
47	59.6263	76.8179	100.3965	132.9454	178.1194	241.0986	329.2244
48	61.2226	79.3535	104.4084	139.2632	188.0254	256.5645	353.2701
49	62.8348	81.9406	108.5406	145.8337	198.4267	272.9584	378.9990
50	64.4632	84.5794	112.7969	152.6671	209.3480	290.3359	406.5289

Periods	8%	9%	10%	11%	12%	13%	14%
1	1.0000	1.0000	1.0000	1.0000	1.0000	1.0000	1.0000
2	2.0800	2.0900	2.1000	2.1100	2.1200	2.1300	2.1400
3	3.2464	3.2781	3.3100	3.3421	3.3744	3.4069	3.4396
4	4.5061	4.5731	4.6410	4.7097	4.7793	4.8498	4.9211
5	5.8666	5.9847	6.1051	6.2278	6.3528	6.4803	6.6101
6	7.3359	7.5233	7.7156	7.9129	8.1152	8.3227	8.5355
7	8.9228	9.2004	9.4872	9.7833	10.0890	10.4047	10.7305
8	10.6366	11.0285	11.4359	11.8594	12.2997	12.7573	13.2328
9	12.4876	13.0210	13.5795	14.1640	14.7757	15.4157	16.0853
10	14.4866	15.1929	15.9374	16.7220	17.5487	18.4197	19.3373
11	16.6455	17.5603	18.5312	19.5614	20.6546	21.8143	23.0445
12	18.9771	20.1407	21.3843	22.7132	24.1331	25.6502	27.2707
13	21.4953	22.9534	24.5227	26.2116	28.0291	29.9847	32.0887
14	24.2149	26.0192	27.9750	30.0949	32.3926	34.8827	37.5811
15	27.1521	29.3609	31.7725	34.4054	37.2797	40.4175	43.8424
16	30.3243	33.0034	35.9497	39.1899	42.7533	46.6717	50.9804
17	33.7502	36.9737	40.5447	44.5008	48.8837	53.7391	59.1176
18	37.4502	41.3013	45.5992	50.3959	55.7497	61.7251	68.3941
19	41.4463	46.0185	51.1591	56.9395	63.4397	70.7494	78.9692
20	45.7620	51.1601	57.2750	64.2028	72.0524	80.9468	91.0249
21	50.4229	56.7645	64.0025	72.2651	81.6987	92.4699	104.7684

Periods	8%	9%	10%	11%	12%	13%	14%
22	55.4568	62.8733	71.4027	81.2143	92.5026	105.4910	120.4360
23	60.8933	69.5319	79.5430	91.1479	104.6029	120.2048	138.2970
24	66.7648	76.7898	88.4973	102.1742	118.1552	136.8315	158.6586
25	73.1059	84.7009	98.3471	114.4133	133.3339	155.6196	181.8708
26	79.9544	93.3240	109.1818	127.9988	150.3339	176.8501	208.3327
27	87.3508	102.7231	121.0999	143.0786	169.3740	200.8406	238.4993
28	95.3388	112.9682	134.2099	159.8173	190.6989	227.9499	272.8892
29	103.9659	124.1354	148.6309	178.3972	214.5828	258.5834	312.0937
30	113.2832	136.3075	164.4940	199.0209	241.3327	293.1992	356.7868
31	123.3459	149.5752	181.9434	221.9132	271.2926	332.3151	407.7370
32	134.2135	164.0370	201.1378	247.3236	304.8477	376.5161	465.8202
33	145.9506	179.8003	222.2515	275.5292	342.4294	426.4632	532.0350
34	158.6267	196.9823	245.4767	306.8374	384.5210	482.9034	607.5199
35	172.3168	215.7108	271.0244	341.5896	431.6635	546.6808	693.5727
36	187.1021	236.1247	299.1268	380.1644	484.4631	618.7493	791.6729
37	203.0703	258.3759	330.0395	422.9825	543.5987	700.1867	903.5071
38	220.3159	282.6298	364.0434	470.5106	609.8305	792.2110	1030.9981
39	238.9412	309.0665	401.4478	523.2667	684.0102	896.1984	1176.3378
40	259.0565	337.8824	442.5926	581.8261	767.0914	1013.7042	1342.0251
41	280.7810	369.2919	487.8518	646.8269	860.1424	1146.4858	1530.9086
42	304.2435	403.5281	537.6370	718.9779	964.3595	1296.5289	1746.2358
43	329.5830	440.8457	592.4007	799.0655	1081.0826	1466.0777	1991.7088
44	356.9496	481.5218	652.6408	887.9627	1211.8125	1657.6678	2271.5481
45	386.5056	525.8587	718.9048	986.6386	1358.2300	1874.1646	2590.5648
46	418.4261	574.1860	791.7953	1096.1688	1522.2176	2118.8060	2954.2439
47	452.9002	626.8628	871.9749	1217.7474	1705.8838	2395.2508	3368.8380
48	490.1322	684.2804	960.1723	1352.6996	1911.5898	2707.6334	3841.4753
49	530.3427	746.8656	1057.1896	1502.4965	2141.9806	3060.6258	4380.2819
50	573.7702	815.0836	1163.9085	1668.7712	2400.0182	3459.5071	4994.5213

Periods	15%	16%	17%	18%	19%
1	1.0000	1.0000	1.0000	1.0000	1.0000
2	2.1500	2.1600	2.1700	2.1800	2.1900
3	3.4725	3.5056	3.5389	3.5724	3.6061
4	4.9934	5.0665	5.1405	5.2154	5.2913
5	6.7424	6.8771	7.0144	7.1542	7.2966
6	8.7537	8.9775	9.2068	9.4420	9.6830
7	11.0668	11.4139	11.7720	12.1415	12.5227
8	13.7268	14.2401	14.7733	15.3270	15.9020
9	16.7858	17.5185	18.2847	19.0859	19.9234
10	20.3037	21.3215	22.3931	23.5213	24.7089

Periods	15%	16%	17%	18%	19%
11	24.3493	25.7329	27.1999	28.7551	30.4035
12	29.0017	30.8502	32.8239	34.9311	37.1802
13	34.3519	36.7862	39.4040	42.2187	45.2445
14	40.5047	43.6720	47.1027	50.8180	54.8409
15	47.5804	51.6595	56.1101	60.9653	66.2607
16	55.7175	60.9250	66.6488	72.9390	79.8502
17	65.0751	71.6730	78.9792	87.0680	96.0218
18	75.8364	84.1407	93.4056	103.7403	115.2659
19	88.2118	98.6032	110.2846	123.4135	138.1664
20	102.4436	115.3797	130.0329	146.6280	165.4180
21	118.8101	134.8405	153.1385	174.0210	197.8474
22	137.6316	157.4150	180.1721	206.3448	236.4385
23	159.2764	183.6014	211.8013	244.4868	282.3618
24	184.1678	213.9776	248.8076	289.4945	337.0105
25	212.7930	249.2140	292.1049	342.6035	402.0425
26	245.7120	290.0883	342.7627	405.2721	479.4306
27	283.5688	337.5024	402.0323	479.2211	571.5224
28	327.1041	392.5028	471.3778	566.4809	681.1116
29	377.1697	456.3032	552.5121	669.4475	811.5228
30	434.7451	530.3117	647.4391	790.9480	966.7122
31	500.9569	616.1616	758.5038	934.3186	1151.3875
32	577.1005	715.7475	888.4494	1103.4960	1371.1511
33	664.6655	831.2671	1040.4845	1303.1253	1632.6698
34	765.3654	965.2698	1218.3684	1538.6878	1943.8771
35	881.1702	1120.7130	1426.4910	1816.6516	2314.2137
36	1014.3457	1301.0270	1669.9945	2144.6489	2754.9143
37	1167.4975	1510.1914	1954.8936	2531.6857	3279.3481
38	1343.6222	1752.8220	2288.2255	2988.3891	3903.4242
39	1546.1655	2034.2735	2678.2238	3527.2992	4646.0748
40	1779.0903	2360.7572	3134.5218	4163.2130	5529.8290
41	2046.9539	2739.4784	3668.3906	4913.5914	6581.4965
42	2354.9969	3178.7949	4293.0169	5799.0378	7832.9808
43	2709.2465	3688.4021	5023.8298	6843.8646	9322.2472
44	3116.6334	4279.5465	5878.8809	8076.7603	11094.4741
45	3585.1285	4965.2739	6879.2907	9531.5771	13203.4242
46	4123.8977	5760.7177	8049.7701	11248.2610	15713.0748
47	4743.4824	6683.4326	9419.2310	13273.9480	18699.5590
48	5456.0047	7753.7818	11021.5002	15664.2586	22253.4753
49	6275.4055	8995.3869	12896.1553	18484.8251	26482.6356
50	7217.7163	10435.6488	15089.5017	21813.0937	31515.3363

EXHIBIT L

Present Value of an Ordinary Annuity Table

Periods	1%	2%	3%	4%	5%	6%	7%
1	.9901	.9804	.9709	.9615	.9524	.9434	.9346
2	1.9704	1.9416	1.9135	1.8861	1.8594	1.8334	1.8080
3	2.9410	2.8839	2.8286	2.7751	2.7232	2.6730	2.6243
4	3.9020	3.8077	3.7171	3.6299	3.5460	3.4651	3.3872
5	4.8534	4.7135	4.5797	4.4518	4.3295	4.2124	4.1002
6	5.7955	5.6014	5.4172	5.2421	5.0757	4.9173	4.7665
7	6.7282	6.4720	6.2303	6.0021	5.7864	5.5824	5.3893
8	7.6517	7.3255	7.0197	6.7327	6.4632	6.2098	5.9713
9	8.5660	8.1622	7.7861	7.4353	7.1078	6.8017	6.5152
10	9.4713	8.9826	8.5302	8.1109	7.7217	7.3601	7.0236
11	10.3676	9.7868	9.2526	8.7605	8.3064	7.8869	7.4987
12	11.2551	10.5753	9.9540	9.3851	8.8633	8.3838	7.9427
13	12.1337	11.3484	10.6350	9.9856	9.3936	8.8527	8.3577
14	13.0037	12.1062	11.2961	10.5631	9.8986	9.2950	8.7455
15	13.8651	12.8493	11.9379	11.1184	10.3797	9.7122	9.1079
16	14.7179	13.5777	12.5611	11.6523	10.8378	10.1059	9.4466
17	15.5623	14.2919	13.1661	12.1657	11.2741	10.4773	9.7632
18	16.3983	14.9920	13.7535	12.6593	11.6896	10.8276	10.0591
19	17.2260	15.6785	14.3238	13.1339	12.0853	11.1581	10.3356
20	18.0456	16.3514	14.8775	13.5903	12.4622	11.4699	10.5940
21	18.8570	17.0112	15.4150	14.0292	12.8212	11.7641	10.8355
22	19.6604	17.6580	15.9369	14.4511	13.1630	12.0416	11.0612
23	20.4558	18.2922	16.4436	14.8568	13.4886	12.3034	11.2722
24	21.2434	18.9139	16.9355	15.2470	13.7986	12.5504	11.4693
25	22.0232	19.5235	17.4131	15.6221	14.0939	12.7834	11.6536
26	22.7952	20.1210	17.8768	15.9828	14.3752	13.0032	11.8258
27	23.5596	20.7069	18.3270	16.3296	14.6430	13.2105	11.9867
28	24.3164	21.2813	18.7641	16.6631	14.8981	13.4062	12.1371
29	25.0658	21.8444	19.1885	16.9837	15.1411	13.5907	12.2777
30	25.8077	22.3965	19.6004	17.2920	15.3725	13.7648	12.4090
31	26.5423	22.9377	20.0004	17.5885	15.5928	13.9291	12.5318
32	27.2696	23.4683	20.3888	17.8736	15.8027	14.0840	12.6466

Periods	1%	2%	3%	4%	5%	6%	7%
33	27.9897	23.9886	20.7658	18.1476	16.0025	14.2302	12.7538
34	28.7027	24.4986	21.1318	18.4112	16.1929	14.3681	12.8540
35	29.4086	24.9986	21.4872	18.6646	16.3742	14.4982	12.9477
36	30.1075	25.4888	21.8323	18.9083	16.5469	14.6210	13.0352
37	30.7995	25.9695	22.1672	19.1426	16.7113	14.7368	13.1170
38	31.4847	26.4406	22.4925	19.3679	16.8679	14.8460	13.1935
39	32.1630	26.9026	22.8082	19.5845	17.0170	14.9491	13.2649
40	32.8347	27.3555	23.1148	19.7928	17.1591	15.0463	13.3317
41	33.4997	27.7995	23.4124	19.9931	17.2944	15.1380	13.3941
42	34.1581	28.2348	23.7014	20.1856	17.4232	15.2245	13.4524
43	34.8100	28.6616	23.9819	20.3708	17.5459	15.3062	13.5070
44	35.4555	29.0800	24.2543	20.5488	17.6628	15.3832	13.5579
45	36.0945	29.4902	24.5187	20.7200	17.7741	15.4558	13.6055
46	36.7272	29.8923	24.7754	20.8847	17.8801	15.5244	13.6500
47	37.3537	30.2866	25.0247	21.0429	17.9810	15.5890	13.6916
48	37.9740	30.6731	25.2667	21.1951	18.0772	15.6500	13.7305
49	38.5881	31.0521	25.5017	21.3415	18.1687	15.7076	13.7668
50	39.1961	31.4236	25.7298	21.4822	18.2559	15.7619	13.8007

Periods	8%	9%	10%	11%	12%	13%	14%
1	.9259	.9174	.9091	.9009	.8929	.8850	.8772
2	1.7833	1.7591	1.7355	1.7125	1.6901	1.6681	1.6467
3	2.5771	2.5313	2.4869	2.4437	2.4018	2.3612	2.3216
4	3.3121	3.2397	3.1699	3.1024	3.0373	2.9745	2.9137
5	3.9927	3.8897	3.7908	3.6959	3.6048	3.5172	3.4331
6	4.6229	4.4859	4.3553	4.2305	4.1114	3.9976	3.8887
7	5.2064	5.0330	4.8684	4.7122	4.5638	4.4226	4.2883
8	5.7466	5.5348	5.3349	5.1461	4.9676	4.7988	4.6389
9	6.2469	5.9952	5.7590	5.5370	5.3283	5.1317	4.9464
10	6.7101	6.4177	6.1446	5.8892	5.6502	5.4262	5.2161
11	7.1390	6.8052	6.4951	6.2065	5.9377	5.6869	5.4527
12	7.5361	7.1607	6.8137	6.4924	6.1944	5.9176	5.6603
13	7.9038	7.4869	7.1034	6.7499	6.4235	6.1218	5.8424
14	8.2442	7.7862	7.3667	6.9819	6.6282	6.3025	6.0021
15	8.5595	8.0607	7.6061	7.1909	6.8109	6.4624	6.1422
16	8.8514	8.3126	7.8237	7.3792	6.9740	6.6039	6.2651
17	9.1216	8.5436	8.0216	7.5488	7.1196	6.7291	6.3729
18	9.3719	8.7556	8.2014	7.7016	7.2497	6.8399	6.4674
19	9.6036	8.9501	8.3649	7.8393	7.3658	6.9380	6.5504
20	9.8181	9.1285	8.5136	7.9633	7.4694	7.0248	6.6231
21	10.0168	9.2922	8.6487	8.0751	7.5620	7.1016	6.6870

Exhibit L. Present Value of an Ordinary Annuity Table   **353**

Periods	8%	9%	10%	11%	12%	13%	14%
22	10.2007	9.4424	8.7715	8.1757	7.6446	7.1695	6.7429
23	10.3711	9.5802	8.8832	8.2664	7.7184	7.2297	6.7921
24	10.5288	9.7066	8.9847	8.3481	7.7843	7.2829	6.8351
25	10.6748	9.8226	8.0770	8.4217	7.8431	7.3300	6.8729
26	10.8100	9.9290	9.1609	8.4881	7.8957	7.3717	6.9061
27	10.9352	10.0266	9.2372	8.5478	7.9426	7.4086	6.9352
28	11.0511	10.1161	9.3066	8.6016	7.9844	7.4412	6.9607
29	11.1584	10.1983	9.3696	8.6501	8.0218	7.4701	6.9830
30	11.2578	10.2737	9.4269	8.6938	8.0552	7.4957	7.0027
31	11.3498	10.3428	9.4790	8.7331	8.0850	7.5183	7.0199
32	11.4350	10.4062	9.5264	8.7686	8.1116	7.5383	7.0350
33	11.5139	10.4644	9.5694	8.8005	8.1354	7.5560	7.0482
34	11.5869	10.5178	9.6086	8.8293	8.1566	7.5717	7.0599
35	11.6546	10.5668	9.6442	8.8552	8.1755	7.5856	7.0700
36	11.7172	10.6118	9.6765	8.8786	8.1924	7.5979	7.0790
37	11.7752	10.6530	9.7059	8.8996	8.2075	7.6087	7.0868
38	11.8289	10.6908	9.7327	8.9186	8.2210	7.6183	7.0937
39	11.8786	10.7255	9.7570	8.9357	8.2330	7.6268	7.0997
40	11.9246	10.7574	9.7791	8.9511	8.2438	7.6344	7.1050
41	11.9672	10.7866	9.7991	8.9649	8.2534	7.6410	7.1097
42	12.0067	10.8134	9.8174	8.9774	8.2619	7.6469	7.1138
43	12.0432	10.8380	9.8340	8.9886	8.2696	7.6522	7.1173
44	12.0771	10.8605	9.8491	8.9988	8.2764	7.6568	7.1205
45	12.1084	10.8812	9.8628	9.0079	8.2825	7.6609	7.1232
46	12.1374	10.9002	9.8753	9.0161	8.2880	7.6645	7.1256
47	12.1643	10.9176	9.8866	9.0235	8.2928	7.6677	7.1277
48	12.1891	10.9336	9.8969	9.0302	8.2972	7.6705	7.1296
49	12.2122	10.9482	9.9063	9.0362	8.3010	7.6730	7.1312
50	12.2335	10.9617	9.9148	9.0417	8.3045	7.6752	7.1327

Periods	15%	16%	17%	18%	19%
1	.8696	.8621	.8547	.8475	.8403
2	1.6257	1.6052	1.5852	1.5656	1.5465
3	2.2832	2.2459	2.2096	2.1743	2.1399
4	2.8550	2.7982	2.7432	2.6901	2.6386
5	3.3522	3.2743	3.1993	3.1272	3.0576
6	3.7845	3.6847	3.5892	3.4976	3.4098
7	4.1604	4.0386	3.9224	3.8115	3.7057
8	4.4873	4.3436	4.2072	4.0776	3.9544
9	4.7716	4.6065	4.4506	4.3030	4.1633
10	5.0188	4.8332	4.6586	4.4941	4.3389

Periods	15%	16%	17%	18%	19%
11	5.2337	5.0286	4.8364	4.6560	4.4865
12	5.4206	5.1971	4.9884	4.7932	4.6105
13	5.5831	5.3423	5.1183	4.9095	4.7147
14	5.7245	5.4675	5.2293	5.0081	4.8023
15	5.8474	5.5755	5.3242	5.0916	4.8759
16	5.9542	5.6685	5.4053	5.1624	4.9377
17	6.0472	5.7487	5.4746	5.2223	4.9897
18	6.1280	5.8178	5.5339	5.2732	5.0333
19	6.1982	5.8775	5.5845	5.3162	5.0700
20	6.2593	5.9288	5.6278	5.3527	5.1009
21	6.3125	5.9731	5.6648	5.3837	5.1268
22	6.3587	6.0113	5.6964	5.4099	5.1486
23	6.3988	6.0442	5.7234	5.4321	5.1668
24	6.4338	6.0726	5.7465	5.4509	5.1822
25	6.4641	6.0971	5.7662	5.4669	5.1951
26	6.4906	6.1182	5.7831	5.4804	5.2060
27	6.5135	6.1364	5.7975	5.4919	5.2151
28	6.5335	6.1520	5.8099	5.5016	5.2228
29	6.5509	6.1656	5.8204	5.5098	5.2292
30	6.5660	6.1772	5.8294	5.5168	5.2347
31	6.5791	6.1872	5.8371	5.5227	5.2392
32	6.5905	6.1959	5.8437	5.5277	5.2430
33	6.6005	6.2034	5.8493	5.5320	5.2462
34	6.6091	6.2098	5.8541	5.5356	5.2489
35	6.6166	6.2153	5.8582	5.5386	5.2512
36	6.6231	6.2201	5.8617	5.5412	5.2531
37	6.6288	6.2242	5.8647	5.5434	5.2547
38	6.6338	6.2278	5.8673	5.5452	5.2561
39	6.6380	6.2309	5.8695	5.5468	5.2572
40	6.6418	6.2335	5.8713	5.5482	5.2582
41	6.6450	6.2358	5.8729	5.5493	5.2590
42	6.6478	6.2377	5.8743	5.5502	5.2596
43	6.6503	6.2394	5.8755	5.5510	5.2602
44	6.6524	6.2409	5.8765	5.5517	5.2607
45	6.6543	6.2421	5.8773	5.5523	5.2611
46	6.6559	6.2432	5.8781	5.5528	5.2614
47	6.6573	6.2442	5.8787	5.5532	5.2617
48	6.6585	6.2450	5.8792	5.5536	5.2619
49	6.6596	6.2457	5.8797	5.5539	5.2621
50	6.6605	6.2463	5.8801	5.5541	5.2623

Exhibit M

Net Working Capital Adjustment Example

Section 2.8 Net Working Capital Adjustment.

1. <u>Estimated Closing Net Working Capital</u>. At least three (3) Business Days prior to the Closing Date, Seller shall provide to Buyer a statement ("Estimated Closing Net Working Capital Statement") setting forth its estimate of Net Working Capital as of Closing ("Estimated Closing Net Working Capital"), prepared in the same manner as which the Final Closing Net Working Capital will be determined pursuant to Section 2.8(3) below. The determination of the Estimated Closing Net Working Capital will be subject to the consent of Buyer, which consent shall not be unreasonably withheld, and the parties agree to use their best commercial efforts to come to an agreement on the determination of the Estimated Closing Net Working Capital.

2. <u>Closing Adjustment</u>. The Interim Net Working Capital Adjustment shall be equal to the amount by which the Estimated Closing Net Working Capital exceeds or is less than the Required Net Working Capital, with such difference being added to the Purchase Price set forth in Section 2.2 if the Estimated Closing Net Working Capital exceeds the Required Net Working Capital and being subtracted from the Purchase Price set forth in Section 2.2 if the Estimated Closing Net Working Capital is less than the Required Net Working Capital.

3. <u>Final Closing Working Capital</u>. Within forty-five (45) days after the Closing Date, Buyer shall prepare and deliver to Selling Stockholders a statement ("Final Closing Net Working Capital Statement") setting forth Net Working Capital as of the close of business on the day before the Closing Date but giving effect to payments made simultaneously with the Closing ("Final Closing Net Working Capital"), prepared in accordance with GAAP consistently applied and in a manner consistent with the methodologies and policies used in the preparation of the Required Net Working Capital and Estimated Closing Net Working Capital Statements. After the Closing Date, at Selling Stockholders' request, Buyer shall provide any information reasonably requested by Selling Stockholders that was used by Buyer in its preparation of the Final Closing Net Working Capital Statement.

4. <u>Objections; Resolutions of Disputes</u>. [**This section intentionally omitted.**]

5. <u>Post-Closing Adjustment</u>.
   a. If the Final Closing Net Working Capital is greater than the Estimated Closing Net Working Capital, then Buyer and Selling Stockholders shall jointly instruct the Escrow Agent to pay the difference for immediate distribution to Selling Stockholders; provided, however, that in no event shall such payment exceed the sum of $1,250,000.
   b. If the Final Closing Net Working Capital is equal to the Estimated Closing Net Working Capital, no further payment shall be made pursuant to this Section 2.8(5); and

c. If the Final Closing Net Working Capital is less than the Estimated Closing Net Working Capital, then Buyer and Selling Stockholders shall jointly instruct the Escrow Agent to pay such difference to Buyer from the Escrow Account.

6. <u>Net Working Capital</u>. The term "Net Working Capital" means Total Current Assets, excluding cash, less Total Current Liabilities. The terms "Total Current Assets" and "Total Current Liabilities" mean the consolidated total current assets, excluding cash, and total current liabilities, other than the current portion of long-term debt and accrued interest on any debt of Seller, calculated in the same way, using the same accounting principles, practices, methodologies, and policies, as the line items comprising total current assets and total current liabilities on the Required Net Working Capital Statement; provided, however, that Total Current Assets and Total Current Liabilities shall be adjusted to the extent necessary so as to exclude any purchase accounting adjustments to the accounting books and records for financial reporting purposes that may be recorded by Seller as a result of the transactions contemplated by this Merger Agreement. For the avoidance of doubt, deductions, losses, credits, or other Tax benefits (other than prepayments of Taxes) shall be excluded from the determination of Total Current Assets; provided, however, that any such Tax benefits shall be included in the computation of net taxable income or gain for purposes of determining Total Current Liabilities.

Earn-Out Example

Section 1.8 Earn-Out Consideration

1. Earn-Out Consideration. Selling Stockholders shall be entitled to receive, as additional cash consideration for the transfer of the Shares, additional cash payments ("Earn-Out Consideration") based on the Actual Revenues of Seller during each of the two consecutive 12-month periods following the Closing Date (each, an "Earn-Out Period," and the entire period, the "Earn-Out Term"), as described below:

2. Earn-Out Consideration Determination. Selling Stockholders shall receive the Earn-Out Consideration, as defined and calculated in accordance with Sections 1.8(2)(a) and 1.8(2)(b) below, for each Earn-Out Period:

    a. In the event that during the first Earn-Out Period, Purchaser generates Actual Revenues (such Actual Revenues, the "First Earn-Out Revenue") in an amount equal to or greater than Twenty Million Dollars ($20,000,000) ("First Earn-Out Target"), then Buyer shall, on a one-time basis, pay to Selling Stockholders an amount determined as follows ("First Earn-Out Payment"):

        (i) If the First Earn-Out Revenue is equal to the First Earn-Out Target, the First Earn-Out Payment shall be Five Hundred Thousand Dollars ($500,000); or

        (ii) If the First Earn-Out Revenue is greater than the First Earn-Out Target, but less than Twenty-Five Million Dollars ($25,000,000), then the First Earn-Out Payment shall be Six Hundred Thousand Dollars $600,000); or

        (iii) If the First Earn-Out Revenue is equal to or greater than Twenty-Five Million Dollars ($25,000,000), then the First Earn-Out Payment shall be Six Hundred Seventy-Five Thousand Dollars ($675,000).

    b. In the event that during the second Earn-Out Period, Purchaser generates Actual Revenues (such Actual Revenues, the "Second Earn-Out Revenue") in an amount equal to or greater than Twenty-Three Million Dollars ($23,000,000) ("Second Earn-Out Target"), then Buyer shall, on a one-time basis, pay to Selling Stockholders an amount determined as follows ("Second Earn-Out Payment"):

        (i) If the Second Earn-Out Revenue is equal to the Second Earn-Out Target, the Second Earn-Out Payment shall be Five Hundred Fifty Thousand Dollars ($550,000); or

        (ii) If the Second Earn-Out Revenue is greater than the Second Earn-Out Target, but less than Twenty-Eight Million Dollars ($28,000,000), then the Second Earn-Out Payment shall be Six Hundred Seventy-Five Thousand Dollars ($675,000); or

        (iii) If the Second Earn-Out Revenue is equal to or greater than Twenty-Eight Million Dollars ($28,000,000), then the Second Earn-Out Payment shall be Seven Hundred Fifty Thousand Dollars ($750,000).

c. Notwithstanding anything to the contrary contained in this Merger Agreement, the maximum possible amount of all Earn-Out Payments for the Earn-Out Term required to be made by Buyer pursuant to this Section 1.8, in the aggregate, shall in no case exceed One Million Four Hundred Twenty-Five Thousand Dollars ($1,425,000) ("Earn-Out Cap").

3. Actual Revenues. The term "Actual Revenues" means, for any period, the aggregate revenues directly attributable to the Business during the period derived in the ordinary course of business from sales of the Business Products as determined in accordance with GAAP, as consistently applied by Buyer and calculated in the same way, using the same accounting principles, practices, methodologies, and policies as Seller used prior to the Closing Date.

4. Earn-Out Statement. [**This section intentionally omitted.**]

5. Earn-Out Dispute and Resolution. [**This section intentionally omitted.**]

Glossary

Accounting Accounting is the measurement, processing, communicating, and reporting of financial information regarding an entity and its business operations.

Accounting Equation The accounting equation (or fundamental accounting equation) offers a simple way to understand how Assets, Liabilities, and Equity relate to each other as follows:

$$Assets = Liabilities + Equity$$

or

$$Assets - Liabilities = Equity$$

Accounting Standards Codification (ASC) The ASC, effective September 15, 2009, is the source of authoritative Generally Accepted Accounting Principles recognized by FASB.

Accounts Payable Accounts payable are an entity's short-term obligations to pay for products and services that it purchased on credit.

Accounts Receivable Accounts receivable are the amounts due an entity from customers who have purchased goods or services from the entity on credit.

Accounts Receivable Turnover Accounts receivable turnover measures the number of times each year the entity collects, or turns over, its accounts receivable.

Accrual Basis Accounting Accrual basis accounting is the method of recording revenues when earned and expenses as incurred, versus waiting on the cash receipt or expenditure before recording.

Accrue (Accruals) To accrue means to record and reflect in an entity's financial records those earned revenues or incurred expenses that have not yet been received or paid, respectively.

Accumulated Depreciation Accumulated depreciation is a contra account to fixed assets on the balance sheet and reflects the total depreciation expense accumulated for those particular fixed assets.

Accumulated Loss Accumulated loss is a balance sheet account that reflects the total net loss accumulated for the entity since it began operations (*see also* "Retained Earnings").

Acid Test The acid test compares the quick assets to current liabilities to determine an entity's ability to meet its short-term obligations.

Additional Paid-in-Capital (APIC)   Additional paid-in-capital is a balance sheet account and reflects the aggregate amount paid for the entity's issued stock that exceeds the par value for each share sold.

Adjusting Entries   Adjusting entries are journal entries recorded at the end of an accounting period to adjust account balances to reflect accrual basis accounting.

Adverse Opinion   An adverse opinion is an opinion given by an auditors stating that the financial statements are materially misstated, misrepresented, or misleading and do not fairly present the financial condition of the entity.

American Bar Association Statement of Policy   The American Bar Association Statement of Policy is a policy issued by the American Bar Association in 1976 that provides guidelines on the manner in which lawyers should respond to the audit inquiry letter regarding a client's contingencies, meaning pending litigation, claims, and assessments, as well as unasserted claims.

American Institute of Certified Public Accountants (AICPA)   The AICPA is an organization that represents the CPA profession and develops the standards and rules for audits of private entities and other services provided by CPAs, as well as represents the CPA profession through advocacy.

Amortization   Amortization is the accounting method used to allocate the cost of an intangible asset over its expected life.

Analyst Report   An analyst report is a report created by a financial analyst that makes a recommendation regarding whether to buy, sell, or hold a particular security.

Annuity   An annuity is a series of fixed payments made at regular intervals.

Annuity Due   An annuity due is a series of equal and fixed payments, with the payments made at the same time at the beginning of each period such as the first day of the year, quarter, or month.

Annuity in Advance   *See* "Annuity Due."

Annuity in Arrears   *See* "Ordinary Annuity."

Asset   An asset is an item of economic value owned by an entity that can be measured and that is expected to yield a benefit to the entity in future periods.

Asset Turnover Ratio   The asset turnover ratio compares the total revenues to average total assets of an entity and indicates how efficiently an entity uses its assets to generate sales.

Asset Valuation Approach   The asset valuation approach is a valuation method used to measure the value of a business based on the entity's asset values.

At-the-Money   At-the-money indicates that the market price of a security is equal to the strike price of an option for that security.

Audit Inquiry Letter The audit inquiry letter is the primary method that auditors use to obtain information from their client and its lawyers regarding litigation, claims, and assessments that their client may be facing.

Audited Financial Statements Audited financial statements are the financial statements of an entity that have been examined and audited by a certified public accountant (CPA), who issues a formal audit opinion.

Auditing Standards (AS) Auditing Standards are those standards established by the PCAOB that registered public accounting firms must follow in the preparation and undertaking of audits of publicly traded or reporting entities, brokers, and dealers.

Auditor's Opinion An auditor's opinion is a formal statement made by the auditors concerning a client's financial statements and their presentation of the financial condition and results of operations of the entity's business.

Authorized Shares Authorized shares represent the maximum number of shares a company is legally allowed to issue as provided in its corporate charter.

Balance Sheet The balance sheet is a report that summarizes an entity's assets, liabilities, and equity as of a given point in time.

Balance Sheet Insolvency Balance sheet insolvency is a modern dividend test that assesses an entity's solvency based on its balance sheet and, in particular, whether total assets exceed total liabilities. It is used by the board of directors of an entity to determine if the entity may legally declare and issue a dividend.

Bond A bond is a debt security issued by a corporation or government entity to investors, who are called bond holders, creating an obligation on the part of the issuer to repay the face value of the bond in the future at maturity.

Book Value Book value of an asset is an asset's original cost less any accumulated depreciation or amortization. Book value of an entity is the amount by which total assets exceed total liabilities (i.e., stockholders' equity).

Bookkeeping Bookkeeping involves the recording of an entity's financial transactions in the entity's general ledger or record keeping system.

Business Valuation Business valuation is the process used to establish an estimate of the economic value of an entity's business, whether the whole business or a portion.

Call Option A call option gives the option holder the right to purchase the underlying item, such as stock, at a specified price in the future.

Callable Bond A callable bond is one that gives the issuer the right to call the bond and buy it back from the investor prior to its maturity date at a specified price.

Capital Asset Pricing Model (CAPM) CAPM is a financial model used to estimate the cost of equity.

Capital Lease   A capital lease is a lease in which the lessor transfers most of the benefits and risks of leasing the property or asset to the lessee, resulting in the lessee recording the lease as an asset of its business.

Capital Markets   The capital markets are comprised of the primary and secondary markets where the purchase and sale of long-term investments occur between willing participants.

Capital Stock   Capital stock comprises all of the types of stock (common and preferred) and classes or series issued by a corporation and is a line item recorded in the stockholders' equity section of the balance sheet, which amount represents the number of shares issued (or sold) multiplied by the shares' par value.

Cash Basis Accounting   Cash basis accounting is the practice of only recording revenue when cash has been received and only recording expenses when the cash has been paid.

Cash Dividend   A cash dividend is a distribution of a cash payment by an entity to shareholders based on their pro rata ownership in the entity.

Cash Flows Statement   The cash flows statement is a financial report that reflects the cash flows of the entity from its operating, investing, and financing activities and shows how changes in the balance sheet accounts and income statement accounts affect the cash account balance during the accounting period.

Certified Public Accountant (CPA)   A certified public accountant is an accountant who has passed all parts of the CPA exam, as administered by the AICPA, and who has completed all additional work and educational requirements of his or her state accounting regulatory agency.

Chart of Accounts   A chart of accounts is the list of all possible accounts an entity can use to record its financial transactions in its general ledger or record keeping system.

Closing Entry   Closing entries are journal entries used to zero out the balances in temporary accounts at the end of the accounting period and transfer their balances into permanent accounts, such as closing the balances of all the income statement accounts into the retained earnings or accumulated loss balance sheet account.

Codification   *See* "Accounting Standards Codification."

Commercial Loan   A commercial loan is a debt financing arrangement between the entity and a financial institution or a syndicate of financial institutions that allows the entity to borrow funds for its business and operations.

Commercial Paper   Commercial paper is a debt instrument that is issued by an entity to raise money for its short-term needs and is unsecured and matures in nine months or less.

Commitment   A commitment is a future obligation to purchase items pursuant to a contractual arrangement between an entity and a third party.

Commodity Futures Trading Commission (CFTC)   The CFTC is an independent agency that regulates the derivatives markets with the goal of protecting market users and their funds.

Common Size Analysis   Common-size analysis reflects each line item on a financial statement as a percentage of a base figure, generally "total assets" for the balance sheet and "revenues" for the income statement, and allows for comparisons of financial results with entities of different sizes.

Common Stock   Common stock is an ownership interest in a corporation that entitles its holders to vote on shareholder matters and at shareholder meetings and provides the shareholder with the opportunity to receive dividends on a pro rata basis, if the entity declares dividends.

Compound Interest   Compound interest is interest that is calculated on the principal plus any accrued interest or calculated on the amount invested plus any interest earned.

Consignee   A consignee is the party that accepts the consignor's goods on consignment and agrees to sell them on behalf of the consignor. The consignee does not take legal title to the goods, but simply acts as the middle person in the sale.

Consignment   A consignment is an arrangement whereby the consignor (the party who owns the item) contracts with the consignee (a third party who acts as an agent) to undertake the task of selling an item for the consignor, generally for a commission or fee.

Consignor   A consignor is the owner of the goods placed on consignment with the consignee and the party who retains legal title to the goods until the consignee sells the goods to another party.

Contingency   A contingency is an event or circumstance that poses an uncertain future outcome as to a potential gain or loss as a result of that event or circumstance.

Contra Account   A contra account is an account that has an opposite balance from the account to which it is related or paired, such as the contra account of "accumulated depreciation" to its paired fixed asset account. A contra account reduces the balance of the account to which it is related or paired.

Convertible Bond   A convertible bond is a type of bond that has an option that allows the bond holder to convert that bond into some type of equity interest in the issuing entity at a specified price or conversion ratio.

Cost of Capital   The cost of capital refers to the opportunity cost of making a specific investment as opposed to an alternative investment. The cost of capital also refers to the entity's costs associated with its debt and equity, or all of its capital.

Cost of Debt   The cost of debt is the amount an entity must pay to borrow money, such as the interest rate, and reflects the rate of return the investor or lender requires over the term of the debt financing.

Cost of Equity   The cost of equity represents the cost of the next dollar of equity to be raised by the issuer and reflects the minimum that the investor is willing to accept in return for making the investment in the entity.

Cost of Goods Sold (COGS)   The cost of goods sold are the direct costs incurred by the entity to produce the goods sold by the entity and the terminology generally used by manufacturers.

Cost of Services (COS)   The cost of services are the direct costs incurred by the entity to provide the goods sold by the entity and the terminology often used by retailers.

Coupon Date   The coupon date is the date on which bond coupon payments (interest) are made.

Coupon Payment   The coupon payment is the amount of interest the issuer pays to the bond holder on the coupon date.

Credit   A credit is an accounting entry on the right-hand side of an account that either increases a liability, equity, revenue, or gain account, or decreases an asset, expense, or loss account.

Credit Default Swap   A credit default swap is a particular type of swap that offers a guarantee and thus transfers the risk of nonpayment.

Cumulative Dividend   A cumulative dividend is a right of preferred shareholders to receive payment of unpaid past dividends and current dividends before common shareholders can receive a dividend. In other words, the dividends accumulate until paid in full.

Current Assets   Current assets are those assets that can be readily converted to cash within one year.

Current Liabilities   Current liabilities are those liabilities that must be paid within one year.

Current Ratio   The current ratio compares current assets to current liabilities to assess an entity's ability to meets its short-term obligations.

Days Inventory on Hand   "Days inventory on hand" reflects the average number of days that inventory is held by the entity before sold to customers.

Days Sales Outstanding   "Days sales outstanding" reflects the average number of days it takes for the entity to collect its accounts receivable, or credit sales.

Debenture   A debenture is a debt instrument, issued by entities to borrow money, that is typically unsecured.

Debit   A debit is an accounting entry on the left-hand side of an account that either increases an asset, expense, or loss account, or decreases a liability, equity, revenue, or gain account.

Debt-to-Asset Ratio The debt-to-asset ratio compares total debt to total assets and measures the proportion of assets of the entity paid for with debt.

Debt-to-Equity Ratio The debt-to-equity ratio compares total debt to total stockholders' equity and measures the amount of debt an entity uses to finance its business as compared to the amount of equity it uses.

Declaration Date The declaration date is the date on which the board of directors declares the dividend and the corporation becomes obligated to pay it.

Default Risk Premium The default risk premium is the premium portion of the interest rate meant to compensate the lender in the event that the borrower defaults.

Defer (Deferral) To defer means to delay the recognition of prepaid revenues (unearned revenues) or prepaid expenses to the accounting period in which the revenues are earned or the expenses are incurred.

Depletion Depletion is the accounting method used to allocate the cost of extracting natural resources that are mined, extracted, or otherwise removed from the environment for use.

Depreciation Depreciation is the accounting method used to allocate the cost of a fixed asset over its useful life.

Derivative A derivative is a contract between parties whose value or price is derived from one or more underlying assets, such as stock, or from a financial or economic variable, such as a foreign currency.

Diluted Earnings Per Share Diluted earnings per share represents the portion of the entity's profits allocated to each share of issued and outstanding common stock that takes into account all issued and outstanding shares of common stock plus any financial instruments of the entity that can be converted into or exercised for common stock.

Disclaimer of Opinion A disclaimer of opinion is a formal statement by the auditors that they are unable to express an opinion on the entity's financial statements and position.

Discount Rate The discount rate is the interest rate the Federal Reserve charges a depository institution to borrow money directly. The discount rate also refers to the rate used to discount a future cash lump sum payment or stream of future cash flows to their present value.

Dividend A dividend is a distribution made to shareholders that is in proportion to the number of shares each shareholder owns, meaning on a pro rata basis.

Dividend Payment Date The dividend payment date is the day on which the entity issues the dividend payment to those shareholders who were owners on the record date.

Double-Entry Bookkeeping Double-entry bookkeeping is a record keeping system under which each financial transaction is recorded in at least two accounts that are equal and opposite amounts, meaning at least one debit entry and one credit entry.

Earn-Out   An earn-out is a type of purchase price adjustment in a merger transaction that provides for a portion of the purchase price to be paid after the transaction has closed, and is based upon certain financial metrics being met after closing.

Earned Surplus   Earned surplus is an entity's earnings not distributed as dividends or what is reflected as retained earnings in the entity's stockholders' equity section of the balance sheet.

Earnings Before Interest and Taxes (EBIT)   EBIT is an entity's profit or earnings before taking into account its interest and income tax expenses.

Earnings Before Interest, Taxes, Depreciation, and Amortization (EBITDA)   EBITDA is an entity's profit or earnings before taking into account its interest, income tax, depreciation, and amortization expenses.

Earnings Per Share   Earnings per share represent the portion of the entity's profit allocated to each share of issued and outstanding common stock without taking into account any dilutive events. Earnings per share are calculated using the weighted average of the common stock issued and outstanding during the period.

Equity   Equity is the amount of funds invested in a business by its owners, plus any retained earnings or less any accumulated loss, and less treasury stock. It is the difference between total assets and total liabilities on an entity's balance sheet.

Equity Insolvency   Equity insolvency is a modern dividend test that assesses an entity's solvency based on a number of factors, such as whether the entity is liquid, is financially able to operate in the normal course, and can meet its short-term and long-term obligations. It is used by the board of directors of an entity to determine if the entity may legally declare and issue a dividend, and is often assessed in conjunction with balance sheet insolvency.

Exchange-Traded Derivative   An exchange-traded derivative is a derivative that is traded on a regulated exchange and utilizes a standard agreement.

Ex-Dividend Date   The ex-dividend date is the date that is two business days before the record date and sets the cutoff date for new purchasers of the corporation's shares to receive a dividend distribution.

Expense   An expense is a cost of the entity's business resulting from some aspect of its operating activities.

Face Value   The face value is the amount that a bond is worth at maturity or what the issuer pays the bond holder at maturity.

Fair Market Value   Fair market value is the price that a willing buyer would pay a willing seller under no pressure in the open market.

Federal Funds Rate The federal funds rate is the rate of interest at which a depository institution lends funds to other depository institutions on an overnight basis.

Federal Reserve Board The Federal Reserve Board is made up of those individuals who control the policies of the U.S. Federal Reserve System, and consists of seven members nominated by the president and confirmed by Congress, 12 regional Federal Reserve Banks, and other financial institution members.

Financial Accounting Standards Board (FASB) FASB is an independent, non-profit organization that establishes financial accounting and reporting standards for use by public and private companies that follow Generally Accepted Accounting Principles (GAAP).

Financial Analyst A financial analyst is a professional with expertise in evaluating and assessing the financial condition of a business, securities, or potential investments.

Financial Covenant Financial covenants are promises by the borrower to comply with certain restrictions, whether negative or affirmative, placed on the borrower pursuant to a commercial loan, indenture, or similar type of agreement.

First-In, First-Out (FIFO) FIFO is an inventory valuation method that assumes the first goods purchased (or the oldest goods) are the first goods sold.

Fiscal Year A fiscal year is the 12-month period that an entity uses for accounting purposes and does not have to be the calendar year.

Fixed Charges (Fixed Expenses) A fixed charge is a fixed expense of a business that occurs on a regular basis, such as rent, salaries, or loan payments, and does not fluctuate due to changes in revenues.

Form 10-K The Form 10-K is an annual report publicly reporting entities must file with the SEC containing comprehensive disclosures regarding the entity, its business, management, and financial condition.

Forward Contract A forward contract is a customized contract that requires the buyer and seller to purchase and sell the underlying asset at an agreed upon price on a specified future date.

Forward Stock Split A forward stock split is a stock split that results in an increase in the number of shares issued and outstanding.

Freight on Board (or Free on Board) (FOB) FOB is a shipping term that indicates which party is responsible for the transportation costs.

Freight on Board Destination FOB destination means that the seller retains legal title to the goods until the goods reach the buyer's location (or their destination), and so the seller bears the risk of loss.

Freight on Board Shipping Point FOB shipping point means the buyer takes legal title to the goods when the goods leave the seller's shipping dock (or the departure point), and so the buyer bears the risk of loss.

Future Value Future value is the amount that cash will be worth or grow to as of a date in the future based on an assumed growth rate.

Futures Contract A futures contract is a standardized forward contract traded on one of the public exchanges.

Generally Accepted Accounting Principles (GAAP) GAAP is an established framework of accounting standards, rules, and procedures that companies follow in preparing financial statements.

Generally Accepted Auditing Standards (GAAS) GAAS are standards established by the AICPA that constitute the foundation of auditing, under which an audit is performed and against which the quality of an audit is judged.

General Ledger The general ledger is the list of accounts that are currently in use by the entity and reflects the summary of all the financial transactions that have occurred and been recorded.

Goodwill Goodwill is an intangible asset that represents the excess amount of the purchase price paid by the entity for the assets of a business or the entire business that exceeds the total value of those assets or business.

Governmental Accounting Standards Board (GASB) The GASB is an independent, nonprofit organization that establishes accounting and financial reporting standards for U.S. state and local governments.

Gross Profit Gross profit is the difference between revenues or net revenues and COGS or COS.

Gross Profit Margin The gross profit margin represents the percentage of profits the entity achieved based on its revenues and the expenses directly associated with its primary products or services.

Guarantee A guarantee is a promise or obligation by the guarantor to be responsible for another entity's financial obligation if the other entity fails to meet such obligation.

Guaranteed Dividend A guaranteed dividend is a dividend that the entity is required to pay to its preferred shareholders before common shareholders can receive a dividend. A guaranteed dividend can be cumulative or noncumulative.

Hedge (Hedging) A hedge is an investment intended to counterbalance against a perceived risk associated with another investment and its price movements in order to reduce risk exposure.

Historical Cost Historical cost is the original cost of an asset as recorded in an entity's accounting records and as reflected on its balance sheet.

Horizontal Trend Analysis   Horizontal trend analysis is a technique of analyzing an entity's financial statements that provides insight into changes in amounts and results over periods of time.

Income Statement   The income statement is a report that summarizes an entity's revenues and gains and its expenses and losses for a given period of time and shows the entity's net profit (or net loss) for the accounting period.

Income Valuation Approach   The income valuation approach is a valuation method used to measure the value of a business based on the entity's ability to generate future economic benefits through cash flows.

Indenture   An indenture is a legal contract between the bond issuer and bond holder that sets forth the terms and features of the bond.

Inflation Premium   The inflation premium is the premium portion of the interest rate that is meant to compensate the lender for the anticipated rate of inflation over the term of the loan.

Insolvency   Insolvency is a condition in which an entity cannot meet its obligations as they come due for payment.

Intangible Asset   An intangible asset is a non-physical asset such as intellectual property or goodwill.

Interest   Interest is the charge or fee paid by the borrower to the lender to use or borrow money and is generally expressed as an annual percentage rate.

Interest Coverage Ratio   The interest coverage ratio measures the entity's ability to cover its interest payments with its earnings before interest and taxes (EBIT) and indicates how many times the entity could meet its interest obligations with EBIT.

Interest Rate Swap   An interest rate swap is a type of contract that allows parties to swap or exchange one interest rate stream for another interest rate stream.

Internal Revenue Service (IRS)   The IRS is a government agency organized to carry out the responsibilities of the Secretary of the U.S. Treasury and is the primary tax collection service of the federal government of the United States. The IRS administers the Internal Revenue Code.

International Accounting Standards Board (IASB)   The IASB is an independent, nonprofit organization that develops and approves the International Financial Reporting Standards used by entities in many countries throughout the world.

International Financial Reporting Standards (IFRS)   IFRS are standards established by the IASB that provide a global framework that public companies follow in preparing financial statements.

In-the-Money   In-the-money indicates that the market price is above the option's strike price in regard to a call option and that the market price is below the option's strike price in regard to a put option.

Inventory   Inventory is an asset of the business that consists of the merchandise or products the entity intends to sell and includes raw materials, work-in-progress, and finished goods.

Inventory Turnover Ratio   The inventory turnover ratio measures the number of times each year that the entity sells, or turns over, its inventory.

Issue Price   The issue price is the price at which a bond is originally sold.

Large Stock Dividend   A large stock dividend is a stock dividend of 25 percent or more of the shares of the same class of stock currently issued and outstanding.

Last-In, First-Out (LIFO)   LIFO is an inventory valuation method that assumes the last goods purchased (the newest ones) are the first goods sold.

Liability   A liability is an entity's legally binding obligation owed to a third party that is expected to yield an economic benefit to that third party in the future.

Liquidation Preference   The liquidation preference establishes the order in which different creditors are paid in the event of an entity's liquidation.

Liquidity   Liquidity refers to how readily or easily an asset can be converted to cash or an entity's ability to meet its obligations with cash or assets that can be converted to cash.

London Interbank Offer Rate (LIBOR)   LIBOR is the short-term interest rate that world banks charge each other for short-term loans and is similar to the federal funds rate in the United States.

Long-Term Assets   Long-term assets are those assets that are not readily converted to cash or expected to be consumed within one year.

Long-Term Liabilities   Long-term liabilities are those liabilities that are not due within the next 12 months.

Lower of Cost or Market (LCM)   LCM is an approach to inventory valuation that requires an entity to reflect the value of its inventory at the lower of its historical cost or its current market value in certain situations.

Management's Discussion and Analysis (MD&A)   MD&A is the section of an entity's annual report on Form 10-K where management, from its perspective, provides an overview and year-by-year comparison of the results of operations and the financial condition of the entity.

Marked-to-Market   Marked-to-market is the process of settling the profits or losses on a futures contract on a daily basis.

Market Valuation Approach   The market valuation approach is a valuation method used to measure the value of an entity's business based on the values of comparable transactions.

Maturity Date   The maturity date is the date on which a bond matures and the issuer must pay the bond holder the bond's face value.

Money Markets　The money markets are the marketplaces where the purchase and sale of short-term investments occur between willing participants.

Multiple　A multiple is the multiplier that is applied to a financial metric, such as revenues or EBIT, to determine a valuation for the entity's business.

Municipal Bond　Municipal bonds are bonds issued by states, municipalities, or counties.

Net Income　Net income is the entity's profit for the accounting period and occurs when all revenues and gains exceed all expenses and losses as reflected on the income statement during the accounting period.

Net Loss　Net loss is the entity's loss, or failure to make a profit, for the accounting period and occurs when all expenses and losses exceed all revenues and gains as reflected on the income statement during the accounting period.

Net Profit Margin　The net profit margin represents the percentage of profits the entity achieved after taking into account all of its revenues and gains and expenses and losses for the period and shows the proportion of total profits as compared to revenue.

Net Realizable Value (NRV)　NRV is the value that can be realized from selling an asset less the reasonable costs associated with that sale. NRV is used in conjunction with the inventory concept of lower of cost or market.

Nominal Interest Rate　*See* "Real Rate of Interest."

Noncumulative Dividend　A noncumulative dividend is a term tied to preferred stock that means the preferred shareholders do not have the right to receive any unpaid or past dividends before common shareholders can receive a dividend. It means the preferred shareholders do not have a right to dividends that accumulate.

Operating Income　Operating income is the entity's income before taking into account interest or taxes and indicates the profit the entity makes from its business operations. Operating income often equals EBIT.

Operating Lease　An operating lease is a lease in which the lessor leases property or an asset to the lessee to use for a period of time, but does not transfer an ownership interest to the lessee.

Opportunity Cost Premium　The opportunity cost premium is the premium portion of the interest rate that is meant to compensate the lender for lending money to a particular borrower and thus forgoing the opportunity to use the money for another purpose or loan.

Option　An option is a contract between two parties that gives the option holder the right, but not the obligation, to engage in the specified transaction (either purchase or sell the underlying asset) with the option writer, or counterparty, at a predetermined price on or before a specified date in the future.

Ordinary Annuity   An ordinary annuity is a series of equal and fixed payments, with the payments made at the same time at the end of each period, such as the last day of the year, quarter, or month.

Out-of-the-Money   Out-of-the-money indicates that the market price is below the option's strike price in regard to a call option and that the market price is above the option's strike price in regard to a put option.

Over-the-Counter Derivative   An over-the-counter derivative is a derivative that is privately negotiated and allows for the contract to be tailored by the parties to their specific needs and is not traded on a regulated exchange.

Par Value   Par value is the face value of a share of stock as stipulated in the corporate charter or by the board of directors, or the face value of a bond or other security instrument.

Periodic Inventory System   The periodic inventory system is a system whereby the entity does not keep an accurate count of inventory on a continuous basis, but instead updates the inventory accounts after it conducts a physical count of its inventory to determine the amount of inventory it has on hand at the end of the accounting period or updates the inventory accounts based on an estimate of the amount of inventory the entity has on hand at the end of the accounting period.

Perpetual Annuity   A perpetual annuity, or a perpetuity, is a type of annuity that has no end or a stream of payments that continue forever, or into perpetuity.

Perpetual Inventory System   The perpetual inventory system is a system whereby an entity keeps an accurate count of inventory on a continuous basis and updates the inventory accounts after each purchase or sale of inventory.

Potentially Responsible Party (PRP)   A PRP is an individual or entity that is potentially liable for payment of environmental cleanup costs.

Preferred Stock   Preferred stock is an ownership interest in a corporation that entitles its holders to a higher priority claim on the entity's assets and earnings than a common shareholder and often has a guaranteed dividend and/or liquidation preference, but does not entitle the holder to vote.

Prepaid Expense   A prepaid expense is an expense that has been paid in advance by the entity, but not yet used up, and is reflected as an asset of the entity until used or benefited from by the entity.

Present Value   Present value is the current value of a future lump sum of money or future sum of a series of payments based on an assumed discount rate.

Price-to-Earnings Ratio   The price-to-earnings ratio compares the market price of an entity's common stock to its earnings per share and is an indication of how much an investor is willing to pay for each $1.00 of the entity's earnings or profit.

Primary Market   The primary market is the market where the entity issues or sells its financial instruments directly to the public, meaning investors, for the first time and receives the cash consideration. It is sometimes referred to as the initial public offering (IPO) market.

Prime Rate   The prime rate is the short-term rate of interest in the United States used as an index by banks to price loans and is the rate that banks may charge their most stable and creditworthy customers or borrowers.

Pro Rata   Pro rata means a proportionate allocation or distribution and from a dividend perspective is based on the shareholder's percentage ownership interest based upon all the shares of that class that are issued and outstanding.

Property, Plant, and Equipment (PP&E)   PP&E are the tangible long-term, or fixed assets, of an entity that are expected to be used in its business operations for the longer term.

Public Company Accounting Oversight Board (PCAOB)   The PCAOB is a non-profit organization that protects investors by overseeing the audits of public companies, brokers, and dealers.

Purchase Price Adjustment   A purchase price adjustment is an adjustment to the purchase price in a merger transaction to account for fluctuations in the value of the target's business.

Put Option   A put option is an option that gives the option holder the right to sell the underlying item, such as stock, at a specified price in the future.

Qualified Opinion   A qualified opinion is an opinion given by the auditors stating that either (i) the audit was limited in scope, but the financial statements are otherwise fairly presented; or (ii) the entity did not meet or conform to GAAP.

Quick Assets   Quick assets are those assets that are highly liquid and can be readily converted to cash in a short amount of time and so excludes current assets such as inventories and prepaid expenses that are not as quickly convertible to cash.

Quick Ratio   *See* "Acid Test."

Real Rate of Interest   The real rate of interest is the interest rate that a lender would charge if there was no risk.

Record Date   The record date is the cutoff date established by an entity to determine the shareholders who own stock on that date and are entitled to receive the dividend distribution.

Residual Value   The residual value is the estimated amount that an asset will be worth at the end of its useful life.

Retained Earnings   Retained earnings are the profits that a company has earned to date less any dividends or other distributions paid to investors, and are reflected in the stockholders' equity section of the balance sheet (*see also* "Accumulated Loss").

Return on Assets Ratio   The return on assets ratio compares an entity's net income to total assets and indicates the amount of profit earned on each $1.00 of total assets of the business.

Return on Common Equity Ratio   The return on common equity ratio compares an entity's net income to common stockholders' equity and indicates the amount of profit on each $1.00 of common stockholders' equity invested in the business.

Return on Equity Ratio   The return on equity ratio compares an entity's net income to total stockholders' equity and indicates the amount of profit on each $1.00 of total stockholders' equity invested in a business.

Return on Investment (ROI)   Return on investment is a measurement of the amount of return (or profit) on an investment as compared to its cost.

Revenues   Revenues are the income of the entity from the sale of its primary goods or services associated with its main business operations.

Reverse Stock Split   A reverse stock split is a stock split that results in a decrease in the number of shares issued and outstanding.

Salvage Value   The salvage value is an estimate of the amount that the entity believes a fixed asset will be worth at the end of its useful life.

Secondary Market   The secondary market is the market where previously issued financial instruments are bought and sold by investors and the selling holder (or investor) receives the cash consideration. It is sometimes referred to as the aftermarket.

Securities and Exchange Commission (SEC)   The SEC is a United States independent, government agency that enforces federal securities laws and regulates the securities markets with the intent of protecting investors.

Shareholder   A shareholder is any person that that owns shares of a corporation.

Short-Term Assets   *See* "Current Assets."

Short-Term Liabilities   *See* "Current Liabilities."

Simple Interest   Simple interest is interest that is calculated only on the principal due or the amount invested, meaning interest does not compound or is not calculated on interest.

Small Stock Dividend   A small stock dividend is a dividend of less than 25 percent of the shares of the same class of stock currently issued and outstanding.

Specific Identification   Specific identification is an inventory valuation method that assigns costs to the specific goods to which those costs relate.

Spoilage   Spoilage is waste, scrap, or damaged material arising from the production process. In accounting, normal spoilage is included in cost of goods sold, while abnormal spoilage is charged as an expense when incurred.

Statement of Cash Flows   *See* "Cash Flows Statement."

Statement of Changes in Stockholders' Equity   The statement of changes in stockholders' equity is a report that reflects changes that occurred in the stockholders' equity accounts for a given period of time.

Stockholders' Equity *See "Equity."*

Stock Dividend A stock dividend is a dividend payment by a corporation in the form of additional shares of stock to the shareholders based on their pro rata ownership interest.

Stock Split A stock split is an issuance of new shares of stock to the shareholders based on their pro rata ownership interest that increases the number of shares issued and outstanding in a forward split or decreases the number of shares issued and outstanding in a reverse split.

Strike Price The strike price is the price at which the put or call option can be exercised at some point in the future.

Swap A swap is a privately negotiated derivative contract between two parties who agree to exchange financial instruments.

T-Account A T-account is a visual representation of a general ledger account in the form of a capital "T" where debit entries are depicted on the left side of the "T" and credit entries are depicted on the right side of the "T."

Tangible Asset A tangible asset is a physical asset such as a building or piece of equipment.

Terminal Value The terminal value represents the present value of the stabilized cash flow stream of an entity.

Time Value of Money The time value of money concept states that cash received today is more valuable than cash received at some point in the future or "a dollar today is worth more than a dollar tomorrow."

Treasury Bill (T-Bill) A treasury bill is a short-term debt security issued by the U.S. government that matures in less than one year.

Treasury Bond (T-Bond) A treasury bond is a debt security issued by the U.S. government that matures in ten years or longer.

Treasury Note (T-Note) A treasury note is a debt security issued by the U.S. government that matures in one to ten years.

Treasury Stock Treasury stock is the portion of the entity's shares that it retains in its treasury and generally results from a repurchase of its stock.

Unearned Revenue Unearned revenue is money received in advance by the entity for goods or services that have not yet been provided and is reflected as a liability of the entity until it ships the goods or provides the services and can recognize the revenue.

Unqualified Opinion An unqualified opinion is an opinion given by the auditors stating that the entity's financial statements are fairly presented and in accordance with GAAP.

U.S. Federal Reserve System (The Federal Reserve) The Federal Reserve is the central bank of the United States.

Useful Life Useful life is the estimated amount of time a fixed asset is expected to contribute to the entity's business operations.

Weighted Average The weighted average is an inventory valuation method that uses an average that is calculated by dividing the cost of the units available for sale by the number of units available for sale to determine the cost per unit.

Weighted Average Cost of Capital The weighted average cost of capital is a method that an entity uses to determine its cost of capital or the rate the entity expects to pay on average to all of its security holders to finance the cost of its assets.

Working Capital Working capital is the difference between an entity's current assets and its current liabilities and reflects the entity's short-term liquidity.

Working Capital Ratio *See* "Current Ratio."

Vertical Trend Analysis *See* "Common-Size Analysis."

Zero Coupon Bond A zero coupon bond is a type of bond that does not include a coupon payment (interest) and is sold at a deep discount.

Index